Polycentric Governance
and Development

INSTITUTIONAL ANALYSIS

Editors, Michael D. McGinnis and Elinor Ostrom

Institutions link political, economic, social, and biophysical processes. *Institutional Analysis* was established to encourage multi-disciplinary, multi-level, and multi-method research on institutions for collective action, public services, resource management, development, and governance. Each book in this series investigates the origins and operation of institutions in particular empirical contexts or their broader roles in the constitution of order in human societies.

Titles in the Series:

Polycentric Governance and Development:
Readings from the Workshop in Political Theory and Policy Analysis
Michael D. McGinnis, editor

Polycentricity and Local Public Economies:
Readings from the Workshop in Political Theory and Policy Analysis
Michael D. McGinnis, editor

Polycentric Games and Institutions:
Readings from the Workshop in Political Theory and Policy Analysis
Michael D. McGinnis, editor

Related Titles on the Analysis of Institutions:

The Meaning of Democracy and the Vulnerability of Democracies:
A Response to Tocqueville's Challenge
Vincent Ostrom

Rules, Games, and Common-Pool Resources
Elinor Ostrom, Roy Gardner, and James Walker,
with Arun Agrawal, William Blomquist, Edella Schlager, and Shui-Yan Tang

Trust, Ethnicity, and Identity: Beyond the New Institutional Economics
of Ethnic Trading Networks, Contract Law, and Gift-Exchange
Janet Tai Landa

Laboratory Research in Political Economy
Thomas R. Palfrey, editor

POLYCENTRIC GOVERNANCE AND DEVELOPMENT

Readings from the Workshop in Political Theory and Policy Analysis

Michael D. McGinnis, Editor

Ann Arbor

THE UNIVERSITY OF MICHIGAN PRESS

2002   2001   2000   1999   4   3   2   1

A CIP catalog record for this book is available from the British Library.

Library of Congress Cataloging-in-Publication Data

Polycentric governance and development : readings from the Workshop in
   Political Theory and Policy Analysis / Michael D. McGinnis, editor.
       p.   cm. — (Institutional analysis)
   Includes bibliographical references and index.
   ISBN 0-472-11039-X (alk. paper). — ISBN 0-472-08623-5 (pbk. :
alk. paper)
       1. Political science—Congresses.   I. McGinnis, Michael D.
(Michael Dean)   II. Indiana University, Bloomington.   Workshop in
Political Theory and Policy Analysis.   III. Series.
JA71.P675   1999
351—dc21   99-24422
                                                                     CIP

Contents

Figures

Tables

Series Foreword

Michael D. McGinnis

From its current location in a few scattered office buildings on the Bloomington campus of Indiana University, the Workshop in Political Theory and Policy Analysis lies at the heart of a worldwide network of scholars who use institutional analysis to understand and to strengthen the foundations of self-governance. Over the past twenty-five years the political scientists, policy analysts, economists, lawyers, anthropologists, sociologists, psychologists, biologists, ecologists, and policymakers associated with the Workshop have investigated diverse research topics. Results of these research programs have been published in books and journals from several disciplines. A portion of this work has been gathered in this volume; two related volumes are scheduled to be published at approximately the same time.

Each of these edited volumes exemplifies what is special and distinctive about *institutional analysis* as it has been developed and practiced by Workshop scholars. Institutions are ubiquitous in contemporary society, and the fields of political science and economics have experienced a recent renaissance in the study of institutions. The Workshop approach is uniquely multidisciplinary, drawing on the complementary strengths of a wide range of social science methodologies: field studies, laboratory experiments, formal models, comparative case studies, opinion surveys, archival research, philosophical investigations, physical measurements, computer simulations, and, most recently, satellite imagery. Institutions affect all aspects of social life. Major Workshop research programs have focused on (1) police services in metropolitan centers in the United States; (2) the management of fisheries, irrigation systems, forests, and other common-pool resources from California to Nepal (and many places in between); and (3) the macro structure of constitutional order from imperial China to the contemporary international system, with particular emphasis given to the nature of American democracy.

Beneath this bewildering variety lies a core message, buttressed by reinforcing methodological and political foundations. Politically, the goal is to establish and sustain capacities for *self-governance,* by which is meant the structured ways communities organize themselves to solve collective problems, achieve common aspirations, and resolve conflicts. Methodologically, the goal is to understand the institutional foundations of self-governance, that is, to determine which conditions strengthen and which conditions undermine community capacities for self-governance.

In practice these goals have inspired a series of careful, detailed studies of narrow ranges of empirical phenomena. Yet, since each study draws on a single framework of analysis, the overall product has import far beyond the confines of these particular settings. The aggregate lesson of these empirical analyses is clear: many, many self-governing communities thrive, in all parts of the world.

By focusing on community efforts to resolve local problems, the writings of Workshop scholars are sometimes misinterpreted as lending credence to the "small is beautiful" slogan. For many public purposes local community action will be effective, but other circumstances require coordinated policies at the regional, national, or international levels. It is important to remember that public officials at all levels of aggregation have important roles to play in helping communities provide for their own needs.

Shouting slogans about the desirability of decentralization or civil society contributes little toward the crucially important task of sustaining capacities for self-governance. The challenge of institutional analysis lies in producing solid research findings, based on rigorous empirical tests of hypotheses grounded in carefully articulated theories and models. Institutional analysts have a responsibility to combine policy relevance and scientific rigor.

A basic tenet of institutional analysis is that multiple arenas, or centers, of interaction and participation need to be considered simultaneously. Self-governance works best if the overall governance structure is *polycentric*. The word itself may be awkward, but it encapsulates a way of approaching the study of politics and policy analysis that stands in sharp contrast to standard modes of thought. Governance does not require a single center of power, and governments should not claim an exclusive responsibility for resolving political issues. Instead, politics should be envisioned as an activity that goes on in many arenas simultaneously, at many scales of aggregation. Implications of polycentric governance for particular empirical and theoretical contexts are detailed in the readings included in these volumes.

To illustrate the *coherence* of the theoretical approach that underlies applications to a wide array of empirical domains, a selection of previously published articles and book chapters have been collected into three books with similar titles: *Polycentric Governance and Development, Polycentricity and Local Public Economies,* and *Polycentric Games and Institutions.* Each book addresses a separate audience of scholars and policy analysts, but all of them will be of interest to anyone seeking to understand the institutional foundations of self-governance.

The essays in *Polycentric Governance and Development* demonstrate that empirical analyses of the management of irrigation systems, fisheries, groundwater basins, and other common-pool resources have important implications for development policy. Long before "sustainable development" became an over-used slogan, scholars associated with the Workshop were trying to understand the myriad ways self-governing communities had already achieved that goal in practice.

After an initial section on the general conceptual framework that has influenced research on the full array of Workshop research topics, *Polycentricity and Local Public Economies* presents essays published from the first major empirical project associated with the Workshop, a comparative study of the performance of police agencies in metropolitan areas of the United States. Although most of the research results included in this volume date from over a decade ago, they remain relevant today. Recent trends toward community policing, for example, reflect the continuing influence of factors identified in this research program.

In *Polycentric Games and Institutions* the general concepts that guided these empirical analyses themselves become the focus of analysis. Workshop scholars use game theory and laboratory experiments to understand how individuals behave in the context of diverse political and economic institutions. Results from laboratory experiments and field settings show that individuals draw upon an extensive repertoire of rules or strategies from which they select different strategies, given their understanding of the nature of the situation at hand.

By collecting readings on similar topics that were originally published in scattered outlets, we hope to highlight the contribution these research programs have made to their respective fields of study. Any evaluation of the scholarly contribution of *institutional analysis* as a whole, however, must be partial and incomplete, for the Workshop remains an active place. Each of these research themes is being pursued by scholars who have long been associated with the Workshop and by a new generation of scholars.

Each article or book chapter is reprinted without changes, except for a few minor corrections to the published versions. To avoid duplication of material and improve the flow of this presentation, textual deletions have been made in a few of the selections. Citations to forthcoming books and articles have been updated, and cross-references to essays included in the other volumes have been added. Otherwise, reference and footnote conventions used in the original sources have been left intact.

Selection of an appropriate set of readings was a daunting task, for the list of publications is long and diverse. I enjoyed digging through the extensive files of reprints, and I wish we could have included many more readings, but that would have defeated the purpose of compiling accessible surveys of selected Workshop research programs. I tried to minimize overlap with the most influential and widely available books that have emerged from these research programs. Each edited volume includes an integrative introductory essay, in which frequent references are made to the many other books and journals in which the results of these diverse research projects are reported. Each book also includes an annotated list of suggested readings.

One final caveat is in order. Elinor Ostrom and Vincent Ostrom are authors or coauthors of many of the readings in all three books. Both have served jointly as co-directors since its establishment in 1973. Without doubt, these two individuals have been absolutely crucial to the success of the Workshop. Even so, they would be the first to insist that they have *not* been the only reason for its success. Collaboration has always been a hallmark of the Workshop. Many individuals have made essential contributions, as will be apparent throughout the readings in these books. Yet it is impossible to imagine how the Workshop could have been established or sustained without the tireless efforts of Elinor and Vincent Ostrom. Their influence will continue to shape the future direction of the Workshop for years to come.

Acknowledgments

In an edited volume composed of essays written over a span of thirty years, the help and assistance of a many, many people and institutions deserves to be acknowledged. Fortunately, the contributors have already thanked those who assisted in the original preparation of each of the journal articles or book chapters reprinted here.

As editor, I am going to start my acknowledgments with Patty Dalecki. Her assistance has been invaluable, her contributions legion and long-standing. As a staff member of the Workshop for more years than either of us cares to admit, she used several generations of word-processing programs to prepare many of the original manuscripts included here. To put them all into a single format for this book, she managed the long process of scanning all of the original publications and checking them for errors. Her record keeping is immaculate, giving me (or any other interested scholar) easy access to the diverse array of Workshop publications. She kept track of copyright permissions from authors and publishers, comments from contributors, and my frequent changes in the list of readings to be included. Finally, she typeset the complete manuscript. She truly has been in on this project from start to finish, and the quality of the final product directly reflects her skill and her own inimitable style.

I also want to thank all of the staff members who helped Patty and I at various stages in this process. Amber Cleveland, Sara Colburn, Ray Eliason, Anne Leinenbach, Bob Lezotte, David Wilson, and Cynthia Yaudes all helped in scanning and proofreading the manuscripts or in posting drafts of the introduction and contents list on the web. One of the strengths of the Workshop has always been our competent, hard-working, and friendly staff.

At the other end of the publication process, I am deeply appreciative of the support and guidance offered by Colin Day, director of the University of Michigan Press. His comments and suggestions were crucial, all the way from initial planning of the volumes to preparation of the final manuscript. The introduction and other new material was ably copyedited by Elizabeth Gratch. Sujai Shivakumar contributed a first draft of listings for the index. I would also like to thank two anonymous reviewers for their helpful comments and suggestions on drafts of the introduction and on the overall organization of the volume.

None of this activity would have been possible if the contributors to this volume had not written such excellent research reports in the first place. I thank each of the contributors for providing the foundational material out of which this book was constructed. They all returned corrections to the scanned versions in short order, helping us complete this book in a remarkably short period of time.

I also want to say a few words to those scholars associated with the Workshop whose work I was not able to include in this volume. I wish the book could have been twice as long, and I repeatedly found it necessary to restrain my enthusiasm for including more essays. I especially want to express my appreciation to those authors who were willing to proof essays that, for whatever reason, had to be cut from the final list.

Two of the contributors play uniquely pivotal roles. Elinor and Vincent Ostrom have inspired, encouraged, and supported all of the research included in this volume. Each has had a major impact on my own career, helping to broaden my interests and to sharpen my analytical skills. I can't thank them enough.

Introduction

Michael D. McGinnis

Fisheries, irrigation systems, and groundwater basins may seem unpromising subjects for a book on governance and development, but the management of commonly held resources requires political skill. When one person appropriates a portion of a *common-pool resource* (CPR), that portion is no longer available for another person's use. Efforts to exclude others from appropriation can be very costly in terms of the time and effort required to establish rules, monitor compliance, and sanction rule violators. Thus, any CPR user group faces a basic dilemma of collective action: how can the common goal of sustaining secure access to this resource be realized despite individual incentives to free ride on the efforts of others or to overexploit common resources for private gain? This is an inherently political issue, no matter how narrow the scope of that resource or how small the community affected by it.

Governance is the way society as a whole manages the full array of its political, economic, and social affairs. By shaping the incentives facing individuals and local communities, governance either facilitates or hinders economic development. If the overall governance structure reinforces the capability of local groups to deal with their own problems, then user groups have an incentive to manage their own common-pool resources wisely. Under these circumstances development is likely to be sustainable. Conversely, if local rules are routinely superseded by the policies of higher authorities, then it will be much more difficult to restrain individual appropriators from engaging in opportunistic behavior. In those circumstances any effort to develop the national economy as a whole will rest on shaky foundations at the local level.

Over the past few decades scholars associated with the Workshop in Political Theory and Policy Analysis at Indiana University have studied how CPR user groups in many parts of the world have managed a diverse array of common-pool resources. This volume includes several of these empirical studies, supplemented by a few essays on alternative forms of constitutional order. In this introduction I explain why analyses of local patterns of resource management can have profound implications for broader issues of development and governance.

The basic lesson of the interrelated research programs conducted by Workshop scholars is that community efforts to manage common-pool resources work best in the context of *polycentric governance*. A political order is polycentric when there exist many overlapping arenas (or centers) of authority and responsibility. These arenas exist at all scales, from local community groups to national governments to the informal arrangements for governance at the global level.

Although originally developed to characterize the nature of governance in metropolitan areas in the United States (V. Ostrom, Tiebout, and Warren 1961), polycentricity is a general concept that encapsulates a distinctive way of looking at political, economic, and social order (McGinnis 1999a, b; V. Ostrom 1997). A sharp contrast is drawn against the standard view of sovereignty as connoting a single source of political power and authority that has exclusive responsibility for determining public policy. The responsibility for development policy, for example, is typically taken to fall within the exclusive purview of national governments or, increasingly, international funding agencies.

Contributors to this volume adopt a different viewpoint. Development must occur at all scales simultaneously, with input from individuals and local communities welcomed at all levels of political interaction. This concern for the "nesting" of local arrangements within the overarching political, economic, and cultural order is distinctive. Many development policy analysts focus on what happens at the national level, especially political developments in national capitals. Workshop scholars agree that these activities are important but primarily for their effects on shaping or constraining the ability of local communities to address their own problems. Free elections may help end a tradition of single-party rule, but serious dangers may arise if elections degenerate into shouting matches dominated by ideologies, ethnic hatreds, or other forms of political symbolism. Similarly, if all community groups are prepared to do is to lobby the government for special privileges or assistance, then the mere existence of civil society may not contribute much toward the solution of practical problems. Only polycentric governance can nurture and sustain the self-governing capabilities of local communities.

Some collective efforts to manage common-pool resources fail. A *tragedy of the commons* (Hardin 1968) occurs when individual appropriators selfishly extract excessive levels from a CPR and thereby undermine the long-term sustainability of that resource. Instances of overuse and destruction of common-pool resources have been well documented, but in other cases local users have effectively managed resources over long periods (E. Ostrom 1990; E. Ostrom, Gardner, and Walker 1994).

In one sense this observation is hardly surprising. If no communities of fishers or farmers had found a way to cope with practical problems of collective action, then none of them would be around today for us to study. In another sense this observation is revolutionary, for the ability of local groups to manage their own resources effectively is often overlooked by policy analysts. To an unfortunate extent the standard literature on development policy fixates on markets and states. By treating privatization and centralized state control as the primary means of responding to problems of CPR management, policy analysts overlook the many alternative institutional arrangements designed and implemented by self-governing communities throughout the world.

An implicit theme in the development policy literature is that, if people in the developing world want to emulate the successes of advanced industrial society, then they need to learn how to make efficient use of their physical, human, and institutional resources. But the processes of learning need not be unidirectional. Communities in the developing world can contribute important insights to a developed world that is just beginning to confront severe problems of resource depletion.

Workshop scholars have implemented research programs on the institutional foundations of self-governance in widely scattered locales throughout the world. The diversity of these institutional arrangements can be initially overwhelming, but the readings included in this book develop a means of understanding the factors shared in common by successful efforts. This community of scholars has developed methods of *institutional analysis* (McGinnis 1999a, b) that help observers understand the ways in which local communities manage those resources that are most important to their own survival or prosperity.

The first section of this introduction outlines the theoretical framework that has emerged from the collaborative activities of Workshop scholars. This framework draws an explicit connection between micro-level processes of resource management and macro-level structures of constitutional order. The remaining four sections of this introduction provide summaries of the journal articles and book chapters reprinted in this volume. The essays in part I are arranged chronologically, to illustrate the historical development of the Workshop research program on common-pool resources. Part II shifts to a thematic focus, by specifying alternative forms of constitutional order and illustrating each form with examples from Africa. The essays in part III use examples from several countries to illustrate the importance of informal institutions and local associations on the prospects for sustainable development. These essays use analytical concepts developed by Workshop scholars, in particular the idea that development needs to be seen as a process of "coproduction" in which local residents take a fully active role. Finally, the volume concludes with two essays in part IV that highlight the creative nature of the process of institutional design and analysis. The deep philosophical issues raised there have direct and practical consequences, for those policy analysts who restrict their advice to the state-market dichotomy threaten to undermine the very basis of self-governance.

Some readers may be discomforted by the frequent changes in scale and mode of analysis in this book, but Workshop scholars have grown accustomed to juxtaposition of highly detailed, empirical analyses of irrigation systems with broad-ranging, philosophical investigations of alternative forms of constitutional order. Movement up and down levels of aggregation, and movement across standard disciplinary boundaries, is essential if we are to understand the human capacity for self-governance. In short, local self-governance is sustainable only if macro-level political, economic, cultural, and epistemic orders support these practices.

Institutions for Resource Management, Development, and Governance

In polycentric governance the efforts of user groups to manage common-pool resources are granted the same status as individual or corporate rights to private property. Just as individuals are presumed to be the best judge of their own tastes, user groups should be presumed to be capable of managing their common property. A basic tenet of public policy should be that those groups who are able to manage CPRs effectively should be allowed to do so, if at all possible. In this view government intervention should be limited to two sets of circumstances: (1) when user groups fail to manage their resources effectively; or (2) if user groups violate basic standards of fairness, accountability, or other issues of concern to society as a whole. Instead of presuming that governmental officials or scientific experts know best how to manage CPRs, user groups should be given the benefit of the doubt and encouraged to govern their own affairs.

The Workshop approach to institutional analysis complements well-known results from the literature on "new institutional economics" concerning the importance of property rights. Influential research by Douglass North (1981, 1990; North and Thomas 1973) has demonstrated that a clear definition of private property rights is essential before market processes can operate at anywhere near efficient levels. Economic growth requires investor confidence, because individuals or private corporations will make investments to improve the productive capacity of their assets only if they can expect to enjoy the benefits of these investments. Rarely, however, is this conclusion extended to a clarification of property rights over commonly held assets, including the common-pool resources that are the subject of most of the research included in this volume (see also E. Ostrom 1999).

This analogy between group and private property rights is very close. Those groups of resource users who have successfully managed their common resources have done so at the cost of establishing and enforcing rules that call for significant sacrifices on the part of individual members of that group. They are unlikely to continue to pay those costs if governmental officials are expected to establish or enforce a different set of rules. Without this assurance group cooperation will break down, and individuals may succumb to the temptations to overexploit the resource. The resulting destruction of the resource will hurt society as a whole. By the same line of argument, then, group rights to common-pool resources need to be just as well protected as are individual (or corporate) rights to private property.

Protection of group rights is particularly crucial if the policy goal is sustainable development and not just economic growth per se. Resource sustainability is not a new idea: groups of fishers, farmers, and herders throughout the world have always had to cope with sustainability problems. Governmental officials and policy analysts should remain open to the possibility that they can learn from user groups about the conditions for successful resource management.

The macro-level structure of governance directly impacts the prospects for successful user group management of common-pool resources. Yet even a detailed picture of the institutional arrangements at all scales of aggregation would not suffice. Workshop scholars have long realized the importance of considering the physical nature of the good, the attributes of the community, and the institutional rules-in-use within that community as they cope with those physical problems. This threefold structure has been summarized in the *Institutional Analysis and Development* (IAD) framework. Kiser and Ostrom (1982; reprinted in McGinnis 1999b) provide the most extensive discussion of the rationale behind this framework, and Oakerson (1992) uses the framework to organize an extended set of case studies sponsored by the Research Committee of the National Research Council. Because this framework has been discussed in great detail in several sources, only a brief overview is necessary here. Figure 1 illustrates this framework (Ostrom, Gardner, and Walker 1994: 47).

The IAD framework differentiates among operational, collective choice, and constitutional levels (or arenas) of interaction. At the operational level concrete actions are undertaken by those individuals most directly affected or by public officials. These actions directly impact the world in some demonstrable manner, resulting in observable policy outcomes. (In fig. 1 dashed lines with arrows denote feedback from outcomes to all the steps in the process.) The rules that define and constrain the activities of individual citizens and officials in operational arenas have been established at the collective choice level. The rules by which these rules themselves are subject to modification are determined at the constitutional level of analysis.

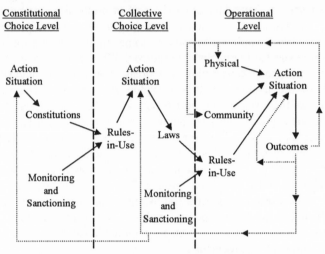

Fig. 1. Linking levels of analysis

At each level individual and collective choice is constrained to some range of strategic options. The point of this demarcation of levels is to highlight some fundamental similarities among political processes at different levels of analysis. At each level actors confront an *action situation* with strategic options and role expectations as defined at higher levels, and the choices of actors at one level jointly produce patterns of interactions and outcomes.

In short, institutions link levels by defining the roles that individual or collective actors fulfill. Clearly, all three levels of interactions are involved in any one particular process. Analysts of development or governance must take factors and processes at all three levels into account, for interactions at the operational, collective choice, and constitutional levels are going on concurrently. In normal circumstances foundational constitutional questions are not in doubt for routine operational decisions. Yet this level cannot be entirely ignored, since it determines who has the capability or the responsibility to participate in collective choice and operational decisions.

Furthermore, in many empirical settings these analytical arenas cannot be so clearly demarcated. Consider the activities undertaken by a small group of fishers deciding how to allocate rights to fishing locations. Participants may be simultaneously considering who should be allowed to fish and the quality of the spots to be allocated to each participant. Still, this analytical distinction remains a valuable aid to understanding.

This concern for embedding operational decisions within broader institutional settings, and local studies within larger constitutional orders, is reflected in the organization of this set of readings. Taken as a whole, the research programs of Workshop scholars cover the full spectrum of scales from "nano-level" studies of local irrigation systems to the large-scale organization of the global economy. Any one research project, however, is focused on a more restricted range for obvious reasons. This collection of readings is designed to illustrate how all the pieces fit together and to suggest connections among multiple levels and modes of analysis that can inspire even more research.

Part I. Resource Management

Essays in part I show how Workshop research programs on common-pool resource management developed over the span of the last five decades. Although this research program now encompasses research sites dispersed throughout the world, it began close to home. While a doctoral student at UCLA and a junior faculty member at the Universities of Wyoming and Oregon, Vincent Ostrom (1953b, c) began his studies of political institutions and the physical nature of water resources in the American West. When Elinor Ostrom completed her Ph.D. dissertation (1965), also at UCLA, her topic was groundwater management in California. Shortly after the Ostroms moved to Indiana University, the Workshop was established to coordinate collaborative research projects on policing in nearby Indianapolis (and related subjects). Clearly, the importance of local knowledge was recognized from the very start.

The origins of the Workshop approach to institutional analysis can be illustrated with a brief discussion of an essay not included in this volume. In "State Administration of Natural Resources in the West" Vincent Ostrom (1953a) surveys the legal underpinnings of the role of American states in natural resource management. Although the details of his presentation are now dated, it is fascinating to see how the overall structure of the Workshop approach was presaged in this article, published twenty years before its establishment. In the opening paragraphs Ostrom directs attention to the imperatives imposed by the physical nature of the good, that is, the characteristics of the physical and climatic environment of the American West. The second paragraph bears quoting in its entirety:

> American institutional arrangements, sustenance patterns and resource policies were conceived in humid England and developed in the humid

regions of the United States. However, the general aridity of the West stands in marked contrast to the humidity that prevailed in the physical environment where American social institutions and traditions were formed. This alteration of the physical environment has caused an important shift in the balance of human ecology requiring significant modification in institutional arrangements and social policy, especially in regard to the control and development of natural resources. (478)

He argues that state jurisdictions bear little relationship to natural water management zones and that institutional arrangements must be selected that are consistent with this physical reality.

As units of government, the states were not conceived in terms that are relevant to resources administration. Only California constitutes an adequate hydrologic unit permitting multiple-purpose administration of an integral watershed area. Major land-use patterns transcend state boundaries and cause the states to determine the nature of their resource programs by a standard of competitive relationships with each other.

The states as constitutional units within the American federal system of government are inclined to conceive of their relationships with one another and, to some extent, with the federal government on the basis of concepts of sovereignty and states' rights which presume inherent authority and power to decide. . . . Yet the major problems of resource administration require regional solutions that transcend state boundaries. (492)

This concern for matching institutions to the physical environment (and to the characteristics of the community) lies at the heart of the IAD framework later developed at the Workshop. Although he discusses the relevant legal context, Ostrom places much more emphasis on whether legal rules are in fact consistent with the likely behavior of the relevant actors, that is, with the rules-in-use. This theme recurs throughout the corpus of Workshop research programs.

In this article Ostrom pays particular attention to the nature of the property rights in natural resources. He doubts that state governments have the institutional capacity to deal with natural resource issues that transcend the limits of any state's legal jurisdiction. These issues were of more than passing, theoretical interest. In subsequent years he evaluated resource problems in the transition to statehood in Hawaii, and he helped craft the natural resource article of the Alaskan state constitution.

The first selection included in this volume is taken from a popular magazine published in 1967. In "Water and Politics California Style" (chap. 1)

Vincent Ostrom briefly summarizes the historical process by which water rights and resource management patterns were first established in California. He points to the important precedents established when miners simply grabbed all the water they needed for their mining operations. Eventually, the interests of many other segments of the community were integrated into cooperative arrangements of various kinds. This accessible overview should help ease the reader into the more abstract analyses to follow.

In "Legal and Political Conditions of Water Resource Development" (chap. 2) Vincent and Elinor Ostrom provide more detail about the specific actors involved in the West Basin area around Los Angeles. After a brief overview of the technical, economic, and legal context, the authors summarize the results of Elinor Ostrom's doctoral dissertation (1965) on the role of public entrepreneurs in devising groundwater institutions in southern California. In this work Elinor Ostrom concluded that the use of equity proceedings in state courts facilitated the negotiation of complex patterns of interagency arrangements to prevent saltwater erosion from the ocean and to ensure the replenishment of groundwater supplies. Through in-depth interviews, archival research, and nonparticipant observation she determined that one factor crucial to this success was the existence of institutional arrangements at the state level that authorized local associations, special districts, and public and private agencies to deal with these problems. Also, effective conflict mechanisms were made available to reach consensual arrangements that secured clear property rights.

Since the next reading in this part was published ten years after the initial establishment of the Workshop in 1973, a brief digression on the intervening years seems in order. Despite their initial interest in natural resources and groundwater management, the first large-scale empirical research program of the Workshop dealt with police services in urban America (McGinnis 1999b). Upon their arrival in Bloomington the Ostroms were intrigued by a long-standing political debate over metropolitan organization that had just come to a head. In 1969 city and county governments in the Indianapolis metropolitan area were consolidated into a single government, called "Unigov." This consolidation was incomplete, however, in the sense that a few suburban municipalities elected to remain outside this new arrangement. Thus, these social scientists had a unique opportunity to compare the production of public goods and services by large and small agencies serving consolidated and nonconsolidated communities that were virtually identical in all other ways.

In a long series of related research projects the Ostroms and their faculty and student colleagues demonstrated that citizens were more satisfied with the performance of smaller or intermediate-sized police forces (see McGinnis 1999b). Yet larger-scale operations remained an important aspect of this success, especially for training and crime lab facilities. In short, these research programs demonstrated the benefits of polycentric governance in metropolitan America.

When they returned to the study of the management of natural resources, the Ostroms brought with them a renewed appreciation of the myriad advantages of allowing self-governing communities to address their own collective problems in the way they saw most fit. It is safe to say that they decided to study police not because of an inherent interest in the subject but because it was a good vehicle to explore theoretical ideas.

On its own terms this research program on metropolitan governance has been (and still is) very successful (McGinnis 1999b). For purposes of the present volume it is important to recognize the methodological legacy of those studies: a unique combination of insistence on scientific rigor and policy relevance, openness to multiple techniques of empirical and formal analysis, and sensitivity to nested levels of analysis. The early Workshop research programs demonstrated that public services can be most efficiently provided under a system of multiple and overlapping jurisdictions, by enabling producers of public services to operate at the scale most efficient for particular activities. These empirical results were consistent with the nature of the American constitutional order, as originally envisioned by the founders (V. Ostrom 1987). As they began to examine problems of resource development in more detail, Workshop scholars began to find that polycentric governance was equally effective for empirical settings that could not be further removed from metropolitan centers in the United States, namely, some of the poorest regions of the developing world.

In many ways common-pool resources turned out to be a more effective focus for empirical explorations of these theoretical concerns. Anyone evaluating police performance in urban areas can scarcely avoid emotion-laden controversies over race relations and welfare policy. Also, one prominent issue concerns the appropriate role for the national government in the fight against urban blight. Not only does the management of fisheries, irrigation systems, and most common-pool resources occupy a lower level of salience, but, in many cases, these resources are physically remote from urban centers or national capitals. In these more isolated communities it is easier to identify the reasons why some communities manage to solve their own problems while other communities flounder or fail.

Whereas urban politics evoke ideological statements more easily than rigorous analyses, policy analysts often adopt a problem-solving attitude toward CPR management. Ideologically tinged debates certainly occur between advocates of privatization and centralized management, especially when treated in the abstract. Still, resource management issues lie at the far periphery of most political scientists' range of interests. Thus, for many common-pool resources it is possible to maintain a focus on practical problems of a manageable scope.

None of this means that CPR management is unimportant. For those whose lives or livelihoods depend on the continued availability of plentiful water or fish stocks, nothing could be more important. Politics is surely involved but rarely in the form of noisy confrontations between competing ideologies, which would most likely result in confusion and destruction.

In recent years issues of the environment and resource management have gained a new urgency in political debates. Global environmental issues, in particular, have emerged as an important new topic of political contention. Unfortunately, global environmental debates often degenerate into ideological confrontations, far removed from the physical realities they are supposedly meant to address (see McGinnis and Ostrom 1996).

Many years before sustainable development became a ubiquitous slogan, Workshop scholars were already seeking to understand the conditions under which resources can be managed in a sustainable manner. Now that the world of national and international politics has caught up with the Workshop, it has important insights to offer. As shown in this volume, long-standing and ongoing research programs on the management of common-pool resources have given us a clearer understanding of the requisites for the successful implementation and sustenance of self-governance.

In "Institutional Capacity and the Resolution of a Commons Dilemma" (chap. 3) Elinor Ostrom, in collaboration with William Blomquist, returned to the issues of groundwater management with which she began her career. Blomquist went on in his own book, *Dividing the Waters* (1992), to compare the institutional arrangements for eight groundwater basins, including one that Elinor Ostrom had examined in depth three decades earlier. Another of his cases had been the focus of Weschler (1968), a dissertation completed by one of Elinor Ostrom's fellow graduate students at UCLA. Comparisons between these two periods are made more explicitly in Blomquist's contribution to E. Ostrom, Gardner, and Walker (1994). Revisiting the sites of earlier research has become a Workshop tradition, one that, if continued over the next few decades, will enable analysts to make valid inferences based on comparison of the same area across multiple time periods.

This 1985 essay presages the underlying principles of the design of successful common-pool resource regimes that Elinor Ostrom summarizes in her influential book *Governing the Commons* (1990). Her list of eight design principles is probably the most widely cited aspect of that pathbreaking book. At the time of the publication of her essay with William Blomquist, these principles had not yet taken their final form, but the way in which the two authors go through the many informational and other requirements that would have to be satisfied for the successful operation of a market-based resource management scheme should help readers understand how Elinor Ostrom eventually came up with her famous list. She didn't yet have the answer, but she was already asking the right questions.

In her Presidential Address to the International Association for the Study of Common Property, "Design Principles in Long-Enduring Irrigation Institutions" (chap. 4), Elinor Ostrom succinctly states the design principles that encapsulate her extensive comparisons of institutional arrangements in mountain meadows and forests in Switzerland and Japan, irrigation systems in Spain and the Philippines, fisheries in Sri Lanka and Turkey, and groundwater management in California. These design principles have been discussed by a vast array of scholars in diverse areas of study. For example, McGinnis and Ostrom (1996) and the contributors to Keohane and Ostrom (1995) discuss the potential relevance of these design principles to global governance.

Ostrom concludes that all of the successful, long-lasting cases of CPR management included some mechanism for monitoring and sanctioning the behavior of participants in that community. This finding implies that self-governance requires more than a simple agreement to cooperate. Instead, some means must be found to ensure the continuation of cooperative behavior in the face of individual incentives to take advantage of the situation for personal gain. Communities of common understanding can support appropriate monitoring arrangements that help encourage individuals to use these resources in a fair and equitable manner. Self-governance cannot eliminate opportunistic behavior entirely, but it can limit its negative effects.

Ostrom's book synthesizes the results of a vast array of case studies, several of which were still under way at that time. The Workshop has published extensive bibliographies on CPR research (see Suggested Further Readings at the end of this volume). Also, reference sources are regularly updated on the Workshop's web page, <http://www.indiana.edu/~workshop>. The range of empirical cases of common-pool resource regimes studied by scholars associated with the Workshop is far too diverse to cover here. This part concludes with two essays that exemplify development of this research program in recent years.

In "Property Rights Regimes and Coastal Fisheries: An Empirical Analysis" (chap. 5) Edella Schlager and Elinor Ostrom examine the nature of property rights in fisheries. After laying out the general properties of any property rights system, they detail the combinations of rules that different groups of fishers have used to satisfy the design principles defined in the previous reading. Their analysis of the legal components of the system of rules that define property rights builds on basic distinctions laid out in the earlier essays included in this part of the volume. Clearly, many conceptual advances were made as these research programs progressed.

The authors use a comprehensive data set on the physical and institutional characteristics of a set of coastal fisheries to draw conclusions about the determinants of long-term success or failure in the management of this common-pool resource. They conclude that in-shore fishery regimes characterized by some, but not all, of the attributes of private property are more effective means of governing local fisheries.

In "Mobile Flows, Storage, and Self-Organized Institutions for Governing Common-Pool Resources" (chap. 6) Edella Schlager, William Blomquist, and Shui-Yan Tang shift the focus to a particular characteristic of common-pool resources, namely, the extent to which that resource can be stored for later use. Their comparative analysis of irrigation systems, fisheries, and groundwater basins is based on the application of similar data coding forms to the physical and institutional characteristics of these very different resources. They present a useful taxonomy of different types of CPR problems and conclude that the same solution cannot be expected to apply to all kinds of common-pool resources.

As discussed earlier, a major goal of institutional analysis has been to break apart the state-market dichotomy that so dominates policy debates. Workshop scholars have clearly demonstrated the effectiveness of alternative institutional forms for the management of common-pool resources. Just as neither markets nor centralized management are appropriate in all circumstances, no single institutional arrangement can work for the full range of common-pool resource problems.

In recent years many Workshop scholars have begun to study resources governed by multiple user groups. In the International Forestry Resources and Institutions (IFRI) Research Program the IAD framework and multiple modes of empirical analysis are applied to many different uses of forest resources: timber, fuel, food, water, mining, and tourism. With the support of United Nations, United States, and private funding agencies, scholars associated with IFRI have developed and field-tested a rigorous method of measuring the characteristics of resource use and institutions for the management of forested areas (Thomson 1992). The first fruits of this research program have just been brought together into a book containing research reports from Bolivia, Ecuador, Guatemala, Nepal, Uganda, and the United States, all using the same set of methods (Gibson, McKean, and Ostrom forthcoming). The central goal of this project is to understand what combinations of institutional arrangements are most likely to allow sustainable development of forestry resources. Again, rigorous comparison lies at the heart of the method, as the coding form generated for this project includes measures of more than a hundred variables on the physical, economic, and institutional characteristics of specific forested regions. Furthermore, the data and analytical conclusions from the IFRI project are made freely available to local communities for use in their own development projects. This spirit of collaboration with the communities they study is a long-standing Workshop tradition.

The IFRI project is now associated with an even more comprehensive project. Elinor Ostrom and Emilio Moran, an anthropologist, serve as co-directors of the Center for the Study of Institutions, Population, and Environmental Change (CIPEC) at Indiana University. This collaborative undertaking by the Workshop and three other research centers in anthropology, demography, and environmental science is funded by the National Science Foundation as part of its major program on global environmental change. CIPEC research programs combine state-of-the-art satellite positioning and imagery systems with a variety of field methods based on rigorous sampling techniques. In this way CIPEC scholars increase the rigor of empirical analyses of environmental conditions and institutions specifically related to the management of forests throughout the Western Hemisphere. The work of this center has only just begun, but it promises to make a major contribution to these important areas of research and policy.

Part II. Constitutional Order

This brief overview of forestry and global environmental change research programs leads naturally to consideration of the ways in which Workshop scholars approach the study of macro-level political and economic orders. One hallmark of the Workshop has been a sustained effort to integrate factors operating at different scales of aggregation. Detailed examinations of small-scale common-pool resource regimes are undertaken with an eye toward the implications such analysis might have for issues of development and governance. Of particular relevance are conditions conducive to the establishment and maintenance of the local capacities for self-governance and sustainable development. Both the big picture and the details need to be understood.

For example, McGinnis and Ostrom (1996) argue that the same principles of design that make it possible for local communities to manage common-pool resources may also apply to efforts to manage global environmental change. The analogy between local and global commons, however, is not exact (Keohane and Ostrom 1995). The benefits of person-to-person interaction in the management of common-pool resources at the local level, for example, cannot be duplicated at the global level. Gibson, Ostrom, and Ahn (1998) investigate the extent to which behavioral regularities identified at one level can be "scaled up" for application to higher levels of aggregation. They conclude that some extensions are defensible but that caution must be taken against overgeneralization. One principle that does scale up is that both monitoring and sanctioning remain critical for the implementation of international agreements to protect the environment.

Even if different sets of design principles turn out to be most relevant for different levels of aggregation, it is still important to ensure that institutional arrangements at different levels reinforce one another rather than working at cross-principles. Elinor Ostrom's list of design principles (see chap. 4) recognizes the importance of the ways in which local rules are "nested" within the context of higher-level patterns of governance. For if groups are not given at least a minimal right to organize, then resource management schemes may not be grounded in locally generated knowledge. Elsewhere, Oakerson and Walker (1997) argue that nesting is essential to any meaningful reform of institutional arrangements at the macro level. This concern for nesting is the glue that ties micro-level analyses of resource management to macro-level development policy.

The readings in part II move the locus of analysis to macro-level concerns about constitutional choice. No matter how closely one scales up the same principles or insists on a consistent nesting of principles at different levels, there is no reason to require institutional analysts to apply the same mode of analysis at all scales of aggregation. As shown in the readings in this part, institutional analysis at the macro level takes on a more philosophical tenor. No longer is there as much direct concern for the nature of physical goods; instead, focus shifts to efforts to comprehend the overall implications of how a society organizes itself at the most fundamental level. A certain level of abstraction is required, but these abstractions should not become fodder for vacuous debates over ideological slogans. It may be a different mode of analysis, but the same normative and analytical approach underlies applications at all levels.

In "A Forgotten Tradition: The Constitutional Level of Analysis" (chap. 7) Vincent Ostrom argues that it is important to understand the overall context within which specific policy debates take place, because constitutional order can either support or undermine the foundations for self-governance. Vincent Ostrom has written a series of books (1987, 1989, 1991, 1997) that each, in different ways, offer polycentricity as an alternative to standard notions of sovereignty. Under unitary sovereignty the government can impose a uniform set of laws that do not take account of local variation in physical conditions. Under polycentricity different physical realities would be reflected in the rules designed by the affected communities. Diverse sets of local rules set the stage for conflict among alternative worldviews and rule systems, but this conflict can be constructive rather than destructive. Indeed, contestation lies at the very heart of polycentricity.

In this essay Vincent Ostrom contrasts the model of polycentric governance in *The Federalist* with a paternalistic vision of public administration closely associated with Woodrow Wilson. For Wilson and other reform-minded politicians and policy analysts the role of government is to produce public goods in the most efficient manner, as determined by expert opinion. Public opinion plays a role in selecting leaders and setting general guide-lines, but beyond that the public is a passive recipient of government policies.

In polycentric governance political authorities should act to support the capacity of self-governance for groups and communities at all levels of aggregation. Within such a constitutional order individuals form corpora-tions to produce private goods and join myriad associations to produce public goods and manage common-pool resources. Governmental authorities at all levels play important roles, all of which are supportive in nature. Just as they are expected to provide a stable legal foundation for the smooth operation of economic markets, public officials should also devote them-selves to nurturing group capacities for self-governance. Generally, govern-ment officials should concentrate on the *provision* of public goods and services, but they need not be directly involved in the *production* of that good. (The distinction between provision and production is detailed in Ostrom, Tiebout, and Warren 1961; McGinnis 1999b.)

Perhaps the most important role of government in a polycentric order is to help local jurisdictions resolve their conflicts of interest in a way that remains consistent with societal standards of fairness. If a CPR user group unfairly restricts access to their resources to a very small group of people who benefit materially from that restriction, then higher political authorities should act to open up the process to broader participation. In other words, public authorities should act to prevent self-governing communities from taking unfair advantage of their ability to coordinate their actions.

Unfortunately, under paternalistic governance, the government itself can become a form of private property. For if sovereignty is assumed to reside in a single center of power, then politics becomes a simple question of determining who wields that power or who "owns" that office. Once the ability to impose laws and regulations becomes a source of revenue for public officials, great importance is attached to winning power and remain-ing in office. If elections degenerate to a competition among self-interested agents seeking to access the levers of sovereign power, then even a liberal democratic order can become a form of tyranny.

The danger inherent in paternalistic governance can be illustrated by an admittedly loose analogy to problems of common-pool resource manage-ment. To some extent a government's budget or a nation's entire resource base can be thought of as a common-pool resource. These resources can be used efficiently, in ways that enhance social welfare, or they can be captured by small groups to satisfy their own narrow interests. The same concern for opportunism that permeates institutional analysis of a CPR user group becomes translated into concerns for predatory behavior by governmental authorities. If too many public officials act too selfishly, then society as a whole can suffer grave consequences. Since monitoring and sanctioning are essential activities to effective CPR management, how governmental authorities are to be deterred from engaging in excessive opportunism is the key question of governance.

The problems in autocratic political orders are even more extreme. In "Cryptoimperialism, Predatory States, and Self-Governance" (chap. 8) Vincent Ostrom argues that Hobbes's *Leviathan* remains an important influence on contemporary events. Hobbes's vision of a single, overwhelming source of power remains a strong inspiration for rulers in many countries. In particular, Ostrom shows that Lenin's writings contain an especially pure distillation of the logic of Hobbesian sovereignty.

The main point of this essay is to draw attention to a more subtle influence of Hobbes on today's world. Vincent Ostrom introduces the term *cryptoimperialism* to designate the insidious phenomenon by which the rulers of developing countries are influenced by the ideas of the foreign donors upon which they have come to depend so heavily. Since the most influential individuals in governments on both sides of the Cold War and in international lending institutions see the paternalistic form of government as natural, this attitude is naturally passed on to their clients. The consequence is a natural tendency toward the establishment of "predatory states" in many parts of the world. Although military force and vast disparities in economic power play obvious roles in maintaining new forms of imperialism, a more subtle prop is the widespread habit of thinking in terms of Hobbesian sovereignty.

Contemporary problems of governance have deep historical roots. In *The Emergence of Autocracy in Liberia: Tragedy and Challenge* (1992) Amos Sawyer, a former president of Liberia, concurs with Vincent Ostrom's concerns about the dangers of cryptoimperialism. This book, completed while Sawyer was a visiting scholar at the Workshop, documents how a community of freed slaves ironically came to establish a constitutional order that concentrated power in a single position, the president. The tragic civil wars his country experienced in recent years are a direct consequence of the widespread acceptance of this conceptualization of governance as domination.

Sawyer's book is one of several books in which the Workshop approach to the study of governance has been applied to a remarkably diverse set of political regimes. Subjects include constitutional order in Communist regimes (Kaminski 1989, 1992), imperial Russia (Obolonsky 1996), imperial China (Yang 1987), and military regimes in Latin America (Loveman 1993). The same principles have been applied in shorter works on other parts of Africa (Duany 1992, 1994; Jinadu 1994). Contributors to Wunsch and Olowu (1995) survey the vast array of problems that can be attributed to the general adoption of the centralized, Hobbesian state throughout postcolonial Africa. In each of these works the authors have been deeply influenced by the work of Vincent Ostrom.

A related line of research on the nature of governance in Africa has been most closely associated with Robert Bates, whose relationship with the Workshop has been primarily through his doctoral students: Arun Agrawal, Kathryn Firmin-Sellers, and Clark Gibson. Bates (1981, 1983) portrays most postcolonial African regimes as disassociated from their own people. To the extent that these regimes are sustained by foreign aid, the rulers are absolved of any need to provide a full range of public services for their own people. Quite to the contrary, their interests lie in appropriating as many resources as they can for their own personal wealth. At best they will spread these resources to just enough groups for them to stay in power. Given this proprietary attitude toward government office, it is hardly surprising that the record of African development has been so woeful.

In the next selection, "The Concentration of Authority: Constitutional Creation in the Gold Coast, 1950" (chap. 9), Kathryn Firmin-Sellers shows the process of constitutional choice in action. She shows how the relevant actors were willing to set up a centralized political order because each thought they had a good chance to dominate the system once it was in place. Her interpretation of these events draws on concepts and analytical tools developed in the field of research known as the new institutional economics, especially Knight's (1992) contention that distributional consequences are the most important determinants of institutional change.

The single most important lesson of these analyses of macro-level constitutional order is that national governments can either support and enhance the self-governing capacities of local communities or else they can undermine local capacities by adopting a predatory attitude. In practice nearly all governments do a little bit of both. Some groups are granted the right to manage their own affairs or to protect their own resources from the encroachments of other groups. Meanwhile, the resources controlled by other groups serve as the target of expropriation. This essay by Kathryn Firmin-Sellers reminds us that constitution making is an inherently political process, in which some groups gain at the expense of others. Similarly destructive conflicts can occur in the operational and collective choice arenas of interactions whenever participants (and policy analysts) forget that the essential purpose of government is to help peoples solve their problems rather than to select winners and losers. This problem-solving attitude is difficult to sustain given the competitive thrust of much political interaction and policy analysis.

E. Ostrom (1999) notes that strong conceptualizations sometimes make it hard for analysts even to acknowledge the existence of certain kinds of organizations. In "Local Organizations and Development: The African Experience" (chap. 10) Dele Olowu, a Nigerian scholar who has made extended visits to the Workshop, demonstrates that local forms of self-governance are alive and well in many parts of Africa. These organizations tend to be overlooked, however, because they do not fit into the standard categories of state, market, or civil society.

One of the more subtle problems concerns the ways in which policies of decentralization have been applied in several African countries. On the face of it, decentralization seems congruent with calls for self-governance, but in practice all that has changed is the locus of public decision making. Just because a governmental unit is smaller in scope does not necessarily mean that the people are going to be involved in governing their own affairs. Dele Olowu discusses several examples that illustrate the subtle yet fundamental differences between decentralized administration and genuine self-governance.

Finally, Dele Olowu concludes that the findings from the studies of metropolitan governance undertaken at the Workshop could be fruitfully applied in the African context. He points to the existence of long-standing traditions of local resource management regimes while still recognizing the problems of sustaining these traditions in the context of the modern, centralized state imported to Africa from the West.

Part III. Development

This diagnosis of an overreliance on centralized authority might seem to lead directly to the conclusion that efforts must be undertaken to reform the political order as a whole, to remake society from the ground up. But it is not quite that simple, because Workshop scholars tend to be skeptical of grand plans for reform.

Vincent Ostrom (1991, 1997) cautions that many "great experiments," such as those undertaken by Marxist-Leninist regimes, result in the "monumental failures" of war, famine, or repression. Utopian ideals of equality provided the groundwork for the terrible costs of totalitarianism in the Soviet Union, Eastern Europe, China, and elsewhere in the world. Even the high ideals of democratization and national self-determination can result in terrible suffering for the average person, as was clearly shown in the post–Cold War history of the former republics of Yugoslavia.

The danger of monumental failure does not mean that reform should not be pursued. After all, absence of reform can, in some circumstances, be equally disastrous (see Eggertsson 1996). Instead, the lesson should be that reform should be undertaken with full acceptance of the limited ability of humans to grasp the full consequences of their actions (see V. Ostrom 1991, 1997). Rather than try to impose a single utopian ideal on society as a whole, his preferred solution is to design institutions that help local communities help themselves. This attitude leads to a form of policy analysis more concerned with process than with ends. Still, designing open-ended institutions that nurture self-governing capacities should lay a solid foundation for sustainable development. Part III includes several examples of the Workshop approach to the design of development institutions.

In "Institutional Analysis and Decentralization: Developing an Analytical Framework for Effective Third World Administrative Reform" (chap. 11) James Wunsch reiterates Dele Olowu's concerns that decentralization per se does not guarantee self-governance. Just as the state-market dichotomy is unnecessarily limiting, he argues that a similar fixation on a centralization-decentralization dimension will lead policy analysts to overlook potentially relevant alternative institutions. After explaining the implications of all of the major components of institutional analysis in the context of African development, Wunsch uses these methods to explain the general failings of the centralized, administrative state in much of Africa. Wunsch offers suggestions for training future administrators to be more creative and open-ended in their consideration of alternative options. Wunsch also highlights conceptual similarities between the problems of development and the results of previous Workshop research on police service provision in metropolitan areas in the United States (McGinnis 1999b).

The crucial issue is not the degree of centralization but the configuration of incentives that motivate individual and collective actions. The next essay explicitly compares alternative institutional arrangements for the governance of irrigation systems. In "Improving the Performance of Small-Scale Irrigation Systems: The Effects of Technological Investments and Governance Structure on Irrigation Performance in Nepal" (chap. 12) Wai Fung (Danny) Lam demonstrates that irrigation systems built and managed by the central government or international financial lending institutions tend to be less long-lasting or effective than irrigation systems built and maintained by local farmers. This difference holds even when the government-funded systems are much larger and technologically more sophisticated.

The explanation of this puzzle is simple. Even the latest technology cannot survive without regular maintenance, and the incentives have to be right if local participants are going to exert the effort needed to maintain an irrigation system. Lam examines the problems raised by asymmetries between "headenders" and "tailenders," that is, between farmers whose crops are located close to the headworks of the irrigation system and those who farm areas near the end of the line. As he shows, establishment of sophisticated headworks may exacerbate these asymmetries, and tailenders who benefit little from these improvements may not be willing to help maintain the system as a whole. Conversely, both groups would be motivated to maintain less sophisticated improvements in the lining of the irrigation channels, since their failure to do so could mean that none of them will receive sufficient water. Lam shows that, counter to the expectations of most external observers, farmers can undertake all the maintenance, monitoring, and sanctioning activities needed for many successful irrigation systems.

This essay, if read in isolation, might be misconstrued as supporting an ideological aversion to big government. "Small is beautiful" is not an appropriate slogan, however, for advocates of polycentric governance. In hopes of belaying any misunderstanding, the next selection, by this same author, shows how governmental officials and local farmers can work together toward the common goal of development.

In "Institutional Design of Public Agencies and Coproduction: A Study of Irrigation Associations in Taiwan" (chap. 13) Danny Lam argues that an overlooked source of Taiwan's economic success is the autonomy granted local farmers' associations in managing their own irrigation systems. Governmental officials play generally supportive roles, since aspects of Taiwan's bureaucratic structure limit their incentives to engage in predatory behavior. As a consequence, government authorities act primarily to support the conditions under which local arrangements can be implemented.

Whereas the essays in part I evaluate the physical properties of a wide array of irrigation systems and other common-pool resource regimes, this one provides an in-depth analysis of the reasons why local irrigation associations work as institutions. Lam illustrates the ways in which the complementary interests of participants are encapsulated within an effective governance structure. The national governments fulfill several important roles: arbiter of conflicting interests, a source of finance, and "epistemic leader."

The next selection continues with the case of Taiwan but moves to an examination of other forms of institutions. When Workshop scholars consider problems of the developing world, they focus on the contributions of informal networks of political and economic entrepreneurs typically overlooked by policy analysts. Although typically denounced as illegal "black markets," individual entrepreneurs rarely have much of a choice in the matter. Under conditions of the widespread government corruption and incompetence typical of predatory states, the informal sector can be a most effective alternative to officially recognized transactions. De Soto's book *The Other Path* (1989) is the most widely known analysis of the "informal sector" in the developing world. Within the community of Workshop scholars, Landa (1994) places special emphasis on trading networks organized around ethnic identifications.

In "Informal Credit Markets and Economic Development in Taiwan" (chap. 14) Shui-Yan Tang argues that informal credit markets were key to the economic success of Taiwan. One general implication of this analysis is that similar institutional arrangements should be encouraged in other developing countries seeking to emulate Taiwan's economic success. Too often policy analysts fixate on the presence of a secure legal system or the occurrence of regular elections, but Tang's analysis reminds us that development is primarily local in nature.

This essay illustrates an important lesson of Workshop research. Although analysts regularly use terms like *the government* to refer to the actions of particular sets of officials, the reality is much more complex. Any analysis of the operation of governments would show that most (if not all) are themselves organized in a polycentric manner. Despite the presumption that top leaders can command subordinates to carry out particular policies, many difficulties are associated with monitoring the behavior of bureaucratic agents. Also, informal contacts among bureaucratic officials are often crucial to policy implementation. The complexity of the policy implementation process is well recognized, but the Workshop approach to institutional analysis tries to bring some coherence to our understanding of the interactions that take place in both formal organizations and in more informal settings.

The term *civil society* is often used very loosely, but the essays by Lam and Tang illustrate how the operation of informal organizations can further the process of development. Another now popular term, *sustainable development,* is closely related to the concept of "coproduction" developed nearly two decades ago by Workshop scholars investigating the determinants of the successful provision of police services (see McGinnis 1999b). In a regular production process a commodity is produced by one actor and consumed by another. Under a process of coproduction both must interact to produce the desired result. For example, if police officials and neighborhood residents coordinate their efforts to monitor crime in that neighborhood, then public safety results from a process of coproduction. It's not simply a matter of police supplying their customers with a better product but, rather, a consequence of continuing cooperation between police officers and members of the community.

Several of the readings included in this volume make use of the concept of coproduction. In the final reading in part III, "Crossing the Great Divide: Coproduction, Synergy, and Development" (chap. 15), Elinor Ostrom discusses the general implications of conceptualizing development as a process of coproduction. Her discussion of specific examples of development from two different continents supports her contention that participation by local communities is a key to the success of sustainable development. This essay, as well as the earlier essays by Wunsch and Olowu, refers to specific conclusions from earlier Workshop research programs on public perceptions of policing in metropolitan areas of the United States (McGinnis 1999b). This convergence demonstrates that the principles of polycentric governance transcend the many obvious differences between rural areas of the developing world and urban America.

Part IV. Polycentric Governance

The Workshop approach to development is more fully explicated in a textbook written by Elinor Ostrom, Larry Schroeder, and Susan Wynne (1993). This book places rural infrastructure at the very heart of development issues. E. Ostrom (1992) uses these same principles to guide community "crafting" of institutions for the management of irrigation systems. Oakerson and Walker (1997), students from two different generations of the Workshop, discuss the general implications of Workshop research for the reform of institutions in developing countries. They draw extensively on the IAD framework (Kiser and Ostrom 1982; Oakerson 1992; McGinnis 1999a) to illustrate broader issues of development. Walker (1994) uses this framework to examine the gritty details of fertilizer distribution in Cameroon as an example of institutional analysis applied to a practical policy program.

In all of these works the authors stress that policy analysts must approach institutional reform in an open and creative fashion, rather than relying on standard categories. Yet, it is not just the policy analysts who need to adopt a broader frame of reference. A community's common conceptualization of the meaning of development is a crucial factor in its likely success. The final two readings address these matters directly.

In "Artisanship and Artifact" (chap. 16) Vincent Ostrom reminds institutional analysts that all institutions are social creations, grounded in shared understandings. Just as an individual craftsman or artist must imagine a tool or artwork before he or she can bring that creation to life, communities of individuals cannot govern themselves without some shared set of beliefs and norms, some shared conceptualizations. In an earlier work Vincent Ostrom (1987[1971]) summarizes the political theory behind the design of the U.S. Constitution. In his more recent work Ostrom (1997) has been concerned about the institutional creations that go on every day, in communities of all sizes. Constitutional order at the macro level is grounded in the conceptualizations and understandings of the ultimate micro-level actor, the individual.

In the final selection in this volume Vincent Ostrom sounds a cautionary note. Once self-governance has been achieved, there is no reason to assume that the shared understandings that support self-governance will be automatically maintained. Tocqueville, in particular, was gravely concerned that a tendency toward a leveling equality might eventually undermine the spirit of self-governance by the voluntary associations that he saw as the very foundation of American democracy. In "Problems of Cognition as a Challenge to Policy Analysts and Democratic Societies" (chap. 17) Vincent Ostrom reiterates Tocqueville's concern about the difficulties inherent in intergenerational transmission of the "habits of heart and mind" that support a democratic, self-governing society. He calls on institutional analysts to contribute to the maintenance of self-governance by not allowing their analyses and policy recommendations to be colored by an unthinking adherence to the Hobbesian notion of unitary sovereignty. In this way scholars can make an important, even essential, contribution to the achievement and sustainability of self-governance.

In these works Vincent Ostrom advises institutional analysts to pay careful attention to language. The IAD framework and the terminology of polycentric governance provide, in effect, a "new language" for the study of the new "art and science of association" that Tocqueville saw as the essential foundation of any understanding of democracy. The terms we use to analyze institutions and policies must, ultimately, be consistent with this vision or else self-governance cannot be sustained.

The IAD framework (see fig. 1) lays out the magnitude of the task facing institutional analysts. It is no easy matter to match up institutional solutions to the physical realities of the situation, the attributes of the community, and the political relationships defined at the constitutional level. Design and establishment of a polycentric governance structure is not something that can happen overnight. It is not simply a matter of making markets work well, for it is also necessary to facilitate group management of common-pool resources. It is not simply a matter of providing law and order, because communities must be encouraged to take responsibility for their own conditions of life. Public officials must arrange for the provision of public goods, either by producing them directly or by contracting with other producers. Citizens need to be self-reliant yet also willing to work with government officials to solve collective problems. This balance is very difficult to sustain.

As artisans, institutional analysts need to recognize and appreciate the creative capacity of people to cope with their own collective problems. Rather than relying exclusively on abstract theory to tell us which policy instrument works best in any given situation, policy analysts must familiarize themselves with the diverse array of institutional arrangements that local communities have developed. This book illustrates some of the efforts of this community of scholars to do exactly that, to acquaint themselves with institutions that work.

Their tendency to focus on local solutions has made Workshop scholars deeply appreciative of the remarkable successes achieved by peoples throughout the developing world. It is appropriate to let the founders of the Workshop have the final word in this introduction to a volume of research reports by scholars personally inspired by their own unstinting efforts. In a guest editorial in the January 1994 issue of *Research and Creative Activity* (a publication of Indiana University Graduate School) Vincent and Elinor Ostrom succinctly articulate the guiding vision that has united the diverse strands of research undertaken by scholars associated with the Workshop during the first twenty-five years of its existence:

> Once we understood the logic of the use of land and water in paddy agriculture, for example, we came to appreciate the marvel of hillside terraces in Nepal and elsewhere that would justify their being considered among the Wonders of the World. In a contrary way, intelligent people can perversely reduce urban landscapes to rubble. How people think of themselves, structure their relationships with others, and pursue the opportunities that they see as available to them may make the difference between a sustainable and meaningful way of life and one reduced to rubble. Working with others to gain mutual advantage under changing conditions of life requires substantial use of knowledge, moral sensitivity, skills, and intelligence in the exercise of self-organizing and self-governing capabilities.

REFERENCES

Bates, Robert H. 1981. *Markets and States in Tropical Africa: The Political Basis of Agricultural Policies.* Berkeley: University of California Press.

———. 1983. *Essays on the Political Economy of Rural Africa.* Cambridge: Cambridge University Press.

Blomquist, William. 1992. *Dividing the Waters: Governing Groundwater in Southern California.* San Francisco: ICS Press.

De Soto, Hernando. 1989. *The Other Path: The Invisible Revolution in the Third World.* Trans. June Abbott. New York: Harper and Row.

Duany, Wal. 1992. "The Nuer Concept of Covenant and Covenantal Way of Life." *Publius* 22, no. 4 (Fall): 67–89.

———. 1994. "The Problem of Centralization in the Sudan." *Northeast African Studies* 1, nos. 2–3: 75–102.

Eggertsson, Thráinn. 1996. "No Experiments, Monumental Disasters: Why It Took a Thousand Years to Develop a Specialized Fishing Industry in Iceland." *Journal of Economic Behavior and Organization* 30, no. 1 (July): 1–24.

Gibson, Clark, Margaret McKean, and Elinor Ostrom, eds. Forthcoming. *People and Forests: Communities, Institutions, and the Governance of Forests.* Cambridge: MIT Press.

Gibson, Clark, Elinor Ostrom, and T. K. Ahn. 1998. "Scaling Issues in the Social Sciences." Report for the International Human Dimensions Programme (IHDP) on Global Environmental Change, IHDP Working Paper no. 1, Bonn, Germany.

Hardin, Garrett. 1968. "The Tragedy of the Commons." *Science* 162:1243–48.

Hobbes, Thomas. 1962 [1651]. *Leviathan or the Matter, Forme, and Power of a Commonwealth Ecclesiasticall and Civil*, ed. Michael Oakeshott. New York: Collier Books.

Jinadu, L. Adele. 1994. "Federalism and the Structure of the Nigerian Federation: Some Recurrent Issues." *Nigerian Journal of Federalism* 1, no. 2 (Dec.): 57–66.

Kaminski, Antoni. 1989. "Coercion, Corruption, and Reform: State and Society in Soviet-type Socialist Regime." *Journal of Theoretical Politics* 1, no. 1 (Jan.): 77–102.

———. 1992. *An Institutional Theory of Communist Regimes: Design, Function, and Breakdown*. San Francisco: ICS Press.

Keohane, Robert O., and Elinor Ostrom, eds. 1995. *Local Commons and Global Interdependence: Heterogeneity and Cooperation in Two Domains*. London: Sage.

Kiser, Larry L., and Elinor Ostrom. 1982. "The Three Worlds of Action: A Metatheoretical Synthesis of Institutional Approaches." In *Strategies of Political Inquiry*, ed. Elinor Ostrom, 179–222. Beverly Hills, CA: Sage. Reprinted in McGinnis 1999a.

Knight, Jack. 1992. *Institutions and Social Conflict*. Cambridge: Cambridge University Press.

Landa, Janet T. 1994. *Trust, Ethnicity, and Identity: Beyond the New Institutional Economics of Ethnic Trading Networks, Contract Law, and Gift-Exchange*. Ann Arbor: University of Michigan Press.

Loveman, Brian. 1993. *The Constitution of Tyranny: Regimes of Exception in Spanish America*. Pittsburgh: University of Pittsburgh Press.

McGinnis, Michael D., ed. 1999a. *Polycentric Games and Institutions: Readings from the Workshop in Political Theory and Policy Analysis*. Ann Arbor: University of Michigan Press.

———, ed. 1999b. *Polycentricity and Local Public Economies: Readings from the Workshop in Political Theory and Policy Analysis*. Ann Arbor: University of Michigan Press.

McGinnis, Michael, and Elinor Ostrom. 1996. "Design Principles for Local and Global Commons." In *The International Political Economy and International Institutions*, vol. 2, ed. Oran Young, 464–93. Cheltenham, UK: Edward Elgar.

North, Douglass C. 1981. *Structure and Change in Economic History*. New York: Norton.

———. 1990. *Institutions, Institutional Change and Economic Performance*. Cambridge: Cambridge University Press.

North, Douglass C., and Robert Paul Thomas. 1973. *The Rise of the Western World: A New Economic History*. Cambridge: Cambridge University Press.

Oakerson, Ronald J. 1992. "Analyzing the Commons: A Framework." In *Making the Commons Work: Theory, Practice, and Policy*, ed. Daniel W. Bromley et al., 41–59. San Francisco: ICS Press.

Oakerson, Ronald J., and S. Tjip Walker. 1997. "Analyzing Policy Reform and Reforming Policy Analysis: An Institutionalist Approach." In *Policy Studies and Developing Nations: An Institutional and Implementation Focus*, vol. 5, ed. Derick W. Brinkerhoff, 21–51. Greenwich, CT: JAI Press.

Obolonsky, Alexander. 1996. *The Drama of Russian Political History: System against Individuality.* Bloomington: Indiana University, Workshop in Political Theory and Policy Analysis.

Ostrom, Elinor. 1965. *Public Entrepreneurship: A Case Study in Ground Water Management.* Ph.D. diss., University of California at Los Angeles.

———. 1990. *Governing the Commons: The Evolution of Institutions for Collective Action.* New York: Cambridge University Press.

———. 1992. *Crafting Institutions for Self-Governing Irrigation Systems.* San Francisco: ICS Press.

———. 1999. "Coping with Tragedies of the Commons." *Annual Review of Political Science* 2, forthcoming.

Ostrom, Elinor, Roy Gardner, and James Walker. 1994. *Rules, Games, and Common-Pool Resources.* Ann Arbor: University of Michigan Press.

Ostrom, Elinor, Larry Schroeder, and Susan Wynne. 1993. *Institutional Incentives and Sustainable Development: Infrastructure Policies in Perspective.* Boulder, CO: Westview Press.

Ostrom, Vincent. 1953a. "State Administration of Natural Resources in the West." *American Political Science Review* 47, no. 2 (June): 478–93.

———. 1953b. *Water and Politics: A Study of Water Policies and Administration in the Development of Los Angeles.* Los Angeles: Haynes Foundation.

———. 1953c. *Water Supply.* Los Angeles: Haynes Foundation. (Metropolitan Los Angeles: A Study in Integration, vol. 8).

———. 1987 [1971]. *The Political Theory of a Compound Republic: Designing the American Experiment.* 2d rev. ed. San Francisco: ICS Press.

———. 1989 [1973]. *The Intellectual Crisis in American Public Administration.* 2d ed. Tuscaloosa: University of Alabama Press.

———. 1991. *The Meaning of American Federalism: Constituting a Self-Governing Society.* San Francisco: ICS Press.

———. 1997. *The Meaning of Democracy and the Vulnerability of Democracies: A Response to Tocqueville's Challenge.* Ann Arbor: University of Michigan Press.

Ostrom, Vincent, Charles M. Tiebout, and Robert Warren. 1961. "The Organization of Government in Metropolitan Areas: A Theoretical Inquiry." *American Political Science Review* 55 (Dec.): 831–42. Reprinted in McGinnis 1999b.

Sawyer, Amos. 1992. *The Emergence of Autocracy in Liberia: Tragedy and Challenge.* San Francisco: ICS Press.

Thomson, James T. 1992. *A Framework for Analyzing Institutional Incentives in Community Forestry.* Rome, Italy: FAO.

Tocqueville, Alexis de. 1969 [1835]. *Democracy in America.* Edited by J. P. Mayer, trans. George Lawrence. Garden City, NY: Anchor Books.

Walker, S. Tjip. 1994. "Crafting a Market: A Case Study of USAID's Fertilizer Sub-Sector Reform Program." Decentralization: Finance and Management Project Report. Burlington, VT: Associates in Rural Development.

Weschler, Louis F. 1968. *Water Resources Management: The Orange County Experience*. Davis: University of California, Davis, Institute of Governmental Affairs, California Government Series no. 14.

Wunsch, James S., and Dele Olowu, eds. 1995. *The Failure of the Centralized State: Institutions and Self-Governance in Africa*. 2d ed. San Francisco: ICS Press.

Yang, Tai Shuenn. 1987. "Property Rights and Constitutional Order in Imperial China." Ph.D. diss., Indiana University, Department of Political Science.

Part I
Resource Management

CHAPTER 1

Water and Politics California Style

Vincent Ostrom

The California water industry is the product of a century's effort by the people of California to solve their water problems. Its foundations were forged in frustration—frustrations derived from the uncertainties produced by contradictory decisions by different state authorities. Contradictory doctrines of water law had been allowed to stand; and the law of the highwayman became the effective law of water rights in California: "Take what you can get and defend what you have got."

The miners of the Sierras engaged in as contentious rivalry over water as they did for gold. Water was essential for separating the precious metal from worthless gravel amid the placers of the gold fields. The death of the California gold industry came in 1884 as the direct result of a federal court order enjoining miners from disposing of debris in any tributary of the Sacramento River system and from, thus, causing injury to downstream settlers.

The cattle kings built and maintained their empires by a vigilant defense of their claims to available water supplies. The Kern Land and Cattle Company and Miller and Lux, Inc., were among those who succeeded. Homesteaders struggled with cattle barons to secure enough water to irrigate their croplands. Some failed, but, in the long run, most succeeded. Many of the cattle barons eventually became land developers selling subdivided parcels with appertaining water rights to new settlers. In turn, the building of cities in this arid region was accompanied by a quest for the water coveted by the homesteader and the highlanders. Each saw his control over water as an essential ingredient in realizing his hopes and aspirations for the future.

Some of these conflicts provoked a release of energy which spent itself in exhaustion, without much to show for the effort. Some culminated in

Originally published in *Arts and Architecture* 84 (July–August 1967): 14–16, 32. Reprinted by permission of the author.

Author's note: I am indebted to Resources for the Future, Inc., Washington, DC for support of much of my recent research on California water problems. I alone am responsible, however, for any of the conclusions or opinions expressed in this article.

tragedy. Much more frequently the struggles were rewarded in some small measure by a resolution, a settlement or an agreement pointing the way to a new approach or to a new method for organizing human enterprise in the utilization and development of the water resources of an arid land.

Many of these innovations have been used in the development of water institutions in other states and in other countries. Most western states, for example, drew upon the principles developed in the rules of the California mining camps for formulating their basic law of water rights. Enterprises in many other areas have been modelled after California mutual water companies and the irrigation districts of California. Contemporary development in state water planning has drawn its inspiration more from the traditions of the State Water Plan in California than from the New Deal's efforts to develop state counterparts to its National Resources Planning Board.

The work of the Chaffey brothers in designing the institutional structures for the settlement of Upland and Ontario, California, was used to plan the colonization of the Murray River region of Australia. Elwood Mead, a professor of irrigation institutions at the University of California, was employed as a commissioner of water rights in Australia to help fashion their system of water law before returning to the United States to become the U.S. Commissioner of Reclamation. H. W. Grunsky, a colleague of Mead's in California, helped reformulate the basic water legislation for the Canadian province of British Columbia at the turn of the century. California innovations have, in short, been incorporated into the general pattern of water institutions in many different lands. This process of institutional innovation is best observed in the general configuration of water institutions which form today's California water industry. It is a multibillion dollar system of works and enterprises. The superstructure is composed predominantly of governmental agencies or public enterprises of one form or another. The substructure is composed of millions of water consumers of whom many tens of thousands function as independent water producers with their own systems of water supply. The growth and prosperity of the state as a whole is immediately dependent upon the performance of this strange admixture of public—federal, state, local—and private enterprises forming the California water industry.

Two large-scale producers, the U.S. Corps of Engineers and the U.S. Bureau of Reclamation, each operates water works that represent a cumulative capital investment in California of more than one billion dollars.

The California Department of Water Resources is becoming the third large-scale producer. Its Feather River works will store water for release into the Sacramento River system, and its California Aqueduct will divert water from the Sacramento River delta to southern California with service to intermediate points. An investment of more than two billion dollars will be required before the state's water works system becomes operational in the 1970s.

The intermediate water service agencies are also gargantuan in proportions. The largest of these, the Metropolitan Water District of Southern California, is predominantly a water wholesaler serving the southern California metropolitan region with a network of aqueducts, reservoirs and watermains extending to the Colorado River and girding the southern California coastal plain. This system represents an investment in plant and equipment of more than a half billion dollars, and a 1.3 billion–dollar expansion program is planned.

The Los Angeles Department of Water and Power is the largest combined municipally owned, water and power utility system in the United States. Its independent water supply system includes most of the water yield from Mono Basin, Owens Valley and the upper Los Angeles Basin with a network of aqueducts, tunnels and diversion works that extends nearly 400 miles into Mono Basin on the eastern slope of the Sierra Nevadas. The San Francisco Municipal Water Department and the East Bay Municipal Utility District have comparable systems that take water from the western slope of the Sierra Nevadas to supply the metropolitan communities of the San Francisco Bay region.

Most urban communities in California are served by municipal water departments, public water districts or cooperatively owned mutual water companies. Rural areas are usually served by irrigation districts, other public water districts, or mutual water companies. Private enterprise engaged in the water business as a profitable endeavor is the exception rather than the rule. Altogether there are nearly 1,500 mutual water companies and perhaps an equal number of public water districts and municipal water supply systems. The cooperative mutual water companies tend to be small-scale operations by comparison to most public water district and municipal systems.

As the structure of the California water industry has developed it has tended to become more fragmented. Local water suppliers have become more specialized in distribution of water services to the ultimate consumer and in functions of retailing. The intermediate agencies have tended to become wholesalers, while the large-scale state and federal water resource management agencies have become more specialized in the operation of major production facilities and diversion works at the sources of water supply.

Horizontal segmentation in the organization of water institutions has occurred with the development of two or three distinct types of water systems—supply, storm drain and flood control, sanitation and water quality control—for every highly developed area of human habitation in California, each system managed by a separate and independent set of agencies.

Finally, another group of agencies manages certain in-the-channel or flow resources in California's rivers, reservoirs, lakes and ground water pools, for example, the fish and wildlife agencies, the park and recreation agencies, harbor and navigation agencies as well as the large-scale water production agencies which use their facilities to supply water for in-the-channel uses as well as for diversion purposes.

Thus, the picture of the California water industry stands in sharp contrast to the American ideal represented by the Tennessee Valley Authority: a single regional authority responsible for the comprehensive planning and integrated management of a river basin on a multiple use basis. And yet the California water industry has transformed an arid desert region into a land of unparalleled agricultural productivity and industrial growth. Perhaps this industry of assorted public and private enterprises provides us with a different model of organization for water resource development deserving of serious attention and study.

Amid the political and legal frustrations, contradictory decisions and doctrines, private property rights under California law of water rights did not perform their economic function of allocating a scarce resource to the highest bidder. Instead, water rights were used as a political means of giving each claimant a voice in the course of action to be taken in the solution of mutual water problems. Litigation over water rights has been a major preoccupation in California but in the course of time, the folk wisdom of the water industry came to reflect the futility of seeking court decisions as an effective means to exclude an adversary's claim. An expression of frustration, "Law suits never produced a drop of water," became the motto of the industry.

The preferred solution was to find a mutually agreeable arrangement for increasing the available water supply for all of the interests involved from some new supplementary source of supply. Along with an engineering plan to increase the available supply of water came the task of designing an appropriate structure for the organization of an enterprise to carry out the engineering solution and to continue to represent the community of water producers in the government of that enterprise. If demand exceeded the yield of a local water supply and if all water producers had equal access to that local supply, the development of a supplementary source of supply would be of mutual benefit only if all producers shared in the cost of acquiring the new supply. If one producer could hold out and satisfy his demands from local supplies while others met their increased demand from the new, more costly source of supply, the hold-out would then be able to gain the benefits without paying his share of the costs for expanding the available water supply. If one hold-out could free-load, so could others, and the viability of a physical solution to common water supply problems would dissolve in vindictive bickering and rivalry.

The solution to this type of problem in designing the structure of an enterprise to undertake the development of a supplementary water supply was facilitated by the use of the organizational form of a public as opposed to private instrumentality. A public enterprise can be organized to include a whole community of people who will benefit from a common undertaking without having to gain the voluntary subscription or willing consent of each and every potential beneficiary. The public enterprise formula solves the problem of the hold-out. A public enterprise also has the power of taxation, and the costs of securing a joint water supply can in part be recovered by levying taxes as well as by charging a price for water services. Finally, the organization of the internal political structure of a public enterprise provides an opportunity to represent those it serves by giving them a continuing voice in the government of its affairs.

Each new physical solution to a water problem in California is accompanied by the negotiation of a new political solution among water users. The primary burden for fashioning both the physical solution and the political solution is usually assumed by entrepreneurs representing the community of people who will become the principal beneficiaries. Solutions are fashioned in numerous rounds of discussion and of negotiation at the conference table. A settlement is reached when an effective bargain is struck. Litigation is used only when the processes of accommodation and negotiation break down. Similarly, decisions by legislative bodies or decisions by the electorate are sought only when a proposed solution requires formal validation by political authorities. Within the water industry it is universally assumed that substantial consensus among water users is the essential condition for assuring the political feasibility of any new undertaking. In the absence of consensus among a community of water users the judgment is frequently expressed that, "We are not ready to go to Sacramento yet."

At any particular level of development those responsible for organizing and conducting the enterprise and for implementing the engineering solution will seek to exploit the opportunities which they have created both by expanding the domain of their enterprise and by seeking new sources of water supply when justified by growing demand. This imperialist stage of growth and expansion proceeds until checkmated by competitive rivals. The checkmating is accomplished when a rival or a coalition of rivals is able to nail down a veto position through governmental action, either through court action, legislative action, popular referenda or a combination of these methods.[1]

The stalemate is then resolved by seeking a new solution within the context of a still broader community of political interests. The political task is one of converting frustrated rivalries into a cooperative game against nature. The new solution must include both the engineering of a new scheme for a new source of water supply as well as the political negotiation of a new pattern of organization to govern the new enterprise.

This process can again be illustrated by the development of a new source of water supply for southern California from the Colorado River. When the city of Los Angeles began to explore the importation of a new supply of water from the Colorado River, the venture had been conceived as a municipal undertaking. In order to establish the political feasibility of the new undertaking and secure appropriate authorizations both in the California legislature and in Congress, a new political solution had to be devised to solve the water problems of its erstwhile rivals as well as those of the city of Los Angeles. The organization of the Metropolitan Water District of Southern California represents the political solution which was negotiated by representatives of these diverse southern California communities to undertake the importation of Colorado River water to the southern California coastal plain.

With the consolidation and expansion of Metropolitan, checkmating strategies occurred on two different fronts. One involved Arizona's efforts to checkmate California interests; the other involved northern California efforts to checkmate southern California. Both efforts to establish veto points and develop bargaining positions based upon those veto points were successful; and the conditions for negotiating a new pattern of political settlements were established.

An accommodation between northern and southern California interests was attained not by Metropolitan going it alone to develop a new source of supply on the Russian or the Eel River as Metropolitan had proposed, but through a state program to develop the Feather River and build an aqueduct to southern California both to serve Metropolitan and to supply other service areas along the aqueduct route. The political settlement also involved a commitment to sustain a program of water resource development in the mountain counties of northern California at the sources of supply.

When the solutions become state-wide or inter-state in character, the political aspect of the solution takes on a different structure. The political settlement is no longer incorporated into the charter of a self-governing public water district such as the Metropolitan Water District Act. Instead the settlement is represented by a whole series of inter-agency agreements formulated in contractual undertakings and in legislative authorizations. The general political community of interest is no longer represented in a governing board like Metropolitan's board of directors but is organized in the context of various water users' associations and interagency committees representing the several agencies and communities of interest involved in the common undertakings. The Pacific Southwest Inter-Agency Committee is an illustration of such a group concerned with inter-state aspects of water resource development in the Pacific Southwest. The California water industry is still governed primarily by negotiations with recourse to appropriate governmental authorities when negotiations break down. General reliance upon governmental authorities for reaching decisions in the absence of negotiated settlements is so very costly that most decisions are reached by some form of negotiated settlement. Governmental authorities are relied upon primarily to establish veto points, to determine bargaining positions, and to validate negotiated settlements.

A political settlement of the water demands of the budding political community in the tri-state area of the Pacific Southwest is still in the making. California has now embraced Arizona within a common community of interest in an effort to establish the feasibility of a new Southwest water plan. The ultimate shape of the engineering solution and of the political solution remains to be determined. On the basis of prior experience we might expect a new league of the Southwest to scan the distant horizons for a new source of water supply. Where will they go? Who will become the new rivals? When will the processes of consolidation and expansion be checkmated? How will the new political settlements shape the constitutions of new communities of political interest as the California water industry comes to find its niche among Western water institutions?

Has public entrepreneurship in the California water industry produced the right results in the development of the state's water resources? The methods of public entrepreneurship have been most productive in yielding a generous supply of water to meet the demands of an extraordinary pattern of growth in an arid region. The California water industry has earned a badge of special merit for its dynamic performance. An ample supply of water has been available to meet most requirements for growth and development.

A number of economists, however, have recently questioned some of the industry's methods. Rapid expansion may lead to over-production, and over-production may lead to a wasteful or uneconomic use of scarce resources. If this is the case, what are the elements in the California practice of public entrepreneurship that lead to this result? What do these conclusions imply for the future of water and politics—California style?

With the very high rate of economic growth and development which has occurred in California during the past several decades, public bodies responsible for supplying water to meet these demands have had every incentive to attempt to preempt as much water as they can reasonably justify. The reasonableness of their justification has often depended as much upon the veto position of a potential rival as upon appropriate standards of economic justification. Frequently an agency joining in a new development will hedge against the future and attempt to assure its own independence of action by holding some potential source of water supply in an undisclosed reserve. The availability of such undisclosed reserves has either meant that the reserve supply was not being put to economic use; or if brought into production concurrently with a new source of supply, the development of the undisclosed reserve would then tend to lower demand and weaken the viability of the new undertaking.

The Department of Water and Power in the city of Los Angeles has had recourse to such a strategy on two separate occasions. The first instance occurred when the city proceeded independently in tapping the water supply of Mono Basin *after* commitments had already been made to develop the Colorado River supply. As a result the city of Los Angeles has had only a nominal need for Colorado River water once it developed the Mono supply as a least-cost alternative.

This process is being repeated following the authorization of the $1,750,000,000 bond issue by the people of the state to construct the California Aqueduct and transport northern water to southern California. The Los Angeles Department of Water and Power is currently adding a second barrel to its Los Angeles Owens River Aqueduct and thus expanding the yield from that source of supply.

An additional undisclosed reserve of potential water supply also exists in the water discharged through the sewerage systems of southern California. The feasibility of reclaiming much of this water at less cost than Feather River water has been demonstrated in pilot-plant programs on a number of occasions. This potential source of supply is still largely being held as an unpublicized reserve to hedge against the future.

The incentives for over-development or over-production of water supply in the California water industry have been greatly accentuated in the past 30 or 40 years with the substantial expansion of activity by the large federal water production agencies. The make-work policies of the Depression years led to a substantial expansion of federal expenditures on water works projects. While the W.P.A. and the P.W.A. have long since passed from the American scene, the federal water production agencies, both the Corps of Engineers and the Bureau of Reclamation, are still using programs born in the Depression years to sustain a flow of subsidies for the support of water resource development projects. When this factor is added to the dynamic style of public entrepreneurship in the California water industry, the momentum of development is greatly accelerated.

Are there any dangers in this acceleration of development or do these strategies represent an appropriate hedge against the future by assuring an ample stock of water for whatever course of events the future may hold? An aggressive course of development is faced with three major types of risks in attempting to preempt the future. First, the probability of error is increased the further developments are projected into the future. Plans for the year 2020 can be made with little confidence. Second, as the costs of water production rise in relation to each unit of output, a point will eventually be reached where the cost of transferring water over great distances will exceed the costs of producing water by different methods from alternative sources. For example, eventually the declining cost-curve for desalinization of ocean water will intersect the rising cost-curve for transporting water from great distances.[2] Prospects of increasing water production by weather modification may provide still another alternative source of supply. Third, over-development of vendable water supplies can lead to an imbalance among all of the various uses for water resources. A balanced program of water resource development needs to take account of all of the joint and alternative uses for water—consumptive, recreational, industrial, agricultural, etc.

Rather minor changes would go a long way to establish a better balance in the equilibrium of the California water industry and still preserve the energy and vitality of this complex public enterprise system. First, every effort should be made to maintain the economic principle that the beneficiaries should bear the costs for the goods produced by an enterprise. The result is usually assured in the private sector by the sale of a product for a price. The same principle can be applied to enterprises in the public sector whether the costs are borne by taxes, service charges or a combination of both. Subsidizing cheap water for agriculture does not lead to the economic use of water in a state that is being overwhelmed by urbanization.

Second, more careful economic calculations will occur when the price of water is directly proportioned to the use of water services. Water priced to reflect the quantity used leads to more economic use than water priced by flat rates or paid by tax levies. Conversely, if the quantity and quality of waste water could be metered and priced proportionate to the costs imposed upon the operation of the discharge system, an incentive would be created to reduce waste discharges and to increase the recirculation of water when feasible. Similarly, if fishing license fees were established to reflect the value that fishermen place upon sport fishing there would be less tendency to underestimate the importance of recreation in the development of water resources. As opportunities for leisure grow the modern city dweller may want to measure the relative value of water in other forms than tapwater.

Third, the policy of permitting the free appropriation of "unappropriated" water should be discontinued in the same way that the free homesteading of public land was discontinued several decades ago. Public waters like public lands have a value that should be taken into account in resource management programs. In recognition of the economic value of water at its source, new appropriations should require that an appropriator pay an annual rent or production charge for on-land-use equal to the value of that water for in-the-channel users. Such a policy would create less incentive for water developers to follow strategies of attempting to preempt as much water as possible and to hoard undisclosed reserves for development in the more distant future.

Finally, the diverse agencies operating in each of the more highly developed, water marketing regions with access to two or more independent sources of water supply should be encouraged to follow the example of some southern California communities overlying ground water basins in that region. Water agencies in those areas have taken concerted action to institute coordinated programs for ground water basin management by such measures as (1) adjudicating ground water rights, (2) reclaiming waste water, (3) replenishing ground water supplies, (4) charging a pump tax on ground water production to pay for the replenishment programs, and (5) developing water exchange agreements to facilitate the buying and selling of water rights among local ground water producers. These measures create opportunities for more efficient management of ground water supplies and for the development of market forces in the reallocation of ground water among different producers. As long as one or more independent sources of supply is available to meet long-term demands, local ground water producers should be free to rent or sell their pumping rights to the highest bidder. Ground water supplies would then be made available for their highest economic use, rather than being used as the cheapest source of supply. When Alexis de Tocqueville visited the United States in the early 1830s he recognized that the administration of public affairs in the United States was "full of animation and effort" mobilized in diverse forms of collective enterprise. Today, a Tocqueville might find the California water industry to represent a further fruition of an American system of public enterprise fashioned by a free people in solving their common problems of water supply.

"Water and Politics California Style" has provided the circumstances for fashioning a complex of public enterprises into a dynamic water industry. Ironically its problems are not those of inaction and under-development but of over-production and over-development. A few changes to better proportion the calculation of risks and of costs may lead toward a more efficient performance. It is easier to draw in the reins of a dynamic system of enterprise than to induce the release of productive energy in the absence of enterprise.

NOTES

1. The operation of these political dynamics can be observed in the search for solutions to water problems among the communities of southern California. Los Angeles was able to embark upon its stage of imperialistic growth and expansion by the acquisition of its greatly increased water supply from Owens Valley. This was followed by a great wave of annexations which expanded the city's boundaries to their present proportions. This wave of expansion was first checkmated by the

refusal of people in surrounding communities to approve referenda to consolidate with Los Angeles during its annexation campaigns, and by an intense political storm provoked by Owens Valley interests opposed to the city's water programs.

2. When the desalinization programs were first undertaken some 15 years ago the price target was to produce desalted water for $1 per 1,000 gallons ($326 per acre-foot). Costs have now declined until 30 cents per 1,000 gallons ($97 per acre-foot) is a reasonable estimate of the current cost of desalted water at sea level. The cost of northern California to divert water by comparison, will be something in excess of 20 cents per 1,000 gallons ($65 per acre-foot) when delivered to southern California. Transferring Columbia River water to the Pacific Southwest would almost certainly exceed the future costs of desalting ocean water to supply the coastal communities of California. Salt water is currently (1999) being desalinized to supply water for the city of Avalon, located on Catalina Island.

CHAPTER 2

Legal and Political Conditions of Water Resource Development

Vincent Ostrom and Elinor Ostrom

Control of water to secure maximum supply at costs determined by the economic situation is the engineering problem and that problem is solvable. Ahead of the engineering accomplishment is the engineering of men. The decision of the community at large must be made. For accomplishment, its public body, its semipublic water organizations and its individuals must unite in teamwork to pool, rearrange and compromise existing interests, to legislate and to create a competent organization to carry out the engineering solution. (California Department of Public Works 1928)

The close relationship between the solution to engineering problems and the design of institutional arrangements is clearly set forth in the engineering report quoted above. The "engineering of men" has to do with the institutional arrangements which are used to organize the actions of men in the development and use of water resource systems. The design and operation of human enterprises always occur within the context of legal and political considerations.

Engineers and economists use modes of professional analysis which have become an integral part of decision-making concerned with water resource development. These analyses relate to the design and operation of systems of water works which will transform the behavioral characteristics of water systems and yield a flow of goods and services as a consequence.

Originally published in *Land Economics* 48, no. 1 (February 1972): 1–14. Copyright 1972. Reprinted by permission of the University of Wisconsin Press and the authors.

Authors' note: This essay is based upon presentation made to the Seminar on Resource System Models in Decision-Making at Purdue University. The seminar was organized by Professor G. H. Toebes and sponsored by the Purdue University School of Engineering and Water Resources Research Center. The authors express their appreciation to Professor Toebes and his colleagues and acknowledge the earlier support of their work by Resources for the Future, Inc., the University of California's Water Resources Center and Indiana University's Water Resources Research Center and Office of Research and Advanced Studies.

The engineering problems associated with *the design and operation of water works* as physical facilities are always accompanied by problems in *the design and operation of organizational arrangements* concerned with the conduct of people associated with the enterprise. Any system of water works must be accompanied by a system of human enterprise that involves the allocation, exercise and control of decision-making capabilities in the development and use of water supplies.

Feasibility Criteria

When we recognized the union of relationships involved in the engineering of works and the engineering of institutions for water resource development, at least five sets of criteria became relevant to decision-making. These include the following: (1) *Technical Feasibility:* Can it be done? Is a potential course of action within the realm of possibilities given existing knowledge and technical capabilities? (2) *Economic Feasibility:* Is it worth doing? Will the expected benefits to be derived from any course of action exceed the expected costs including the cost of other opportunities foregone? If this criterion can *not* be met, a course of action will leave people worse off rather than better off. (3) *Financial Feasibility:* Can sufficient revenues be generated with reference to a proposed program of action to cover expenditures? Where products may not be marketable under normal marketing conditions, the financial feasibility of water resource development programs may depend upon funding from tax revenues or the development of politically imposed pricing mechanisms such as user taxes, user charges, etc. (4) *Legal Feasibility:* Is a proposed program of action lawful? Is the proposed program within the legal competence of an entrepreneur to undertake on his own authority? (5) *Political Feasibility:* Can the appropriate decisions be sustained? Conditions of political feasibility may affect decisions bearing upon financial and legal feasibility in the sense that the authorization of a project and the appropriation of funds may be necessary before a program of action may be subject to a continuing series of decisions to sustain its operation.

Law as Decision Rules

The basic architecture of human institutions, social organizations, or enterprises can be conceptualized as a system of decision rules which serve as working rules for ordering human behavior into going concerns. A system of law can thus be defined as the system of decision rules operative in a society. Where a program of action is authorized under a prevailing system of law, that program of action would then be legally feasible.

In a most general sense, a political system is concerned with the *allocation, exercise and control of decision-making capabilities among people.* When people are engaged in activities concerned with the allocation, control and exercise of decision-making capabilities, they are engaged in political activities, that is, activities defined by reference to policy. Any form of action is taken with some presumption of the lawfulness of that action. Where conflict arises from the competing claims of individuals regarding the lawfulness of their actions, recourse must be had to courts or other decision-making facilities to reach a determination about the competing claims and thus to control the exercise of decision-making capabilities.

Any resource development program will need to take account of legal and political considerations which bear upon the exercises of decision-making capabilities among those involved in the development and use of resource potentials. A presumption that one has a valid claim to exercise a decision-making capability must in turn be based upon the strategic calculation that such a claim can be sustained in relation to any potential contest pursued by any other claimant. Any complex undertaking such as the development of a multipurpose, water-resource-development project will involve a substantial reallocation of decision-making capabilities among the community of people involved. A vast new framework of decision rules may have to be fashioned in order to accommodate the heterogeneity of interests inherent in a complex configuration of relationships.

Many theoretical models used by economists and political scientists tend to postulate the existence of legal and political arrangements as given. Economic theory, for example, is predicated upon an assumption that market behavior will be lawful and that a condition of "law and order" exists. This is an appropriate assumption for analyzing market conditions which approximate those of the competitive market model. Where economic relationships radically deviate from a market model, legal and political conditions will have to be manipulated to establish alternative institutional arrangements.

In a similar way, many organization theorists postulate legal and political arrangements as given. Max Weber, for example, postulates the existence of a comprehensive code of law which is fully consistent in the sense of being without contradictions and complete in the sense of being "gapless." On the basis of such a "rational" legal code he then conceptualized bureaucratic organization as an ideal-type organization for maintaining a rational social order (Rheinstein 1967: 61–64).

A Paradigm for Analyzing Legal Relationships

If, instead of postulating legal and political relationships as given, we are to treat those relationships analytically, then we need to characterize legal relationships in terms of their anticipated effect upon human behavior. Decision rules serve as guides for ordering behavior in the sense that the rules of a game structure the strategic opportunities inherent in the play of a game. The decision rules inherent in any system of law provide a basis for calculating strategic opportunities that are available to persons participating in those activities. The calculation of strategic opportunities, when viewed from a gaming context, can be used to estimate the basic "structure," "bias" or "rig" that is "determined" by the rules of the game. Players presumably are able to calculate their strategic opportunities in deciding how proposed courses of action will affect outcomes.

The calculation of strategic opportunities in a gaming context can be viewed as crudely analogous to a cost calculus appropriate to an economic analysis where joint and interdependent actions can be expected to occur with a greater frequency than separate and independent actions. A crude analogy to *benefits* and *costs* in assessing strategic opportunities is formulated in the assignment of *capabilities* and *limitations* for action within the rules of the game. The assignment of a capability to act presumes that the initiative for action resides with those who have an incentive to act. The assignment of limitations in turn implies that constraints and risks are interposed so that the play of a game will be bounded within limits. The assignment of both capabilities and limitations gives "structure" or "rig" to the play of a game and presumably "biases" the game toward some type of socially preferred outcome.

John R. Commons, drawing upon the earlier work of Wesley N. Hohfeld, provides us with a basic paradigm for an analysis of decision rules as these affect the pursuit of strategic opportunities (Commons 1959; Hohfeld 1964; the authors' representations are an adaptation of Commons). Within the context of any operative set of decision rules *authority to act* involves the assignment of a capability or a *right* to act on the part of someone, with a correlative obligation or *duty* on the part of others to act in accordance with the right being asserted. Rights are subject to limits. Limits bearing upon any right define the area of decision-making where a claimant stands *exposed.* Thus, Commons has defined the limit of a right as an *exposure.* The correlative of an exposure is beyond the limit of a *duty.* A person who is no longer under duty is at *liberty* to act. Thus, the correlative of an *exposure* is a *liberty.* When these are represented in a boxed space, as in figure 2.1, the correlatives indicate the reciprocal interdependencies among two different legal parties or sets of legal parties. The limits are applied to each particular party. Taken together the diagonal or reciprocal relationship represented by right and liberty establish the *capabilities* assigned to both party and *duty* and *exposure* establish the *limitations* assigned to their respective decision-maker capabilities.

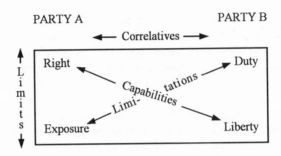

Fig. 2.1. Authorized relationships: Authority to act

Both Commons and Hohfeld refer to a further set of legal relationships which assign decision-making capabilities or authority to *determine, enforce* and *alter* legal relationships. These are represented by figure 2.2. The terminology in figure 2.2 has reference to "power" or "authoritative" relationships in the sense that *authority to determine, enforce, and alter legal relationships* defines power relationships. Authorized relationships as illustrated in figure 2.1 provide only an initial approximation to the general structure of legal relationships. Authority to act without reference to the power relationships defines the structure of "authorized" relationships.

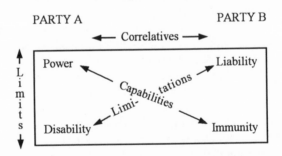

Fig. 2.2. Power or authoritative relationships: Authority to determine, enforce, and alter legal relationships

Power or authoritative relationships may vary from contractual arrangements to a variety of governmental decision-making arrangements for determining, enforcing and altering authorized legal relationships. Under contractual arrangements, persons may participate in a mutually agreeable arrangement in redefining and altering legal relationships in order to accomplish the objectives of some undertaking of mutual interest. Governmental arrangements, inherent in the operation of courts, executive agencies, and legislative bodies, enable a collectivity to sustain efforts to determine, enforce, and alter legal relationships.

The structure of strategic opportunities inherent in the rights, duties, exposures and liberties formulated as authorized relationships provide us with only a first approximation in a conception of legal and political relationships. Any contest, conflict or rearrangement of authorized relationships necessarily involves recourse to power or authoritative relationships to determine, enforce or alter legal relationships. Power relationships thus establish the general scenario for all decision-making. The game of life is one where each player pursues his strategic opportunities and is potentially exposed to the strategic actions of others in a series of interdependent games where the rules of the game are themselves subject to change during the course of play.

In the American political system, where authority is widely dispersed, the range of strategic calculations confronting any individual is very large indeed. Numerous decision structures in a national government, 50 state governments, nearly 100,000 units of local governments and countless corporations, cooperative societies, and voluntary associations indicate some of the potential variety that may be available. The aggregate complexity in rationally calculating strategic opportunities in such a context defies human imagination. Yet human beings are able to acquire a knowledge about the essential rules of the game and make provisional calculations about strategic opportunities as they pursue their respective endeavors. Decision-making under those circumstances always occurs with substantial uncertainty and risk. Such is the necessary price for sustaining ordered relationships which are subject to change.

Institutional Arrangements for Water Resource Development

The problem of devising arrangements appropriate for the development and use of water resources is greatly complicated by the common-pool, flow-resource characteristic of any water system. Water as a liquid is difficult to partition and contain in isolable units that can be packaged for marketable transactions. In addition, any water resource system will involve a complex bundle of potential goods and bads which sustain a high level of interdependency among the various joint and alternative uses (for a further discussion of some of these problems, see V. Ostrom 1968). Some uses may be undertaken by individual proprietorships but many other uses can only be sustained by collective enterprises with access to a public treasury or powers of taxation in order to generate sufficient revenue to establish the financial feasibility of an enterprise.

Income maximizing strategies involve the proportioning of different mixes of goods and services where the jointness of supply requires individuals to act so as to realize a jointness of income and expenditure in the development of that supply. As supply and demand change among the various joint and alternative uses and, as new forms of technology affect the productive potential, substantial legal and political problems are created in rearranging decision-making capabilities. Every new technical solution to a water problem necessarily implies that decision-making capabilities will need rearranging. The wider the ramification of the consequences that flow from any particular technological development the more complex will be the task of rearranging decision-making capabilities in the development of appropriate institutional arrangements within and among communities of users.

The Law of Water Rights as the Institutional Base of Authorized Relationships

The basic structure of institutional arrangements for water resource development is established by the decision rules which comprise the law of water rights. The law of water rights is a form of property law that establishes the authority of persons to use, control, and dispose of claims upon the available water supply. An individual property right to water is usually conceptualized as an individual right to make use of a common property. A common property relationship recognizes both an individuality of interests and a commonality of interests. Under these circumstances individual interests are assumed to have a high level of interdependency with other individual interests within the bounds of the common pool that circumscribe a commonality of interests. The high degree of interdependency among the individual users of a common-pool, flow resource gives rise to a high potential for conflict and a high degree of politicization of institutional arrangements for water resource development.

The basic conception and structure of the law of water rights continues to be a controversial subject in most areas of the United States. Two basically different approaches to the law of water rights have developed in different regions of the United States. The common law doctrine of riparian rights is based upon the presumption that any land owner adjoining a water course or body of water has a right to make a reasonable beneficial use of that water for both consumptive and nonconsumptive purposes subject to the right of other similarly situated proprietors also to make reasonable use of the same water resource system. Each user's right is correlative with the rights of all other users. A contrary system of water law, first developed in the desert regions of the American west, involves the perfection of a water right to specifiable quantities and flows of water for consumptive on-the-land uses.

Such rights are extended to those who were first in time. This doctrine of water law is known as the *prior appropriation* doctrine. Each user's right has a different order of priority and tends to be variant from the rights of each other user. Many variations and permutations of these two doctrines of water rights have developed among the American states. In California, where the prior appropriation doctrine was first developed among early gold miners, both systems of law have been allowed to develop side-by-side. Other states in the humid regions of the United States have remained predominantly riparian in orientation with increased consideration being given to appropriative arrangements.

An examination of the capabilities and limitations inherent in different systems of water law can be used to establish the essential rig of the game for transforming water resource potential into operative economic relationships. Such an examination will lead to an identification of the community of water users in terms of (1) who may claim and for what uses or purposes, (2) exclusiveness or jointness of use, (3) exposure to the claims of others, (4) stability or perishability of the right over time, (5) transferability of the right, (6) burden for bearing the costs or risks of adversity, and (7) the structure of authoritative arrangements for reaching and enforcing determinations in relation to conflicts of interests between individual users and among communities of water users.

An examination of the decision rules inherent in the law of water rights in relation to each of the above variables will reveal the relative priorities and patterns of development which are facilitated. A riparian proprietor will stand relatively exposed to the entry of other riparian proprietors who may initiate new patterns of water use. Each riparian proprietor will stand relatively equally exposed to a reduction in water supply during periods of extreme drought. A junior appropriator would stand exposed to a highly unequal curtailment of his demands in relation to senior appropriators.

Water Rights and Collective Enterprise

These differences may become critical when patterns of development cross the threshold where demands for water exceed the available natural yield. Where no price is established for water at its source we would expect water users having a riparian or a correlative groundwater right to follow a hold-out strategy of taking what they can get with little regard for other users who share in the common property. Costs of litigation are apt to be high. Each proprietor is apt to take an ostrich stance and disregard a threatening situation in the short run without reference to long-term cost calculations. Short-run calculations are apt to predominate over long-run calculations unless recourse can be had to alternative decision structures.

In the absence of other neighborhood effects, a senior appropriator when confronted with a serious impairment of the available supply will be moved to eliminate the demands of the most junior appropriators. The burden for shortages thus would fall disproportionately upon junior appropriators. If other neighborhood effects are present to deter a senior appropriator from seeking to eliminate junior appropriators, then the force of the prior appropriation system would be confused by those neighborhood effects. Where demands exceed the water supply available under a natural regimen, an alternative solution may be available by storing and transferring water from periods or places of surplus to make up the deficits at other times and places. This circumstance provides an opportunity for joint action to expand the usable water supply and significantly improve economic opportunities.

Again the structure of incentives inherent in the capabilities and limitations implicit in different systems of water law creates significantly different predispositions toward such undertakings. A system of riparian or correlative water rights is likely to create incentives toward obfuscation during an interim short-run period while different alternatives including the pursuit of a holdout strategy are explored and clarified. If appropriate strategies including litigation are developed which preclude a holdout strategy then the community of water users sharing a common source of supply as riparian or correlative users has an incentive to join in some collective enterprise where the costs of the enterprise would be borne by each user in proportion to his demand. The solution is to rearrange decision-making capabilities so that the community of water users minimize the prospects of fighting among themselves and direct their energies in undertaking a cooperative venture to increase the aggregate supply of water available to the entire community of users. Each must share and share alike in the costs of the undertaking. To attain that capability would require recourse to some form of public water district or collective enterprise where the cost of the improvement can be assessed against each potential user and thereby eliminate any incentive for individuals to avoid costs by engaging in a holdout strategy. Where such assessments are collectible as taxes a holdout strategy can be foreclosed.

The capabilities and limitations assigned to water users through prior appropriation rights create a substantial incentive for junior appropriators to find alternative means to supplement their water supplies when confronted with shortages. Junior appropriators will thus have incentive to take the initiative in promoting water resource development projects where primary entrepreneurial responsibility rests with some water resource development agencies with access to alternative sources of public funding. Senior appropriators would not be adverse to a supplementary source of water supply so long as they were not burdened with either a higher price for their water supply or with higher tax burdens. This combination of circumstances has been realized in all prior appropriation states through the jurisdiction and water service policies sustained by the United States Bureau of Reclamation.

The structure of incentives inherent in the law of water rights is clearly not sufficient to constitute a variety of collective enterprises capable of increasing the supply of water services available to a community of water users.[1] Such users must have ready access to courts, legislatures and other decision-making facilities capable of taking authoritative decisions in determining, enforcing and in altering decision-making arrangements. If the political costs of collective decision-making by public officials were high, we would expect a smaller number of collective enterprises to be undertaken by communities of water users. Conversely, if the services of judges, legislators and other political officials were available at a relatively low cost, we would expect recourse to an increasing variety of collective enterprises in undertaking diverse water resource development programs.

The organization of collective enterprises for water resource development will increase the dispersion of decision-making capabilities. Each collectivity acquires authority for rearranging decision-making capabilities to adapt to changing conditions among that community of users. Relatively complex systems of collective enterprises can coordinate their actions one with another so long as judicial, legislative and executive remedies are available to process conflicts of interest as they arise among the diverse enterprises.

Exploiting the opportunities for attaining political solutions to problems of water resource development requires a knowledgeable understanding of the strategic opportunities that can be realized through each of the decision-making structures that are available in a political system. Litigation in courts, the organization of voluntary associations, participation in election campaigns, drafting legislative proposals, lobbying for the enactment of legislation, and negotiating arrangements with other water users are but a few of the political strategies pursued by water resource developers in fashioning the institutional arrangements appropriate to the organization and conduct of their endeavors. Perhaps the craftsmanship inherent in the design and articulation of the institutional arrangements for water resource development can be best illustrated by a case study of public entrepreneurship in West Basin, California.

Organization of Institutional Arrangements for Collective Action, West Basin, California

West Basin, California, is a groundwater basin located on the western periphery of the Los Angeles metropolitan area. West Basin is bounded by

Ballona Creek on the north, by the Beverly-Newport Fault extending roughly from Beverly Hills to Newport Beach on the east and by the Pacific Ocean to the west and south. The basin is composed of a series of sedimentary deposits sustaining a net annual yield of about 30,000 acre feet of water in its natural state. Prior to this century, the hydraulic gradient was such that fresh water was transmitted through pressurized acquifers and discharges into the ocean where wave action had eroded impervious strata and exposed the courser sediments. Prior to World War II the pattern of human culture associated with the development of such communities as El Segundo, Manhattan Beach, Redondo Beach, Hermosa Beach, Palo Verdes, Inglewood, Hawthorne, Torrance, Gardena, Compton, and Long Beach had occurred by drawing upon the accumulated reserve of groundwater stored in the West Basin acquirers. A continuing demand in excess of long-term yield reduced the level of the water tables. By the end of World War II the flow of water had reversed so that salt water from the ocean was flowing into sediments previously occupied by fresh water supplies. The threat of salt water intrusion into West Basin created a political crisis of substantial proportions. In addition to its yield of water, the basin has an economic value as a subsurface reservoir to meet seasonal and cyclical peaking demands. The cost of alternative storage facilities is as high as $1,000 per acre foot of storage. Estimates of the capitalized value of the basin for water storage purposes range from 90 to 150 million dollars (Los Angeles County Flood Control District 1961: 98; also statement of Carl Fossette printed in *Daily Breeze,* January 15, 1954). The problem confronting West Basin water users required a substantial rearrangement of decision-making capabilities among the community of water users if they were to "save" the basin from salt water intrusion and develop its potential as a natural reservoir. The courses of action taken by water users in West Basin included the following legal and political efforts.

(1) Formation of a Water Association

In 1945 a group of water producers took a crucial step toward changing the legal and political relationships of water users by creating the West Basin Water Association as a voluntary association of major water producers extracting water from West Basin. The association provided a forum in which water producers could discuss mutual problems, expand the level of knowledge about alternative techniques for increasing their total usable water supply, and investigate a variety of methods for solving their problems through legal and political means. From the beginning, members of the West Basin Water Association were committed to a strategy of cooperation with all existing water agencies.

(2) Creation of a Municipal Water District

Many members of the association considered access to a supplemental source of water to be an essential first step in solving their problem. Water producers would not be motivated to reduce withdrawals from the basin until they had access to an alternate supply to meet demands. Creation of a municipal water district was a means to include the entire basin within one public entity which could then annex to the Metropolitan Water District of Southern California and gain access to Colorado River water. After one unsuccessful attempt to create a district, the West Basin Municipal Water District was voted into existence on November 25, 1947. The first deliveries of Colorado River water were made to West Basin in 1949.

(3) Initiation of Litigation to Curtail Total Groundwater Production

While efforts were being made to form a municipal water district, a simultaneous effort was made to restructure the basic legal relationships of all water producers utilizing groundwaters from the basin. In October 1945, two private water companies and a city filed suit in Superior Court against a long list of known water producers in West Basin.[2] The plaintiffs sought a legal determination of the rights of all users. The case was referred to the Department of Public Works to serve as a referee in determining the physical facts involved. The referee's report was not filed until 1952.[3] At that time the referee recommended that production from the basin be severely curtailed to a safe yield of 30,000 acre feet per year. By 1952 total groundwater production from the basin had reached 90,000 acre feet. Thus, to fulfill the recommendation of the referee, groundwater producers would have been required to reduce their total production from the basin by two-thirds. Most large water producers opposed this recommendation.

Consequently, a legal settlement committee was established by the West Basin Water Association to negotiate a physical settlement agreeable to major water producers. After three years of negotiation, 46 producers responsible for over 75 percent of the total groundwater production in West Basin entered into a voluntary interim agreement to reduce their groundwater production by 25 percent. A water master was appointed by the court to supervise the operation of this interim agreement. An integral part of the agreement was an exchange pool which allowed those who had physical or economic difficulties in complying with the interim agreement to purchase annual rights to withdraw groundwater in excess of their assigned quota from others more able to gain supplemental supplies from alternative sources.

In August 1961, 16 years after the case was originally initiated, the trial court rendered a final judgment on the basis of a stipulated agreement presented to the court by almost all major West Basin water producers. The final judgment was similar to the interim agreement which had been in operation for six years. Water master services were continued to assure adherence to the judgment by all water producers. The final judgment was challenged by only one major producer who had refused to sign the stipulated agreement. The District Court of Appeals upheld the stipulated agreement approved by the trial court and the remaining holdout was enjoined from pumping more water than authorized under the stipulated agreement.[4]

While the final judgment did not require West Basin Water producers to reduce their groundwater production to a safe field, several beneficial results were achieved by the litigation. First, litigation ended the competitive race among water producers by reducing total production to a level equivalent to the demand of 1942. Total groundwater production was stabilized at approximately 60,000 acre feet per year. Second, the question of who would benefit from the continued use of the basin and who would pay for the costs of using an alternative supply was resolved. Adjudicated rights were determined which gave each water user the right to produce a certain quantity of water each year or to sell or lease his claim to that right. If a future curtailment were to be ordered by the court, each water producer would share the cost of this reduction proportionately. Third, litigation was successful in slowing down the rate of salt water intrusion. However, by the 1950s it was apparent that neither litigation nor the creation of the West Basin Municipal Water District would, by themselves, eliminate the problem of salt water intrusion.

(4) Development of a Barrier against the Sea

West Basin was exposed to the ocean along an eleven-mile western front and along an eight-mile southern front. Engineers associated with the Los Angeles County Flood Control District suggested that the creation of an underground fresh water barrier to hold back the sea appeared to be technically feasible. Water users in West Basin appealed to Los Angeles County Flood Control District to undertake a small-scale experiment to ascertain whether fresh water injected into a well under pressure would create a fresh water mound. That experiment was successful. Individuals in West Basin next appealed to the State of California to finance a prototype barrier to determine whether a series of injection wells could prevent salt water intrusion along a one-mile front. The state legislature appropriated $750,000 for this project.[5] By the end of 1953 the prototype barrier was considered to be a technical success. The fresh water injected into that series of wells held back the sea and much of the injected water flowed into the basin to supplement the natural yield. The Flood Control District estimated the capital cost of the barrier at $5,000,000 and annual operating costs at $500,000 exclusive of water costs. Estimated costs of injection water per year varied from $312,000 to $1,040,000 depending on the type of water used (Los Angeles County Flood Control District 1953: 4).

(5) Search for Institutional Arrangements to Fund the Barrier

Members of the West Basin Water Association drafted legislation which would enable West Basin to form a special zone of benefit within the Los Angeles County Flood Control District to coincide roughly with basin boundaries. Revenue could be raised from an *ad valorem* property tax within the zone to help finance construction of the barrier.

(6) Establishment of a Management Enterprise

Revenue raised from the .05 *ad valorem* tax authorized under the Flood Control District's zone-of-benefit would not be sufficient to pay for the entire cost of the barrier. A number of related problems also needed resolution. One problem was a means for allocating cost of groundwater basin development to the diverse beneficiaries. A second problem was the determination of an appropriate long-run boundary to achieve control over the water resource system in West Basin. As individuals in West Basin purchased surface water, reduced their pumping and started the construction of a barrier, their neighbors in Central Basin continued to increase production from this adjacent and interconnected basin. Consequently, the normal subsurface flow from Central Basin into West Basin declined to a substantial degree. An opportunity was available to replenish both basins through the inexpensive means of spreading water at the Los Angeles forebay where water percolates into both Central Basin and West Basin. Water producers in both basins began to acknowledge that the two basins were so interrelated that future efforts to manage water resource development in either basin should be coordinated with actions in the other.

A third set of unresolved problems related to the appropriate mix of agencies to undertake a more ambitious and long-run management program. Several existing agencies including the West Basin Municipal Water District, the Los Angeles County Flood Control District, the Metropolitan Water District, and the State Department of Water Resources were already involved. After extensive negotiation among all the agencies involved and with other individuals prominent in the southern California water industry, legislation authorizing a local area to create a groundwater replenishment district was drafted by a committee of twelve representing local and regional water agencies. This draft legislation was submitted to the state legislature and enacted in 1955.[6] After further negotiation within the West Basin Water Association itself and with Central Basin water producers to establish boundary conditions and an appropriate management plan, a new agency, the Central and West Basin Water Replenishment District, was organized in November 1959. The management plan has quasi-constitutional status in the organization of a replenishment district.

The major source of revenue for the Replenishment District is a replenishment assessment or a "pump tax" levied on all water produced in both basins. This fund is utilized to purchase water for spreading at the Los Angeles forebay and for injection into the West Basin barrier. The cost of the barrier is shared by water users who pay operating costs through the "pump tax" and land owners who pay capital costs through an *ad valorem* property tax.

The Replenishment District has a wide range of powers and sustains an effective management system for the two basins. The Replenishment District, after extensive negotiation with Central Basin, initiated litigation to control groundwater production in Central Basin. A final agreement has been reached in accordance with the principles of the West Basin settlement, approved by the court, and a water master has been appointed to supervise that operation.[7] The Replenishment District is authorized to act jointly with any public or private agency which can help accomplish its purposes economically. The Replenishment District has contracted, for example, with the Los Angeles County Sanitation districts to supply reclaimed waste water from local sewerage systems for spreading at the Los Angeles forebay (Los Angeles County Sanitation District 1963). Extensive interagency negotiation has evolved a management system which includes the participation of the Replenishment District, the Los Angeles County Flood Control District, the Metropolitan Water District, the Los Angeles County Sanitation Districts, the State Regional Water Pollution Control Board, the State Department of Water Resources, a private engineering firm serving as water master and the West Basin Water Association (for a description of the current management system, see Central and West Basin Water Replenishment District 1969). Water resource development in West Basin is conducted by a multi-organizational arrangement where first priority is given to decision-making by voluntary agreement through negotiation but backed up by potential recourse to litigation and legislative action.

The institutional arrangements established by West Basin water producers have enabled them to develop the basin as a reservoir subject to effective control. The replenishment program in operation supplements the natural supply of water to the basin and offsets the demands made upon the basin in excess of safe yield. A large share of the water used in the replenishment program is made available at a cost less than the marginal cost of importing water to the Los Angeles metropolitan region from either the Colorado River or from northern California. The use of a pump tax to cover the cost of water used in the replenishment program means that an administered price has been imposed on water at its source leading to a more efficient utilization of water resources in the area. The operation of the water master service, the definition of the rights of all water producers to a share of the total yield, and the tradition of exchanging or transferring water among producers originally authorized under the Exchange Agreement, have all contributed to the development of a market in the renting or leasing of water rights. (For a more complete description of the set of relationships among public agencies managing West Basin, see Elinor Ostrom 1965.)

Conclusion

The groundwater basin management program in West Basin, California is illustrative of the legal and political strategies involved in reallocating decision-making capabilities among a community of water users under changing conditions of supply and demand. Each new technical solution to a water resource problem is likely to depend upon the formulation of new political solutions in rearranging decision-making capabilities among water users.

Any particular institutional arrangement will afford significant capabilities for approaching some problems but will be subject to serious weaknesses or limitations in approaching other problems. The theory of market mechanics in economics enables us to anticipate where market arrangements can be used to advantage and where market weaknesses and market failure will occur. Recent work on bureaucratic organization enables us to anticipate where a bureaucratic structure can lead to an improvement in economic welfare by sustaining a closely coordinated teamwork among those engaged in an enterprise, and where a bureaucratic arrangement can lead to serious deterioration in human welfare (Coase 1937; Tullock 1965). The high degree of interdependency among joint and alternative uses characteristic of water resource development poses special problems associated with externalities, the theory of public goods, common properties, the organization of collective enterprise and public regulation (V. Ostrom 1968). Such circumstances require recourse to collective decision rules that relax the requirement of willing consent and place increasing reliance upon the type of decision rules associated with governmental action.

A central task among persons associated with problems of water resource development will be one of conceptualizing appropriate institutional solutions that will take account of the heterogeneous sets of interests involved among diverse communities of water users. These efforts will require the collaboration of engineers, lawyers, economists and political scientists in assessing the technical, economic, financial, legal and political feasibility of alternative institutional arrangements in addition to our present preoccupation with the application of feasibility criteria to water works planning.

NOTES

1. Voluntary action among individual property owners would presume a decision rule of unanimity for taking collective action. Mancur Olson (1965) examines the theoretical difficulties inherent in collective action. James Buchanan and Gordon Tullock (1962) examine the theoretical issues associated with the choice of decision rules in constituting a collective enterprise.
2. *California Water Service Company et al.,* v. *City of Compton et al.,* Case No. 506806 in the Superior Court of the State of California in and for the county of Los Angeles
3. California Department of Public Works, *Report of the Referee in California Water Service Company* v. *City of Compton,* Case No. 506806 in the Superior Court of the State of California in and for the county of Los Angeles.
4. *California Water Service Company* v. *City of Hawthorne,* 224, A.C.A. 885.
5. *California Statues,* 1951, ch. 1500, sec. 1, pp. 3483–84.
6. *California Water Code,* Sec. 60220-60250.
7. *Central and West Basin Water Replenishment District* v. *Charles E. Adams,* Case No. 786656 in the Superior Court of the State of California in and for the county of Los Angeles.

REFERENCES

Buchanan, James, and Gordon Tullock. 1962. *Calculus of Consent.* Ann Arbor: University of Michigan Press.
California Department of Public Works, Division of Engineering and Irrigation. 1928. *Santa Ana Investigation, Flood Control and Conservation.* Bulletin No. 19. Sacramento, CA.
Central and West Basin Water Replenishment District. 1969. *Annual Survey Report on Ground Water Replenishment.* Glendale, CA: Central and West Basin Water Replenishment District.
Coase, Ronald H. 1937. "The Nature of the Firm." *Economica* 4:386–405.
Commons, John R. 1959. *Legal Foundations of Capitalism.* Madison: University of Wisconsin Press.
Hohfeld, Wesley N. 1964. *Fundamental Legal Conceptions.* Ed. W. W. Cook. New Haven, CT: Yale University Press.

Los Angeles County Flood Control District. 1953. *Report on the Advisability of Establishing Water Conservation Zone 11 of the Los Angeles County Flood Control District.* Los Angeles: Los Angeles County Flood Control District.

————. 1961. *Report on Required Facilities for Replenishment and Protecting Ground Water Reserves in the Central and West Coast Ground Water Basins.* Los Angeles: Los Angeles County Flood Control District.

Los Angeles County Sanitation District. 1963. *A Plan for Water Re-Use.* Los Angeles: Los Angeles County Sanitation District.

Olson, Mancur. 1965. *Logic of Collective Action.* Cambridge, MA: Harvard University Press.

Ostrom, Elinor. 1965. *Public Entrepreneurship: A Case Study in Ground Water Basin Management.* Ph.D. diss., University of California, Los Angeles.

Ostrom, Vincent. 1968. "Water Resource Development: Some Problems in Economic and Political Analysis of Public Policy." In *Political Science and Public Policy,* ed. Austin Ranney, 123–50. Chicago: Markham.

Rheinstein, Max, ed. 1967. *Max Weber on Law in Economy and Society.* New York: Simon and Schuster.

Tullock, Gordon. 1965. *The Politics of Bureaucracy.* Washington, DC: Public Affairs Press.

CHAPTER 3

Institutional Capacity and the Resolution of a Commons Dilemma

William Blomquist and Elinor Ostrom

This is the story of the fight to supply water for 250,000 people living in 82,000 homes in West Basin. It tells of efforts to find water for industries located here, so that thousands of workers might draw daily wages. . . . Tangible property, with an assessed value of over $250 million, had been developed and established, based on a water supply that was believed to be abundant and constant.

This is the story of depletion and contamination of that water supply. It is the story of reports, studies, investigations, committee meetings, mass meetings, parades, and elections, and also a story of opposing views, of tempers and temperament, of nonsensical argument. Finally, it is a story of success, of community cooperation, of mutual helpfulness, and of buried antagonisms. (Fossette 1950, p. i)

West Basin is an underground water basin located adjacent to the Pacific Coast in Los Angeles County, California. It is the last of several interconnected groundwater basins underlying the south coastal plain. The success of the West Basin water producers in overcoming problems of depletion and contamination of the water resource makes this case relevant for those interested both in water resource management strategies and in more general questions concerning the resolution of commons problems.

As an example of a solution to a commons dilemma situation, not only are the institutional arrangements used in West Basin relevant to a broad class of problems but propositions derived from the theory of commons dilemma situations can be examined for their empirical relevance in this

Originally published in *Policy Studies Review* 5, no. 2 (November 1985): 383–93. Reprinted by permission of the Policy Studies Organization and the authors.

Authors' note: The authors gratefully acknowledge the assistance of the National Science Foundation, NSF SES 83–09829. Views expressed are the authors and not necessarily those of the National Science Foundation. We appreciate the comments we have received from David Feeny, Frank Hoole, John McIver, Margaret McKean, Vincent Ostrom, Roger B. Parks, Paul Sabatier, Norman Uphoff, and L. A. Wilson, on an earlier version of this essay.

natural setting. Commons dilemmas arise from the joint use of a common-pool resource. A common-pool resource provides a finite flow of separable "use-units" over time. Multiple individuals can use a common-pool resource system simultaneously, but each person's consumption subtracts the amount consumed from the quantity available to others.[1]

Not every common-pool resource will necessarily produce a commons dilemma. A commons dilemma is characterized by the overuse, erosion, and deterioration of the resource's ability to continue to provide the valued "use-units." Whether or not a commons dilemma arises in a particular case of a common-pool resource depends upon the behavior of users, which in turn depends upon the structure of their situation and the incentives they face.

Although the theory of commons dilemma situations is incomplete, several scholars have developed dynamic models that predict stable, long-term cooperative solutions (Lewis and Cowens 1983) or the possibility of long-term cooperative equilibria (Axelrod 1981; Taylor 1977; Hardin 1982). Others have presumed the principal—perhaps the only—hope for resolution of the commons dilemma and the preservation of the common resource is the coercive intervention of an external regulator (Carruthers and Stoner 1981). Still others have concerned themselves with the possibilities for "privatizing" the commons by establishing separable and transferable property rights to the commons (Sinn 1984; Welch 1983; Anderson and Hill 1977).

The West Basin case is noteworthy because the actions taken to preserve the commons were primarily designed by the water producers themselves, rather than being imposed on them by a state or national government. Yet in West Basin, strictly private action was not the case either. Public institutions and officials were involved throughout the process of resolution. The ability to use, create, and alter public institutions was critical to the formulation and implementation of the actions agreed upon by the local producers. Thus, resolution to this case by a mixture of private and public institutional arrangements constitutes a promising "middle ground" for the resolution of commons problems.

In this essay we consider the process of resolution of a commons dilemma in dynamic situations involving commons-sharing arrangements without an externally imposed solution, and we give particular attention to a model presented by Lewis and Cowens (1983) and to the conditions necessary to their result of a cooperative private arrangement, privately enforced. A different set permits a variety of processes to resolve a commons dilemma, one of which is illustrated in West Basin. Throughout this presentation, it is our purpose to build upon and contribute to the work of those scholars who have sought means other than an externally coerced solution to such frequent, difficult, and variegated problems.

Conditions for the Resolution of a
Commons Dilemma

At least two ways exist for resolving a commons dilemma in the absence of an externally imposed resolution. One way, which has already been explored in the literature, involves not only the absence of a coercive external regulator but the absence of any public institutions whatever. This approach relies entirely on voluntary, independent decisions made by the participants. Another way, which we propose, allows public institutions to facilitate voluntary agreements.

Resolution without Institutions

The private "resolution without institutions" approach is presented in an important dynamic model by Lewis and Cowens (1983). They model the joint use of an ocean fishery by a group who harvest fish in each time period. Lewis and Cowens attempt to account for cooperative behavior in a commons dilemma in the absence of an imposed solution or external regulation. They search for conditions under which "users may be able to construct a cooperative scheme for conserving the resource that is self-policing," with enforcement by "the threat of retaliation by others" (1983, p. 2). Their conclusion is fundamentally different from that derived from static models. Lewis and Cowens predict an indefinitely extended cooperative equilibrium in the joint use of an open-access fishery. All participants monitor the behavior of rivals and harvest at an efficient rate (for the commons) as long as each observes the others doing so.

In light of their optimistic predictions for the resolution of the commons dilemma, and given their purpose in deriving such a resolution without the involvement of institutions, it is important to examine in some detail the assumptions underlying the Lewis and Cowens's model. Lewis and Cowens's outcome rests upon five necessary conditions. Each of the five conditions—information, communication, symmetry, enforcement, and monitoring—has been widely discussed by scholars concerned with the resolution of commons dilemma situations. For scholars interested in understanding how individuals cope with continuing, long-term commons dilemmas, the particular assumptions made about each of these conditions by Lewis and Cowens are hard to accept. Their assumptions are logical fictions necessary to drive through a proof. One might simply reject them all as unrealistic. We have taken a different approach.

We view each of these five conditions as *variables* that may take on *values* progressively approximating the conditions present in Lewis and Cowens's model. We then ask what type of institutional arrangements might enhance the possibility that this variable would approach a high value in the same direction as the assumption made by Lewis and Cowens. Our focus is on the question: Under what institutional arrangements would the value of this variable tend to approach that posited by Lewis and Cowens?

The Information Condition

Lewis and Cowens presume, as do most formal theorists, that participants have complete information about the structure of the situation they face. Participants are presumed to have information concerning the resource they are using and their own and others' use. They know the capacity and growth rate of the common resource, and thus are able to take future depletion effects into account in assessing the present value of cooperative and noncooperative strategies. Participants know the safe yield of the resource, the total amount of fish harvested by users in each time period, and make comparisons between the two. Therefore, they know if even a single user increases his or her harvest. Participants also know the total number of users, and the amount by which other users would increase their harvest if all defect. Thus, they can calculate the depletion effects of joint noncooperation.

Complete information is necessary in a model that excludes the consideration of institutions. In the absence of an information *source,* one must presume that participants already hold all knowledge necessary to their calculations; learning is not needed. Assuming complete information in a dynamic model places participants in a post-learning mode. They begin their participation in the use of the commons already comprehending all that is important to their decisionmaking.

The Communication Condition

Lewis and Cowens abstract from problems of communication among users by assuming that communication is immediate, undistorted, and costless. Information is shared by all because it is held by each. Threats of retaliation are understood by all because all users are assumed to be identical, facing identical strategic situations resulting from identical amounts of use. This interaction of the information condition discussed above with the symmetry condition discussed below renders communication among users unnecessary, which is the same as assuming perfect and costless communication. Lewis and Cowens note this in their discussion of the effect of the number of harvesters by acknowledging that an increase in the number of participants is usually associated with increased negotiation and monitoring costs (1983, p. 15).

The Symmetry Condition

Lewis and Cowens assume that all users are identical and there is perfect symmetry in use and in benefits from use. The result, an indefinitely extended cooperative equilibrium, is conditioned on the assumption that each user consumes 1/Nth of the present yield of the resource, each user maximizes the same utility function, and each user harvests the same amount from the resource and derives the same utility from that harvest. This condition (1) allows participants to take one another's actions into account and recognize what will succeed in deterring defections and (2) removes from the analysis potentially thorny problems of "fairness" that may arise in the development of a resolution of a commons dilemma that involves unequal division of the commons. This symmetry condition drives the model's private enforcement mechanism a long way: the shared understanding of participants that *all* will cooperate or *all* will defect is premised on the condition that all are alike in the use of the commons and benefits derived therefrom.

The Enforcement Condition—Deterrence

Lewis and Cowens's harvesters enforce their commons-sharing arrangement by individually adapting to a deterrent strategy. The strategy is to restrain one's harvest at the cooperative level unless and until an excessive total harvest is detected. If anyone defects, the best reply that all of the other participants can make is to pursue noncooperative exploitation of the fishery for all subsequent time periods. The deterrent threat is not "tit for tat" but "defect forever if anyone defects once." This strategy is adopted by each of the identical harvesters and satisfies Selten's (1975) perfectness property as the optimal response of all possible histories of play.

The deterrent strategy is what makes the present value of restraint greater than the present value of defection. The recognition that any defection will destroy forever the common resource, keeps one from defecting, as long as future harvests are sufficiently weighted relative to the present harvests.

The Monitoring Condition

One condition that keeps Lewis and Cowens's fish harvesters from a situation in which some retaliate while others do not is the presumption of perfect and costless monitoring. Each harvester monitors the behavior of all others by monitoring the total fish harvest in each time period. Such monitoring is presumed to be without costs, and always correct.

The Cumulative Effect of the Conditions

Lewis and Cowens's model predicts an indefinitely extended cooperative arrangement, which is arrived at and enforced by the participants themselves. These conditions—and their configuration—are *necessary* conditions. All must be satisfied to reach and sustain the cooperative equilibrium.

Yet, each condition is unlikely to be obtained in a natural setting. Lewis and Cowens acknowledge, for instance, that the perfect and costless monitoring assumption is too strong to be satisfied in practice. If each of the conditions taken separately is unlikely to be met by an actual commons dilemma, certainly the odds of ever observing the confluence of all of them must be deemed exceedingly small.

The question then is how to treat these unrealistic conditions and the Lewis and Cowens model in analyzing the prospects for the resolution of a commons dilemma. A frequent stance taken by analysts is to ignore a model (or to criticize it) because its assumptions are unrealistic. An alternative stance is to disregard the assumptions and embrace the model by presuming that the predicted outcome is the most likely outcome in actual settings. Yet a third perspective, which we adopt, is to accept the model as a polar case showing the conditions necessary to an extreme sort of outcome—a purely private resolution privately enforced without institutions—and then to take the conditions it identifies as *variables*. These variables have to take on extreme values to produce the original proof. These variables may exhibit a range of states or values in actual settings. Let us now examine how these five conditions could be reexamined using an institutional framework.

Resolution with Institutions

The Information Condition
If we relax the assumption that all participants with access to the commons already know everything about the resource and its users, then perhaps we should expect that participants will exploit the commons to an initial state of overuse *before* they become concerned with overuse. Detrimental effects of overuse may be the trigger for individuals who value the commons to begin to inquire about its capacity and its use by them and others.

The fact that users do not know all they need to know does not mean they are doomed to a dynamic of destruction. The availability of information can be viewed as a process. Information gathering can be initiated by the participants themselves. Before they find answers, we should expect they must discover the relevant questions. This may start with simple inquiries such as: Why is the water coming out of the well salty now? Or, why are we using more nets and catching fewer fish? When such a point is reached, the process can go in different ways.

If each individual user must undertake an investigation of the commons to discover personally all relevant information, the prospects may be dim indeed. If, on the other hand, a participant or group of participants can invoke an existing institutional arrangement to aid them in finding information about their problem, better prospects may arise. For policy analysts the question to ask may not be: Do all participants know what is going on? Rather, one should ask: Is there some way for participants to find out what is going on? Can participants engage some mechanism for discovery about the causes of their losses? Is there a court system, an agency, or a foundation that might be able to inform the users or undertake an inquiry? Are cost-sharing arrangements available for such efforts?

The Communication Condition

If an information-gathering process is engaged by or on behalf of a subgroup of users, this will not translate into a resolution of a commons dilemma without dissemination to other users. This makes the identification of users and of the boundaries of the resource critical elements of information. In addition, a process of dissemination of information must exist or be developed.

The second dimension of communication is discourse among users about their common problem and possible joint strategies for resolution. If a solution is not externally imposed, and if we cannot expect each user to adopt the same strategy in isolation (as Lewis and Cowens posit), the choice and maintenance of commons-sharing arrangement requires communication among the users.

Such communication will neither be perfect nor costless. Not all users need be involved in the development of proposals or ideas about resolution. A self-selection process may even develop where those most immediately affected by overuse are most likely to seek out or create a forum for discussing possible resolutions. A trade association of fish harvesters or water producers, litigation among claimants to a resource, or some other arrangement, may make possible or require interaction among users. The point is that it may not be necessary to assume perfect and costless communication to obtain a resolution of a commons dilemma. If an imperfect forum provides some sharing of information and some interaction among users for the airing of possible resolutions, prospects will improve. The greater the extent to which such a capacity is used, the greater the likelihood of resolution.

The Symmetry Condition

The symmetry condition raises the question of cost-sharing. Unless one is willing to assume total *a priori* information, (perfect and costless) communication, and costless enforcement monitoring, any resolution of the commons dilemma will involve costs, and thus the issue of cost allocation. The participants in Lewis and Cowens model bear the costs of harvest reduction and deterrence symmetrically since they are identical. In a symmetrical situation, a "prominent" solution (Schelling 1963; also Hardin 1982, p. 90) exists to the allocation problem; everyone bears 1/Nth of the costs. Symmetry of interest in the use of the commons makes agreeing on a cost-sharing rule a trivial matter.

When the interests of joint users are asymmetric, this allocation decision is critically important. Allocation of costs must relate to the distribution of interests among the participants. The aggregation of benefits to participants from a particular cooperative scheme could exceed the aggregation of costs; yet participants still fail to bear the full costs because the *allocation* of costs to some exceeds their benefits. Hardin (1982, p. 92) argues that under conditions of asymmetry no abstract *a priori* cost-sharing rule can avoid conflicts when applied post hoc to an asymmetrical group whose numbers had not previously borne such costs. A cost-sharing rule must be developed and adopted for the particular case in question.

Lack of symmetry of interests is to be expected in actual settings. We believe it highly unlikely that each and every user of a joint facility other than a pure Samuelsonian public good will derive exactly the same benefit from its use and suffer exactly the same loss from its deterioration. If we are to have a theoretical treatment of an iterated commons dilemma capable of predicting anything other than absolute and inevitable destruction, we would have to acknowledge the institutional capacity of users to develop a cost-sharing rule suited to their case as a variable contributing to the structure of the situation and the prospects for resolution.

The Enforcement Condition

The Lewis and Cowens model implicitly makes a structural change in the iterated Prisoners' Dilemma game that has been likened to the commons dilemma. Through their combination of conditions, they produce a situation where it is not possible to defect while all others cooperate. Nor would one cooperate while all others defect. Referring back to the original game structure, this operates as an elimination of the "temptation" and "sucker's" payoffs, leaving each player with a choice only of cooperating while all others cooperate (the second-best payoff) or defecting while all others defect (the third-best payoff). Under such a structure, cooperating dominates defecting. Such a situation yields an indefinitely extended equilibrium.

The question then arises, can such a structural change be made by users? The answer depends upon whether users are capable of making enforceable contracts that eliminate the "temptation" and "sucker" payoffs. A "contingent contract" accomplishes this and therefore can change a commons dilemma into a situation where cooperating dominates defecting.

In the context of an overused common resource, a contingent contract might begin with a proposed curtailment of use by all parties to a prescribed level. Such a proposal is submitted to each participant for ratification with a condition that the arrangement does not become binding upon that participant unless a stated proportion of the other participants also ratify. Participants can agree to such a curtailment, while being protected from being a "sucker," since there is no obligation to cooperate unless enough others do the same.

Once the sufficient number of participants have agreed to cooperate, the agreement takes effect. Like all contracts, it can be enforced by any party against any defector. Enforcement does not have to be private enforcement. The availability of institutions for the enforcement of contracts substitutes the cost of using such institutions for the cost of private enforcement and lowers the threshold of participation in enforcement from all users to as few as one. As monitoring approaches a sufficient degree of accuracy, the "temptation" payoff may be effectively eliminated, or at least reduced below the payoff from cooperating while all others cooperate. Institutional capacity for the making and enforcing of contracts exists in many settings and the recognition of its availability may allow us to eliminate a number of problematic assumptions (e.g., identical users, complete information) necessary to the private-enforcement approach (see discussion by Hardin 1982; Brubaker 1975; and Guttman 1978, on contingent contracting).

The Monitoring Condition

We cannot expect perfect and costless monitoring in a naturally occurring setting. The question is whether participants can structure a capacity that provides sufficient monitoring to deter participants from defecting and to sanction those who do. Every criminal act does not have to result in conviction and incarceration for law enforcement to work nor does every individual who exceeds the maximum allowable water use need to be caught to avoid the depletion of the common resource. The appointment of an outside monitor is also a feasible option in many institutional settings. An outside monitor displaces a considerable amount of the responsibility for enforcing the cooperative arrangement from the participants and can implement time-consuming means of monitoring that might not be feasible if joint users of the commons were the only monitors.

The Conditions as Variables

We have approached Lewis and Cowens's five conditions as a set of variables whose values may be affected by the institutional milieu within which a commons situation occurs. We have argued that the possibilities for cooperative commons-sharing arrangements are enhanced as the values of these five variables approach a sufficient level over time to shift the structure of incentives and constraints faced by joint users of the commons closer to those posited by Lewis and Cowens. But in the analysis of a long-term commons dilemma, it is not necessary to presume all five conditions must be met or the commons will be destroyed. The very fact that in most actual settings, commons dilemmas are iterated allows participants to evolve a solution through a variety of institutional arrangements. What conditions the resolution of a commons dilemma is the capacity to make such changes.

The general institutional arrangements that enhance the capability of participants to reach a particular solution include the institutional capacity to develop:

1. Information about the commons and use-patterns;
2. A forum for communication among those affected;
3. Cost-sharing formulae accepted by most participants as being equitable;
4. Enforceable, contingent contracts; and
5. Effective monitoring of use-patterns.

Individuals facing a commons dilemma situation in an institutional setting where they can develop the above institutions should be more likely to adopt a cooperative commons-sharing arrangement than individuals in an institutional milieu without such capabilities. In the case of the West Basin groundwater commons dilemma, all of these capabilities were developed and used in the evolution of a program for the curtailment of use of the basin.

The West Basin Case and Institutional Capacity

In the West Basin of Southern California's Los Angeles County, joint users of a common resource have, over a number of years, formulated a solution to their iterated commons dilemma. Their solution is neither purely private nor an externally imposed, coercive solution. It involves the development of capacities for communication, cost-sharing, and monitoring, and the use and adaptation of capacities for information provision, contracting and contract enforcement. It involves the interaction of private users, private institutions, and public institutions in a complex set of arrangements that generate a new rule configuration governing behavior in the joint use of the commons.

In a semiarid region such as the Los Angeles metropolitan area, economic development depends on the availability of a dependable water supply. Early economic development in the area was based almost exclusively on the use of groundwater. The "safe yields" of many of these basins were first exceeded in the 1930s. By the early 1940s, overdraft conditions were so severe in some basins that the viability of the basins was threatened. Nonetheless, the water extracted from underground was more attractive in cost and quality than alternative sources. Water users continued to withdraw water and did so at an increasing rate as the area developed. West Basin, being adjacent to the Pacific Ocean and lowest in the series of basins, faced the most severe problems of overdraft and saltwater intrusion.

As individuals in the basin noticed water levels falling and word spread of saltwater intrusion, each pumper's incentive was to continue to increase pumping. Failure to do so would simply mean that one's desired water would be extracted by another user. Water levels steadily lowered, and saltwater intruded further and further along the coast. Unless the participants, or external authorities, restructured the situation faced by the water producers, they would jointly destroy a resource of considerable economic value.

Over approximately a 20-year period, the water producers of West Basin created a successful water management program (see Lipson 1978, for the details of this development). This program involved developing various parts of the commons-sharing arrangement and then fitting them together. The steps toward the resolution of the problem included:

1. The creation of a voluntary association of water producers to share information available from a state water resources division about the boundaries and conditions of the south coastal plain basins, to provide a forum for discussion of the information and of possible alternatives to the present situation, and to relate activities occurring in different public arenas. The association was supported by voluntary dues from producers based on the amount of water each produced from the basin, with votes apportioned accordingly.
2. The use of the available court system for three principal purposes. First, through discovery and reference procedures, to ascertain reliable information on basin supply and use patterns, and to determine the identity of all other users in the basin. Second, to adjudicate rights based on use patterns and the determined safe yield of the basin, which rights were then secure unto the parties and could be worked into an agreement curtailing total use to the safe yield level. Three, to give force and effect to that agreement as an enforceable settlement provided that it was signed by at least 80 percent of users. The cost of the litigation was apportioned among the users based on their rights as determined in the agreement.
3. The establishment of an office of the state water resources agency as Watermaster to serve as a permanent monitor of use in the basin and compliance with the agreement. Two-thirds of the costs of the Watermaster service are assessed on these producers with rights to water and one-third is borne by the State of California.
4. The creation of a public water district covering the basin area to

provide an alternative source of supply—that is, to import sufficient fresh water into the area to make up the difference between ground-water extractions and total water use. Costs of the water district's operation and acquisition are borne by water users according to amount of use with minor reliance on the property tax.

The participants in the West Basin commons dilemma developed the institutional capacities necessary to their commons-sharing arrangement through their adaptation of existing capacities and their creation of new ones. The information condition, for instance, of each participant having complete information about the resource and use patterns was approximated by the adaptation of the data-collection practices of a state agency and the discovery and reference procedures of the court. The provision of information about individual users and the losses they were incurring and their willingness to explore alternatives occurred through the creation of the voluntary association.

The communication condition was approximated in a similar way. The creation of the association provided a forum for information dissemination and for the exploration of alternatives without commitment by various association members. The use of litigation allowed dissemination of information and communication among users and eventual contingent commitment.

Cost-sharing arrangements were developed for each step in the resolution process. The use of proportionate cost-sharing began with the voluntary association. Dues were assessed based on the amount of groundwater extracted. In the court case, costs of investigation and litigation were matched to the benefit obtained in the judgement—that is, the prescribed rights to water. The cost of monitoring compliance with the upper bounds of one's rights was again matched to rights, with a portion borne by the State of California. Citizens of the state have an interest that accurate information be gathered on groundwater conditions and that facilities be maintained that encourage solutions to commons dilemmas. The cost of providing an alternative source of supply was apportioned primarily to water *use,* rather than to production.

The use of contingent contracting to formulate an enforceable commons-sharing arrangement was explicit in the West Basin case. The plan for curtailment which emerged in the course of litigation was not effective unless 80 percent of the parties signed. The plan allowed those who did sign to move toward a cooperative resolution without being committed to a cooperative strategy that could result in a sucker's payoff. When 80 percent did sign, an interim agreement enforceable against signatories took effect. After experience with the interim agreement the final court judgement made it enforceable against *all* parties.

The capacity for effective monitoring of use patterns was developed out of the data collection function performed by the state's water resources division as fact-finding referee in the litigation of the West Basin case. Having formed a history of groundwater production in the basin, and having participated in the identification of all water producers in the basin, the agency was significantly better positioned to perform an ongoing monitoring of individuals' extractions than the individuals were to perform that function with respect to one another. So the agency was, in essence, "hired" as Watermaster to be paid by the parties and the state to monitor compliance with the curtailment agreement (see California Watermaster annual reports for a detailed identification of exactly how much is pumped by each producer each year).

By the close of the process of development of the commons-sharing arrangement, West Basin water producers had put in place and used all of the elements of institutional capacity discussed above—information, communication, cost-sharing, contingent contracting, and monitoring. Through these measures, participants had fundamentally changed the rules structuring their situation in such a way that a cooperative response was more rational than a noncooperative response.

The development of a resolution of the commons dilemma is part of the West Basin story. From the standpoint of theoretical work and the analysis of commons dilemma situations, it is the most important part. But for the application of analytical work to actual settings, an equally important question is whether the commons-sharing arrangement "worked," in the sense of producing the intended results.

Considerable data exist on the historical use-patterns in West Basin and on the water quantity and quality conditions of the Basin. These data extend from approximately 25 years before the initiation of the basin management programs to 30 years thereafter. In a longer, unpublished version of this essay, we have examined this data series using least-squares regression techniques and ARIMA time-series analysis. The results of this testing indicate that aggregate extractions from the Basin have been curtailed to the safe yield of the basin and saltwater intrusion has not further undermined basin water quality. Confidence levels are sufficiently strong to support the conclusion that the basin-management programs developed for West Basin have indeed produced their intended results.

NOTE

1. Thus, a commons is not a pure private good, as it is capable of use by more than one user at a time, and it is not a pure public good in the Samuelsonian sense of

nonsubtractability, as a commons is a finite resource or facility that is susceptible to problems of crowding or overuse (see, e.g., Ostrom and Ostrom 1977). Nonetheless, the behavior of participants sharing a commons may be rather similar to the behavior of members of a group attempting to provide themselves with a public good.

REFERENCES

Anderson, T., and P. J. Hill (1977) From free grass to fences: transforming the commons of the American West. In G. Hardin and J. Baden, eds., *Managing the commons*, 200–16. San Francisco: W. H. Freeman and Co.

Axelrod, R. (1981) The emergence of cooperation among egoists. *American Political Science Review* 75:306–18.

Brubaker, E. (1975) Free ride, free revelation, or golden rule? *Journal of Law and Economics* 18:147–61.

California, State of, Department of Water Resources (series) (1958–83) *Watermaster service in the West Coast Basin*. Annual reports.

Carruthers, I., and R. Stoner. (1981) *Economic aspects and policy issues in groundwater development*. World Bank Staff Working Paper No. 496. Washington, DC: World Bank.

Fossette, C. (1950) *The story of West Basin water*. Hermosa Beach, CA: West Basin Water Association.

Guttman, J. M. (1978) Understanding collective action: matching behavior. *American Economic Review* 68:251–55.

Hardin, R. (1982) *Collective action*. Baltimore: Johns Hopkins Press for Resources for the Future.

Lewis, T. R., and J. Cowens (1983) *Cooperation in the commons: an application of repetitious rivalry*. Vancouver: University of British Columbia, Department of Economics.

Lipson, A. J. (1978) *Efficient water use in California: the evolution of groundwater management in Southern California*. Santa Monica, CA: Rand Corporation.

Ostrom, V., and E. Ostrom (1977) Public goods and public choices. In E. S. Savas, ed., *Alternatives for delivering public services*, 7–49. Boulder, CO: Westview Press. Reprinted in M. D. McGinnis, ed., *Polycentricity and local public economies* (Ann Arbor: University of Michigan Press, 1999).

Schelling, T. (1963) *The strategy of conflict*. New York: Oxford University Press.

Selten, R. (1975) Reexamination of the perfectness concept for equilibrium points in extensive games. *International Journal of Game Theory* 4:25–55.

Sinn, H-W. (1984) Common property resources, storage facilities and ownership structures: A cournot model of the oil market. *Economica* 51:235–53.

Taylor, M. (1977) *Anarchy and cooperation*. London: John Wiley.

Welch, W. P. (1983) The political feasibility of full ownership property rights: the cases of pollution and fisheries. *Policy Sciences* 16:165–80.

CHAPTER 4

Design Principles in Long-Enduring Irrigation Institutions

Elinor Ostrom

Irrigation development must confront the issues of governance and enlist human and other resources and procedures to arrange appropriate institutions and organizations in addition to appropriate irrigation technologies. (Coward 1980, p. 16)

Introduction

For the next several decades, the most important question related to water resource development is that of institutional design rather than engineering design. Institutional design is a different process than that of engineering design. Crafting institutions is an ongoing process that is enhanced when both the users and the suppliers of irrigation water are involved in a design process. The term *crafting,* to refer to the activities associated with the design of institutions, emphasizes (1) the artisanship involved in the design, operation, appraisal and modification of rule-ordered behavior (Ostrom 1980), and (2) the ongoing nature of "getting the process right" (Uphoff 1986).

Originally published in *Water Resources Research* 29, no. 7 (July 1993): 1907–12. Copyright 1993 by the American Geophysical Union. Reprinted by permission of the American Geophysical Union and the author.

Author's note: This essay was originally delivered as the Presidential Address to the International Association for the Study of Common Property at Duke University on September 28, 1990. It is drawn from a longer project report (Ostrom 1992) written for the Decentralization, Finance and Management (DFM) Project that is sponsored by the Office of Rural and Institutional Development of the Bureau for Science and Technology of the U.S. Agency for International Development under contract number DHR–5446–Z–00–7033–00 to Associates in Rural Development, the Metropolitan Studies Program of the Maxwell School of Citizenship and Public Affairs at Syracuse University and the Workshop in Political Theory and Policy Analysis at Indiana University. See Ostrom et al. 1993, for an overview of our activities. The views expressed are those of the author and do not represent the official views of the sponsoring agency. The author deeply appreciates the assistance of Patty Dalecki and Gina Davis and earlier comments of Roy Gardner, Ronald Oakerson, Vincent Ostrom, Larry Schroeder, Louis Siegel, Shui-Yan Tang, and James Thomson.

Crafting institutions related to the supply and use of irrigation systems require skills in understanding how rules, combined with particular physical, economic, and cultural environments, produce incentives and outcomes. A consistent finding of many analysts is that there is no "one best way" to organize irrigation activities (Chambers 1980; Ostrom 1990; Levine 1980; Coward 1979; Uphoff 1986). Given the absence of a single or even a small set of institutional solutions to the problem of organizing irrigation systems, rules to enhance the supply and use of any particular physical system must be devised, tried, modified, and tried again in an ongoing process of institutional artisanship. To do this requires considerable investment of time and resources in learning more about the effects of various institutional rules on the behavior of participants and the results they can achieve. Thus instead of thinking about the choice of institutions as a one-shot decision in a known environment, one needs to think about it as an ongoing investment process in an uncertain environment.

If the users and suppliers of irrigation systems design their own institutional arrangements to cope with the physical, economic, social, and cultural features of each system, the variety of institutional arrangements could be immense. This, indeed, appears to be the case. Major studies of irrigation systems located in different parts of the world illustrate the substantial differences in the rules used on irrigation systems located in different regions (Uphoff 1986; Sengupta 1991; Carruthers 1988; Maass and Anderson 1986).

Examining specific rules of particular systems, however, is like focusing on specific blueprints of successful irrigation projects around the world. No blueprint is the same. No set of rules-in-use is the same either when local participants actively craft rules to fit their own changing circumstances over time. Although blueprints vary, common engineering principles underlie the blueprints used to construct physical structures. Similarly, underlying the specific rules established for particular systems are design principles that users have discovered for themselves as they have faced the problems involved in crafting their own irrigation institutions (see Ostrom et al. 1994).

Recent theoretical and empirical work on institutional design has attempted to elucidate the core design principles used in long-enduring, self-organized irrigation institutions throughout the world (Ostrom 1990). By "design principle" is meant a characteristic that helps to account for the success of these institutions in sustaining the physical works and gaining the compliance of generations of users to the rules in use. By "long enduring" is meant that the irrigation system has been in operation for at least several generations. The methodology used to derive these design principles and a fuller development of their implications are contained in the work by Ostrom (1990). A description of the large number of irrigation systems in the project files and some general patterns of relationships is contained in the work by Tang (1991, 1992). Although it is impossible to evaluate the efficiency of these systems precisely, the repeated willingness of the users of these systems to invest large amounts of labor and other resources is strong evidence that individual farmers receive more benefits from these systems than the costs they assume for maintaining them. These self-organized systems are sustainable over time even though the technical efficiency of many of them could probably be improved. It is not at all unusual for farmers to devote three to four weeks of labor per year to operate and maintain these systems. Farmers who invest valuable time that could be devoted to other activities to clean canal sections, repair diversion works, and operate weirs are "voting" with their backs. They indicate a continued willingness to contribute resources. While all such systems impose sanctions on those who do not contribute agreed-upon resources, the size of these sanctions is sufficiently small that one cannot use coercion as the basis to explain the continuity of the systems.

The following sections will present and discuss eight design principles identified in prior research as characterizing long-enduring irrigation systems.

Design Principle One: Clearly Defined Boundaries

The boundaries of the service area and the individuals or households with rights to use water from an irrigation system are clearly defined.

Defining the boundaries of the irrigation system and of those authorized to use it can be thought of as a foundation for organizing collective action. So long as the boundaries of who has rights to the water remain uncertain, no one knows what they are managing, or for whom. Without defining the boundaries of a system and closing it to "outsiders," local irrigators face the risk that any benefits they produce by their efforts will be reaped by others who do not contribute to these efforts. Thus for irrigators to have a minimal interest in coordinating patterns of appropriation and provision, some users have to be able to exclude other potential users from taking water. The presence of boundaries concerning who is allowed to appropriate from a resource has been used since the work of Ciriacy-Wantrup and Bishop (1975) as the single defining characteristic of "common property" institutions as contrasted to "open access" institutions. The impression is sometimes given that this is all that is necessary to achieve successful regulation. Making this attribute one of eight, rather than a unique attribute, puts its importance in a more realistic perspective.

Simply closing the boundaries is usually not enough. If those irrigators who have authorized access can profitably use more water than is available, farmers at the head end of the system will take so much water that those at the tail end may not have a predictable and adequate flow of water for agricultural use. The actual yield of the system may be far less than it could be even though some farmers reap considerable benefits. Consequently, in addition to closing the boundaries, rules limiting use and/or mandating provision are needed whenever water scarcity is present.

Design Principle Two: Proportional Equivalence between Benefits and Costs

Rules specifying the amount of water that an irrigator is allocated are related to local conditions and to rules requiring labor, materials, and/or money inputs.

Adding well-tailored appropriation and provision rules to boundary rules helps to account for the sustenance of irrigation systems themselves. Different rules are used in self-organizing irrigation systems to mobilize resources for construction, for maintenance, and to pay water guards. In long-enduring systems, those who receive the highest proportion of the water are also required to pay the highest proportion of the costs. Coward (1979) identified this design principle as a major characteristic of the successful irrigation systems he had examined. It was also identified by Olson (1969) as a very general principle, called fiscal equivalence, of any public institution that would achieve efficient use of resources. No single set of rules defined for all irrigation systems in a region would produce this equivalence. Crafting rules to equalize benefits and costs has to take into account many of the unique features of each irrigation system.

Design Principle Three: Collective-Choice Arrangements

Many individuals affected by operational rules are included in the group who can modify these rules.

Irrigation systems that use this principle are better able to tailor rules to local circumstances since the individuals who directly interact with one another and with the physical world can modify their rules over time so as to better fit them to the specific characteristic of their setting. Users who design institutions that are characterized by the first three principles, clearly defined boundaries, benefit-cost congruence, and user participation in collective choice, should be able to devise effective operating rules if they keep the costs of changing these rules relatively low.

The presence of effective operational rules, however, does not account for users following them; nor is the fact that the users themselves designed and initially agreed to the operational rules an adequate explanation for generations of compliance by individuals who were not originally involved in the initial agreement. It is not even an adequate explanation for the continued commitment of those who were part of the initial agreement. Agreeing to follow rules ex ante is an easy "commitment" to make. Actually following rules ex post, when strong temptations are present, is the significant accomplishment. Game-theoretical analyses of the temptation to steal water and the resultant game among irrigators who must monitor the behavior of other irrigators are presented in the works by Weissing and Ostrom (1991a, b; 1993).

The problem of gaining compliance to rules, no matter what their origin, is frequently assumed away by theorists positing all knowing and all powerful external authorities that enforce agreements. In the case of many self-organizing systems, no external authority has sufficient presence to play any role in the day-to-day enforcement of the rules in use. Thus external enforcement cannot be used to explain high levels of compliance. In the long-enduring systems, however, irrigators themselves make substantial investments in monitoring and sanctioning activities. This leads us to consider a fourth and fifth design principle.

Design Principle Four: Monitoring

Monitors, who actively audit physical conditions and irrigator behavior, are accountable to the users and/or are the users themselves.

Design Principle Five: Graduated Sanctions

Users who violate operational rules are likely to receive graduated sanctions (depending on the seriousness and context of the offense) from other users, from officials accountable to these users, or from both.

Now we are at the crux of the problem. In long-enduring systems, monitoring and sanctioning are undertaken not by external authorities but by the participants themselves. The initial sanctions used in these systems are also surprisingly low. Even though it is frequently presumed in modern theoretical work that participants will not spend time and effort to monitor and sanction each other's performance, substantial evidence exists that irrigators do both in long-enduring user organizations (see Tang 1992).

To explain the investment in monitoring and sanctioning activities that occurs in these robust, self-governing institutions, the term "quasi-voluntary compliance," used by Levi (1988, chap. 3) to describe the behavior of taxpayers in systems where most taxpayers comply, is very useful. Paying taxes is voluntary in the sense that individuals choose to comply in many situations where they are not being directly coerced. On the other hand, it is "quasi-voluntary because the noncompliant are subject to coercion—if they are caught" (Levi 1988, p. 52). Levi stresses the contingent nature of a commitment to comply with rules that is possible in a repeated setting. Strategic actors are willing to comply with a set of rules, Levi (1988) argues, when (1) they perceive that the collective objective is achieved, and (2) they perceive that others also comply. Levi is not the first to stress how individuals who interact with one another over time are able to use contingent behavior to overcome free-riding problems (see, e.g., Axelrod 1981, 1984; Oakerson 1993; Lewis and Cowens 1983). But Levi stresses the importance of coercion as an essential condition to achieve the form of contingent behavior she has identified as quasi-voluntary compliance. In her theory, enforcement increases the confidence of individuals that others are not allowed to be free riders and that those who contribute are not suckers. As long as individuals are confident that others are cooperating and joint benefits are being provided, they comply willingly to provide a collective benefit by contributing resources. On irrigation systems that are owned and operated by government agencies, the agency could also provide the type of monitoring and sanctioning Levi has in mind. Wade (1987) has a similar view of the willingness of many irrigators to comply with reasonable rules if they were assured that others would also comply and that those who did not would be sanctioned.

> In many situations individual irrigators will restrain their water rule breaking *if* they are confident that others will also refrain and *if* they are confident that they will still get as much water as they are fairly entitled to (even if not as much as they would like). They will more likely refrain from cheating if they are confident that by doing so they will not be the "suckers." Where people are motivated by an "I'll restrain if you restrain" calculation, then an institution (such as an irrigation department) that convinces them that these expectations are justified can promote voluntary compliance with the rules. (Wade 1987, p. 178)

In highly developed economies, water users can organize themselves and hire their own monitors. (For an analysis of how groundwater producers organize self-governing institutions, see Blomquist 1992).

To explain commitment in long-enduring water-user organizations, one cannot posit external enforcement as Levi (1988) does. In many instances, irrigators create their own internal enforcement to (1) deter those who are tempted to break rules and thereby (2) assure quasi-voluntary compliers that others also comply. Given the evidence that individuals monitor, then the relative costs and benefits must be different than posited in prior work. Either the costs of monitoring are lower or the benefits to an individual are higher, or both.

The costs of monitoring are low in many long-enduring irrigation systems as a result of the rules in use. Water rotation systems, for example, usually place the two actors most concerned with cheating in direct contact with one another. The irrigator who nears the end of a rotation turn would like to extend the time of his turn (and thus the amount of water obtained). The next irrigator in the rotation system waits nearby for him to finish, and would even like to start early. The presence of the first irrigator deters the second from an early start, and the presence of the second irrigator deters the first from ending late. Neither has to invest additional resources in monitoring activities. Monitoring is a by-product of their own strong motivations to use their water rotation turn to the fullest extent. Many ways that workteams are organized encourage monitoring as a natural by-product.

When monitoring is accomplished by an agent accountable to other users, several mechanisms increase the rewards for doing a good job or exposing slackards to the risk of losing their positions. In some systems, a percentage of the fines is kept by the guards. In other systems, guards are paid a proportion of the crop at the end of the year. With this type of payment, the guard's own payment is dependent on keeping the reliability of the system as high as possible so that the farmers being served can produce as much on their fields as possible. All of the formal guard positions are accountable to the users. Monitors can easily be fired if discovered slacking off. Since the users tend to continue monitoring the guards as well as each other, some redundancy is built into the monitoring and sanctioning system. A failure to deter rule breaking by one mechanism does not trigger a cascading process of rule infractions since other mechanisms are potentially available. Consequently, the costs and benefits of monitoring a set of rules are not independent of the particular set of rules adopted. Nor are they uniform in all settings.

Design Principle Six: Conflict Resolution Mechanisms

Users and their officials have rapid access to low-cost, local arenas to resolve conflict among users or between users and officials.

Applying rules is rarely an unambiguous task. Even such a simple rule as "each irrigator must send one individual for one day to help clean the irrigation canals before the rainy season begins" can be interpreted quite differently by different individuals. Who is or is not an "individual" according to this rule? Does sending a child below 10 or an adult above 70 to do heavy physical work meet this rule? Is a "day" of work fulfilled by someone working for four hours or six hours? Does cleaning the canal immediately next to one's own farm qualify for meeting a community obligation? For individuals who seek ways to slide past or subvert rules, there are always ways to "interpret" the rule in order to argue that they meet it while subverting the intent. Even individuals who intend to follow the spirit of a rule can make errors. What happens if someone forgets about a labor day and does not appear? Or what happens if the only able-bodied worker is sick, or unavoidably in another location?

If individuals are going to follow rules over a long period of time, some mechanism for discussing and resolving what is or is not a rule infraction is necessary to the continuance of rule conformance itself. If some individuals are allowed to free ride by sending less valuable workers to a required labor day, others will consider themselves to be suckers if they send their strongest workers who could be used to produce private goods rather than communal benefits. Over time, only children and old people will be sent to do work that requires strong adults and the system breaks down.

If individuals who make an honest mistake or face personal problems that prevent them from following a rule cannot find mechanisms to make up their lack of performance in an acceptable way, rules can be viewed as unfair and conformance rates decline. While the presence of conflict resolution mechanisms does not guarantee that users are able to maintain enduring institutions, it is difficult to imagine how any complex system of rules could be maintained over time without such mechanisms. In many irrigation systems, conflict resolution mechanisms are informal, and those who are selected as leaders are also the basic resolvers of conflict.

Design Principle Seven: Minimal Recognition of Rights to Organize

The rights of users to devise their own institutions are not challenged by external governmental authorities.

This principle is related to the fact that many water-user groups organize in a de facto manner but are not recognized by national governments as legitimate forms of organization. Consequently, the officials of the organization may not legally open a bank account in the name of the organization or represent the interests of their members before administrative or judicial bodies. Decisions taken by user-group organizations may not be enforced by police or formal courts. Without official recognition of the right to organize, it is quite difficult to hold either user-group officials or members accountable for their actions.

De facto organization is sufficient in isolated locations where irrigation is used primarily for subsistence agriculture. But when roads are constructed that create market opportunities for surplus products, the level of conflict over the allocation of water to different farmers is likely to escalate. If government agents use their authority to support those who refuse to follow the rules of a de facto organization, it is hard for the other participants to continue following the rules either. An effective irrigator organization lacking formal recognition may crumble rapidly when its authority to make legitimate rules for its own members is challenged and not supported by the formal government of a regime.

Design Principle Eight: Nested Enterprises

Appropriation, provision, monitoring, enforcement, conflict resolution, and governance activities are organized in multiple layers of nested enterprises.

Long-enduring, large, and complex irrigation systems are usually organized into many tiers of nested organizations. Work teams may be established of groups as small as four or five individuals. All irrigators using a particular branch of an irrigation system may be the basis for another level of organization. A third layer may involve all farmers served by one headworks. A fourth layer may involve all systems served by the same river. If the seventh and eighth design principles hold, all of these irrigation organizations would be recognized and nested in externally organized political jurisdictions. (See Coward 1979, for his discussion of various aspects of this design principle; see also Ostrom 1989, 1991, 1993.)

By nesting layers of organization within one another, irrigators can take advantage of many different scales of organization. Small-scale work teams are an effective technique for overcoming free riding. Everyone monitors everyone else in situations where shirking is obvious. Large-scale enterprises allow systems to take advantage of economies of scale where they are relevant and to aggregate capital for investment. By using more than a single scale of organization, many farmer-managed irrigation systems have sustained large-scale irrigation systems for long periods of time relying primarily on their own resources without extensive help from external agencies. Projects that have been constructed by external agencies without any investment by the irrigators themselves could learn substantially from the successful efforts of farmers to sustain their own complex systems over time (see Maass and Anderson 1986; Siy 1982; Pradhan 1989a, b).

Conclusion

These eight design principles are quite general. The specific ways that suppliers and users of long-enduring irrigation systems have crafted rules to meet these principles vary substantially in their particulars. Successful, long-enduring irrigation institutions that appear to be quite different apply similar design principles in different ways. For example, long-enduring irrigation systems develop methods to equate the costs of building and maintaining the irrigation system to the benefits that are achieved, or to design principle 2. Some examples may help the reader understand the diversity of specific rules that meet design principle 2.

The Zanjeras of the Northern Philippines

These self-organized systems obtain use rights to previously unirrigated land from a large landowner by building a canal that irrigates the landowner's land and that of a zanjera. At the time that the land is allocated, each farmer willing to abide by the rules of the system receives a bundle of rights and duties in the form of atars. Each atar defines three parcels of land located in the head, middle, and tail sections of the service area where the holder grows his or her crops. Responsibilities for construction and maintenance are allocated by atars, as are voting rights. In the rainy seasons, water is allocated freely. In a dry year, water may be allocated only to the parcels located in the head and middle portions. Thus everyone receives water in plentiful and scarce times in rough proportion to the amount of atars they possess (see Siy 1982; Coward 1979).

Thulo Kulo in Nepal

When this system was first constructed in 1928, 27 households contributed to a fund to construct the canal and received shares to the resulting system proportionate to the amount they invested. By selling additional shares, the system has been expanded several times. Measurement and diversion weirs or gates are installed at key locations. Water is automatically allocated to each farmer according to the proportion of shares owned. Routine monitoring and maintenance is allocated to workteams so that everyone participates proportionately (see Martin and Yoder 1983; Martin 1986).

The Huerta of Valencia in Spain

In 1435, 84 irrigators served by two interrelated canals in Valencia gathered at the monastery of St. Francis to draw up and approve formal regulations to specify who had rights to water from these canals, how the water would be shared in good and bad years, and how responsibilities for maintenance would be shared. The modern Huerta of Valencia, composed of these plus six additional canals, now serves about 16,000 ha and 15,000 farmers. The right to water inheres in the land itself and cannot be bought and sold independently of the land. Rights to water are approximately proportionate to the amount of land owned as are obligations to contribute to the cost of monitoring and maintenance activities (see Maass and Anderson 1996; Ostrom 1990).

These three systems differ substantially from one another. The zanjeras are institutional devices for landless laborers to acquire use rights to land and water. They could be called communal systems. The Thulo Kulo system comes as close to allocating private and separable property rights to water as is feasible in an irrigation system. The Valencian Huerta has maintained centuries-old land and water rights that forbid the separation of water rights from the land being served. The Valencian system differs from both "communal" and "private property" systems because water rights are firmly attached to private ownership of land. Underlying these major differences, however, is the basic design principle that the costs of constructing, operating, and maintaining these systems are roughly proportional to the benefits that the irrigators obtain.

It is important to keep these differences in mind in any effort to do policy analysis. Slogans, such as "privatization," may mask important underlying principles rather than providing useful guides for reform. Strict privatization of water rights is not a feasible option within the broad institutional framework of many countries. On the other hand, authorizing the suppliers and users of irrigation water to have more voice in the design of their own systems, design principles 3 and 7 combined, is a feasible reform within the broad institutional frame of many countries. If those involved are authorized to devise their own rules and are encouraged to learn about how others have successfully overcome difficult design problems, we can expect that many of those who are most motivated will find solutions to the highly salient problems that they face. The proportion of successful self-organized systems can be greatly increased by the investment of central governments in general institutional facilities that enhance the capabilities of those directly involved to learn new ways of governing and managing their systems, to create enforceable rules, and to sanction behavior contrary to these rules.

REFERENCES

Axelrod, R. 1981. The emergence of cooperation among egoists. *Am. Pol. Sci. Rev.* 75:306–18.

————. 1984. *The Evolution of Cooperation.* New York: Basic Books.

Blomquist, W. 1992. *Dividing the Waters: Governing Groundwater in Southern California.* San Francisco: Institute for Contemporary Studies Press.

Carruthers, I. 1988. Irrigation under threat: A warning brief for irrigation enthusiasts. *IIMI Rev.* 2:8–11, 24–25.

Chambers, R. 1980. Basic concepts in the organization of irrigation. In *Irrigation and Agricultural Development in Asia: Perspectives from the Social Sciences,* ed. E. W. Coward Jr., pp. 28–50. Ithaca, NY: Cornell University Press.

Ciriacy-Wantrup, S. V., and R. C. Bishop. 1975. "Common property" as a concept in natural resources policy. *Nat. Resour. J.* 15:713–27.

Coward, E. W., Jr. 1979. Principles of social organization in an indigenous irrigation system. *Hum. Org.* 38, no. 1: 28–36.

————. 1980. *Irrigation and Agricultural Development in Asia: Perspectives from the Social Sciences.* Ithaca, NY: Cornell University Press.

Levi, M. 1988. *Of Rule and Revenue.* Berkeley: University of California Press.

Levine, G. 1980. The relationship of design, operation and management. In *Irrigation and Agricultural Development in Asia: Perspectives from the Social Sciences,* ed. E. W. Coward Jr., pp. 51–62. Ithaca, NY: Cornell University Press.

Lewis, T. R., and J. Cowens. 1983. Cooperation in the commons: An application of repetitious rivalry. Dept. of Econ., Univ. of British Columbia, Vancouver.

Maass, A., and R. L. Anderson. 1986. . . . *and the Desert Shall Rejoice: Conflict, Growth and Justice in Arid Environments.* Malabar, FL: Robert E. Krieger.

Martin, E. G. 1986. Resource mobilization, water allocation, and farmer organization in hill irrigation systems in Nepal. Ph.D. diss., Cornell Univ., Ithaca, NY.

Martin, E. G., and R. Yoder. 1983. The Chherlung Thulo Kulo: A case study of a farmer-managed irrigation system. In *Water Management in Nepal: Proceedings of the Seminar on Water Management Issues, July 31–August 2,* app. I, pp. 203–17. Kathmandu, Nepal: Ministry of Agriculture, Agricultural Projects Services Centre, and the Agricultural Development Council.

Oakerson, R. J. 1993. Reciprocity: A bottom-up view of political development. In *Rethinking Institutional Analysis and Development: Issues, Alternatives, and Choices,* ed. V. Ostrom, D. Feeny, and H. Picht, pp. 141–58. San Francisco: Institute for Contemporary Studies Press.

Olson, M. 1969. The principle of "fiscal equivalence": The division of responsibilities among different levels of government. *Am. Econ. Rev.* 59, no. 2: 479–87.

Ostrom, E. 1990. *Governing the Commons: The Evolution of Institutions for Collective Action.* New York: Cambridge University Press.

————. 1992. *Crafting Institutions for Self-Governing Irrigation Systems.* San Francisco: Institute for Contemporary Studies Press.

Ostrom, E., R. Gardner, and J. Walker. 1994. *Rules, Games, and Common-Pool Resources.* Ann Arbor: University of Michigan Press.

Ostrom, E., L. Schroeder, and S. Wynne. 1993. *Institutional Incentives and Sustainable Development.* Boulder, CO: Westview.

Ostrom, V. 1980. Artisanship and artifact. *Publ. Admin. Rev.* 40:309–17. Reprinted as chap. 16 of this volume.

————. 1989. *The Intellectual Crisis in American Public Administration,* 2d ed. Lincoln: University of Nebraska Press.

————. 1991. *The Meaning of American Federalism: Constituting a Self-Governing Society*. San Francisco: Institute for Contemporary Studies Press.

————. 1993. Cryptoimperialism, predatory states, and self-governance. In *Rethinking Institutional Analysis and Development: Issues, Alternatives, and Choices,* ed. V. Ostrom, D. Feeny, and H. Picht, pp. 43–68. San Francisco: Institute for Contemporary Studies Press. Reprinted as chap. 8 of this volume.

Pradhan, P. 1989a. *Patterns of Irrigation Organization in Nepal*. Colombo, Sri Lanka: International Irrigation Management Institute.

————. 1989b. *Increasing Agricultural Production in Nepal: Role of Low Cost Irrigation Development through Farmer Participation*. Kathmandu, Nepal: International Irrigation Management Institute.

Sengupta, N. 1991. *Managing Common Property: Irrigation in India and the Philippines*. London: Sage.

Siy, R. Y., Jr. 1982. *Community Resource Management: Lessons from the Zanjera*. Quezon City: University of the Philippines Press.

Tang, S.-Y. 1991. Institutional arrangements and the management of common-pool resources. *Publ. Admin. Rev.* 51, no. 1: 42–51.

————. 1992. *Institutions and Collective Action: Self-Governance in Irrigation*. San Francisco: Institute for Contemporary Studies Press.

Uphoff, N. 1986. *Improving International Irrigation Management with Farmer Participation: Getting the Process Right*. Boulder, CO: Westview.

Wade, R. 1987. Managing water managers: Deterring expropriation or equity as a control mechanism. In *Water and Water Policy in World Food Supplies,* ed. W. R. Jordon, pp. 117–83. College Station: Texas A&M University Press.

Weissing, F., and E. Ostrom. 1991a. Irrigation institutions and the games irrigators play: Rule enforcement without guards. In *Game Equilibrium Models II: Methods, Morals, and Markets,* ed. R. Selten, pp. 188–262. New York: Springer-Verlag.

————. 1991b. Crime and punishment: Further reflections on the counterintuitive results of mixed equilibria games. *J. Theor. Pol.* 3, no. 3: 343–50.

————. 1993. Irrigation institutions and the games irrigators play: Rule enforcement on government- and farmer-managed systems. In *Games in Hierarchies and Networks: Analytical and Empirical Approaches to the Study of Governance Institutions,* ed. Fritz W. Scharpf, pp. 387–428. Boulder, CO: Westview. Reprinted in *Polycentric Games and Institutions,* ed. M. D. McGinnis (Ann Arbor: University of Michigan Press, 1999).

CHAPTER 5

Property Rights Regimes and Coastal Fisheries: An Empirical Analysis

Edella Schlager and Elinor Ostrom

Political economists' understanding of property rights and the rules used to create and enforce property rights shape perceptions of resource degradation problems and the prescriptions recommended to solve such problems. Ambiguous terms blur analytical and prescriptive clarity. The term *common-property resource* is a glaring example of a term that is repeatedly used by political economists to refer to varying empirical situations including: (1) property owned by a government, (2) property owned by no one, and (3) property owned and defended by a community of resource users.[1] The term is also used to refer to any common-pool resource used by multiple individuals regardless of the type of property rights involved. The purpose of this essay is to develop a conceptual schema for arraying property rights regimes that distinguishes among diverse bundles of rights that may be held by the users of a resource system. We define a property rights schema ranging from authorized user, to claimant, to proprietor, and to owner. We do *not* find that "owners" are the only resource users who make long-term investments in the improvement of resource systems. Proprietors face incentives that are frequently substantial enough to encourage similar long-term investments. Even claimants may manage use patterns to an extent not predicted by a simpler property rights dichotomy. We apply this conceptual schema to analyze findings from a variety of coastal fisheries.

Originally published in Terry L. Anderson and Randy T. Simmons, eds., *The Political Economy of Customs and Culture: Informal Solutions to the Commons Problem* (Lanham, MD: Rowman and Littlefield, 1993), 13–41. Reprinted by permission of Rowman and Littlefield and the authors. Portions of this chapter are reprinted by permission of the University of Wisconsin Press, Edella Schlager and Elinor Ostrom, "Property Rights Regimes and Natural Resources: A Conceptual Analysis," *Land Economics* 68, no. 3 (1992): 249–62. Copyright 1992.

Authors' note: This essay has benefited from the critical and helpful comments from many colleagues at Indiana University and elsewhere. In particular, we would like to thank William Blomquist, Ed Connerley, Louis DeAlessi, David Feeny, Howard Frant, Roy Gardner, Larry Kiser, Ron Oakerson, Vincent Ostrom, Tai-Shuenn Yang, and two anonymous reviewers. Financial support provided by the National Science Foundation (grant no. SES–8921884) is gratefully acknowledged.

Rules, Rights, and Property Regimes

As individuals conduct day-to-day activities and as they organize these activities, they engage in both operational and collective choice levels of action (Kiser and Ostrom 1982).[2] Operational activities are constrained and made predictable by operational-level rules regardless of the source of these rules. By "rules" we refer to generally agreed-upon and enforced prescriptions that require, forbid, or permit specific actions for more than a single individual (Ostrom 1986).[3] Examples of operational rules are those used by fishers to specify the types of fishing equipment authorized or forbidden at particular locations within a fishing ground.

Operational rules are changed by collective choice actions. Such actions are undertaken within a set of collective choice rules that specify who may participate in changing operational rules and the level of agreement required for their change. Changing the types of fishing equipment authorized or forbidden at different locations within a resource is an example of a collective choice action. The particular set of operational rules that are actually in use and enforced may have been devised in multiple arenas. Operational rules related to inshore fisheries are as apt to be devised in a local meeting place, even a tavern, as they are in a court, a legislature, or a governmental bureau.[4]

The terms *rights* and *rules* are frequently used interchangeably in referring to uses made of natural resources. Clarity in analysis is enhanced by recognizing that "rights" are the product of "rules" and thus not equivalent to rules. *Rights* refer to particular actions that are authorized (Ostrom 1976). *Rules* refer to the prescriptions that create authorizations. A property right is the authority to undertake particular actions related to a specific domain (Commons 1968). For every right an individual holds, rules exist that authorize or require particular actions in exercising that property right. In addition, all rights have complementary duties. To possess a right implies that someone else has a commensurate duty to observe this right (Commons 1968). Thus rules specify both rights and duties.

In regard to common-pool resources, the most relevant operational-level property rights are "access" and "withdrawal" rights. These are defined as:

Access: The right to enter a defined physical property.
Withdrawal: The right to obtain the "products" of a resource (e.g., catch fish, appropriate water, etc.).[5]

If a group of fishers hold rights of access, they have the authority to enter a resource. Rules specify the requirements the fishers must meet in order to exercise this right. For instance, fishers may be required to reside in a specified jurisdiction and to purchase a license before entering a fishing ground. In addition, fishers, through a lottery, may be assigned particular fishing spots (Faris 1972; Martin 1973). The assignment of fishing spots is an operational-level withdrawal right authorizing harvesting from a particular area.[6]

Individuals who have access and withdrawal rights may or may not have more extensive rights authorizing participation in collective choice actions. The distinction between rights at an operational-level and rights at a collective choice level is crucial. It is the difference between exercising a right and participating in the definition of future rights to be exercised. The authority to devise future operational-level rights is what makes collective-choice rights so powerful. In regard to common-pool resources, collective-choice property rights include management, exclusion, and alienation. They are defined as follows:

Management: The right to regulate internal use patterns and transform the resource by making improvements.

Exclusion: The right to determine who will have an access right, and how that right may be transferred.

Alienation: The right to sell or lease either or both of the above collective choice rights.

The right of management is a collective choice right authorizing its holders to devise operational-level withdrawal rights governing the use of a resource. Individuals who hold rights of management have the authority to determine how, when, and where harvesting from a resource may occur, and whether and how the structure of a resource may be changed. For instance, a group of fishers who devise a zoning plan that limits various types of harvesting activities to distinct areas of a fishing ground are exercising rights of management for their resource (see, e.g., Davis 1984; and Cordell 1972).

The right of exclusion is a collective choice right authorizing its holders to devise operational-level rights of access. Individuals who hold rights of exclusion have the authority to define the qualifications that individuals must meet in order to access a resource. For instance, fishers who limit access to their fishing grounds to males above a certain age who live in a particular community and who utilize particular types of gear are exercising a right of exclusion.[7]

The right of alienation is a collective choice right permitting its holder to transfer part or all of the collective choice rights to another individual or group. Exercising a right of alienation means that an individual sells or leases the rights of management, exclusion, or both.[8] Having alienated those rights, the former rights-holder can no longer exercise these authorities in relation to a resource or a part thereof.

Arraying these rights, as shown in figure 5.1, enables us to make meaningful distinctions among four classes of property rights holders related to fisheries. The five property rights are independent of one another but, in relation to fisheries, are frequently held in the cumulative manner arrayed in figure 5.1. It is possible to have entry rights without withdrawal rights, to have withdrawal rights without management rights, to have management rights without exclusion rights, and to have exclusion rights without the rights of alienation.[9] In other words, individuals or collectivities may, and frequently do, hold well-defined property rights that do not include the full set of rights defined here. On the other hand, to hold some of these rights implies the possession of others. The exercise of withdrawal rights is not meaningful without the right of access; alienation rights depend upon having rights to be transferred.

	Owner	Proprietor	Claimant	Authorized User
Access and withdrawal	✓	✓	✓	✓
Management	✓	✓	✓	
Exclusion	✓	✓		
Alienation	✓			

Fig. 5.1. Bundles of rights associated with positions

We call individuals holding operational-level rights of access and withdrawal "authorized users."[10] If specified in operational rules, access and withdrawal rights can be transferred to others either temporarily, as in a lease arrangement, or permanently when these rights are assigned or sold to others. Transfer of these rights, however, is not equivalent to alienation of management and exclusion rights as we discuss below.

The rights of authorized users are defined by others who hold collective-choice rights of management and exclusion. Authorized users lack the authority to devise their own harvesting rules or to exclude others from gaining access to fishing grounds. Even though authorized users may be able to sell their harvesting rights, nevertheless, they lack the authority to participate in collective action to change operational rules.

An example of authorized users are the salmon and herring fishers of Alaska. In 1972, the Governor's Study Group on Limited Entry was created to research and develop limited entry legislation, which the Alaskan legislature adopted in 1973 (Adasiak 1979, 771). The Alaskan limited entry system divides Alaskan salmon and herring fisheries into a number of different fisheries. An Entry Commission determines the number of permits available for each fishery. The Commission can make adjustments in the numbers as circumstances change, either by issuing additional permits or by buying back existing permits. Fishers cannot hold more than one permit per fishery. The permits are freely transferable, but cannot be used as collateral. The Alaskan fishers who hold permits are authorized users. The Alaskan legislature in conjunction with a study group devised the fishers' rights of access and withdrawal, which fishers can transfer. The fishers do not directly participate in making collective choices, and thus cannot devise their own operational-level rules concerning the use of their fisheries.

We define as "claimants" individuals who possess the same rights as authorized users plus the collective choice right of management.[11] With the right of management, claimants have the collective choice authority to devise operational-level rights of withdrawal. They cannot, however, specify who may or may not have access to resources, nor can they alienate their right of management.

For instance, the net fishers of Jambudwip, India, are claimants (Raychaudhuri 1980). Jambudwip is an island in the Bay of Bengal which is only occupied during fishing seasons when fishers establish camps and fish off its southwestern shore. The Jambudwip fishers, exercising management rights, have devised a set of withdrawal rules that permit them to coordinate their use of the fishing grounds. At the beginning of a fishing season each crew chooses a spot on which to set their net. A large bag net is suspended between two posts which are then driven into the ocean floor. Rules, as well as environmental conditions, govern the placing of nets. As Raychaudhuri explains:

> According to the convention of the fisherfolk, one is not allowed to set his net in a line, either in front or behind another's net. But there is no bar to set on any side of it. . . . If one net is set in front of another, both lose the catch, either of the tide or of the ebb. (1980, 174)

In addition, a spot once claimed by a fishing crew belongs to that crew for the remainder of the fishing season. Even if the crew removes its net from the spot and moves to another spot, no other crew can fish the abandoned spot unless first gaining permission from the original crew (Raychaudhuri 1980, 167–68). While the Jambudwip fishers have exercised management rights by devising rules that define withdrawal rights, they do not exercise the authority to decide who can and who cannot enter the fishing grounds that they utilize. Consequently, the Jambudwip fishers are claimants and not "proprietors."

"Proprietors" are defined as individuals who possess collective choice rights to participate in management and exclusion. Proprietors authorize who may access resources and how resources may be utilized, however, they do not have the right to alienate either of these collective choice rights. Scholars who have recently undertaken theoretical and empirical research on "common-property regimes" focus primarily on those regimes organized by proprietors (National Research Council 1986; Berkes 1989; McCay and Acheson 1987; Ostrom 1990). To use the same term for regimes composed of proprietors, who possess four bundles of property rights, and regimes composed of individuals who possess no property rights, clearly confounds the capacity to communicate about important scientific and policy issues.

The fishers who participate in the cod trap fisheries of Newfoundland are proprietors. Cod trap berths are allocated by lottery. To gain access to a berth, a fisher must participate in a lottery. "Only fishermen from the local community are allowed to participate in the lottery" and to sit on the local cod trap berth committee that operates the lottery (Martin 1979, 282). The lottery system is significant in that "the organization of cod trap committees since 1919 has legally codified the boundaries of the fishing space over which a community has political jurisdiction" (Martin 1973, 15).

Turkish fishers who harvest from coastal lagoons are also proprietors. The Turkish government leases lagoons to fishers' cooperatives. For instance, it leases the Ayvalik-Haylazli lagoon to a fishers' co-op of the same name. To access and harvest fish from the lagoon, a fisher must belong to the co-op. In order to belong to the co-op a fisher must reside in one of the three adjacent villages for at least six months and not have wage employment income. The fishers of Ayvalik-Haylazli lagoon

> have exclusive and legal rights to the fish of the lagoon and the lagoon's adjacent waters. All fishermen are cooperative members, and all cooperative members are active fishermen. They protect their rights by patrolling the boundary of their fishing area and chasing off or apprehending intruders. (Three outside fishing boats were apprehended in 1983.) (Berkes 1986, 72)

Neither the fishers of Ayvalik-Haylazli lagoon nor the cod fishers of Newfoundland, however, can sell or lease their rights of management and exclusion.

If, in addition to collective choice rights of management and exclusion, individuals also hold the right of alienation, that is, they can sell or lease their collective choice rights, then they are defined as "owners."[12] For instance, fishers of Ascension Bay, located in Quintana Roo State, Mexico, are members of the Vigia Chico cooperative. Co-op members have divided Ascension Bay into "individually held capture areas ('parcelas' or 'campos') ranging from 0.5 to more than 3 km^2" from which they harvest lobster (Miller 1989, 190). Each co-op member holds complete sets of rights over specific areas. The fishers may transfer their rights of management and exclusion over their particular spot to other fishers of Ascension Bay. "Several campos are sold or bartered each season and such transactions are common knowledge. On occasion, sales are registered with the co-op" (192). Once having sold their campos, however, fishers no longer can exercise rights of exclusion or management in relation to Ascension Bay lobster-grounds.

De Facto and *De Jure* Property Rights

The sources of the rights of access, withdrawal, management, exclusion, and transfer are varied. They may be enforced by a government whose officials explicitly grant such rights to resource users. If so, such rights are *de jure* rights in that they are given lawful recognition by formal, legal instrumentalities. Rights-holders who have *de jure* rights can presume that if their rights were challenged in an administrative or judicial setting, their rights would most likely be sustained.

Property rights may also originate among resource users. In some situations resource users cooperate to define and enforce rights among themselves. Such rights are *de facto* as long as they are not recognized by government authorities. Users of a resource who have developed *de facto* rights act as if they have *de jure* rights by enforcing these rights among themselves. In some settings *de facto* rights may eventually be given recognition in courts of law if challenged, but until so recognized they are less secure than *de jure* rights.[13]

Within a single common-pool resource situation a conglomeration of *de jure* and *de facto* property rights may exist which overlap, complement, or even conflict with one another. A government may grant fishers *de jure* rights of access and withdrawal, retaining the formal rights of management, exclusion, and alienation for itself. Fishers, in turn, may cooperate and exercise rights of management and exclusion, defining among themselves how harvesting must take place, and who may engage in harvesting from their fishing grounds. In many situations where local fishers possess *de jure* authorized user or claimant rights, field researchers have found *de facto* proprietor arrangements that are commonly understood, followed, and perceived as legitimate within the local community (Cordell and McKean 1987; Berkes 1986, 1989; Davis 1984; Acheson 1975).

In many instances government officials simply pay little attention to inshore fisheries, leaving fishers with sufficient autonomy to design workable arrangements. For many years this was the case for fishers of Valenca, Brazil, who fished from the adjacent estuary (Cordell 1972). These fishers held *de jure* rights of access and withdrawal when they first developed the fishery at the beginning of this century. Initially, they experienced a number of problems due to the diverse technologies in use. Gear became entangled and was destroyed, leading to violence among the fishers. In addition, fishers fought over the choicest fishing spots (Cordell 1972, 105). Over a period of time fishers designed harvesting arrangements that addressed many of the problems they had experienced. The fishers divided the estuary among different technologies so that diverse gears were not utilized within the same area (42). In addition, fishers allocated fishing spots by drawing lots to determine the order of use of a particular spot. The Valenca fishers did not initially experience exclusion problems. No other fishers exhibited interest in fishing the estuary. While the Valenca fishers were *de jure* authorized users, they were *de facto* claimants.

The Brazilian government, in an attempt to "modernize" fisheries, made nylon nets available to anyone who qualified for a bank loan arranged by the government through the *Banco do Brasil*. The Valenca fishers did not qualify for bank loans and could not purchase nets. A number of wealthy individuals around Valenca did qualify, and purchased nets. These individuals hired men to fish with the nets, men who had no prior fishing experience. The men invaded the Valenca estuary. Conflict erupted between the established fishers and the new entrants. Fishers were shot and equipment destroyed. The *de facto* property rights crumbled as fishers fought for whatever fishing spots they could gain. The fishery was overharvested and eventually was abandoned (Cordell 1978).[14]

De facto property systems are important for several reasons. First, the resource economics literature examining property rights and fishery regulation is generally pessimistic about the likelihood of fishers undertaking self-regulation so as to avoid inefficient economic outcomes, such as rent dissipation and the extinction of valuable species. And yet, an extensive empirical literature exists that documents a diversity of indigenous institutions devised by fishers without reference to governmental authorities (Alexander 1977; Berkes 1986, 1989; Cordell 1972; Davis 1984; Faris 1972; Forman 1970; Martin 1979; McCay and Acheson 1987; Pinkerton 1989). Many of these *de facto* arrangements substantially reduce the incentives to overinvest in harvesting effort and to dissipate rent that fishers face in an open access fishery. Understanding the *de facto* arrangements that have enabled some fishers to reduce inefficient use of resources permits the development of better explanations of the conditions that inhibit or enhance effective self-organized collective solutions.

Second, self-organized collective choice arrangements can produce operational rules closely matched to the physical and economic conditions of a particular site. Within the context of *de facto* proprietor regimes fishers have devised maps of their fishing territories that could not be generated by central authorities. The maps reflect local knowledge of where fish spawn, their habits in particular waters, and where technologies can be used without the efforts of one boat adversely affecting the success of another boat (see, e.g., Cordell 1972; or Berkes 1986). The knowledge needed to establish agreement concerning a set of productive fishing spots is achieved by a community of fishers who learn from their accumulated daily experience on a particular fishing ground. The cost of assigning a government official to devise a similar arrangement would be prohibitive. Nor is such an arrangement enforceable without the commitment of the fishers to the legitimacy of their self-imposed constraints (see, e.g., McGuire and Langworth 1991).

Third, since the professional literature is so pessimistic about fishers adopting effective self-regulation, this literature is used by policy analysts to recommend sweeping reforms. These reforms, however, may "sweep away" successful human efforts to solve extremely difficult problems (see, e.g., Berkes 1989 and Davis 1984).

Fourth, since the regulation of these *de facto* proprietor regimes is undertaken by local fishers who benefit from these regimes, the costs of regulation are largely borne by these same beneficiaries. Institutional arrangements that internalize the costs of monitoring and exclusion among beneficiaries reduce inefficiencies.

Property Rights, Incentives, and Outcomes

Different bundles of property rights, whether they are *de facto* or *de jure*, affect the incentives individuals face, the types of actions they take, and the outcomes they achieve. An important difference often discussed in economics is that between owners, who hold a complete set of rights, and all other users who do not hold complete rights. In particular, the right of alienation is believed crucial for the efficient use of resources.[15] Alienation rights, combined with rights of exclusion, produce incentives for owners to undertake long-term investments in a resource. Through sale or lease of all or part of the property rights owners hold, they can capture the benefits produced by long-term investments. In addition, alienation permits a resource to be shifted from a less productive to a more productive use (Posner 1975). Ownership, however, does not guarantee the survival of a resource. If owners use a relatively high discount rate, they may still destroy a resource (Clark 1973, 1974) or engage in activities leading to substantial "over-exploitation, resource abuse, and overcapitalization" (van Ginkel 1989, 102; see also Larson and Bromley 1990).

Owners of natural resources often invest in the physical structure of resources that maintain or increase the productivity of the resource. For instance, the fishers of Ascension Bay, discussed earlier, place artificial habitats, called casitas, on the sea floor in each of their campos, which attract lobsters. Lobsters are attracted because they "are gregarious; because they remain in dens during the day; and because they do not modify existing habitat or build new habitat" (Miller 1989, 190). In addition, casitas may enhance the productivity of the campos because they provide "refuge sites from predators," and those located near feeding grounds of lobsters "have the potential to reduce predation risk" (Miller 1989). Fishers of Ascension Bay regularly make long-term investments in their fishing grounds.

Rights of alienation, however, are not the only important distinction among rights-holders. Another important difference is that between claimants and authorized users on the one hand, and proprietors and owners on the other hand, based on the right of exclusion. The right of exclusion produces strong incentives for owners and proprietors to make current investments in resources. Because proprietors and owners can decide who can and cannot enter a resource, they can capture for themselves and for their offspring the benefits from investments they undertake in a resource.[16] Owners and proprietors are reasonably assured of being rewarded for incurring the costs of investment (Posner 1975). Such investments are likely to take the form of devising withdrawal rights that coordinate the harvesting activities of groups of owners or proprietors so as to avoid or resolve common-pool resource dilemmas. In addition, owners and proprietors devise access rights that allow them to capture the benefits produced by the withdrawal rights (Dahlman 1980).

Claimants, because of their rights of management, face stronger incentives than do authorized users to invest in governance structures for their resources even though their incentives are weaker than proprietors or owners. Claimants can devise operational-level rights of withdrawal for their situation. Without collective choice rights of exclusion, however, they can no longer be assured of being rewarded for investing in withdrawal rights. Consequently, whether claimants exercise their rights of management depends upon whether they act within a set of circumstances that allows them to capture the benefits of coordinating their activities even without rights of exclusion.

For instance, claimants may utilize resources that no other groups are interested in using, or claimants may be physically isolated from other populations so that exclusion is not problematic. In such situations, claimants are likely to be able to capture the benefits from exercising their rights of management. The fishers of Valenca, Brazil, discussed earlier, even though claimants, utilized fishing grounds of no interest to other potential users. Over a period of time the fishers devised a number of withdrawal rights that resolved the common-pool resource dilemmas that they faced. For several decades the Valenca fishers enjoyed the benefits produced from coordinating their use of the Valenca estuary. Of course, such arrangements are vulnerable to external invasion as the Valenca fishery attests.

Finally, authorized users possess no authority to devise their own rules of access and withdrawal. Their outcomes are dependent primarily upon the operational-level rights that others define for them. Whether the incentives they face induce them to act so as to achieve efficient outcomes depends upon the institutional design skills of those who hold the collective choice rights. Since authorized users do not design the rules they are expected to follow, they are less likely to agree to the necessity and legitimacy of the rules. Authorized users may engage in a game with rule enforcers, seeking to gain as much as possible. This leads to an overinvestment in the fishery and inefficient outcomes.

Common-Pool Resource Dilemmas

The institutional arrangements fishers may invest in to govern the use of their fishing grounds are often designed to address and resolve common-pool resource (CPR) dilemmas (Schlager 1990). CPR dilemmas that fishers typically experience are appropriation externalities, technological externalities, and assignment problems (Schlager 1994). Assuming a homogeneous distribution of fish over space and time, and identical fishers harvesting from the stock of fish, the dilemma that arises is one of appropriation externalities. The dilemma arises because fishers are withdrawing fish from a common stock without taking into account the effects of their harvesting upon each other. When a fisher harvests fish, he subtracts from the amount of fish available to be harvested increasing the marginal costs of appropriating additional fish and lowering the marginal product of additional fishing effort. Thus, the increased costs of harvesting due to reducing the stock not only affect the fisher who harvested the fish—the fisher who generated the costs—but all fishers who fish that stock. As Wilson explains:

> each individual fisherman cannot perceive the marginal external costs of his fishing activity on the rest of the fleet. Consequently, fishermen as a whole tend to commit too much capital and labor to the fishery, i.e., too much fishing effort. (1982, 423–24)[17]

Another dilemma fishers potentially face is technological externalities. Technological externalities are produced when fishers physically interfere with each other in harvesting fish. Wilson defines technological externalities as:

gear conflicts or other forms of physical interference which arise because fishermen often find it advantageous to fish very close to one another. (1982, 423)

Technological externalities may also be produced by indirect physical interference. Gear does not become entangled or destroyed, but it is set so close together that the flow of fish among gear is obstructed. As Smith explains:

externalities may also enter via crowding phenomena: If the fish population is highly concentrated the efficiency of each boat may be lowered by congestion over the fishing grounds. (1968, 413)

A third dilemma that coastal fishers potentially face are assignment problems. Fish are unevenly distributed across fishing grounds, congregating in areas that provide food and shelter. Consequently, particular areas or spots of fishing grounds are more productive than others, with fishers desiring to fish the most productive spots. Assignment problems occur when fishers, in their uncoordinated choice of a fishing spot, do not allocate themselves efficiently across spots. Problems arise over who should have access to the productive spots and how access should be determined. Failing to solve assignment problems can lead to violence among fishers and increased production costs.

Combining the above arguments concerning property rights and CPR dilemmas, a general research question emerges that will be carefully examined in the following sections.

The more complete the bundle of property rights fishers hold in relation to a fishing ground the more likely fishers are to invest in institutional arrangements that govern their access and harvesting activities of that ground; the institutional arrangements fishers adopt are designed to address and resolve typical CPR dilemmas fishers face; consequently, fishers who adopt institutional arrangements to govern the use of their fishing ground are much less likely to face CPR dilemmas.

Data from the Field

The above research question will be examined using data collected from case studies of coastal fishing grounds located around the world (see table 5.1).

The data were extracted from these case studies using a set of detailed coding forms containing mostly close-ended questions that captured the physical, institutional, and community attributes of coastal fishing grounds and the fishers who utilize them (see Tang 1992 and Schlager 1990).

In choosing case studies two criteria were used. First, the study had to describe a coastal fishery dilemma. Second, the study had to contain information on the rules that fishers used to organize their harvesting activities. After searching through hundreds of documents, *thirty* in-depth coastal fishery case studies were identified for their completeness and coded.

These case studies are not a random sample from the population of coastal fishing grounds located throughout the world. Consequently, one must be cautious in generalizing these findings. On the other hand, a consistent set of variables were collected across the cases permitting controlled comparisons.

The unit of analysis used is the subgroup. A subgroup is a group of fishers who harvest from the same fishing ground and who are relatively similar in relation to the following five characteristics:

1. Their legal rights to appropriate fish.
2. Their withdrawal rate of fish.
3. Their exposure to variation in the supply of fish.
4. Their level of dependency on fish withdrawn from the resource.
5. Their use of the fish they harvest.

This definition of a subgroup depends on the sharing of similar characteristics and not on the presence or absence of an organization of fishers. More than one subgroup of fishers may utilize the same fishing grounds simultaneously. Forty-four subgroups utilize the thirty fishing grounds listed in table 5.1.

Property Rights and Rules

Among the forty-four subgroups of fishers, the set of property rights each possesses varies (see table 5.2). One subgroup possesses all five rights, those of access, withdrawal, management, exclusion, and alienation. The fishers of this subgroup reside at Punta Allen in Quintana Roo State in Mexico and harvest lobster from Ascension Bay, and are owners of their grounds (Miller 1982, 1989). Twenty-six of the subgroups are proprietors, possessing the four rights of access, withdrawal, management, and exclusion. Another ten subgroups are claimants. These subgroups do not possess the rights of exclusion or alienation. Finally, the remaining seven subgroups are authorized users, possessing only rights of access and withdrawal.

TABLE 5.1. Coastal Fishing Grounds Case Studies

Country	Location	Fish Harvested	Sub-groups	Positions	Documentation
Belize	Caye Caulker	Lobster	1	Claimants	Sutherland (1986)
	San Pedro	Lobster	2	Proprietors	Gordon (1981)
Brazil	Arembepe	Mixed	1	Authorized Users	Kottak (1966)
	Coqueiral	Mixed	1	Proprietors	Forman (1966, 1970)
	Valenca	Mixed	5	Claimants, Authorized Users	Cordell (1972, 1974, 1978, 1983, 1984)
Canada	Baccalaos Cove	Cod	2	Proprietors	Powers (1984)
	Cat Harbour	Cod	2	Proprietors	Faris (1972)
	Fermeuse	Cod	2	Proprietors	Martin (1973, 1979)
	James Bay	Whitefish	1	Proprietors	Berkes (1977, 1987)
	Petty Harbour	Cod	2	Proprietors	Shortall (1973)
	Port Lameroon, Pagesville	Lobster	1	Proprietors	Davis (1975, 1984)
	Port Lameroon, Pagesville	Mixed	1	Proprietors	Davis (1975, 1984)
Greece	Messolonghi Etolico	Mullet, Seabream	2	Claimant, Authorized User	Kotsonias (1984)
India	Jambudwip	Mixed	2	Claimants	Raychaudhuri (1980)
Jamaica	Fraquhar Beach	Mixed	1	Proprietors	Davenport (1956)
Japan	Ebibara	Shrimp	1	Claimants	Brameld (1968)
Korea	Kagoda	Anchovy	1	Proprietors	Han (1972)
Malaysia	Kampong Mee	Mixed	1	Authorized Users	Anderson and Anderson (1977)
	Perupok	Mixed	1	Proprietors	Firth (1966)
Mexico	Andres Quintana Roo	Mixed	1	Authorized Users	Miller (1982)
	Andres Quintana Roo	Lobster	1	Proprietors	Miller (1982)
	Ascension Bay	Lobster	1	Owners	Miller (1982, 1989)
Nicaragua	Tasbapauni	Turtle	2	Proprietors	Nietschmann (1972, 1973)
Sri Lanka	Gahavalla	Mixed	3	Proprietors, Claimants	Alexander (1982)
Thailand	Rusembilan	Mackerel	1	Claimants	Fraser (1960, 1966)
Turkey	Alanya	Mixed	1	Proprietors	Berkes (1986)
	Ayvalik-Haylazi	Mixed	1	Proprietors	Berkes (1986)
	Tasucu	Mixed	1	Proprietors	Berkes (1986)
Venezuela	Chigauan	Lisa	1	Authorized Users	Breton (1973)
United States	Mount Desert Island	Lobster	1	Proprietors	Grossinger (1975)

TABLE 5.2. Guttman Scale of Property Rights

Access	Withdrawal	Manage	Exclusion	Transfer	Number of Subgroups
Yes	Yes	Yes	Yes	Yes	1
Yes	Yes	Yes	Yes	No	26[a]
Yes	Yes	Yes	No	No	10[b]
Yes	Yes	No	No	No	7

CR (coefficient of reproductivity) = 1
[a] Eighteen subgroups hold *de facto* rights of exclusion
[b] Five subgroups hold *de facto* rights of management

Authority and Scope Rules

How these collectively held rights are exercised is important. Rules define how fishers within a group can exercise their rights in relation to each other and in relation to nongroup members. Without rule definition, even given a more complete set of property rights, a group of fishers can utilize the resource inefficiently, and even possibly destroy it, if they do not organize their harvesting activities. Rule definition, however, is more likely to take place as fishers possess more complete sets of rights in their fishing grounds. More complete sets of rights grant fishers greater authority to make decisions concerning the use of the grounds. They are more likely to capture the benefits of investments they make in rules that order their harvesting activities.

Among the forty-four subgroups of fishers this expectation holds (see table 5.3). Subgroups that possess at least the right of management are much more likely to devise authority and scope rules—rules that define how harvesting is to take place.[18] Among proprietors and owners, 88 percent devised authority and scope rules. Ninety percent of the claimants devised authority and scope rules, whereas only one group of authorized users use authority and scope rules.

As shown in table 5.4, five different types of authority and scope rules are used in these groups: location rules, size rules, season rules, order rules, and time-slot rules. Subgroups frequently rely on more than one authority or scope rule. The most often used rule is a scope rule that limits harvesting activities to specific locations or spots. Every subgroup in the sample used a location rule to determine how choice fishing spots are distributed. Access to fishing spots is dependent on meeting any of a variety of requirements. The gear that a fisher uses may determine where the fisher can locate it (Davis 1975). Or a fisher may gain access to a choice fishing spot through a lottery (Faris 1972).

TABLE 5.3. Required Authority Rules by Property Rights Holders

	Authorized Users	Claimants	Owners, Proprietors	Total
No Required Rules	86% (6)	10% (1)	11% (3)	(10)
Required Rules	14% (1)	90% (9)	89% (24)	(34)
Total	100% (7)	100% (10)	100% (27)	(44)

Gamma = .75

TABLE 5.4. Required Authority and Scope Rules

Type of Rule	Number of Subgroups Using Rule ($N = 34$)	% of Subgroups Using Rule
Withdraw at Specific Locations/Spots	34	100
Withdraw Fish of at Least a Specific Size	9	26
Withdraw in a Fixed Order	7	21
Withdraw Only during Specific Seasons	7	21
Withdraw at a Fixed Time Slot	4	12

The second most frequently used rule is a size rule requiring that fishers harvest fish greater than a minimum size. The rule is typically used to ensure that fish achieve maturity and have a chance to spawn before being harvested. Nine of the thirty-three subgroups utilize this rule. In all but one instance an external authority has imposed the size rule on the fishers.[19]

The third most frequently used rules are seasonal restrictions and harvesting in a fixed order. Seasonal restrictions forbid the harvesting of fish during specific times of the year, typically when fish spawn. In the case of seasonal restrictions, all but one of the rules was devised by a government authority. Harvesting in a fixed order defines how choice spots on the grounds can be accessed and harvested from. Often times the rule requires that fishers take turns in accessing particular spots. All of the order rules were devised by fishers.

The fourth most frequently used rule is a fixed time slot rule. This rule is often combined with a fixed order rule or a location rule. It limits the amount of time that a boat can remain on a choice fishing spot. Typical limits involve one casting of a net, or one day (Alexander 1982; Cordell 1972).

The authority and scope rules reveal a clear attempt on the part of fishers to resolve CPR dilemmas. Assignment problems are addressed by location rules that allocate choice spots, minimizing destructive competition among fishers. Relegating particular technologies to different areas of a fishing ground addresses technological externalities by separating incompatible types of gear.

Boundary Rules

In addition to authority and scope rules that define how rights of withdrawal may be exercised, boundary rules are also used among the fishers. Boundary rules define how rights of access may be exercised. The required boundary rules reveals attempts on the part of fishers to limit the number of fishers who can access fishing grounds and the types of technology that can be utilized (see table 5.5).

TABLE 5.5. Required Boundary Rules among Fishers

Type of Rule	Number of Subgroups Using Rule ($N = 44$)	% of Subgroups Using Rule
Residency—Local	34	77
Use of Particular Technology	27	61
Membership in an Organization	15	34
License	8	18
Ownership of Property Related to Harvesting (i.e., fishing berths)	7	16
Lottery	5	11
Race	6	14
Registration on Lottery Eligibility List	5	11
Continuing Usage of Access Rights	3	7
Ethnicity	7	16
Ownership or Leasing of Land in Area	7	16
Caste	2	5

Twelve different types of boundary rules are utilized among the forty-four subgroups. The rules used by most subgroups (34 out of 44) are residency rules that require fishers to reside in a particular village to gain access to particular grounds. After residency requirements, twenty-seven subgroups (61 percent) limit access to their fishing grounds on the basis of the type of technology used. Boundary rules based on gear assist in alleviating technological externalities. By limiting the types of gear that can be brought into the grounds, interference among gears is minimized.

Note, however, that boundary rules can have an indirect effect upon appropriation externalities. Limiting both the number of individuals who can access a ground and the type of technologies they can utilize limits the amount of fishing effort applied in harvesting, and thereby possibly affecting the magnitude of appropriation externalities.

Performance of Institutional Arrangements

While fishers have adopted institutional arrangements that appear to address CPR dilemmas, have fishers successfully resolved such problems?[20] In table 5.6 property rights holders are arrayed by the level of assignment problems.[21] Altogether, nineteen subgroups, at some point in time faced assignment problems. But, as table 5.6 illustrates, fishers have been very successful in addressing and resolving them. Of the nineteen subgroups of fishers who faced assignment problems, 74 percent, or 14, of the groups have resolved them. The successful resolution of assignment problems is particularly high among proprietors and owners. Of those eleven subgroups, ten, or 91 percent, have minimized such problems. Among the claimants, 67 percent no longer face problems of assignment. Authorized users, however, continue to experience assignment problems.

TABLE 5.6. Property Rights Holders by Level of Assignment Problems

	Owners, Proprietors	Claimants	Authorized Users	Total
Minimal Assignment Problems	91% (10)	67% (4)	0% (0)	(14)
Moderate Assignment Problems	9% (1)	33% (2)	100% (2)	(5)
Total	100% (11)	100% (6)	100% (2)	(19)

Gamma = .85

The finding that institutional arrangements make a difference in resolving assignment problems also holds for the resolution of technological externalities.[22] Table 5.7 arrays property rights holders by the level of technological externalities. Of the forty-four subgroups, twenty-one have experienced technological externalities. Of the twelve subgroups that are proprietors or owners, 67 percent no longer experience problems with technological externalities. The outcomes for claimants is quite different. Of the six subgroups, 17 percent, or one, has resolved its technological externality problems, while five, or 83 percent, have not. Not one of the three subgroups of authorized users have resolved their problems of technological externalities. Clearly, the types of institutional arrangements fishers have devised affect whether they are able to solve technological externalities.

TABLE 5.7. Property Rights Holders by Level of Technological Externalities

	Owners, Proprietors	Claimants	Authorized Users	Total
No Technological Externalities	67% (8)	17% (1)	0% (0)	(9)
Technological Externalities	33% (4)	83% (5)	100% (3)	(12)
Total	100% (12)	100% (6)	100% (3)	(21)

Gamma = .68

Conclusion

DeAlessi (1980, 42) argues that "differences in the structures of rights to use resources affect behavior systematically and predictably." Clearly, this assertion holds true for the forty-four subgroups of fishers examined here. Fishers who hold more complete sets of property rights are more likely to invest in authority and scope rules that define how they exercise their right of withdrawal. Defining how fishing grounds may be used substantially affects whether fishers resolve common-pool resource dilemmas. Owners, proprietors, and claimants fare much better than do authorized users. Another important difference emerges between owners and proprietors who possess the right of exclusion and claimants who have no such right. Owners and proprietors are more successful in resolving assignment problems and technological externalities. Being able to exclude is an important right.

Since different bundles of rights affect the behavior of resource users it is crucial that in analyzing common-pool resources the types of property rights held by users be made explicit. The term *common property* cannot begin to capture the diversity of rights held in common by resource users. Instead, a more precise language must be developed that captures meaningful differences among different property rights regimes. We have begun such a process through the schema presented here.

NOTES

1. The confusion in the use of the term *common property* has been addressed frequently in the past (Ciriacy-Wantrup and Bishop 1975; Bromley 1982, 1986, 1989; Runge 1981) without much impact on its careless usage. Even scholars, who are meticulous theorists and observers of behavior related to natural resource systems, use the terms *open access* and *common-property systems* interchangeably (see Johnson and Libecap 1982, 1005; for other examples, see Agnello and Donnelly 1975; Bell 1972; Christy 1975; Gordon 1954; Scott 1955; Scott and Christy 1965; Smith, Weber, and Wiesmeth 1991; Sinn 1988).

2. A third level of action is also available and that is the constitutional level. Constitutional choice actions entail devising collective choice rules. In establishing an organization or changing the process by which operational rules are to be devised within an existing organization, individuals engage in constitutional choice actions. Fishers creating a marketing cooperative is an example of a constitutional choice action.

3. A plan adopted by an individual for how that individual wishes to undertake future actions is better thought of as a "strategy" rather than as a "rule." The concept of "rule" relates to shared understandings about prescriptions that apply to more than a single individual. A marriage contract can be viewed as a set of rules authorizing and forbidding future actions for the two individuals involved. A court decision outlawing some types of agreements among fishers using inshore fisheries is a set of rules affecting future actions for all individuals using the coastal fisheries under that court's jurisdiction. Rules, be they operational, collective choice, or constitutional choice, instruct individuals to take actions that are required or permitted, or to avoid taking action that is forbidden (Gardner and Ostrom 1991; Ostrom 1986). See Buck 1989, for an analysis of the rules creating property rights in the American Southwest.

4. Not all actions taken in collective choice arenas affect rules-in-use. Passing a new law or writing a new regulation is not the equivalent of establishing a new rule. Laws and regulations must be enforced to become rules (see Ostrom 1991). To be effective they must be accepted as legitimate by resource users.

5. Rules defining the rights of access and withdrawal may or may not permit those rights to be transferred.

6. See Copes 1986, for an analysis of quota systems in relation to fisheries. See Wilson 1982, for an effective critique of standard economic theory's limited view of institutional alternatives in relation to fisheries.

7. If these same fishers revise the conditions that constitute the right of access by expanding the number of fishers who can enter their fishery, they have not exercised a right of alienation. They have not transferred their own rights to additional individuals. Rather, they have exercised their right of exclusion to redefine who may or may not enter. The right of alienation refers only to the authority to alienate collective choice rights, that is, to sell or lease such rights.

8. By alienation we specifically mean the authority to sell or lease collective-choice rights. We do not include the ability to bequeath. In most common-property regimes, users have the ability to bequeath their rights in a resource. Rights rarely die with an individual. In many situations, however, resource users do not have the right to sell or lease their rights to others. Limiting alienation to sale or lease also

brings it closer to its economic usage. The importance of a right of alienation for many economists is that it provides the possibility that resources will be transferred to their highest valued use. While being able to sell or lease collective choice rights provides that potential, the right to bequeath these rights is usually presumed by economists to be an insufficient property right to achieve full efficiency. Larson and Bromley (1990) effectively challenge this commonly held view and argue that much more needs to be known about the specific values of a large number of parameters in a particular setting before analysts can make careful judgements whether the right of alienation leads to higher levels of efficiency than the right to bequeath. See also Anderson and Hill 1990, for an analysis of three different alienation rules that the U.S. government used in transferring public lands to individuals.

9. While theoretically it is possible to hold entry rights without withdrawal rights, in practice this rarely occurs. The distinction between access and withdrawal becomes crucial at a collective choice level. Often times individuals who hold rights of management and thereby define withdrawal rights are not the same individuals who hold rights of exclusion and thereby define access rights. We provide a number of examples throughout the remainder of the essay.

10. One could also define a position called "squatter" to consist of individuals who possess no rights at any level in relation to a common-pool resource. Squatters use natural resources, such as fisheries, but they do so at their own risk. If challenged by a person who holds collective choice or operational rights, squatters lack authority to enforce their claims. Squatters stand entirely exposed to the actions of others as concerns the use of a resource.

11. Alchian and Demsetz refer to the possession of the right of management but not exclusion or alienation as "communal rights" (1973, 19).

12. The rights of alienation can be exercised in total or to a limited set of rights for a limited duration. Given the latter capability, "hybrid" legal arrangements related to the same resource are possible and occur frequently. Alchian and Demsetz (1973, 18) point out that some of the "ambiguity in the notion of state or private ownership of a resource" occurs "because the bundle of property rights associated with a resource is divisible." In fact, all coastal fisheries in the U.S. are apt to be hybrid legal arrangements of one or another variety since the ownership rights to the coastal waters are vested in states. Each state decides whether to assign claimant status to all residents, to all residents who obtain licenses, or to allow various forms of proprietorship to come about through self-organization or through formal lease-hold arrangements.

13. Note that unchallenged *de facto* rights are as much a factor affecting action as are *de jure* rights. Only if *de facto* rights are challenged do the differences between the two classes of rights become apparent.

14. See Matthews 1988; and Matthews and Phyne 1988, for discussions of the impact Canadian fishing policies are having on the institutional arrangements devised by fishers in Newfoundland.

15. By efficiency, we focus in this essay on the level of resource rents that are obtained by fishers and not dissipated through overinvestment or other inefficient practices. Copes (1972) points out that in relation to fisheries, however, not only can resource rent be dissipated but producer and consumer surplus can be lost, depending upon the institutional arrangements that govern the use of a fishery. We have not

attempted to expand our analysis of efficiency to that of total social surplus, as we are not examining property rights to resource units in commodity markets.

16. See Larson and Bromley (1990) for an important analysis of the "bequest motives" that exist under common property versus the "market incentives that exist under private property." They conclude: "There is no scientific knowledge that can rank the relative magnitudes of the terminal value under private property . . . and common property . . . even assuming a perfect land market" (254).

17. Anderson (1986, 47) defines stock externalities as follows: "The individual fishermen do not consider the effect that their production will have on the production of all others in the current period. . . . At the same time, however, the stock is being nonoptimally depleted because individual operators do not consider the user cost they are imposing on harvesters in future periods." Smith (1968, 413) states that stock externalities occur because: "No individual competitive fisherman has control over population size as a private decision variable yet it enters as a parameter in each fisherman's cost function." Gordon (1953, 451) argues that stock externalities arise because: "It is not the relative *marginal* productivities of the two grounds but their *average* productivities. The fisherman does not ask what allocation of effort will maximize the aggregate production of the fishing fleet but what action will give him, individually, the greater yield."

18. See Ostrom 1986, for a complete discussion of rule types.

19. That exception is the Cree Indians in northern Canada as reported by Berkes (1977, 1987).

20. Appropriation externalities are not examined because of measurement problems and a lack of data. Obtaining a measure of production externalities is highly problematic. Not only do fishers have little information concerning stock dynamics and the effects of their actions upon each other's harvest, but neither do most researchers. Thus, direct measures of production externalities are not reported in the case studies. The only information reported in the case studies that may relate to production externalities is whether the stock of fish appeared to be abundant. Stock abundance is not, however, a good measure of production externalities since declining stocks of fish may be due to environmental factors and not necessarily the harvesting activities of fishers. Since no reliable measure of production externalities is available, whether fishers organize when confronted with production externalities will not be explored.

The following discussion of assignment problems and technological externalities involves thirty-one distinct subgroups. Ten subgroups have experienced assignment problems only, twelve have faced technological externalities only, and nine have experienced both. For thirteen subgroups, not enough information was presented to determine the type of problem the fishers experienced.

21. This discussion involves nineteen subgroups—ten of which have experienced assignment problems only and nine of which have experienced both.

22. The question concerning technological externalities appears on the operational level form and is worded as follows: *As of the beginning and end of this period, what is the extent of technical externalities resulting from the appropriation activities of participants from this resource? (1) the level of technical externalities is quite low, (2) the level of technical externalities is relatively low, (3) modest levels of technical externalities exist, (4) relatively high levels of technical externalities*

exist, (5) very high levels of technical externalities exist. For table 5.7 we collapsed answers 1 and 2 as no technological externalities and answers 3, 4, and 5 as technological externalities.

REFERENCES

Acheson, James M. 1975. The lobster fiefs: Economic and ecological effects of territoriality in the Maine lobster industry. *Human Ecology* 3, no. 3: 183–207.

Adasiak, A. 1979. Alaska's experience with limited entry. *Journal of the Fisheries Research Board of Canada* 36, no. 7: 770–82.

Agnello, Richard, and Lawrence Donnelly. 1975. Property rights and efficiency in the oyster industry. *Journal of Law and Economics* 18:521–33.

Alchian, Armen, and Harold Demsetz. 1973. The property rights paradigm. *Journal of Economic History* 33, no. 1: 16–27.

Alexander, Paul. 1977. South Sri Lanka sea tenure. *Ethnology* 16:231–55.

———. 1982. *Sri Lankan fishermen: Rural capitalism and peasant society.* Canberra: Australian National University.

Andersen, Raoul. 1979. Public and private access management in Newfoundland fishing. In *North Atlantic maritime cultures*, 299–336. New York: Mouton.

Anderson, Eugene N., Jr., and Marja L. Anderson. 1977. *Fishing in troubled waters: Research on the Chinese fishing industry in West Malaysia.* Taipei: Chinese Association for Folklore.

Anderson, Lee. 1986. *The economics of fisheries management,* 2d ed. Baltimore: Johns Hopkins University Press.

Anderson, Terry, and Peter Hill. 1990. The race for property rights. *Journal of Law and Economics* 33:117–97.

Bell, Frederick W. 1972. Technological externalities and common property resources: An empirical study of the U.S. lobster industry. *Journal of Political Economy* 80:148–58.

Berkes, Fikret. 1977. Fishery resource use in a subarctic Indian community. *Human Ecology* 5, no. 4: 289–307.

———. 1986. Marine inshore fishery management in Turkey. In *Proceedings of the conference on common property resource management*, National Research Council, 63–38. Washington, DC: National Academy Press.

———. 1987. Common property resource management and Cree Indian fishermen in subarctic Canada. In *The question of the commons: The culture and ecology of communal resources*, ed. Bonnie J. McCay and James M. Acheson, 66–91. Tucson: University of Arizona Press.

———, ed. 1989. *Common property resources: Ecology and community-based sustainable development.* London: Belhaven Press.

Brameld, Theodore. 1968. *Japan: Culture, education, and change in two communities.* New York: Holt, Rinehart, and Winston.

Breton, Yvan D. 1973. A comparative study of rural fishing communities in Eastern Venezuela: An anthropological explanation of economic specialization. Ph.D. diss., Michigan State University.

Bromley, Daniel. 1982. Land and water problems: An institutional perspective.

American Journal of Agricultural Economics 64 (December): 834–44.

————. 1986. Closing comments at the conference on common property resource management. In *Proceedings of the conference on common property resource management*, National Research Council, 591–97. Washington, DC: National Academy Press.

————. 1989. *Economic interests and institutions: The conceptual foundations of public policy*. Oxford: Basil Blackwell.

Buck, Susan J. 1989. Cultural theory and management of common property resources. *Human Ecology* 17:101–16.

Christy, Francis T. 1975. Property rights in the world ocean. *Natural Resources Journal* 15, no. 4: 695–712.

Ciriacy-Wantrup, S. V., and Richard C. Bishop. 1975. Common property as a concept in natural resource policy. *Natural Resources Journal* 15, no. 4: 711–27.

Clark, Colin W. 1973. Profit maximization and the extinction of animal species. *Journal of Political Economy* 81, no. 4: 950–61.

————. 1974. The economics of overexploitation. *Science* 181:630–34.

Commons, John R. 1968. *Legal foundations of capitalism*. Madison: University of Wisconsin Press.

Copes, Parzival. 1972. Factor rents, sole ownership, and the optimum level of fisheries exploitation. *Manchester School of Economics and Social Studies* 41:145–63.

————. 1986. A critical review of the individual quota as a device in fisheries management. *Land Economics* 62 (August): 278–89.

Cordell, John C. 1972. The developmental ecology of an estuarine canoe fishing system in Northeast Brazil. Ph.D. diss., Stanford University.

————. 1974. The lunal-tide fishing cycle in northeastern Brazil. *Ethnology* 13:379–92.

————. 1978. Carrying capacity analysis of fixed territorial fishing. *Ethnology* 17 (January): 1–24.

————. 1983. Social marginality and sea tenure in Brazilian fishing. Occasional Papers in Latin American Studies Association, no. 7, 1–21. Stanford, CA: Joint Center for Latin American Studies.

————. 1984. Traditional sea tenure and resource management in Brazilian coastal fishing. In *Management of coastal lagoon fisheries*, ed. James M. Kapetsky and G. Lasserre, GFCM Studies and Reviews, no. 61, 429–38. Rome: FAO.

Cordell, John C., and Margaret A. McKean. 1987. Sea tenure in Bahia, Brazil. In *Proceedings of the conference on common property resource management*, National Research Council, 85–114. Washington, DC: National Academy Press.

Dahlman, Carl J. 1980. *The open field system and beyond: A property rights analysis of an economic institution*. Cambridge: Cambridge University Press.

Davenport, William H. 1956. A comparative study of two Jamaican fishing communities. Ph.D. diss., Yale University.

Davis, Adam F. 1975. The organization of production and market relations in Nova Scotian inshore fishing community. Ph.D. diss., University of Manitoba.

Davis, Anthony. 1984. Property rights and access management in the small boat fishery: A case study from Southwest Nova Scotia. In *Atlantic fisheries and coastal communities: Fisheries decision-making case studies*, ed. Cynthia Lamson and Arthur J. Hanson, 133–64. Halifax: Dalhousie Ocean Studies Programme.

DeAlessi, Louis. 1980. The economics of property rights: A review of the evidence. *Research in Law and Economics* 2:1–47.

Dewar, Margaret E. 1990. Federal intervention in troubled waters: Lessons from the New England fishers. *Policy Studies Review* 9 (Spring): 485–504.

Faris, James. 1972. *Cat harbour: A Newfoundland fishing settlement.* Newfoundland Social and Economic Studies, no. 3. Toronto: University of Toronto Press.

Firth, Raymond. 1966. *Malay fishermen: Their peasant economy,* 2d ed. London: Routledge and Kegan Paul.

Forman, Shepard L. 1966. Jangadeiros: Raft fishermen of Northeastern Brazil. Ph.D. diss., Columbia University.

————. 1970. *The raft fishermen: Tradition and change in the Brazilian peasant economy.* Bloomington: Indiana University Press.

Fraser, Thomas M., Jr. 1960. *Rusembilan: A Malay fishing village in Southern Thailand.* Ithaca, NY: Cornell University Press.

————. 1966. *Fishermen of South Thailand: The Malay villagers.* New York: Holt, Rinehart and Winston.

Gardner, Roy, and Elinor Ostrom. 1991. Rules and games. *Public Choice* 70, no. 2: 121–49.

Gardner, Roy, Elinor Ostrom, and James Walker. 1990. The nature of common-pool resource problems. *Rationality and Society* 2, no. 3: 335–58.

Gordon, Edmund T. 1981. Phases of development and underdevelopment in a Caribbean fishing village: San Pedro, Belize. Ph.D. diss., Stanford University.

Gordon, H. Scott. 1953. An economic approach to the optimum utilization of fishery resources. *Journal of the Fisheries Research Board of Canada* 10:442–57.

————. 1954. The economic theory of a common property resource: The fishery. *Journal of Political Economy* 62 (April): 124–42.

Grossinger, Richard. 1975. The strategy and ideology of lobsterfishing on the back side of Mount Desert Island, Hancock County, Maine. Ph.D. diss., University of Michigan.

Han, Sang-Bok. 1972. Socio-economic organization and change in Korean fishing villages: A comparative study of three fishing communities. Ph.D. diss., Michigan State University.

Johnson, Ronald N., and Gary D. Libecap. 1982. Contracting problems and regulation: The case of the fishery. *American Economic Review* 72, no. 5:1005–22.

Kiser, Larry L., and Elinor Ostrom. 1982. The three worlds of action: A metatheoretical synthesis of institutional approaches. In *Strategies of political inquiry,* ed. Elinor Ostrom, 179–222. Beverly Hills, CA: Sage. Reprinted in *Polycentric games and institutions,* ed. M. D. McGinnis (Ann Arbor: University of Michigan Press, 1999).

Kotsonias, G. 1984. The Messolonghi-Etolico Lagoon of Greece: Socioeconomic and ecological interactions of cooperatives and independent fishermen. In *Management of coastal lagoon fisheries,* ed. James M. Kapetsky and Georges Lasserre, GFCM Studies and Reviews, no. 61, 521–28. Rome: FAO.

Kottak, Conrad. 1966. The structure of equality in a Brazilian fishing community. Ph.D. diss., Columbia University.

Larson, Bruce A., and Daniel W. Bromley. 1990. Property rights, externalities, and resource degradation: Locating the tragedy. *Journal of Development Economics* 33:235–62.

Martin, Kent 0. 1973. "The law in St. John's says . . .": Space division and resource allocation in the Newfoundland fishing community of Fermeuse. Master's thesis, Department of Anthropology, Memorial University of Newfoundland.

―――. 1979. Play by the rules or don't play at all: Space division and resource allocation in a rural Newfoundland fishing community. In *North Atlantic maritime cultures: Anthropological essays on changing adaptations,* ed. R. Anderson, 276–98. The Hague: Mouton.

Matthews, R. 1988. Federal licensing policies for the Atlantic inshore fishery and their implementation in Newfoundland, 1973–1981. *Acadiensis: Journal of the History of the Atlantic Region* 17:83–108.

Matthews, R., and J. Phyne. 1988. Regulating the Newfoundland inshore fishery: Traditional values versus state control in the regulation of a common property resource. *Journal of Canadian Studies* 23:158–76.

McCay, Bonnie J., and James M. Acheson. 1987. *The question of the commons: The culture and ecology of communal resources.* Tucson: University of Arizona Press.

McGuire, Thomas R., and Mark Langworth. 1991. Behavioral and organizational modification of enforcement/avoidance theories: The fisheries case. MS, Department of Anthropology, University of Arizona.

Miller, David. 1982. Mexico's Caribbean fishery: Recent change and current issues. Ph.D. diss., University of Wisconsin–Milwaukee.

―――. 1989. The evolution of Mexico's spiny lobster fishery. In *Common property resources ecology and community-based sustainable development,* ed. Fikret Berkes, 185–98. London: Belhaven Press.

National Research Council. 1986. *Proceedings of the conference on common property resource management.* Washington, DC: National Academy Press.

Nietschmann, Bernard. 1972. Hunting and fishing focus among the Miskito Indians, Eastern Nicaragua. *Human Ecology* 1, no. 1: 41–67.

―――. 1973. *Between land and water: The subsistence ecology of the Miskito Indians, Eastern Nicaragua.* New York: Seminar Press.

Ostrom, Elinor. 1986. An agenda for the study of institutions. *Public Choice* 48:3–25. Reprinted in *Polycentric games and institutions,* ed. M. D. McGinnis (Ann Arbor: University of Michigan Press, 1999).

―――. 1987. Institutional arrangements for resolving the commons dilemma: Some contending approaches. In *The question of the commons: The culture and ecology of communal resources,* ed. Bonnie J. McCay and James Acheson, 250–65. Tucson: University of Arizona Press.

―――. 1990. *Governing the commons: The evolution of institutions for collective action.* New York: Cambridge University Press.

Ostrom, Elinor, Roy Gardner, and James Walker. 1994. *Rules, games, and common-pool resources.* Ann Arbor: University of Michigan Press.

Ostrom, Vincent. 1976. John R. Commons' foundations for policy analysis. *Journal of Economic Issues* 10, no. 4: 839–57.

―――. 1991. *The meaning of American federalism: Constituting a self-governing society.* San Francisco: Institute for Contemporary Studies Press.

Pinkerton, E., ed. 1989. *Co-operative management of local fisheries: New directions for improved management and community development.* Vancouver: University of British Columbia Press.

Posner, Richard. 1975. Economic analysis of law. In *Economic foundations of property law*, ed. Bruce Ackerman. Boston: Little, Brown and Co.

Powers, Ann M. 1984. Social organization in a Newfoundland fishing settlement on the Burin Peninsula. Ph.D. diss., State University of New York, Stony Brook.

Raychaudhuri, Bikash. 1980. *The moon and the net: Study of a transient community of fishermen at Jambudwip.* Anthropological Survey of India. Calcutta: Government of India Press.

Runge, C. Ford. 1981. Common property externalities: Isolation, assurance and resource depletion in a traditional grazing context. *American Journal of Agricultural Economics* 63:595–606.

Schlager, Edella. 1990. Model specification and policy analysis: The governance of coastal fisheries. Ph.D. diss., Indiana University.

———. 1994. Fishers' institutional responses to common-pool resource dilemmas. In *Rules, games, and common-pool resources*, ed. Elinor Ostrom, Roy Gardner, and James Walker, 247–65. Ann Arbor: University of Michigan Press.

Scott, Anthony D. 1955. The fishery: The objectives of sole ownership. *Journal of Political Economy* 63 (April): 116–24.

Scott, Anthony D., and Francis T. Christy, Jr. 1965. *The common wealth in ocean fisheries.* Baltimore: Johns Hopkins University Press.

Shortall, D. 1973. Environmental Perception in two local fisheries: A case study from Eastern Newfoundland. Master's thesis, Memorial University of Newfoundland.

Sinn, Hans-Werner. 1988. The Sahel problem. *Kyklos* 41:187–213.

Smith, J. Barry, Shlomo Weber, and Hans Wiesmeth. 1991. Heterogeneity, interdependence and equilibrium industry structure in fisheries. MS, Department of Economics, York University, Toronto.

Smith, Vernon. 1968. Economics of production from natural resources. *American Economic Review* 58, no. 3: 409–31.

Sutherland, Anne. 1986. *Caye Caulker: Economic success in a Belizean fishing village.* Boulder, CO: Westview Press.

Tang, Shui-Yan. 1992. *Institutions and collective action: Self-governance in irrigation.* San Francisco: Institute for Contemporary Studies Press.

van Ginkel, Rob. 1989. Plunders into planters: Zeeland oystermen and the enclosure of the marine commons. In *Dutch dilemmas: Anthropologists look at the Netherlands*, ed. Jeremy Boissevain and Jojada Verrips, 89–105. Assen/Maastricht, the Netherlands: Van Gorcum.

Wilson, James. 1977. A test of the tragedy of the commons. In *Managing the commons*, ed. Garrett Hardin and John Baden, 96–111. San Francisco: Freeman.

———. 1982. The economical management of multispecies fisheries. *Land Economics* 58 (November): 417–34.

CHAPTER 6

Mobile Flows, Storage, and Self-Organized Institutions for Governing Common-Pool Resources

Edella Schlager, William Blomquist, and Shui-Yan Tang

I. Introduction

Considerable progress has been made in the past decade in the analysis of common-pool resource (CPR) problems (National Research Council 1986; McCay and Acheson 1987; Berkes 1989; Pinkerton 1989; Feeny et al. 1990; Ostrom 1990; Bromley 1991). For instance, much attention has been devoted to clarifying the differences between CPRs in which rules of access and use are undefined (i.e., open access), and those in which the users have devised governing arrangements (Ciriacy-Wantrup and Bishop 1975; Bromley and Cernea 1989; Feeny et al. 1990). A major finding emerging from these efforts is that resource users possess considerable capacity to maintain or enhance the resource by devising workable rules that govern access and use. In fact, there are hundreds of documented cases of self-organized institutions developed to govern common-pool resources (Martin 1989, 1992).

Another major finding from recent research efforts is that many attempts by external authorities to impose uniform solutions to CPR problems have suffered from serious institutional weaknesses and failures (Ostrom 1990; Ostrom, Gardner, and Walker 1994). Many of these externally imposed rules are based on overly simplified models that assume that only a limited number of optimal rules are available for improving CPR performance. These rules frequently turn out to be incompatible with the specific physical characteristics of resources. Thus, the time is ripe for the next step

Originally published in *Land Economics* 70, no. 3 (August 1994): 294–317. Copyright 1994. Reprinted by permission of the University of Wisconsin Press and the authors.

Authors' note: We would like to thank Roy Gardner, Elinor Ostrom, James Walker, Rick Wilson, and two anonymous reviewers for this journal for their many helpful comments. Financial support provided by the National Science Foundation (Grant No. SES–8921884) is gratefully acknowledged.

in developing a better understanding of how the incentives and performance of rules are affected by various physical characteristics.

A useful approach in developing a systematic understanding is to examine the variation in rules users of different types of CPRs develop to govern their resources. Having examined fisheries, irrigation systems, and groundwater basins, we find that users of these resources pursue different strategies and design different institutional arrangements.[1] We contend that the differences in strategies and in institutions are connected to two physical distinctions among these resources—the degree of mobility of the flow units and the existence of storage capacity.[2] These two physical characteristics affect the quantity, quality, and costliness of information users possess about their resources and the problems they experience; and users' ability to coordinate their activities and capture the benefits created from such coordination. In other words, the degree of mobility of the flow units and the presence of storage affect the types of institutional arrangements resource users adopt.

In making such an argument, we do not contend that institutional arrangements are "determined" or "induced" by the physical characteristics of the resources. Resource users face a number of interacting constraints in attempting to coordinate their use of common-pool resources. Rather, the physical characteristics of mobility and storage shape the opportunities and constraints that users face in attempting to resolve problems, making some strategy choices more likely than others.

In this essay we do four things: (1) define mobility, storage, and the problems CPR users often experience; (2) examine the interactions between mobility and storage and common-pool problems; (3) explore the implications of these interactions for the strategies resource users adopt to solve common-pool problems; and (4) provide supporting evidence from empirical research on different types of CPRs. In so doing, we present a typology of CPRs for understanding and anticipating resource users' strategies in confronting and solving common-pool problems. We conclude by examining the policy implications of our findings.

II. Mobile Flows, Storage, and Common-Pool Problems

Common-pool resources, which share the defining characteristics of difficult exclusion and subtractable yields, may differ on two important physical characteristics. The first is whether the resource units yielded by the CPR are stationary or mobile. This distinction refers to spatial movement of the units, *apart from any harvesting activity by resource users.*[3] The second is whether the resource has storage capacity that enables users to capture and retain unharvested units.[4] Storage capacity may be an inherent part of a resource, as in groundwater basins; or it may be in the form of human-made structures, as in some canal irrigation systems where reservoirs or tanks have been constructed. Speaking generally, pelagic and demersal fisheries and some canal irrigation systems are CPRs with mobile flows and without storage capacity; some canal irrigation systems have mobile flows and storage; and groundwater basins have relatively stationary flow units and storage capacity (see table 6.1).

TABLE 6.1. A Typology of CPRs

	Flow Units	
Storage	Fugitive	Stationary
Absent	Cell 1 (Fisheries, Some Irrigation Systems)	Cell 2 (Grazing Areas)
Present	Cell 3 (Some Irrigation Systems)	Cell 4 (Groundwater Basins)

No matter the type of common-pool resource, users can experience a variety of problems. Following Ostrom, Gardner, and Walker (1994), we categorize common-pool problems as appropriation problems and provision problems (see table 6.2). Appropriation problems involve allocating the yield of a resource in an efficient and equitable manner. Problems that emerge in this respect include appropriation externalities, technological externalities, and assignment problems. Appropriation externalities arise from excessive harvesting of the flow units from a resource leading to increased harvesting costs per unit of output. Excessive harvest in one year may also reduce or destroy the availability of resource units in future years.[5] Technological externalities and assignment problems involve resource users physically interfering with each other as they engage in harvesting. The issue here is not one of excessive harvesting, rather it is one of actual physical interference in harvesting. In the case of assignment problems, resource users fight over control of the most productive areas in a resource (Cordell 1972). In the case of technological externalities, appropriators use their harvesting technologies in ways that interfere with each other's harvesting; for example, using mobile and fixed fishing gears in the same area within a fishing ground.

Provision problems relate to the optimal size of the stock of flow units as well as the productive nature of the resource. Provision problems generally arise from deficient investments in the development, maintenance, and protection of common-pool resources. Development failures represent opportunities foregone. Resources are not developed to their optimal productivity level. Deficient investments in maintenance of either the physical facilities or the stock of flow units can result in erosion of a CPR's productive or regenerative capacity and deterioration of the status quo. Degradation problems emerge when flow units are not adequately protected from a variety of threats and their quality and value are diminished.

TABLE 6.2. Types of CPR Problems

Appropriation Problems
    Appropriation externalities
    Technological externalities
    Assignment problems
Provision Problems
    Development failures
    Maintenance problems
    Degradation problems

Source: Ostrom, Gardner, and Walker (1994: 8–15).

The two characteristics of mobility and storage affect (1) the severity of the appropriation and provision problems resource users face, (2) the relative ease with which users can resolve those problems, and (3) the kinds of institutional arrangements they are likely to develop and implement. These effects are due to the impact of the physical characteristics on (1) the information users have about their common-pool resources and the problems they are experiencing, (2) the likelihood that users will be able to capture the benefits that issue from their efforts to solve problems, and (3) their assurance about the behavior of other users.[6]

III. Degree of Mobility and Common-Pool Resource Problems

Mobile flows aggravate appropriation externalities and provision problems that relate directly to the intensity of effort applied to harvesting flow units.[7] These types of problems are difficult for users of mobile flows to address because of information complexity and cost, and the difficulty of capturing the benefits of individual or collective action.

For instance, appropriation externalities present compounded difficulties when users are harvesting mobile flows. In order to address appropriation externalities, resource users must possess information on the size of the population, the population dynamics of the flow units, the number of units being harvested, and the effect of each resource user's harvest upon every other resource user's harvests; *and* from this information determine the optimal harvest level. In a CPR with mobile flows, flows which often fluctuate unpredictably, such information may be very difficult, if not impossible, to obtain.[8] It is difficult for resource users to accurately assess the extent of variations in flow, to determine whether an observed flow decline is merely temporary or part of a longer-term phenomenon, and to diagnose the cause of the decline.

Even if users correctly observe a flow decline, and become convinced that the decline is not just an aberration, diagnosing its cause is problematic. The effects of users' harvesting activities in one period on the flow of units in another period is not as clear in a resource with mobile flows. Other plausible hypotheses often present themselves: perhaps some migratory or precipitation patterns have shifted, perhaps some infestation or pestilence is at work, perhaps someone or something outside the area has affected the flow, and so on.[9]

When the cause of their problems cannot be determined clearly, it is difficult for resource users to gain consensus on what would constitute beneficial institutional arrangements, and users have greater incentives to reject or cheat upon agreements to limit harvesting. At a minimum, a rational user's incentive to limit harvesting in order to restore the stock and reduce the externality is diminished in CPRs with mobile flows. Users are less certain that they will reap the benefits of their efforts to respond to appropriation externalities.

These difficulties are compounded if the mobile flows actually exit the boundaries of one resource and traverse across multiple locations, as do migrating species of fish and wildlife. Migration aggravates common-pool problems in four ways: (1) users are more likely to attribute flow declines to the behavior of users elsewhere in the system; (2) the users in any one location cannot control the flow even if they act collectively; (3) because no one group can control the flow and capture the benefits of collective action, users in any one location are less likely to provide benefits for users elsewhere in the system by restraining their own appropriation activities; and (4) coordinating activities with users in other locations raises transaction costs.[10]

For many of the reasons just stated in relation to appropriation problems, users of CPRs with mobile flows are also less likely to take action to solve provision problems. Maintenance efforts may be more difficult to achieve because it is harder for users to correctly diagnose the source of the provision problem—for example, whether declining stocks result from excessive appropriation, maintenance failure, neither, or both—and thus whether increased maintenance efforts this period will mean that flows will exist or be more abundant in future periods. Mobile flows also have deleterious effects on users' ability to diagnose and resolve degradation problems. The incentives for users to take actions or make contributions to protect a mobile flow—whether to protect the quality of water in a surface stream, a migratory species habitat, etc.—are sharply attenuated. The negative consequences of degradation are (from an individual user's viewpoint, literally) passed on to others. Finally, provision problems are exacerbated by the fact that multiple resources are involved. Migration compounds the uncertainty about the incidence and causes of provision problems, and resource users are less certain to capture the benefits from investments made in the protection or enhancement of the resource.

The considerable information and transaction costs that users of resources with mobile flows face may overwhelm any attempt to develop governing structures that allow them to manage the flow units and thereby *directly* address appropriation externalities and provision problems. Instead, such users face powerful incentives to pursue "first capture," or "use it or lose it," strategies. In such situations, it is only through capture that resource users can actually "bank" fugitive flows.[11]

Not all common-pool problems subject users of mobile flows to such extraordinary transaction costs as do appropriation externalities and most provision problems. Assignment problems and technological externalities present very different opportunities for resolution because they often occur within the context of a single resource, and because such problems occur repeatedly under similar circumstances (Wilson 1982). Given these two conditions, users can, over time, accumulate information concerning the causes of such problems. Since users possess more information and can exert greater control over the resource, at least more control than over the units flowing through it, technological externalities and assignment problems are more readily solved. Oftentimes solutions are based on spatial allocations that rely primarily on knowledge of the resource system and not on knowledge of the dynamics of the flow of resource units.

Users of resources that naturally produce stationary resource units have a substantial advantage over users of a resource that naturally produce mobile units. Even though the annual yield from a resource with stationary units may vary dramatically from one year to the next, because of variations in rainfall and temperature, the costs of assessing the quantity of units available for harvest will be less than if the units were mobile. For instance, in relation to a grazing area, experienced individuals can assess the safe fodder yield during a particular year at a relatively low cost.[12] When the cost of assessing the availability of resource units is relatively low, it is much easier to develop allocation rules that assign quantities to individuals in order to minimize appropriation externalities.

Parallel observations apply to the effect of stationary units on provision problems. Appropriators relying on stationary units, who engage in activities that enhance the supply of resource units, can collect information concerning the effects of their efforts and consequently experiment with a variety of supply enhancing methods. In addition, because stationary units do not flow through multiple resources, appropriators can capture the benefits from engaging in supply enhancement activities. Thus, for instance, in many mountain grazing commons, appropriators spend time and effort enhancing the productivity of the commons by weeding out undesirable species, transplanting, and caring for more desirable species (McKean 1992). Groundwater users in locations throughout the United States have engaged in artificial replenishment efforts; they can reasonably anticipate that water stored underground and left unpumped in the present period will be available in the near future (U.S. ACIR 1991).

In general, users of resources with stationary units face lower information and transaction costs both in learning about the dynamics of the flow units, and in negotiating and devising governing arrangements, than do users of resources with fugitive flows. Because stationary units are more readily inventoried and monitored and because they do not flow through multiple locations, resource users can more readily identify solutions to common-pool problems and capture the benefits of such solutions.

IV. Storage Capacity and Common-Pool Problems

The presence of storage capacity in a CPR allows users to capture and contain flow units, at least temporarily. Therefore, storage capacity can help users of CPRs with mobile flows overcome some of their appropriation and provision problems. Users may not only be in a better position to understand the relationship between current appropriation activities and future flows, but to exercise some control over that relationship. If users can store flows, cycles of depletion may be interrupted before they pass a critical threshold and move toward extinction.

The availability of storage enlarges the range of options on which users may agree in addressing appropriation externalities. In a resource with storage capacity, users can "bank" flow units, reducing the powerful incentives to engage in "first capture" strategies. Instead, a variety of quantity assignments may be agreed on, from fixed quotas to assigned shares in the total available harvest. And, agreements may be reached to temporarily draw down the number of units in storage during low-flow periods, with harvesting decreased in later periods to replenish the number of units in storage.

Storage capacity can also reduce technological externalities arising from multiple harvesters' activities occurring within the same space and time. In resources with storage, users may be more willing to defer or relocate their harvesting activities and less likely to conflict with each other's efforts, because the availability of flow units is less a function of space and time.

With respect to provision problems, storage may be expected to increase users' willingness to contribute to resource development and maintenance efforts, because users are more certain of being able to capture and enjoy the benefits of their efforts. Depending on the institutional arrangements for governing the use of the storage capacity, users can have greater confidence that actions taken to augment or maintain the resource and its flows will provide them with greater availability of valued flow units in the future.

Of course, the presence of storage adds to the number of aspects of a CPR system that must be maintained. CPR storage facilities (natural or human-made) themselves must be maintained, which increases the possibilities for some kind of maintenance failure to occur. And users of CPRs with storage capability must learn about that capability in order to take advantage of it, which raises other information costs. Regulation of storage capacity and the allocation of stored flow units are additional items that users will have to resolve, with some attendant increase in transaction costs. No a priori estimation can be made of whether the maintenance benefits of storage in a typical CPR will outweigh these additional costs.

Thus, the physical characteristics of mobility and storage interact with CPR problems in definite ways that affect the types of problems resource users are likely to address and the types of rules they are likely to adopt to govern their harvesting activities. Our first proposition is that in resources in which there are no storage capabilities and in which resource units are mobile, resource users are more likely to address problems related to the physical structure of the resource than they are problems that relate to the flow of resource units. In resources in which storage is present or in which the resource units are stationary, resource users are more likely to address the full range of CPR problems, including those that relate to flow of resource units, than are resource users who are dependent upon mobile units. Recognizing that characteristics of CPRs condition, but do not induce or determine the choices of users, we propose table 6.3.

A second proposition is that the four CPR types can be related to the kinds of resolutions of CPR problems, *particularly appropriation problems*, users are likely to reach. In attempting to resolve appropriation problems, users of some CPRs will be more likely to rely on access limitations, or spatial or temporal restrictions on use of the CPR. In other CPRs, users will be more likely to devise individual quotas or quantity restrictions on use. Our anticipation about these relationships is shown in figure 6.1. Users of CPRs with stationary flows will be more likely to reach resolutions involving quantity restrictions than users of CPRs with mobile flows, and users of CPRs with storage will be more likely to reach resolutions involving quantity restrictions than users of CPRs without storage.

TABLE 6.3. Types of Problems Users of Different Resources Address

	Cell 1	Cell 2	Cell 3	Cell 4
Appropriation Problems				
Technological externalities	+	+	+	+
Assignment problems	+	+	+	+
Appropriation externalities	−	+	−	+
Provision Problems				
Development failures	−	−	+	+
Maintenance problems	−	+	+	+
Degradation problems	−	?	?	+

Note: + = users more likely to address; − = users less likely to address; ? = unknown.

V. Evidence from Fisheries, Irrigation Systems, and Groundwater Basins

We have conducted research on three of the four types of CPRs identified in table 6.1. We have not analyzed empirical evidence concerning examples in Cell 2—CPRs with stationary units but for which storage is absent, such as grazing areas and forests.[13] We relate evidence from fisheries and some canal irrigation systems as examples of CPRs in Cell 1 (mobile flows, storage absent), some canal irrigation systems as examples from Cell 3 (mobile flows, storage present), and groundwater basins as examples from Cell 4 (stationary flows, storage present).

Research Design

The fisheries and irrigation data were collected through a research project conducted at the Workshop in Political Theory and Policy Analysis at Indiana University. A part of the research project involved a systematic analysis of in-depth case studies on common-pool resources. As members of the research project, and in conjunction with others involved, we developed a series of in-depth coding forms, containing mostly closed-ended questions, to capture key physical, community, and institutional attributes of common-

Cell 1	Cell 3	Cell 2	Cell 4

←——→

Access limitations/Spatial/temporal restrictions on use   Quantity restrictions on use

Fig. 6.1. Types of resolutions of appropriation problems

pool resources. These forms were used to code data provided by the in-depth case studies.[14]

Extensive efforts were undertaken by the project to identify theoretical and empirical studies in irrigation systems, fisheries, and other common-pool resources (Martin 1989, 1992). Cases were selected for coding only if they contained detailed information about: (1) participants in the resource, (2) strategies used by participants, (3) the condition of the resource, and (4) rules in use for the resource. Cases were also selected in such a way as to include in the sample as much diversity in terms of physical, community and institutional attributes, and collective outcomes as possible.

The fisheries and irrigation data are based on 48 coded cases—25 fishery and 23 irrigation.[15] The profiles of these cases are shown in tables 6.4, 6.5, 6.7, and 6.9. Since these 48 cases, along with 7 case studies of groundwater basins in southern California, are the basic evidence of this study, the generalizations derived from the study pertain to what has been reported in the cases.

Cell 1: Fisheries

The defining characteristic of many fisheries is their mobile flows. The types of common-pool problems that fishers will attempt to address are heavily influenced by this characteristic. Fishers are more likely to address problems that arise in relation to fishing grounds, and much less likely to address problems that arise in relation to the mobile flows of fish through their fishing grounds.[16] In so doing, fishers are more likely to use time, location, and gear restrictions, as opposed to quotas (Schlager 1990, 1994).

Data collected from in-depth case studies of 25 inshore fishing grounds located around the world will be used to examine the above assertions (see table 6.4 for a listing and a description of the case studies).[17] The unit of analysis is the subgroup. A subgroup is a group of fishers who harvest from the same fishing ground and who are relatively similar in relation to the following five characteristics:

1. their legal rights to appropriate fish,
2. their withdrawal rate of fish,
3. their exposure to variation in the supply of fish,
4. their level of dependency on fish withdrawn from the resource,
5. their use of the fish they harvest.

This definition of a subgroup depends on the sharing of similar characteristics and not on the presence or absence of an organization of fishers. More than one subgroup of fishers may utilize the same fishing grounds simultaneously.

TABLE 6.4. Description of Fishery Case Studies

Country	Location	Fish Harvested	Subgroups	Documentation
Brazil	Arembepe	Mixed	1	Kottak (1966)
Brazil	Coqueiral	Mixed	1	Forman (1966, 1970)
Brazil	Valenca	Mixed	5	Cordell (1972, 1978, 1983, 1984)
Canada	Baccalaos Cove	Cod	2	Powers (1984)
Canada	Cat Harbour	Cod	2	Faris (1972)
Canada	Fermeuse	Cod	2	K. O. Martin (1973, 1979)
Canada	James Bay	Whitefish	1	Berkes (1977, 1987)
Canada	Petty Harbour	Cod	2	Shortall (1973)
Canada	Port Lameroon, Pagesville	Mixed	1	Davis (1975, 1984)
Greece	Messolonghi Etolico	Mullet, Seabream	2	Kotsonias (1984)
India	Jambudwip	Mixed	2	Raychaudhuri (1972)
Jamaica	Fraquhar Beach	Mixed	1	Davenport (1956)
Japan	Ebibara	Shrimp	1	Brameld (1968)
Korea	Kagoda	Anchovy	1	Han (1972)
Malaysia	Kampong Mee	Mixed	1	Anderson and Anderson (1977)
Malaysia	Perupok	Mixed	1	Firth (1966)
Mexico	Andres Quintana Roo	Mixed	1	Miller (1982, 1989)
Nicaragua	Tasbapauni	Turtle	2	Nietschmann (1972, 1973)
Sri Lanka	Gahavalla	Mixed	3	Alexander (1982)
Thailand	Rusembilan	Mackerel	1	Fraser (1960, 1966)
Turkey	Alanya	Mixed	1	Berkes (1986)
Turkey	Ayvalik-Haylazi	Mixed	1	Berkes (1986)
Turkey	Tasucu	Mixed	1	Berkes (1986)
Venezuela	Chigauan	Lisa	1	Breton (1973)

Thirty-four subgroups utilize the 25 fishing grounds. The types of common-pool resource problems that the 34 subgroups of fishers have faced or continue to face are technological externalities; assignment problems; declines in stocks of fish, which may indicate appropriation externalities or maintenance problems; and declines in the quality of fish harvested, which may indicate maintenance or degradation problems (see table 6.5).[18]

One approach to understanding the types of CPR problems fishers attempt to address is to examine the rules fishers have adopted to govern their harvesting activities. Subgroups of fishers collectively invest in the creation and monitoring of rules directed at constraining particular forms of undesirable behavior. For instance, rules that govern the use of the physical resource indicate direct attempts on the part of the fishers to address problems related to the physical structure of a resource. On the other hand, rules that govern the intensity of harvesting of fish indicate direct attempts on the part of fishers to address problems related to the flow of units in a resource.

TABLE 6.5. Common-Pool Problems and Rules—Fishery Cases

Country	Location	Problems	Rules
Brazil	Arembepe	Data Missing	None
Brazil	Coqueiral	Technological Externalities	Specific Location
Brazil	Valenca		
	Subgroup 1	Assignment, Technological Externalities, Appropriation Externalities and/or Maintenance Problems	Specific Location, Fixed Order, Fixed Time
	Subgroup 2	Assignment, Technological Externalities, Appropriation Externalities and/or Maintenance, or Degradation Problems	Specific Location, Fixed Order, Fixed Time
	Subgroup 3	Assignment, Technological Externalities, Appropriation Externalities and/or Maintenance, or Degradation Problems	None
	Subgroup 4	Assignment, Technological Externalities, Appropriation Externalities and/or Maintenance, or Degradation Problems	None
	Subgroup 5	Assignment, Technological Externalities, Appropriation Externalities and/or Maintenance, or Degradation Problems	None
Canada	Baccalaos Cove		
	Subgroup 1	Assignment, Technological Externalities, and Maintenance or Degradation Problems	Specific Location
	Subgroup 2	Assignment, Technological Externalities, and Maintenance or Degradation Problems	Specific Location
Canada	Cat Harbour		
	Subgroup 1	Assignment	Specific Location
	Subgroup 2	Assignment	Specific Location
Canada	Fermeuse		
	Subgroup 1	Assignment	Specific Location
	Subgroup 2	Assignment	Specific Location
Canada	James Bay	Technological Externalities	Specific Location, Fixed Order, Specific Size
Canada	Petty Harbour		
	Subgroup 1	Assignment, Technological Externalities, and Appropriation Externalities and/or Maintenance, or Degradation Problems	Specific Location
	Subgroup 2	Assignment, Technological Externalities, and Appropriation Externalities and/or Maintenance, or Degradation Problems	Specific Location
Canada	Port Lameroon, Pagesville	Technological Externalities, Appropriation Externalities or Maintenance Problems	Specific Location
Greece	Messolonghi Etolico		
	Subgroup 1	Technological Externalities, Appropriation Externalities and/or Maintenance Problems, Degradation Problems	Specific Location
	Subgroup 2	Technological Externalities, Appropriation Externalities and/or Maintenance Problems, Degradation Problems	Specific Location

(continued)

TABLE 6.5. — *Continued*

Country	Location	Problems	Rules
India	Jambudwip		
	Subgroup 1	Assignment, Appropriation Externalities or Maintenance Problems	Specific Location
	Subgroup 2	Assignment, Appropriation Externalities or Maintenance Problems	Specific Location
Jamaica	Fraquhar Beach	Maintenance or Degradation Problem	Specific Location
Japan	Ebibara	Technological Externalities, Appropriation Externalities or Maintenance Problems	Specific Location, Specific Size
Korea	Kagoda	Data Missing	None
Malaysia	Kampong Mee	Technological Externalities, Appropriation Externalities and/or Maintenance or Degradation Problems	None
Malaysia	Perupok	Data Missing	Specific Location
Mexico	Andres Quintana Roo	Data Missing	Specific Location
Nicaragua	Tasbapauni		
	Subgroup 1	Appropriation Externalities and/or Maintenance Problems, Degradation Problems	None
	Subgroup 2	Appropriation Externalities and/or Maintenance Problems, Degradation Problems	None
Sri Lanka	Tasbapauni		
	Subgroup 1	Technological Externalities	Specific Location, Fixed Order
	Subgroup 2	Technological Externalities	Specific Location, Fixed Order
	Subgroup 3	Technological Externalities	Specific Location, Fixed Order
Thailand	Rusembilan	Data Missing	None
Turkey	Alanya	Assignment, Appropriation Externalities and/or Maintenance Problems	Specific Season, Specific Location, Fixed Order
Turkey	Ayvalik-Haylazi	Data Missing	Specific Location
Turkey	Tasucu	Technological Externalities, Appropriation Externalities and/or Maintenance Problems	Specific Location, Specific Size
Venezuela	Chigauan	Appropriation Externalities and/or Maintenance Problems, Degradation Problems	None

Among the 34 subgroups that have faced one or more common-pool resource problems, fishers of 27 subgroups have cooperated to devise rules that govern the use of their fishing grounds. A frequency count of the rules used by fishers in the 27 subgroups is shown in table 6.6. Six different types of rules are used in these groups: location rules, size rules, season rules, order rules, technology rules, and time-slot rules. Subgroups frequently rely on more than one rule.

TABLE 6.6. Rules Used by Fishers

Type of Rule	Subgroups Using Rule ($N = 27$)	
Withdraw at Specific Locations	27	(100%)
Withdraw in a Fixed Order	7	(26%)
Withdraw Fish of at Least a Specific Size	3	(11%)
Withdraw at a Fixed Time Slot	2	(7%)
Withdraw during a Specific Season	1	(3%)

The two most often used rules limit harvesting activities to specific locations or spots and limit the types of technologies that can be used. Every subgroup in the sample used a location rule to determine how choice fishing spots are distributed. Seventeen of the subgroups limited technologies. Access to fishing spots is dependent on meeting any of a variety of requirements. In some instances different types of gear are relegated to different areas of the fishing ground, in part, as a method of minimizing technological externalities, if multiple types of technologies are permitted. For example, the fishers of Port Lameroon Harbour, Nova Scotia, have divided their fishing grounds among different technologies. "A rectangularly shaped area stretching from the Gate Rocks to the Half Moons and out to the Fairway Buoy is reserved primarily for herring and mackerel gillnets," whereas the area around Brazil Rock is reserved for handlining for cod (Davis 1984, 141–43).

In other instances, rules requiring fishers to harvest from specific spots within a fishing ground allocate scarce productive spots and thereby resolve assignment problems. Often times specific spot rules will be combined with other types of rules such as "harvest in a specific order," the third most often used rule, so that all fishers have equal opportunities of harvesting from the most productive spots over the course of a year. For instance, the fishers of the estuary adjacent to Valenca, Brazil, would draw lots to determine the order in which each boat would harvest from a productive spot. Each boat crew was permitted to cast their net once and then they were required to move off of the spot so that the next boat in turn could harvest from the spot (Cordell 1972, 42).

The fourth most frequently used rule is a size rule requiring that fishers harvest fish greater than a minimum size. This rule is typically used to ensure that fish achieve maturity and have a chance to spawn before being harvested. Only 3 of the 27 subgroups utilize this rule. Among those 3 subgroups, only 1 voluntarily adopted such a rule, in the other 2 cases an external authority imposed the rule.[19]

The fifth most frequently used rule is a fixed time slot rule. This rule is often combined with a fixed order rule or a location rule. It limits the amount of time that a boat can remain on a choice fishing spot. Typical limits involve one casting of a net, or one day (Alexander 1982; Cordell 1972). Finally, one subgroup uses seasonal restrictions. Seasonal restrictions forbid the harvesting of fish during specific times of the year, typically when fish spawn.

Most of the fishers in this sample are not free to engage in harvesting of fish in any manner they desire. They have adopted a host of rules to coordinate their use of fishing grounds. These rules directly address assignment problems and technological externalities by allocating space within fishing grounds. Fishers focus on assignment problems and technological externalities because they can readily identify the causes of these problems.

Most of the fishers harvest from the same set of fishing grounds over their lifetimes, the same set of fishing grounds that their fathers and grandfathers harvested from (Davis 1984). Consequently, they possess extensive knowledge of the structure of their grounds. Given the daily interactions among fishers, and their extensive knowledge concerning the problems that arise in relation to their use of their fishing grounds, fishers can more easily devise and experiment with rules to resolve such problems.

In addition, many of these rules are easily monitored by fishers as they engage in harvesting. To address assignment problems, rules allocate choice fishing spots across fishers. That is, fishers are required to fish a particular spot. Such behavior is easily monitored by other fishers while they are harvesting. They only need look at each other's positions to determine whether the rules are being followed.

On the other hand, among the 27 subgroups that have devised rules, no subgroup has devised rules that limit the amount of fish that fishers can harvest. Fishers have not devised quota rules that would limit their catch levels.[20] By limiting the amount of fish (i.e., mobile flow units) that may be harvested, quotas are the most direct means of addressing appropriation externalities and maintenance failures that arise in relation to the flow units. Yet, rules devised by fishers do not usually focus on the allocation of quotas.

Cell 1: Canal Irrigation Systems without Storage

Many small-scale canal irrigation systems depend on water flowing in from other resources such as nearby rivers and ditches that are unstable in water flows. If these systems are not equipped with such facilities as reservoirs and ponds for capturing and storing water, irrigators have little control over the amount of water available for use at any particular time. They need to develop water allocation rules that can be effectively enforced regardless of the current water level in the system. Similar to the fisheries cases examined earlier, irrigators in this kind of irrigation system seldom develop rules that assign specific quantities of water, that is, water quotas, to individuals.

Data collected from in-depth case studies of 23 farmer-managed irrigation systems are examined (see table 6.7).[21] All of these systems are small in scale and lack sizable facilities for water storage.[22] A frequency count of the allocation rules used in this sample of farmer-managed irrigation systems is shown in table 6.8. Three types of rules are most frequently used—fixed time slot rules, fixed order rules, and fixed percentage rules.[23] In four of these cases, more than one rule is used. In the other three, no rule is used (see table 6.9).

TABLE 6.7. Description of Irrigation Cases

Country	System Name	Command Area (in hectares)	Major Crop	Documentation
Iran	Deh Salm	300	Other Grains	Spooner (1971, 1972, 1974)
Iran	Nayband	Data Missing	Rice	Spooner (1971, 1972, 1974)
Nepal	Raj Kulo	94	Rice	Martin and Yoder (1983a, 1983b, 1986)
Nepal	Thulo Kulo	39	Rice	Martin and Yoder (1983a, 1983b, 1986)
Nepal	Char Hazar	200	Rice	Fowler (1986)
Nepal	Chhahare Khola	20	Other Grains	Water and Engineering Commission (1987)
Nepal	Naya Dhara	55	Rice	Water and Engineering Commission (1987)
Philippines	Agcuyo	9	Rice	de los Reyes et al. (1980a)
Philippines	Cadchog	3	Rice	de los Reyes et al. (1980a)
Philippines	Calaoaan	150	Rice	de los Reyes et al. (1980a)
Philippines	Mauraro	15	Rice	de los Reyes et al. (1980a)
Philippines	Oaig-Daya	100	Rice	de los Reyes et al. (1980a)
Philippines	Sabangan Bato	94	Rice	de los Reyes et al. (1980a)
Philippines	Silag-Butir	114	Rice	de los Reyes et al. (1980a)
Philippines	San Antonio 1	23	Rice	de los Reyes et al. (1980b)
Philippines	San Antonio 2	7	Rice	de los Reyes et al. (1980b)
Philippines	Tanowong T	Data Missing	Rice	Bacdayan (1980)
Philippines	Tanowong B	Data Missing	Rice	Bacdayan (1980)
Philippines	Zanjera Danum Sitio	45	Rice	Coward (1979)
Switzerland	Felderin	19	Meadow	Netting (1974, 1981)
Tanzania	Kheri	260	Other Grains	Gray (1963)
Thailand	Na Pae	64	Rice	Tan-kim-yong (1983)
Thailand	Chiangmai	Data Missing	Rice	Potter (1976)

TABLE 6.8. Rules Used by Irrigators

Type of Rule	Systems Using Rule (N = 25)
Withdraw in a Fixed Order	11 (44%)
Withdraw at a Fixed Time Slot	10 (40%)
Withdraw a Fixed Percentage	5 (20%)
No Rule	3 (12%)

TABLE 6.9. Irrigation Allocation Rules (Most Restrictive)

System Name	Fixed Order	Fixed Time Slot	Fixed Percentage	No Rule
Deh Salm		X		
Nayband		X		
Raj Kulo	X		X	
Thulo Kulo	X		X	
Char Hazar	X			
Chhahare Khola				X
Naya Dhara		X		
Agcuyo	X			
Cadchog	X			
Calaoaan		X		
Mauraro				X
Oaig-Daya		X		
Sabangan Bato	X			
Silag-Butir	X			
San Antonio 1			X	
San Antonio 2				X
Tanowong T	X			
Tanowong B	X			
Zanjera Danum	X		X	
Sitio				
Felderin		X		
Kheri		X		
Na Pae		X	X	
Chiangmai		X		
TOTAL	10	9	5	3

The first most frequently used rule is a fixed order rule that requires individuals to take turns getting water. In some systems, one's water turn may depend on the location of one's fields. For instance, those with land located in the headend of the distributory canal may be entitled to get as much water as they want before those further down the canal can get their water. In other systems, some officials may be responsible for deciding which plots of land can get water first, based on their judgment about the most efficient way of diverting water.

The second most frequently used rule is withdrawing water at fixed time slots. The length of the time slot for each irrigator may depend on different premises such as amount of land held, amount of water needed for cultivation, number of shares held, historical pattern of use, location of fields, or officials' discretion. The length of the time slot for an irrigator, for example, may be determined by the amount of land an irrigator holds; that is, the more land he holds, the more time to which he is entitled. The advantage of this rule is that it is relatively easy to enforce. If each irrigator knows his time slot, he will show up at the right spot and divert water to his field when his time slot begins. Since each farmer has an incentive to guard his own time slots against water theft, the arrangement may be self-enforcing and require minimal supervision.[24]

The third most frequently used rule is a fixed percentage rule according to which the water flow is divided into fixed proportions by some physical device. In Thulo Kulo in Nepal, for example, water is divided by the use of saachos—beams with several notches of equal depth but various widths cut into the top. A saacho is "installed in a canal such that all the water flows through the notches causing the flow to be divided proportionally relative to the ratio of the widths of the notches" (Martin and Yoder 1983a, 14).

Absent from the list of allocation rules used in these 23 farmer-managed systems are rules that assign to each irrigator specific amounts of water, that is, water quotas. Quota rules are infeasible because irrigators in these systems lack effective control over the total amount of water available in the system. To accommodate variations in water flows, the three most frequently used rules—fixed time slot, fixed order, and fixed percentage—are so designed that they can be implemented regardless of the actual amount of water available at a particular time. A major function of the rules is to divide up the available water among irrigators with minimum degrees of technical externalities and assignment problems. Similar to the fisheries cases, the rules adopted by these systems reflect irrigators' adaptation to their physical environment. Instead of controlling the volume of the water flow directly, they try to control space (e.g., location) and time (e.g., time slots) as the major means of reducing potential conflict.

Cell 3: Canal Irrigation Systems with Storage

Some canal irrigation systems are equipped with storage structures such as reservoirs and tanks. Once water is captured and stored in these facilities, the peaks and valleys of the flow can be somewhat evened out and excess water at one time can be made available at another time. Irrigators can inventory the water flow and estimate the amount available for appropriation at particular times.

Water storage capacities vary among irrigation systems. Those systems with reservoirs and tanks, for example, have greater storage capacities than those with only gates across canals. Greater storage capacities help to increase irrigators' control of water, that is to reduce uncertainty in the water flow.

Storage facilities may exist at different levels of an irrigation system, from above the headworks down to the watercourse level. Storage facilities, for example, may exist in the form of a major storage dam above the headworks. If the dam is equipped with effective opening and closing devices, farmers can control the quantities of water available within the canal system during any period of time. The Alicante system in Spain, as described by Maass and Anderson (1986), is an example of such a system. In this system, farmers buy and sell rights to specific time slots. When farmers know the amount of water to be released from the major dam, they know the actual quantity of water they can get during specific time slots. Such an arrangement allows for the development of effective water markets among farmers.

Storage capacities also make water quotas a viable alternative for water allocation. In Northeastern Colorado, as described by Maass and Anderson (1986), some water companies deliver reservoir water to farmers by means of quotas. In such irrigation systems, individual farmers own shares of the company. Each year a company allocates a quantity of water per share. When a farmer wants a certain amount of water, he notifies the company in advance. The company then arranges to deliver that amount of water to his fields at some prearranged time. Since individual farmers own specific amounts of water available in the storage system, they can sell or rent their allotments to others. Such an arrangement creates flexibility for farmers because delivery can be made on demand and water can be delivered from the reservoir to multiple canal systems.

Storage facilities may exist in the form of local water tanks within the canal system. Irrigators are more confident in their irrigation practices if there is a local water tank to serve as an inventory buffer. Even though the amount of water delivered to their watercourse may suddenly drop, farmers can still rely on the tank water to irrigate their crops for a while. This inventory buffer is especially important during certain stages of the crop growth when insufficient water will be detrimental to crop yields.

In large-scale irrigation systems, storage tanks at the watercourse level help to reduce the coordination load of the system-level management (Wade and Seckler 1990). With these tanks, irrigators are able to match water supplies to local irrigation needs more precisely, which may not be possible if the system-level management has to bear all the information and transaction costs needed to fine-tune water supplies to various watercourses.

Storage facilities at the watercourse level also induce irrigators to conserve water because the water can be retained for future uses. Irrigators have less incentive to pursue "first capture" if they can be assured that they have a reliable access to at least a certain amount of water. With their increased ability in water control, irrigators are more likely to cooperate in water allocation and maintenance activities in their watercourses. Canal irrigation systems in such East Asian countries as Taiwan, Korea, and Japan normally consist of linked series of small reservoirs and canals, which are mostly absent in irrigation systems in South Asia. This, according to Wade (1988), makes irrigation systems in East Asia generally easier to manage than those in South Asia.

Although extra storage facilities may increase confidence among irrigators, they also create additional provision problems. Regular maintenance of the storage facilities becomes another CPR problem for irrigators. Furthermore, although storage may facilitate water control, the actual utility of the storage facilities depends on the proper operation of gates and other physical devices that control the flow of water. Sometimes, such control potentials generate other types of governance problems: who is to be responsible for opening and closing of gates? Unless a system exists to ensure whoever operates the gates will do so in accordance with the needs of irrigators, such facilities may be counterproductive.

Cell 4: Groundwater Basins

Cell 4 CPRs, such as groundwater basins, have relatively stationary flow units plus storage. The subterranean movement of water into, out of, and through a groundwater basin is so slow as to be relatively stationary from a user's perspective. Groundwater basins also have capacity to store water, although the amount and usefulness of that capacity differs among basins.

The evolution of institutional arrangements in seven southern California groundwater basins demonstrates the effects of stationary units and storage on the collective decisions taken by users. All seven basins experienced severe CPR problems, which became most acute in the middle decades of this century, as irrigated agriculture competed with, and ultimately yielded to, the rapid development of the southern California metropolis.

Collective action to address severe overdraft problems began in two of the basins during the 1930s. In the Orange County basin (Blomquist 1992), users initially organized for the provision-side activity of augmenting the supply of water to the basin by increasing the inflow of the principal surface stream that replenished the basin water supply, and by improving the stream channel to raise the rate of replenishment. Users created a public jurisdiction—the Orange County Water District—to pursue these development activities. Those activities reflected the opportunities created by stationary resource units and storage capacity. Users perceived the advantages of taking fugitive surface water flows and moving them underground, where they could be appropriated as needed by pumpers. In the 1950s, water users further institutionalized these arrangements by authorizing the Orange County Water District to tax groundwater pumping in order to finance purchases of replenishment water.

Users chose a different approach in the nearby Raymond Basin in Los Angeles County (Blomquist 1992). No collective efforts were made to augment the basin flow. Instead, an adjudication resulted in the determination of specific pumping rights based on historic use. Each pumper was assigned a specific share of available water, and total pumping rights were limited to a fixed estimate of the basin's annual "safe yield." The overdraft ceased, and the decline in underground water levels halted, and even reversed. After a few years' experience under the pumping restrictions, it appeared to pumpers that the estimate of the basin's safe yield had been too low. Individual and total pumping rights were adjusted upward slightly, and have remained at that modified level for 35 years.

Water users in two other Los Angeles County groundwater basins followed the Raymond Basin example between the mid-1940s and the mid-1960s. Adjudications in the West and Central basins produced determinations and limitations of pumping rights based on historic use (Blomquist 1992). However, users in these two basins went beyond mere quantity restrictions in three important ways. First, they authorized the leasing or sale of pumping rights, so individual quotas were transferable. Second, they adopted a program of taxing pumping to pay for imported water for basin replenishment, which facilitated users' willingness to accept the pumping restrictions. Third, because West and Central basins are coastal basins, they faced serious degradation problems due to saltwater intrusion from the ocean, which users addressed by constructing and operating freshwater injection barriers along the coast. (Subsequently, the Orange County Water District, which also governs a coastal basin, constructed barrier projects, too.)

New concepts in groundwater basin management, focusing on the active use of basin storage capacity, appeared during the 1960s. Thereafter, three more major groundwater basins in and around the Los Angeles area were adjudicated, but on a substantially different basis. The Main San Gabriel and San Fernando Valley basins in Los Angeles County were adjudicated during the 1960s and 1970s (Blomquist 1992), and the Chino Basin in the west end of San Bernardino County in the 1970s (Blomquist 1992). In these basins, instead of being assigned fixed pumping rights aggregating to a fixed safe yield, pumpers are assigned shares or proportions in a variable "operating safe yield" set each year in each basin by court-appointed watermasters. The "operating safe yield" is determined on the basis of both the basin's normal yield and water storage conditions within the basin. Watermasters are obliged to monitor the basin's available storage capacity and to maintain water in storage within desirable ranges. Furthermore, certain types of water users (overlying water districts in the Main San Gabriel Basin, municipalities in the San Fernando Valley Basin, and municipalities and other appropriators in the Chino Basin) are authorized to enter into agreements with their respective watermasters to store water in the basin for later use. Users in the Chino Basin may even sell their stored water to other pumpers.

On the other hand, it must be stated that water storage in a basin adds to the complexity of the basin management system, with potential for erroneous calculations. In the Chino Basin, for example, the Chino Basin Watermaster increased the amount of water in storage so much that water in the lower portion of the basin rose near the land surface, and users in that area complained that their water supplies were being contaminated by nitrate concentrations in the upper soil layers.

The relative lack of mobility of groundwater and storage capacity of groundwater basins has influenced the evolution of institutional arrangements for managing these basins in southern California. Users in six of the seven basins assigned rights to specific quantities of pumping from the basin, a flow allocation scheme that is substantially easier to devise, implement, and enforce with stationary flows. In the seventh basin, Orange County, pumpers are not limited to specific quantities of pumping, but are required to record and report their water production to the Orange County Water District and to pay taxes upon it. The district uses differential tax rates on pumpers to encourage conservation as necessary.

Conservation (i.e., restraint on pumping) in all seven basins is facilitated by the stationary flows and the availability of storage capacity. All seven basins authorize users to engage in "in lieu replenishment" of the basin (withholding pumping from the groundwater basin in certain periods in exchange for a reduced price on purchases of surface water when it is available in adequate quantities), and the six adjudicated basins permit users to "carry over" unused pumping rights from one year to the next. Neither of these management options would be as feasible if flows were fugitive or could not be stored within the basin.

Finally, the availability of storage has encouraged users to engage in provision-side activities for CPR management in addition to appropriation-side activities. In most of the basins, programs have been instituted for replenishing and storing water within the basin to augment future flows. In the three coastal basins (West, Central, and Orange County), users have financed very expensive barrier projects to halt the degradation of water quality resulting from seawater intrusion. These options also would be considerably more problematic were flows not relatively confined, making users more confident that they would reap the benefits of their provision action.

VI. Conclusion

The physical characteristics of mobility and storage affect the types of CPR problems resource users attempt to resolve, and the kinds of resolutions they adopt. Users of resources characterized by mobile flows and an absence of storage (Cell 1 of fig. 6.1) can exert little direct control over such flows. Thus, they are more likely to grapple with problems that arise when multiple individuals, attempting to capture mobile flows, interact within a defined area. If they are successful in adopting rules that coordinate their harvesting, those rules typically allocate space and/or time slots that ensure access to mobile flows while reducing conflict. For instance, fishers often allocate access to particularly productive spots through lotteries, or through taking turns (Faris 1972; Cordell 1972). Such rules promote predictable access and discourage fighting over spots (Berkes 1986). Or irrigators, in systems that lack storage, may allocate access to water by allocating time slots, with the length of the time slot determined by the amount of land irrigators hold.

Users of Cell 1 types of resources, in many instances, do not attempt to directly manage the mobile flows, since such flows are often unpredictable, and what benefits users would produce may be captured by others who also have access to those flows. Users of Cell 2, 3, and 4 types of resources, because of storage and/or stationary flows, however, can exert direct control over the flow units, and do, as is exhibited by the types of allocation rules that such users adopt. Instead of allocating access to flow units through time slots, access may be achieved by granting fixed or proportionate shares of the flow units to each resource user. For instance, in each of the California groundwater basins examined, except for one, pumpers owned transferable shares of water.

Control over flow units also affects means of addressing provision problems. Whereas Cell 1 resource users oftentimes cannot capture benefits produced by enhancing flow units, or by protecting them from degradation. Cell 2, 3, and 4 resource users can capture such benefits. Groundwater pumpers that prevent the intrusion of saltwater into their groundwater basins through the use of injection wells capture the benefits of preventing the degradation of their water. Those benefits do not flow into multiple basins to be enjoyed by others. Thus, in Cell 2, 3, and 4 CPRs, resource users may move beyond allocating access to flow units to actively managing the productivity of the resource, whether augmenting flow units, or preventing their degradation.

Depending on the physical characteristics of the resource, users may be better positioned to deal with one type of common-pool resource problem than with other types of problems. This means that government authorities have multiple roles to play in the effective governance of CPRs. In some situations resource users may be incapable of directly addressing troublesome problems. Consequently, government officials may have to play an active role by defining and enforcing rules that users themselves would have found too costly to define and enforce on their own. For instance, fishers from several different fishing grounds, all of which share flows of migratory fish, have few incentives to reduce their rate of harvesting, even though easing harvesting pressure would promote the maintenance of the fish stocks. It would be too costly for the fishers using spatially separate fishing grounds to obtain accurate information about patterns of fish migration, fish population changes, and harvesting activities of other fishers, not to mention negotiating agreements on a fair allocation of fishing effort, and then enforcing such agreements. Government authorities may be in a better position to collect crucial information, to force some type of an agreement on harvesting effort, and to enforce such agreements.

In other situations, resource users may be capable of designing and adopting institutional arrangements that address a variety of problems, but need some assistance from government authorities, either in providing a relatively predictable environment, or in providing critical types of information. For instance, Chambers (1988) argues that the key to improving the performance of many government-owned canal irrigation systems in South Asia is not just to organize irrigators below outlets, at the watercourse level, to solve appropriation problems. Rather, it is crucial that main system management be improved so that irrigators below outlets can expect a reasonably reliable supply of water from the main system. If irrigators expect a more predictable supply of water, they are more motivated to organize and solve provision problems that are within their competence, such as the regular maintenance of canals and ditches within their watercourse.

Or, in some cases government authorities are in a position to provide information that is necessary for users to develop institutional arrangements. For instance, conducting a geological survey of a groundwater basin is technically complex and very costly. The State of California and/or the U.S. Geological Survey provided the technical expertise and a portion of the funding for surveys of groundwater basins (Blomquist 1992). Groundwater pumpers then had the necessary information concerning the capacities of the basins, and the rate of depletion, to agree upon a "safe yield," and to devise specific pumping rights. Thus, the action of government officials need not be so direct that they devise and enforce rules at the watercourse level, or at the basin level. As mentioned in the introduction, resource users have considerable capacity to devise workable rules, in some instances they may simply need assistance in tapping that capacity.

Finally, government authorities may provide an environment that is supportive of resource users devising their own governing institutions. Government authorities can recognize and enforce agreements made among resource users. They can also provide arenas in which to resolve conflict peaceably. For instance, the fishers who participate in the cod trap fisheries of Newfoundland are permitted to organize and sit on cod trap berth committees. The committees operate a lottery that allocates cod trap berth spaces. The government of Newfoundland recognizes such committees and the fishing space over which they have jurisdiction, and allows fishers to use its courts to enforce, or challenge, the activities of such committees (Martin 1973). Or, the state of California provided a supportive environment for groundwater pumpers to devise their own solutions. As Ostrom (1990, 110) states, "The solutions to the pumping race, however were not imposed on the participants by external authorities. Rather, the participants used public arenas *to impose constraints on themselves.*"

Resource users are confronted with differing physical characteristics that affect their ability to devise institutional arrangements. The implication for government authorities is that in some instances workable solutions to common-pool resource problems will rely heavily upon time and place information possessed by resource users but not by government authorities. In those instances, the role of authorities should be to provide an environment that is supportive of resource users' efforts at governing themselves. In other instances, workable solutions to common-pool resource problems will rely primarily on resources and expert knowledge of government authorities. In those instances, the role of authorities will be more direct, from providing information to devising rules of use. Thus, the roles of governments, in order to be effective, must be diverse. Appropriately matching the activities of government authorities with the activities of resource users must be further pursued so that the growing body of knowledge concerning common-pool resources can inform and strengthen our understanding of policy decision-making processes (Pinkerton 1989; Ostrom 1990).

NOTES

1. In each of the settings examined, the resource users themselves were the *primary* designers of the institutional arrangements. In relation to the groundwater basins the users had access to formal governmental arrangements, that is, courts, water masters, to help design and enforce their arrangements, and in fisheries and irrigation systems some rules were imposed on users by outside authorities.

2. We do not claim that these are the only physical characteristics that differenti-

ate CPRs. Of course, common-pool resources differ on other physical characteristics, as well: renewability, the distribution of valued flow units throughout the resource, the visibility of the resource, etc. (See, e.g., Cass and Edney [1978] on the effects of visibility and territorial division. See Gilles and Jamtgaard [1981] for the effects of rapid feedback on the quality of resource flows.)

For our purposes, we examine the importance of mobility and storage, but recognize that they are not the only physical characteristics that affect the development of common property solutions. Nor do we claim that we alone have observed the importance of the distinction between stationary and mobile flows. Godwin and Shepard (1979, 277) discussed the relevance of that distinction at length, and concluded that a common error in the CPR literature had been "to treat a fugitive resource as if it were stationary." They added, *"Although it may seem trivial to point out, institutions must be designed to fit the character of the resource involved"* (1979, 277; emph. added).

3. Thus, by definition, fish and wildlife, or water in surface streams, are mobile, while trees and grasses, or water in groundwater basins, are more nearly stationary. Any resource unit—fodder, timber, fish, water, oil—is "mobile" in the sense of being transportable after it has been harvested from the resource.

Also, as suggested by one of the reviewers, the spatial mobility of resources units is only one of several characteristics associated with the flow of a resource. In some resources, for example, the flow of resource units changes over time, as in certain forests or fisheries where the amount of fodder or fish available varies with seasonal changes. While such temporal changes of resource flows are not the focus of this article, they deserve to be carefully studied because they are likely to have significant effects on strategies adopted by resource users.

4. Some resources may be amenable to the addition of human-made storage facilities, so the presence/absence of storage capacity is a somewhat oversimplified dichotomy. As we observe later, adding storage capacity to a CPR may be a strategy that resource users pursue in developing common property arrangements.

Furthermore, a reviewer constructively pointed out that the volume and type of a resource's storage capacity can differ. For example, the viability and efficiency of different strategies for operating an irrigation system will be affected by whether it has a single storage facility at the headworks or several smaller storage facilities distributed throughout. Here we focus on the importance of the presence or absence of storage capacity; more subtle analyses of the distinctions among types of storage need to be undertaken in the future.

5. In the case of fisheries, appropriation externalities are often referred to as stock externalities (Smith 1968).

6. We are not the first to recognize this point in relation to CPRs. There are a number of scholars who are pressing the point that the sparse models, typically grounded in neoclassical microeconomics, that are used to analyze CPRs are too sparse (1) to account for a variety of problems experienced by resource users, and (2) to provide the basis for developing workable policies. For instance, see Edward 1988; Townsend 1986, 1990, 1992; Wilson 1982, 1990. Or, as Wilson (1990, 12) has stated, "Although it may come as a surprise to persons unacquainted with fisheries economics, traditional theory assumes away the problem of finding fish."

7. Eggertsson (1990, 90) explains the distinction between resources and flow

units as follows: "When fishermen are given exclusive rights to patches of the ocean, they do not obtain control over migratory stocks of fish that migrate between the territorial waters of sovereign states. The fish stocks are still de facto common property."

8. As Ludwig, Hilborn, and Walters (1993, 17) point out: "Large levels of natural variability mask the effects of overexploitation. Initial overexploitation is not detectable until it is severe and often irreversible. In such circumstances, assigning causes to past events is problematical, future events cannot be predicted, and even well-meaning attempts to exploit responsibly may lead to disastrous consequences." For discussions of variability of flow units and the problems caused by it in relation to fisheries, see Dickie 1979; Cushing 1981; Wilson 1982.

9. In a fishery, for example, K. O. Martin (1979, 285) describes the views of some Newfoundland cod fishers: "Until very recently, Fermeuse fishermen have seldom thought of anyone's fishing activities, perhaps least of all their own, as having an appreciable effect upon fish populations. 'Queer things' happen, as in years when fish do not appear, but this is explained in terms of natural factors (e.g., a change in water temperature) over which man has no control."

In another Newfoundland fishery case, Shortall (1973, 92) describes a situation in which cod fishers experience both declining numbers and quality of fish available for harvest. The fishers believe that the causes of both problems lie elsewhere: "the main migration has been observed by the fishermen to enter the Petty Harbour area before mid-June and to consist of smaller fish schools and of fish of reduced average size. . . . The smaller size of the fish schools and the reduced average size of the fish, however, are attributed to the growth of the offshore fishing fleets and to the introduction of gillnets in the inshore fishery elsewhere."

10. Hannesson's (1988) review of fishermen's organizations throughout the world found no instances of their involvement in the management of migratory species.

11. In relation to fisheries, Townsend (1990, 372) argues that even attempts on the part of government agencies to address appropriation externalities and provision problems will meet with limited success. "One can argue, however, that it should have been clear (and perhaps was clear to some) that limited entry does not solve the underlying incentives of individual fishermen to catch as many fish as possible as soon as possible. Under virtually all limited entry programs, no fisherman can invest in future catches by delaying current catches. The destructive effects of this inherent competition are constrained by the limits on effort, but the fundamental incentives for individual fishermen are unchanged. Even under ITQs, the fisherman cannot reduce today's catch in return for higher catches tomorrow."

12. Glaser (1987) and Netting (1981) describe systems in the Swiss Alps where local officials make annual assessments of the fodder available and are thus able to regulate the amount harvested with a high degree of accuracy. See also Agrawal's (1994) description of annual assessments of grasses in India.

13. The work of Agrawal (1994), Netting (1981), Glaser (1987) is quite consistent with our analysis.

14. Request copies of coding forms from Julie England, Workshop in Political Theory and Policy Analysis, 513 North Park, Bloomington, IN 47408.

15. The fisheries cases were coded by Schlager. The irrigation cases were coded

by Tang. The reliability of the coding of each case was checked by having another member of the research team review each coding. Disagreements on the proper way of coding were discussed and resolved in regular meetings of the project. In addition, the coding of several cases was reviewed by the case authors themselves, who agreed with the original coding at a very high level. The data are stored in R-Base. Direct inquiries concerning the fisheries data to Schlager and the irrigation data to Tang.

16. Recently, Eggertsson (1990) reviewed some of the literature on institutions and the management of fisheries, and found substantial evidence for inferring that the physical characteristics of fisheries affect strongly the types of institutional arrangements fishers develop. He found that organizations of fishers were substantially less likely to attempt to manage migratory species (1990, 267), and that gear restrictions were generally preferred to individual quotas for most species except for relatively stationary "bottom-dwellers" (1990, 97, 266–67). Eggertsson attributed the differences primarily to enforcement costs, which he argued have been largely ignored by economists advocating individual quotas.

17. Fishers have designed, implemented, and enforced virtually all of the rules that exist in each of the 25 fishing grounds, with the exception of rules that require fishers to harvest fish of at least a minimum size, as discussed later in the text. How fishers have organized themselves to make collective decisions concerning their fishing grounds varies from state sanctioned cooperatives to informal meetings at local coffeehouses (Cordell 1972; Berkes 1986).

18. Four questions were used to identify these four outcomes, respectively:

1. If the quantity or quality of units is regularly better in some of the zones of the resource than in others, has this condition created conflict among the appropriators?
2. Characterize the balance between the quantity of units withdrawn and the number of units available on a 5-point scale ranging from extreme shortage to quite abundant. If a fishing ground was coded as a (1), extreme shortage, or a (2), moderate shortage, the fishers were considered to be experiencing appropriation externalities and/or maintenance problems.
3. Characterize the quality of units being withdrawn on a 5-point scale, ranging from extremely poor quality to extremely high quality. If a fishing ground was coded as a (1), extremely poor quality, or a (2), poor quality, the fishers were considered to be experiencing maintenance problems and/or degradation problems.
4. Characterize the extent of technological externalities resulting from the appropriation activities of participants from this resource on a 5-point scale, ranging from very high levels to quite low levels. If a fishing ground was coded as a (1), very high levels, a (2), relatively high levels, or a (3), modest levels, the fishers were considered to be experiencing technological externalities.

19. That exception is the Cree Indians in northern Canada as reported by Berkes (1977, 1987).

20. That is not to say that individual transferable quotas (ITQs) are never used in fisheries. In fact, it is quite the opposite. ITQs are quickly becoming one of the most

popular regulatory regimes for fisheries (Copes 1986). ITQs, however, are almost always devised, implemented, and enforced by government agencies charged with regulating fisheries. Fishers, in devising self-governing arrangements, rarely adopted such rules. There are, of course, exceptions. See McCay 1980; and Sturgess, Dow, and Belin 1982, for attempts on the part of fishers to influence market prices by devising quotas.

21. Irrigators have designed, implemented, and enforced virtually all of the rules that exist in each of the 23 irrigation systems. The specific governance structures of these systems, however, vary from case to case. For details, see Tang 1992.

22. All of these irrigation systems rely on water coming from nearby rivers, streams, or tunnels. In four of the systems—Calaoaan, Sabangan Bato, Silag-Butir, and Kheri—irrigators have access to spring waters as supplementary sources.

23. In an irrigation system, more than one set of allocation rules may be used for different occasions. In many irrigation systems, a more restrictive set of allocation rules is used during a certain period of time in a year and a less restrictive set is used during another. The allocation rules discussed here are the most restrictive ones reported in the cases.

24. Fixed time slots are especially effective in times when the flow of water in the system is relatively steady. Problems arise when the water flow is highly erratic because an irrigator owning a particular slot is still uncertain about his water supply (see Tang 1991).

REFERENCES

Agrawal, Arun. 1994. "Rules, Rule Making, and Rule Breaking: Examining the Fit Between Rule Systems and Resource Use." In *Rules, Games and Common-Pool Resources*, ed. E. Ostrom, R. Gardner, and J. Walker, 267–82. Ann Arbor: University of Michigan Press.

Alexander, Paul. 1982. *Sri Lankan Fishermen: Rural Capitalism and Peasant Society.* Canberra: Australian National University Press.

Anderson, Eugene N., Jr., and Marja L. Anderson. 1977. *Fishing in Troubled Waters: Research on the Chinese Fishing Industry in West Malaysia.* Taipei: Chinese Association for Folklore.

Anderson, Lee. 1977. *The Economics of Fisheries Management.* Baltimore: Johns Hopkins University Press.

Bacdayan, Albert S. 1980. "Mountain Irrigators in the Philippines." In *Irrigation and Agricultural Development in Asia,* ed. W. Coward. Ithaca, NY: Cornell University Press.

Berkes, Fikret. 1977. "Fishery Resource Use in a Subarctic Indian Community." *Human Ecology* 5, no. 4:289–307.

———. 1986. "Marine Inshore Fishery Management in Turkey." In *Proceedings of the Conference on Common Property Resource Management,* National Research Council, 63–83. Washington, DC: National Academy Press.

———. 1987. "Common Property Resource Management and Cree Indian Fishermen in Subarctic Canada." In *The Question of the Commons: The Culture and*

Ecology of Communal Resources, ed. B. J. McCay and J. M. Acheson, 66–91. Tucson: University of Arizona Press.

————, ed. 1989. *Common Property Resources: Ecology and Community-Based Sustainable Development*. London: Belhaven Press.

Blomquist, William. 1992. *Dividing the Waters: Governing Groundwater in Southern California*. San Francisco: Institute for Contemporary Studies Press.

Brameld, Theodore. 1968. *Japan: Culture, Education, and Change in Two Communities*. New York: Holt, Rinehart, and Winston.

Breton, Yvan D. 1973. "A Comparative Study of Rural Fishing Communities in Eastern Venezuela: An Anthropological Explanation of Economic Specialization." Ph.D. diss., Michigan State University.

Bromley, Daniel W., ed. 1992. *Making the Commons Work: Theory, Practice, and Policy*. San Francisco: Institute for Contemporary Studies Press.

Bromley, Daniel W., and Michael Cernea. 1989. "The Management of Common Property Natural Resources: Some Conceptual and Operational Fallacies." World Bank Discussion Paper No. 57. Washington, DC: World Bank.

Cass, Robert C., and Julian J. Edney. 1978. "The Commons Dilemma: A Simulation Testing the Effects of Resource Visibility and Territorial Division." *Human Ecology* 6, no. 4:371–86.

Chambers, Robert. 1988. *Managing Canal Irrigation: Practical Analysis from South Asia*. New York: Cambridge University Press.

Ciriacy-Wantrup, S. V., and Richard C. Bishop. 1975. "Common Property as a Concept in Natural Resource Policy." *Natural Resources Journal* 15 (Oct.): 713–27.

Copes, Parzival. 1986. "A Critical Review of the Individual Quota as a Device in Fisheries Management." *Land Economics* 62 (Aug.): 278–89.

Cordell, John C. 1972. "The Developmental Ecology of an Estuarine Canoe Fishing System in Northeast Brazil." Ph.D. diss., Stanford University.

————. 1978. "Carrying Capacity Analysis of Fixed Territorial Fishing." *Ethnology* 17 (Jan.): 1–24.

————. 1983. "Social Marginality and Sea Tenure in Brazilian Fishing." Occasional Papers in Latin American Studies Association, No. 7:1–21. Stanford, CA: Joint Center for Latin American Studies.

————. 1984. "Traditional Sea Tenure and Resource Management in Brazilian Coastal Fishing." In *Management of Coastal Lagoon Fisheries*, ed. J. M. Kapetsky and G. Lasserre, 429–38. GFCM Studies and Reviews No. 61. Rome: Food and Agriculture Organization.

Coward, E. Walter, Jr. 1979. "Principles of Social Organization in an Indigenous Irrigation System." *Human Organization* 38, no. 1:28–36.

Cushing, D. H. 1981. *Fisheries Biology: A Study in Population Dynamics*. Madison: University of Wisconsin Press.

Davenport, William H. 1956. "A Comparative Study of Two Jamaican Fishing Communities." Ph.D. diss., Yale University.

Davis, Adam F. (Anthony). 1975. "The Organization of Production and Market Relations in Nova Scotian Inshore Fishing Community." Ph.D. diss., University of Manitoba.

Davis, Anthony (Adam F.). 1984. "Property Rights and Access Management in the Small Boat Fishery: A Case Study from Southwest Nova Scotia." In *Atlantic Fisheries and Coastal Communities: Fisheries Decision-Making Case Studies,* eds. C. Lamson and A. J. Hanson, 133–64. Halifax: Dalhousie Ocean Studies Programme.

de los Reyes, Romana P., et al. 1980a. "Forty-seven Communal Gravity Systems: Organization Profiles." Quezon City, Philippines: Institute of Philippine Culture, Ateneo de Manila University.

de los Reyes, Romana P., S. Bortavian, G. Gatdula, and M. F. Viado. 1980b. "Communal Gravity Systems: Four Case Studies." Quezon City, Philippines: Ateneo de Manila University, Institute of Philippine Culture.

Dickie, L. M. 1979. "Perspectives on Fisheries Biology and Implications for Management." *Journal of the Fisheries Research Board of Canada* 36, no. 7:838–44.

Edwards, Steven. 1988. "Option Prices for Groundwater Protection." *Journal of Environmental Economics and Management* 15, no. 4:475–513.

Eggertsson, Thráinn. 1990. *Economic Behavior and Institutions.* Cambridge: Cambridge University Press.

Faris, James. 1972. *Cat Harbour: A Newfoundland Fishing Settlement.* Newfoundland Social and Economic Studies No. 3. Toronto: University of Toronto Press.

Feeny, David, Fikret Berkes, Bonnie McCay, and James Acheson. 1990. "The Tragedy of the Commons: Twenty-Two Years Later." *Human Ecology* 18, no. 1:1–13.

Firth, Raymond. 1966. *Malay Fishermen: Their Peasant Economy,* 2d ed. London: Routledge and Kegan Paul.

Forman, Shepard L. 1966. "Jangadeiros: Raft Fishermen of Northeastern Brazil." Ph.D. diss., Columbia University.

———. 1970. *The Raft Fishermen: Tradition and Change in the Brazilian Peasant Economy.* Bloomington: Indiana University Press.

Fowler, Darlene, ed. 1986. "Rapid Appraisal of Nepal Irrigation Systems." WMS Report 43. Fort Collins: Colorado State University. Water Management Synthesis Project.

Fraser, Thomas M., Jr. 1960. *Rusembilan: A Malay Fishing Village in Southern Thailand.* Ithaca, NY: Cornell University Press.

———. 1966. *Fishermen of South Thailand: The Malay Villagers.* New York: Holt, Rinehart and Winston.

Gilles, J. L., and K. Jamtgaard. 1981. "Overgrazing in Pastoral Areas: The Commons Reconsidered." *Sociologia Ruralos* 21:129–41.

Glaser, Christina. 1987. "Common Property Regimes in Swiss Alpine Meadows." Presented at the Conference on Comparative Institutional Analysis, Inter-University Center of Postgraduate Studies, Dubrovnik, Yugoslavia, 19–23 Oct.

Godwin, R. Kenneth, and W. Bruce Shepard. 1979. "Forcing Squares, Triangles and Ellipses into a Circular Paradigm: The Use of the Commons Dilemma in Examining the Allocation of Common Resources." *Western Political Quarterly* 32, no. 3:265–77.

Gray, Robert. 1963. *The Sonjo of Tanganyika.* Oxford: Oxford University Press.

Han, Sang-Bok. 1972. "Socio-Economic Organization and Change in Korean Fishing

Villages: A Comparative Study of Three Fishing Communities." Ph.D. diss., Michigan State University.

Hannesson, Rögnvaldur. 1988. "Studies on the Role of Fishermen's Organizations in Fisheries Management: Theoretical Considerations and Experiences from Industrialized Countries." *FAO Fisheries Technical Paper* 300:1–27.

Kotsonias, G. 1984. "The Messolonghi-Etolico Lagoon of Greece: Socioeconomic and Ecological Interactions of Cooperatives and Independent Fishermen." In *Management of Coastal Lagoon Fisheries,* ed. J. M. Kapetsky and G. Lasserre, 521–28. GFCM Studies and Reviews No. 61. Rome: Food and Agriculture Organization.

Kottak, Conrad. 1966. "The Structure of Equality in a Brazilian Fishing Community." Ph.D. diss., Columbia University.

Ludwig, Donald, Ray Hilborn, and Carl Walters. 1993. "Uncertainty, Resource Exploitation, and Conservation: Lessons From History." *Science* 260 (Apr.): 17, 36.

Maass, Arthur, and Raymond L. Anderson. 1986. . . . *and the Desert Shall Rejoice: Conflict, Growth, and Justice in Arid Environments.* Malabar, FL: Krieger.

Martin, Edward, and Robert Yoder. 1983a. "Water Allocation and Resource Mobilization for Irrigation: A Comparison of Two Systems in Nepal." Paper presented at the annual meeting of the Nepal Studies Association, Nov. 4–6. University of Wisconsin, Madison.

——. 1983b. "The Chherlung Thulo Kulo: A Case Study of A Farmer-Managed Irrigation System." In *Water Management in Nepal,* app. 1, 203–17. Kathmandu: Ministry of Agriculture.

——. 1986. "Institutions for Irrigation Management in Farmer-Managed Systems: Examples from the Hills of Nepal." Digana Village, Sri Lanka: International Irrigation Research Paper No. 5, Dec.

Martin, Fenton. 1989. *Common Pool Resources and Collective Action: A Bibliography,* vol. 1. Bloomington: Indiana University, Workshop in Political Theory and Policy Analysis.

——. 1992. *Common Pool Resources and Collective Action: A Bibliography,* vol. 2. Bloomington: Indiana University, Workshop in Political Theory and Policy Analysis.

Martin, Kent O. 1973. " 'The Law in St. John's Says . . .': Space Division and Resource Allocation in the Newfoundland Fishing Community of Fermeuse." Master's thesis, Department of Anthropology, Memorial University of Newfoundland.

——. 1979. "Play by the Rules or Don't Play at All: Space Division and Resource Allocation in a Rural Newfoundland Fishing Community." In *North Atlantic Maritime Cultures: Anthropological Essays on Changing Adaptations,* ed. R. Andersen, 276–98. The Hague: Mouton.

McCay, Bonnie. 1980. "A Fisherman's Cooperative: Limited, Indigenous Resource Management in a Complex Society." *Anthropological Quarterly* 53, no. 1:29–38.

McCay, Bonnie J., and James M. Acheson. 1987. *The Question of the Commons: The Culture and Ecology of Communal Resources.* Tucson: University of Arizona Press.

McKean, Margaret. 1992. "Management of Traditional Common Lands (*Iriaichi*) in Japan." In *Making the Commons Work: Theory, Practice, and Policy*, ed. D. W. Bromley, 63–98. San Francisco: Institute for Contemporary Studies Press.

Miller, David. 1982. "Mexico's Caribbean Fishery: Recent Change and Current Issues." Ph.D. diss., University of Wisconsin-Milwaukee.

————. 1989. "The Evolution of Mexico's Spiny Lobster Fishery." In *Common Property Resources Ecology and Community-Based Sustainable Development*, ed. F. Berkes, 185–98. London: Belhaven Press.

National Research Council. 1986. *Proceedings of the Conference on Common Property Resource Management*. Washington, DC: National Academy Press.

Netting, Robert McC. 1974. "The System Nobody Knows: Village Irrigation in the Swiss Alps." In *Irrigation's Impact of Society*, eds. T. Downing and M. Gibson. Tucson: University of Arizona Press.

————. 1981. *Balancing on an Alp: Ecological Change and Continuity in a Swiss Mountain Community*. New York: Cambridge University Press.

Nietschmann, Bernard. 1972. "Hunting and Fishing Focus Among the Miskito Indians, Eastern Nicaragua." *Human Ecology* 1, no. 1:41–67.

————. 1973. *Between Land and Water: The Subsistence Ecology of the Miskito Indians, Eastern Nicaragua*. New York: Seminar Press.

Ostrom, Elinor. 1990. *Governing the Commons: The Evolution of Institutions for Collective Action*. New York: Cambridge University Press.

Ostrom, Elinor, Roy Gardner, and James Walker. 1994. *Rules, Games and Common-Pool Resources*. Ann Arbor: University of Michigan Press.

Pinkerton, Evelyn, ed. 1989. *Co-operative Management of Local Fisheries: New Directions for Improved Management and Community Development*. Vancouver: University of British Columbia Press.

Potter, Jack M. 1976. *Thai Peasant Social Structure*. Chicago: University of Chicago Press.

Powers, Ann M. 1984. "Social Organization in a Newfoundland Fishing Settlement on the Burin Peninsula." Ph.D. diss., State University of New York, Stony Brook.

Raychaudhuri, Bikash. 1972. *The Moon and Net: Study of a Transient Community of Fishermen at Jambudwip*. Calcutta: Anthropological Survey of India.

Schlager, Edella. 1990. "Model Specification and Policy Analysis: The Governance of Coastal Fisheries." Ph.D. diss., Indiana University.

————. 1994. "Fishers' Institutional Responses to Common-Pool Resource Dilemmas." In *Rules, Games and Common-Pool Resources* by E. Ostrom, R. Gardner, and J. Walker, 247–65. Ann Arbor: University of Michigan Press.

Shortall, D. 1973. "Environmental Perception in Two Local Fisheries: A Case Study from Eastern Newfoundland." Master's thesis, Memorial University of Newfoundland.

Smith, Vernon. 1968. "Economics of Production from Natural Resources." *American Economic Review* 58, no. 3:409–31.

Spooner, Brian. 1971. "Continuity and Change in Rural Iran: The Eastern Deserts." In *Iran: Continuity and Variety*, ed. P. J. Chelkowski. New York: New York University, Center for Near Eastern Studies and the Center for International Studies.

————. 1972. "The Iranian Deserts." In *Population Growth: Anthropological Implications*, ed. B. Spooner. Cambridge: MIT Press.

————. 1974. "Irrigation and Society: The Iranian Plateau." In *Irrigation's Impact on Society*, ed. T. Downing and M. Gibson. Tucson: University of Arizona Press.

Sturgess, N. H., N. Dow, and P. Belin. 1982. "Management of the Victorian Scallop Fisheries: Retrospect and Prospect." In *Policy and Practice in Fisheries Management*, ed. N. H. Sturgess and T. F. Meany, 277–316. Canberra: Australian Government Publishing Service.

Tang, Shui-Yan. 1991. "Institutional Arrangements and the Management of Common-Pool Resources." *Public Administration Review* 51, no. 1:42–51.

————. 1992. *Institutions and Collective Action: Self-Governance in Irrigation.* San Francisco: Institute for Contemporary Studies Press.

Tan-kim-yong, Uraivan. 1983. "Resource Mobilization in Traditional Irrigation Systems of Northern Thailand: A Comparison Between the Lowland and the Upland Irrigation Communities." Ph.D. diss., Cornell University.

Townsend, Ralph E. 1986. "A Critique of Models of the American Lobster Fishery." *Journal of Environmental Economics and Management* 13:277–91.

————. 1990. "Entry Restrictions in the Fishery: A Survey of the Evidence." *Land Economics* 66 (Nov.): 359–79.

————. 1992. "A Fractional Licensing Program for Fisheries." *Land Economics* 68 (May): 185–94.

U.S. Advisory Commission on Intergovernmental Relations (U.S. ACIR). 1991. *Coordinating Water Resources in the Federal System: The Groundwater-Surface Water Connection.* Report No. A-118. Washington, DC: U.S. ACIR.

Wade, Robert. 1988. "The Management of Irrigation Systems: How to Evoke Trust and Avoid Prisoner's Dilemma." *World Development* 16, no. 4:489–500.

Wade, Robert, and David Seckler. 1990. "Priority Issues in the Management of Irrigation Systems." In *Social, Economic, and Institutional Issues in Third World Irrigation Management*, ed. R. K. Sampath and R. A. Young, 13–29. Boulder, CO: Westview Press.

Water and Engineering Commission. 1987. *Rapid Appraisal Study of Eight Selected Micro-Areas of Farmers' Irrigation Systems.* Final Report. Kathmandu, Nepal: Ministry of Water Resources.

Wilson, James M. 1982. "The Economical Management of Multispecies Fisheries." *Land Economics* 58 (Nov.): 417–34.

————. 1990. "Fishing for Knowledge." *Land Economics* 66 (Feb.): 12–29.

Part II
Constitutional Order

CHAPTER 7

A Forgotten Tradition: The Constitutional Level of Analysis

Vincent Ostrom

This chapter will attempt to provide some basic theoretical ideas that may be useful for increasing synthesis in the study of political institutions. I proceed on three assumptions. First, political science is concerned with the study of government. Second, government is a matter of human design and choice. Third, the level of choice that applies to the specification of the terms and conditions of governance is one of constitutional choice (Ostrom 1980).

At the constitutional level of analysis, one is concerned with basic questions of why human beings have recourse to political institutions, and what options are available. One is also concerned about what implications follow from alternative possibilities and what criteria are used, or what purposes are served, in the choices that are made among the alternative possibilities. Thus, political theory has a special relevance for the constitutional level of analysis. The constitutional level of analysis has a fundamental role in clarifying the design of structural arrangements that apply to the play of the games of politics. The play of a game is determined by the rules of the game; and the rules establishing the terms and conditions of governance are constitutional in character. The constitutional level of analysis, then, informs the operational level of analysis of who gets what, when, and how (Lasswell 1936).

The American political system was created as the result of a series of relatively self-conscious efforts in design. This design reflects considerations of a distinctive nature that are not characteristic of the organization of all political systems. In particular, the designers of the American system of government used a federal, rather than a unitary, conception as the proper structure for a democratic polity. Yet we confront the puzzling circumstance that the dominant tendencies among American political scientists in the last

Originally published in Judith A. Gillespie and Dina A. Zinnes, eds., *Missing Elements in Political Inquiry: Logic and Levels of Analysis* (Beverly Hills, CA: Sage Publications, 1982), 237–52. Copyright 1982 by Sage Publications, Inc. Reprinted by permission of Sage Publications, Inc., and the author.

151

century have been: (1) to reject the theory upon which the design of the American political system was based, (2) to accept the logic of a unitary state governed in accordance with principles of a Westminster-type parliamentary system as the appropriate model for the organization of a democratic society, and (3) to adopt the methodology of the natural sciences as the appropriate way to study political phenomena. The stance taken by political analysts in the twentieth century poses rather fundamental questions about the relationship of knowledge to the design and construction of political experience. Are artifacts created by design to be studied as though they were natural phenomena? Or does the study of artifacts require that the intentions, conceptions, and calculations of the designers be taken into account in understanding the nature of an artifact? These questions pose important theoretical and methodological problems for political scientists.

In developing this chapter, I shall turn first to the design of the American constitutional system. I shall then turn to the twentieth-century break with that tradition. Finally, I shall explore the issue of how to construe the essential characteristics of the American political system.

The Design of the American Constitutional System

The American Declaration of Independence, as a founding document, serves as a general preamble to the various experiments in constitutional choice that occurred both within the states and in the larger community shared by the several states. The Declaration opens with a presumption that a people, in dissolving the bonds that have connected them with another people, owe an explanation to the rest of mankind for the action being taken. Choice exists and choice is grounded in reason. A reasoned explanation is due to others.

The grounds and criteria justifying the Declaration of Independence are stated in the following language:

> We hold these Truths to be self-evident, that all Men are created equal, that they are endowed by their Creator with certain unalienable Rights, that among these are Life, Liberty, and the pursuit of Happiness—That to secure these Rights, Governments are instituted among Men, deriving their just Powers from the Consent of the Governed, that whenever any Form of Government becomes destructive of these Ends, it is the Right of the People to alter or to abolish it, and to institute new Government, laying its Foundation on such Principles, and organizing its Powers in such Form, as to them shall seem most likely to effect their Safety and Happiness.

In this statement, basic presuppositions are postulated about the human condition. That condition implies both being and becoming. Governments are instituted among human beings to realize potentials. That which is instituted is artifactual in nature. It is created as a conscious effort in design using principles articulated through forms to accomplish specific purposes. The criterion that is appropriate to the exercise of governmental prerogatives is the informed consent of the community of people who are being governed. Whenever governments as artifacts are destructive of the ends for which they are instituted, The Declaration asserts the "Right of the People" to engage in processes of constitutional decision making with a view to altering or abolishing an existing government or of instituting a new government. The design of institutions of government is a subject of choice where human beings can draw upon knowable principles and design structures in appropriate forms to further human aspirations.

Alexander Hamilton makes a similar observation about the problem of design in the opening paragraph of *Federalist* 1:

It has been frequently remarked that it seems to have been reserved to the people of this country, by their conduct and example, to decide the important question, whether societies of men are really capable or not of establishing good government from reflection and choice, or whether they are forever destined to depend for their political constitutions on accident and force. If there be any truth in the remark, the crisis at which we are arrived may with propriety be regarded as the era in which that decision is to be made; and a wrong election of the part we shall act may, in this view, deserve to be considered as the general misfortune of mankind. (3)

Hamilton's observation is much more problematical than the Declaration's assertion of the "Right of the People to alter or to abolish" an existing government "and to institute new Government." Experience with organizing a government under the Articles of Confederation had, so far as Hamilton was concerned, proved to be a failure. The task proclaimed in the Declaration was both more problematical and more revolutionary in the sweep of human history than had been anticipated. A federal union was necessary to the maintenance of peace of the North American continent. Otherwise, a multitude of states could be expected to repeat the experience of Europe in warring upon one another. Their constitutions would then be determined by accident and force. But, confederations had proved a failure. It was necessary to go back to first principles in devising a federal system of government where its structure of concurrent governments would extend to the person of citizens in their individual capacities and be limited by constitutional rules as enforceable laws (see relevant discussions especially in *Federalist* 8, 15, and 16).

The Americans were, thus, to determine whether institutions of government could be designed by reflection and choice or whether it was the fate of mankind to be governed by institutions over which they had little or no control. If Hamilton was correct, the American experiment in constitutional choice represented an epochal development in the human political experiment that was of substantial significance for a political science. Political science would contribute to the design of political institutions fashioned on the basis of reflection and choice.

Madison in *Federalist* 14 takes a similar position when he observes that the American Revolution implied a major break with the past. Madison articulates this contention in the following words:

> Had no important step been taken by the leaders of the Revolution for which a precedent could not be discovered, no government established of which an exact model did not present itself, the people of the United States might, at this moment, have been numbered among the melancholy victims of misguided councils, must at best have been laboring under the weight of some of those forms which have crushed the liberties of the rest of mankind. Happily for America, happily, we trust, for the whole human race, they pursued a new and more noble course. They accomplished a revolution which has no parallel in the annals of human society. They reared the fabrics of governments which have no model on the face of the globe. They formed the design of a great Confederacy, which it is incumbent on their successors to improve and perpetuate. If their works betray imperfections, we wonder at the fewness of them. If they erred most in the structure of the Union, this was the work most difficult to be executed, this is the work which has been new modelled by the act of your convention, and it is that act on which you are now to deliberate and to decide. (Hamilton, Jay, and Madison n.d.: 85)

In presenting their arguments in *The Federalist,* both Hamilton and Madison explicitly assert that they draw upon a body of knowledge identified as a science of politics. They make systematic use of the theory inherent in a science of politics to conduct their analysis and present their arguments. In *Federalist* 9, for example, Hamilton observes that there have been those throughout history who have "decried all free government as inconsistent with the order of society." However, he goes on to observe that innovations have occurred in the design of republican institutions of government that enhance their viability. In doing so he explicitly states:

The science of politics, however, like most other sciences, has received great improvement. The efficacy of various principles is now well understood, which were either not known at all, or imperfectly known to the ancients. The regular distribution of power into distinct departments; the introduction of legislative balances and checks; the institution of courts composed of judges holding their offices during good behavior; the representation of the people in the legislature by deputies of their own election; these are wholly new discoveries, or have made their principle progress towards perfection in modern times. They are means, and powerful means, by which the excellences of republican government may be retained and its imperfections lessened or avoided. (Hamilton, Jay, and Madison n.d.: 48–49)

After having recited these contributions of political science to the design of republican institutions, Hamilton then goes on to advance the contention that a new principle—that of federalism—might be added to the list of new discoveries in a science of politics. It is this principle that provided an important element in the design of the new constitution and was also the primary source of objections to the new constitution.

Both Hamilton and Madison draw upon a structure of axiomatic reasoning that enables them to explain why particular provisions were made in the proposed constitution and what consequences can be expected to follow. In doing so, they are using the logic of theoretical reasoning as a fundamental tool that enables human beings to use their capacity to reason, and thus, to inform choice. Theory is used both to engage in positive analysis to clarify the implications that follow from particular structural characteristics and to clarify normative criteria used in the design of a constitution. Examples of positive analysis include Hamilton's clarification of the implications that follow when governments presume to govern other collectivities rather than reaching to the person of the individual (*Federalist* 15 and 16) or Madison's clarification of the oligarchical tendencies inherent in the size of deliberative assemblies, whether of a direct democracy or of a representative republic (*Federalist* 55 and 58).

Considerations of design also require reference to normative criteria, or considerations of value, in selecting among alternative possibilities. Criteria relevant to human choice generally and to constitutional choice in particular are given explicit attention in *The Federalist*. Madison warns that "choice must always be made, if not of the lesser evil, at least of the GREATER, not the PERFECT, good" (Hamilton, Jay, and Madison n.d.: 260). In *Federalist* 37, he explains the tradeoffs that occur in the design of governmental institutions with reference to such values as energy in government, stability, safety, and republican liberty. In *Federalist* 31, Hamilton gives quite explicit attention to the use of moral and jurisprudential reasoning to considerations of institutional design.

Having contended that serious mistakes had been made in the constitution of the first American confederation, neither Hamilton nor Madison argue that their formulations were infallible. Rather they argue that both the proponents and the opponents of the new constitution "ought not to assume an infallibility in rejudging the fallible opinions of others" (Hamilton, Jay, and Madison n.d.: 226). Language, by its application to classes of events, implies simplification and vulnerability to error. Moreover, in the case of the formation of human institutions, people use words to express ideas whose referents are not the objects of nature but relationships among human beings. The design of human institutions thus depends upon the use of language to conceptualize arrangements that exist and have meaning only in human thought and experience. Greater ambiguities inevitably exist in the use of language as a tool for reasoning about human institutions than about material conditions.

Given these limitations, both Hamilton and Madison contended that the appropriate test for the conceptions being acted upon in formulating the design of the Constitution of 1787 was to try the experiment and see whether concepts yielded the consequences that were anticipated. If the plan of the convention contained errors based upon inadequate experience and understanding, those errors "will not be ascertained until an actual trial shall have pointed them out" (Hamilton, Jay, and Madison n.d.: 235). Hamilton, in the concluding essay of *The Federalist* (574), quotes David Hume to the effect that:

> To balance a large state or society . . . , whether monarchical or republican, on general laws, is a work of so great difficulty, that no human genius, however comprehensive, is able, by the mere dint of reason and reflection, to effect it. The judgments of many must unite in the work; experience must guide their labor; time must bring it to perfection, and the feeling of inconveniences must correct the mistakes which they *inevitably* fall into in their first trials and experiments.

In the course of elaborating the design of a system of government where the exercise of governmental prerogative would be subject to the rule of law, Americans in the revolutionary era were engaged in a novel experiment in human governance of special significance for a science of politics. Thomas Hobbes (1651: chap. 18) had earlier argued that those who exercise the prerogatives of government are the source of law, and, as such, are above the law. They cannot be held accountable to law. Hobbes's theory of sovereignty assumed that the unity inherent in a system of law derived from having a single ultimate source of law. This implies that those who exercise governmental prerogatives have indivisible authority that is not subject to limits.

The American experiment in constitutional choice was based upon radically different conceptions. These conceptions held that the prerogatives of government could be limited by a rule of law provided that several conditions could be met. First, a constitution need be distinguished from ordinary law. A constitution supplies the rules of law applicable to the conduct of government, while ordinary law applies to relationships among individual members of a society. This distinction can be maintained so long as the processes of constitutional decision making are separated from the processes of governmental decision making. A constitution, according to Madison, is "established by the people and unalterable by the government and a law [is] established by the government and alterable by the government" (Hamilton, Jay, and Madison n.d.: 348).

Given the special juridical status of a constitution as law applicable to the organization and conduct of government, the terms and conditions of constitutions might then incorporate those provisions that facilitate the maintenance of a rule of law. This poses a puzzling problem. Laws are without meaning unless they can be enforced. A distinguishing characteristic of government is that those who exercise the prerogatives of government have access to powers of coercion usually symbolized as the sword of justice. Enforcing rules of law upon those who exercise the prerogatives of government implies the enforcement of law upon the enforcers. Conceptualizing a solution to this problem was no small task.

In the American case, this task of establishing rules of law that applied to rulers was accomplished by specifying limits to all exercise of governmental prerogatives through the distribution of authority to diverse decision structures. A separation of powers with reciprocal veto capabilities implies that the authority of each set of governmental decision makers is subject to limits and that no single center of ultimate authority exists in the American system of government. A sharing of powers within the constraints of reciprocal veto positions is necessary in establishing the legal and political feasibility of any course of collective action. In addition, the prerogatives of government are subject to limits that recognize the correlative constitutional rights of individuals both to act separately and collectively in the performance of governmental functions without interference by governmental authorities.

Constitutional provision is also made for both the direct and indirect participation of citizens in decision-making processes of government. Citizen participation through elections is well recognized among political scientists, but we also need to recognize that making provision for trial by jury involves the direct participation of citizens in the judicial process where the implementation of law is being determined.

Finally, both Hamilton and Madison recognize that constitutional provisions and a distribution of powers, "in such a manner as that each may be a check on the other—that the private interest of every individual may be a sentinel over the public rights" (Hamilton, Jay, and Madison n.d.: 337), is insufficient to maintain the enforceability of constitutional law. There comes a point where the maintenance of a constitutional order depends upon the limits enforced by the decisions that citizens take. This is recognized when Hamilton observes:

> Everything beyond this must be left to the prudence and firmness of the people; who, as they will hold the scales in their own hands, it is to be hoped, will always take care to preserve the constitutional equilibrium between the general and the State government. (Hamilton, Jay, and Madison n.d.: 193)

This observation need not be limited to relationships between the national and state governments but might apply to other constitutional equilibria. Madison even anticipates that enterprises of ambition, such as a military coup, might be successfully resisted in the American constitutional system (*Federalist* 41). Hamilton implicitly recognizes the right in individuals to resist enactments of Congress and seek judicial remedies against legislative usurpation of constitutional powers in his discussion of judicial review in *Federalist* 78.

Formal constitutional limits are necessary in creating opportunities for citizens to impose limits and gain access to the exercise of governmental prerogatives. But these necessary conditions are not sufficient. The necessary and sufficient conditions can be met only when citizens share a common understanding of the nature and requirements of a constitutional order and are willing to pay the price of enforcing limits upon officials. In short, the American experiments in constitutional choice cannot be expected to work without reference to the way people, as artisans, make use of constitutional limits as appropriate instruments for their own governance.

The Break with the Federalist Tradition

By the end of the nineteenth and the beginning of the twentieth century, any sense that the American system of government represented a fundamental experiment of epic proportions had been abandoned. Political preoccupations were with machine politics and boss rule, and the fundamental thrust of reform efforts was with the simplification and strengthening of the governmental apparatus. Preoccupation with a range of new problems led to pervasive efforts to question and to reject prior formulations.

The attack upon the theory used in the design of the American constitutional system took different forms. There were those, like Charles A. Beard (1913), who attacked the economic motivations of those who had the greatest influence in framing the constitutional system, and thus cast doubt upon the system as anything other than a self-serving arrangement by a propertied class. There were others, like Frank Goodnow (1900), who rejected constitutions as formalisms having little significance for the way that governments worked. Efforts by other peoples in Latin America and Europe to use the American constitutional formula often resulted in failure. These failures were construed as evidence that constitutions have little, if any, practical significance. There were still others, like Woodrow Wilson, who believed that the early American constitutional experiments were misguided efforts on the part of those who failed to understand the essential nature of the political process. Wilson's argument has probably been the most influential among political scientists. I shall pursue that argument further.

Wilson saw his own generation as opening a new era of constitutional criticism. His was the first generation, Wilson argued, not subject to an unquestioning adoration of the Constitution. Instead, it had freed itself of the shackles of deference and had the privilege to engage in "the first season of free, outspoken, unrestrained constitutional criticism" (Wilson 1885: 27).

Wilson was persuaded that the constitutional structure designed in the eighteenth century had become little more than a formal facade that concealed the fundamental reality of American politics. His thesis was that "the actual form of our present government is simply a scheme of Congressional supremacy" (Wilson 1885: 28), that could no longer be "squared" with traditional constitutional theory.

All niceties of constitutional restriction and even many broad principles of constitutional limitation have been overridden, and a thoroughly organized system of congressional control set up which gives a very rude negative to some theories of balance and some schemes for distributed powers, but which suits well with convenience, and does violence to none of the principles of self-government contained in the Constitution. (31)

Wilson rejects what he refers to as the "literary theories" and "paper pictures" of the Constitution reflected in the writing of John Adams, Alexander Hamilton, and James Madison. He argues that "those checks and balances have proved mischievous just to the extent to which they have succeeded in establishing themselves as realities" (Wilson 1885: 187). He further asserts that "this balance of state against national authorities has proved, of all constitutional checks, the least effectual" (34).

These structures were contrary to the essential nature of government. Wilson argues that "the leading inquiry in the examination of any system of government must, of course, concern primarily the real depositories and the essential machinery of power." He then goes on to assert a basic responsibility in his political science that "there is always a centre of power." The task of the scholar then is to determine "where in this system is that centre? In whose hands is self-sufficient authority lodged and through what agencies does that authority speak and act" (Wilson 1885: 30). If one sets aside formalities and looks at the "practical conduct" of government, Wilson advances the thesis that "the predominant and controlling force, the centre and source of all motive and of all regulative power, is Congress" (31).

The controlling principle in Wilson's political theory is that "the more power is divided the more irresponsible it becomes" (Wilson 1885: 77). His preferred solution is a unitary system of government following the model of the British Parliamentary system in which Parliament, as the representative body, exercises the supreme authority of government. The requirements of self-government can be met if Parliament as the representative body is raised "to a position of absolute supremacy" (203).

Elsewhere Wilson (1885: 181) asserts:

No one, I take it for granted, is disposed to disallow the principle that the representatives of the people are the proper ultimate authority in all matters of government, and that administration is merely the clerical part of government. Legislation is the originating force. It determines what shall be done; and the President, if he cannot or will not stay legislation by the use of his extraordinary power as a branch of the legislature, is plainly bound in duty to render unquestioning obedience to Congress. And if it be his duty to obey, still more is obedience the bounden duty of his subordinates. The power of making laws is in its very nature and essence the power of directing, and that power is given to Congress.

Wilson's political science does not address the same questions as were addressed in *The Federalist*. Wilson rejects form as having little if any practical significance in the conduct of government. Instead, form is, as Bagehot (1867) contended, the exterior facade of government that conceals the reality of power that operates behind the facade. In taking this position, Wilson opens himself to many ambiguities.

On the occasion of the fifteenth printing of *Congressional Government* in 1900, Wilson, for example, found it necessary to call the reader's attention to extensive changes that had taken place in "our singular system of Congressional government" (Wilson 1885: 19). The war with Spain had resulted in important changes "upon the lodgment and exercise of power within our federal system" (22). Increasing power of the president was bringing a fundamental change in the American system of government. Wilson (23) concludes his preface by observing:

> It may be, too, that the new leadership of the Executive inasmuch as it is likely to last, will have a very far-reaching effect upon our whole method of government. It may give the heads of the executive departments a new influence upon the action of Congress. It may bring about, as a consequence, an integration which will substitute statesmanship for government by mass meeting. It may put this whole volume hopelessly out of date.

The "people's parliament" had become "government by mass meeting." The heads of the executive department were exercising a "new influence upon the action of Congress" rather than being "bounden in duty to tender unquestioning obedience to Congress." The power of making laws was no longer "the very nature and essence of the power of directing" (i.e., the power of government). Instead, "the new leadership of the Executive" will "substitute statesmanship for government by mass meeting."

Any close student of *The Federalist* would appreciate that Wilson was using a radically different mode of political analysis than that used in the design of the American constitutional system. Madison's thesis that "the accumulation of all powers . . . in the same hands, whether of one, a few, or many, and whether hereditary, self-appointed, or elective, may justly be pronounced the very definition of tyranny" (Hamilton, Jay, and Madison n.d.: 313) is beyond Wilson's comprehension. Instead, Wilson characterizes such government as "responsible" government because people can then know whom to hold accountable. It never occurs to Wilson that the "new leadership of the Executive" will be anything other than "statesmanship." The possibility of tyranny is alien to his thinking.

The characterization of a unitary authority that exercises ultimate supremacy in all matters of government as a responsible government poses an interesting problem in a theory of sovereignty. To exercise unlimited and ultimate authority in all matters of government implies that no effective remedies are available to hold the supreme authority accountable. Hobbes recognized this clearly in formulating his theory of sovereignty. Yet Wilson, in offering a coherent argument, was confronted with the necessity of specifying the remedies that were available for enforcing responsibility. He would unquestionably have responded that Parliament is responsible to the people. But if Parliament is supreme in all matters of government, can it also be responsible to the people? Or if it is to be responsible to the people, is it supreme in all matters of government?

Wilson's conception of constitutional decision making was radically at variance with that of Hamilton and Madison. Constitutions for Wilson involve the choice of a broad, general form of government rather than specifying rules that establish the terms and conditions of government. Once the general form of government is selected, the basic constitutional task is accomplished, and then the more difficult task of organizing and running a government begins. Wilson (1887: 207) was critical of the American experience when he observed:

> Once a nation has embarked in the business of manufacturing constitutions, it finds it exceedingly difficult to close out that business and open for the public a bureau of skilled, economical administration. There seems to be no end to the tinkering with constitutions.

Wilson's preoccupation with the "realities" of power as determined by practice and the independence of those realities from constitutional limits became the basis for a new political science that was radically different from the political science that had been used to design the American constitutional system. What exists is justified by its existence. There are no generally recognized normative criteria for evaluating the performance of government apart from being in effective control. The study of political science can be a value-free endeavor to determine who exercises power in human societies. The methods of the natural sciences can be used to discover the realities of political power.

The question remains as to how political scientists are to construe the American experiment in constitutional choice. I shall turn to that problem next.

How Do We Construe the Essential Characteristics of the American Political System?

Two fundamentally different conceptions of political experiences emerge in the formulation of those who engaged in the founding of the compound structure of the American republics, and those who have engaged in the study and practice of politics in the twentieth century. Twentieth-century scholars view themselves as being sufficiently free from commitments to engage in an objective, value-free assessment of the realities of power. They advance the contention that form makes little or no difference. Government, as it were, is the result of shifting coalitions, historical accidents, and basic underlying forces within a society that *cause* political developments to occur.

Those who participated in the founding of the American republics, by contrast, argued that human beings could create governments by reflection and choice using knowable principles to create appropriate forms so that people might exercise essential control over the conduct of government. Governments are artifacts that human beings can *design* and *use* so as to serve their aspirations and purposes, subject to control by the community of people being served.

The latter argument is of fundamental importance for political science if political scientists are to be more than contemporary historians preoccupied with the lore of power. If people can create and maintain governments of their own choosing, presumably their artisanship will depend upon the use of a science that can specify relationships between conditions and consequences in establishing the terms and conditions of government. Such knowledge might then be used to select particular terms and conditions that will meet the design criteria for creating an appropriate system of "good" government.

The design of institutions of government would then reflect two types of calculations. One is the calculation of the probable consequences that follow from specifiable conditions. The other is the criteria to be used in selecting from among alternative possibilities. These criteria will then be used in evaluating alternative institutional designs and thus become the basic values or objectives to be realized as a consequence of the choices made and acted upon.

The design of any artifact then is never value-free. Rather, the creation of any artifact depends, first, upon a knowledge of technique and, second, upon choice in which criteria of selection apply to the choices made. The knowledge of techniques is grounded in science. Criteria of selection are grounded in moral considerations pertaining to human preferences and values. Since any artifact is a product of both forms of calculation, a proper understanding of its meaning or significance requires reference to the knowledge of techniques and criteria of selection that were entailed in its creation and use.

In the case of a political science, this implies that an appropriate beginning point is to consider the arguments of those who undertake the fundamental tasks of designing and creating governmental institutions. Such arguments provide explanations for the techniques used and the criteria utilized in formulating the particular design. The operation of the system can then be evaluated where the criteria of choice are used as evaluative criteria to assess performance, and the appropriateness of technique can be determined by its instrumental quality in yielding the desired results.

The capacity to conduct such an inquiry depends on a knowledgeable understanding of the nature of political phenomena, the primary ingredients used in political artisanship, and the way these ingredients work to yield the results they do. All forms of human organization are artifacts that contain their own artisans. Organizations are used to order human relationships in the conduct of joint activities and enterprises. Order is created by reference to rules. Since rules are not self-formulating, self-applying, or self-enforcing, they depend upon the agency of some who exercise the prerogatives of rulership with reference to others. Rules imply both rulers and ruled. The creation and maintenance of a system of rule depend upon a radical inequality between those who are rulers and those who are subject to rule. Instruments of coercion are necessary ingredients in any system of rule and provide an opportunity for those who are rulers to dominate the allocation of values in a society and exploit others to their own advantage. Fundamental tensions exist in all human societies when the prerogatives of rule are used not to sustain a mutually productive relationship among members of a society, but to allow some to exploit others.

The possibility of devising a system of rule in which rulers are themselves subject to the rule of law was the essential nature of the American experiments in constitutional choice. To attempt to realize such a possibility poses design problems of a substantial magnitude. Authority must be distributed in a way that all authority is subject to limits and no one, or no one set of decision makers, is permitted to gain dominance over the rest.

Since rules are not self-applying and self-enforcing, any system of constitutional rule depends upon a knowledgeable use of the prerogatives of government and citizenship to maintain and enforce limits inherent in a system of constitutional law. Knowledge, both of techniques and design criteria, is thus essential to the conduct of the American experiments in constitutional rule. This knowledge provides appropriate criteria to evaluate performance and methods that can be used for officials to check and limit one another, and for citizens to maintain proper limits in their relationships with officials. Any such structure of relationships is vulnerable to the development of coalitions that attempt to dominate all decision structures. The viability of a system of constitutional rule depends, in turn, upon awareness of these exposures and the willingness of others to resist such usurpations of authority.

As we approach the close of the second century of the American experiments in constitutional choice, we need to reconsider the arguments of those who participated in the design of those experiments and their twentieth-century critics who dismissed their arguments as "literary theories" and "paper pictures" unrelated to the realities of political power. The appropriate level of analysis for this purpose is that relevant to constitutional choice. We still confront the question of

> whether societies of men are capable or not of establishing good government from reflection and choice, or whether they are forever

destined to depend for their political constitutions on accident and force. (Hamilton, Jay, and Madison n.d.: 3)

The question still has profound significance for the human race. Perhaps it is time that we return to the constitutional level of analysis and take account of arguments and normative assumptions as they are relevant to an assessment of performance in construing the American experiments in constitutional choice. To develop a lore about the realities of power without knowing how that lore relates to design possibilities and performance criteria is to ignore the basic question of whether societies of men are capable of creating and maintaining self-governing institutions from reflection and choice.

REFERENCES

Bagehot, W. (1867) [1964] *The English Constitution.* London: C. A. Watts.

Beard, C. A. (1913) [1965] *An Economic Interpretation of the Constitution of the United States.* New York: Free Press.

Hamilton, A., J. Jay, and J. Madison. n.d. (1964). *The Federalist.* New York: The Modern Library.

Hobbes, T. (1651) [1960] *Leviathan.* Oxford: Basil Blackwell.

Goodnow, F. J. (1900) *Politics and Administration: A Study in Government.* New York: Macmillan.

Lasswell, H. D. (1936) [1958] *Politics: Who Gets What, When, How.* New York: Meridian.

Ostrom, V. (1980) "Artisanship and Artifact." *Public Administration Review* 40, no. 4 (July–August): 309–17. Reprinted as chap. 16 of this volume.

———. (1987) *The Political Theory of a Compound Republic: Designing the American Experiment.* 2d rev. ed. San Francisco: ICS Press.

———. (1989) *The Intellectual Crisis in American Public Administration.* 2d ed. Tuscaloosa: University of Alabama Press.

Wilson, W. (1887) "The Study of Administration." *Political Science Quarterly* 2 (June): 197–222.

———. (1885) [1959] *Congressional Government.* New York: Meridian.

CHAPTER 8

Cryptoimperialism, Predatory States, and Self-Governance

Vincent Ostrom

Introduction

People everywhere have recognized that the end of World War II presented a major challenge. That war was seen as the end of imperialism and the opening of a new era in civilization, an era that would be marked by the liberation of colonial peoples and the creation of a free world. But the end of imperialism, as associated with the disappearance of self-proclaimed empires, has not been accompanied by the liberation of the world's peoples. The conditions of many of the peoples in the Third World have not been marked by progressive patterns of development but by seriously degenerative tendencies. The world has not been made safe for democracy. Human aspirations have diverged radically from the patterns of development that have actually occurred. Why has this been the case?

In an effort to explain what has happened, I shall argue that coping with "crises" by calling for imperative actions has yielded new forms of cryptoimperialism. The basic formulae for two different types of cryptoimperialism were worked out some years ago. One is advanced in *The Game of Nations* by Miles Copeland, who identifies himself as having been associated with "cryptodiplomacy" (Copeland 1969: 12). Cryptodiplomacy is hidden diplomacy. I have viewed Copeland's reference to cryptodiplomacy as an invitation to extend the use of the prefix *crypto* to imperialism. Cryptoimperialism is the more general structure of relationships that has come to prevail.

Originally published in Vincent Ostrom, David Feeny, and Hartmut Picht, eds., *Rethinking Institutional Analysis and Development: Issues, Alternatives, and Choices* (1988; rpt., San Francisco: ICS Press, 1993), 43–68. Reprinted by permission of the Institute for Contemporary Studies (ICS) Press and the author.

Author's note: A preliminary draft of this essay was presented on March 21, 1985, as a lecture at McMaster University, Hamilton, Ontario. I owe a substantial debt to Mohammed Labib for calling my attention to the "recipe" contained in what I refer to as the Copeland formula and to Miles Copeland's *The Game of Nations: The Amorality of Power Politics* (New York: Simon and Schuster, 1969).

Cryptoimperialism is a theory for creating cryptoempires, hidden empires in which the control apparatus is concealed by a veil of secrecy behind rhetoric about "freedom" and "liberation." The other formula was worked out by V. I. Lenin. The success of Lenin's revolutionary efforts marked the end of Imperial Russia and created the Union of Soviet Socialist Republics and its association with other socialist states governed in accordance with Marxist-Leninist principles. Lenin's approach to revolutionary struggles for liberation yields a form of cryptoimperialism analogous to Copeland's.

The crises associated with cryptoimperialism are also reflected in the ideology used to organize the new nations of the Third World. In the second part of this essay, I use the theory of sovereignty to demonstrate how sovereign states are likely to become predatory states. Wherever liberation efforts draw upon concepts of state-building and state-to-state relationships as the keys to development in the Third World, we can expect extraordinary opportunities to exist for a few to exploit the many. We can begin to understand some of the sources of human tragedy—crises—in the contemporary world.

In continuing this analysis, I suggest that alternatives may be made available by drawing upon principles of self-governance. Understanding those alternatives depends upon a much fuller elaboration of the terms upon which alternatives are available in the constitution of human societies. Such an approach requires as much attention to the role of infrastructures in the fashioning of human societies as to that of the superstructures reflected in institutions of national governments.

The task we confront in seeking to understand the terms on which alternatives are available is one of challenging proportions, beyond the competence of individual human efforts. Instead, that challenge is potentially tractable to inquiry by many people of diverse capabilities. Other papers in this volume begin to explore some of the terms on which alternatives may be available. This approach opens the possibility of choice among alternative institutional possibilities, rather than presuming that human beings can only respond to crises with no-choice imperatives.

Recipes for Constituting "New" Nations

To a significant degree, human beings shape their own social realities. These realities are grounded in conceptions that refer to ordering principles and imply a computational logic. We can thus turn to the explanations that are offered about how to proceed in constituting ordered relationships in human societies as a way of supplying us with the theoretical conjectures that are constitutive of human social relationships. This is why the Copeland formula and the Lenin formula provide us with computational logics for understanding what has happened in the constitution of the new nations that have come into being following the collapse of the major imperial systems after World War II.

The Copeland Formula

Miles Copeland's *The Game of Nations* (1969) is an account of American efforts to establish a stable regime in an unstable situation in Egypt following British efforts to reduce their imperial commitments in the Middle East. Instability is incompatible with both freedom and development; progress in building a free world requires stability. Prior efforts to cope with comparable instabilities in Syria were the immediate background to the Egyptian developments. In Syria, these efforts began with a coup d'état undertaken by Husni el Zaim, the chief of staff of the Syrian army. According to Copeland's account, Zaim was aided by a "political action team" of American cryptodiplomats who "suggested to him the idea of a coup d'état, advised him how to go about it, and guided him through the intricate preparations in laying the groundwork for it" (Copeland 1969: 50). Other coups followed. "The problem, then," as Copeland indicates, "was not of bringing about a change of government" by a military coup, "but of making the change stick" (54).

Working out arrangements for making a change of government "stick" required a much greater elaboration of the necessary structural conditions for doing so. These were worked out in the coup d'état organized by Gamal Abdelnasser who is known to the world today simply as Nasser. According to Copeland's account, a team of cryptodiplomats was intimately involved in preparing the coup and in continuing discussions about how to build a stable structure of relationships that would be secure against further coups and counterrevolutionary efforts.

James Eichelberger, a State Department political scientist, was, according to Copeland's account, assigned directly to the American ambassador "to work out various situation estimates and recommendations for action" (86). Among the papers said to have been prepared by Eichelberger was one called "Power Problems of a Revolutionary Government," which is published as an appendix to Copeland's book. This paper, Copeland says, "was translated into Arabic, commented upon by various members of Nasser's staff, translated back into English for further editing by Eichelberger, and so on back and forth between English and Arabic until a final version was produced." "The final version was passed off to the outside world," in Copeland's account, "as the work of Zakaria Mohieddin, Nasser's most thoughtful and (in Western eyes) reasonable deputy, and accepted at face value by intelligence analysts of the State Department, the CIA, and, presumably, similar agencies of other governments." Copeland also indicates that Eichelberger later "went to great lengths to disown any connection with it" (87).

Since the analysis contained in "Power Problems of a Revolutionary Government" is the foundation for Copeland's analysis in *The Game of Nations* and is published there, I shall refer to it as the Copeland formula even though that statement may have been variously contributed to by Eichelberger, Mohieddin, and others. The statement is of fundamental importance in specifying the basic conditions for achieving stability in a revolutionary government undertaken by a military coup. We can also view the statement as being of constitutional importance by the extent to which this formulation serves as a model for aspiring leaders in the new nations of the Third World.

A constitution can be conceived as specifying the terms and conditions of government. This is what the Copeland formula addresses; it is a recipe for organizing a stable revolutionary government undertaken by the leaders of a military coup. These terms and conditions provide us with an understanding of the way that systems of government have been organized among the "new nations" of the Third World. In fact, some of these nations are, like Egypt, as old as recorded history; others were little more than administrative units in European empires. What they shared in common was colonial dependency in one form or another; and their newness is reflected in claims to independent standing in the family of nations.

The Copeland formula lays down two principles about the maintenance of governmental power. First, power is based on *"repressive* action or on *constructive* action" (284). Second, *"everything that a government does has an effect on its power base"* (285). That power base, in its most essential structure, rests upon instruments for repressive action. All actions, then, need to be assessed for the way that they contribute to control over instrumentalities for repressive action in a society.

Revolutionary governments, the Copeland formula emphasizes, are not bound by considerations of legality. Revolution is by its nature illegal. The task of a revolutionary government is to do whatever is necessary to actualize a maximum of power that is subject to its control. This it does by placing itself in a position to exercise a monopoly over both repressive and constructive measures of collective action. A "policy of drift and compromise," according to the statement, is "dangerous in the extreme" because it forsakes power for popularity (287).

In consolidating its power base, a revolutionary government, according to the Copeland formula, relies upon repressive powers exercised through: (1) legislation, (2) police, (3) an organized intelligence service, (4) propaganda facilities, and (5) military force. Having seized power illegally, a revolutionary government is subject to no legal constraint in exercising a monopoly over all legal political activity. This is done by prohibiting all "organized political activity not favored by the government" (291). All opposition is made illegal. Legislation, in the form of revolutionary decrees, becomes the foundation of state security and formulates the duties and obligations of citizens. Magistrates, according to the Copeland formula, are presumed to be under the control of the revolutionary government.

Since "police are the bulwark of the security system," control over police is a matter of high priority. "This means, essentially, that the police should be 'politicized' and should become, to whatever extent is necessary, a partisan paramilitary arm of the revolutionary government" (292). A carefully concealed intelligence or secret service is the "nerve center of the whole security system of a revolutionary state." This service, disguised within the structure of government or even located outside of government, must have access to the work of all other security and intelligence services and be capable of penetrating and dealing with "any suspected antirevolutionary activity" (293).

Propaganda activity must, according to the Copeland formula, be mobilized to support the use of repressive power and justify its continued use. Steps need to be taken by assigning press officers to all news media to offer guidance about publication. "The authority of these officers can be reinforced when necessary by evoking the security legislation . . . or by threatening the overstrict or 'nuisance' enforcement of various laws or taxes" (293).

The military force deserves special attention to assure "a loyal and efficient army" and to "build a countersubversive intelligence system in the army." Everything should be done to keep a "happy army" (293).

The repressive apparatus has priority in laying the foundations for the constructive measures that are to be initiated on behalf of the revolutionary movement. Of critical importance is the creation of a "mass organization" as an "extragovernmental association in which the leaders of the revolution, together with other officials and employees, join with a large mass of private citizens for the declared purpose of supporting and furthering the accomplishments of the revolution" (295). This mass organization is to serve as a "propaganda front for the government and to build a political party for the future" (296).

The mass organization is to serve as a "clearinghouse" for anyone wishing to influence the government or dealing with governmental officials. The mass organization is a way of obtaining "satisfaction" for citizens having difficulties with the government. In return for its services, "the mass organization can expect the adherence of many people who otherwise might remain indifferent, and financial contributions or other types of active support should be much easier to solicit" (297). Copeland elsewhere identifies such a mass organization as providing citizens with "the freedom to vote without the freedom to argue about what is being voted upon except, that is, within the confines of the one party set up by the state." In these circumstances, "the party is an instrument of the state whereby the state influences the people to think the way the leader of the state wants them to think" (127).

In the Copeland formula, the "working cadre" of the mass organization "can be found in the civil service, for all government employees can and should be required to join on an active basis as the condition of continued governmental employment" (296). Copeland elsewhere emphasizes a principle of "big government." He asserts that the purpose of government "is not so much to serve the public as to keep a large segment of the public off the streets—a segment that could be extremely dangerous if left unemployed" (128). People absorbed into government employment are kept occupied and under surveillance. At the same time they act, in part, as brokers to secure satisfaction for those whose interests are being impeded by other officials; and in part, to influence people to think the way that the leader of the state wants them to think.

As the structure of government is stabilized, the Copeland formula anticipates the preparation of a new constitution. Two features are considered of "utmost importance, however, if the revolutionary power base is to be perpetuated with maximum effect" (297). First, the written constitution should contain only general provisions without legal force. All such provisions should depend upon further legislation. Second, the constitution should depend upon a "strong executive, popularly elected by plurality." The statement anticipates that the revolutionary party as the only lawful political party "will be in a position for some time to come to 'write the constitution' in accordance with its own requirements" and control the selection of the executive. "It is impossible," the statement insists, "to overemphasize the importance of these two propositions—that the formal constitution (the 'written constitution') should consist of broad general provisions, and that it should provide for a strong executive" (298). It warns against "legalistic documents . . . produced by constitutional commissions" composed "largely of professors and jurists" and "drawn up with great regard for complicated concepts of government that appear in textbooks and with the niceties of theoretical justice" (299).

The Copeland formula, viewed as constitutional design, suggests an unlimited center of power that has at its disposal extensive instrumentalities for repressive action. Such a system of government is not bound by lawful limits. Revolutions and coups d'état are by their nature illegal. Those who lead revolutions and coups are free to be outlaws and pursue a wide range of temptation strategies in oppressing and exploiting others. They are capable of exercising dominance over a society where people are told what to think and what to do. The laws in such a society are subject to arbitrary enforcement. They become instruments of harassment for a press that displays independence; and instruments of corruption in the hands of party cadres who are prepared to extend favors in exchange for active support. The scenario for constructive action implies a commitment to wipe out traditional institutions that stand in the way of progress as conceived by the leaders of a revolutionary government; to mobilize an uncritical devotion to the revolutionary cause; and to secure obedience in undertaking those measures proclaimed by the revolutionary leadership as essential to the revolution. A strong executive and a one-party system form the core of the longer-term constitutional structure.

When we take the design formulated in Copeland's account, we have an explanation that enables us to understand the events that have transpired and are transpiring in the Third World. There, coups d'état and revolutions are the standard methods for changing governments. The standard form of government is the "strong executive," that is, some variant of dictatorship. A politicized police, a secret service, a happy army, an inflated bureaucracy, a mass movement organized as a one-party system, and a propaganda service to tell people what to think are the key instrumentalities of control. Citizens are expected to obey and not to oppose measures of the government. Traditional institutions that have helped to sustain a way of life are subject to assault; and new ways that are amenable to mass appeals and maximization of the regime's control over society are put in their place. Revolutionary rhetoric about socialism is used to nationalize economic enterprises and control economic activity. Costs of government escalate, while productivity declines. The tragedies of the Third World ensue. New forms of cryptoimperialism, managed by cryptodiplomats and dictatorial governments, replace the older forms of imperialism run by colonial officers.

The Lenin Formula

Lenin, as an active professional revolutionary, was explicit about the task of organizing a socialist revolutionary movement. Without a theory of revolution, Lenin argued, there can be no successful revolution. Lenin was preoccupied first with organizing a successful revolutionary movement. Then, once the movement was successful, he hoped to transform society. A brief newspaper article, "Where to Begin?" (May 1901) and a more extended account in *What Is to Be Done?* (written 1901–02) provide the basis for understanding how Lenin viewed the task of constituting a revolutionary movement; and *State and Revolution* ([1917] 1932) indicates how political authority should be organized after a successful revolution to achieve the transformation of society.

The organization of government in Imperial Russia relied upon principles of autocracy that gave the tsar ultimate authority to control the apparatus of government. Autocracy also implied "self-rule" on the part of the tsar. No limits to that autocracy were acknowledged. The tsar, as the personification of autocracy, ruled over society.

In "Where to Begin?" Lenin poses the basic revolutionary task as establishing a strongly organized party for the purposes of winning not only a "few concessions, but the very *fortress* of the autocracy" (Lenin [1901] n.d.: 16; my emph.). The stress is upon establishing a fighting organization where "our military forces mainly consist of volunteers and rebels." The effort is a long-term one of fashioning "an organization that will be ready at any moment to support every protest and every outbreak, and to utilize those for the purposes of increasing and strengthening the military forces fit for the decisive battle" (18). The organizers of a revolution must be prepared for the "decisive battle" and "capable of leading that battle" in light of the "spontaneous outbursts" or "unforeseen political complications which constantly threaten it [the tsarist autocracy] from all sides" (22–23).

The core of this effort is to be achieved through the organization of an all-Russian newspaper. A clandestine newspaper will provide an instrument of publicity, the rudiments of a command apparatus in its distributional network, and an intelligence apparatus in its newsgathering arrangements. The appeal of the revolutionary movement must be to create as large a base of support among the population as possible.

> We must take upon ourselves the task of organizing a universal political struggle under the leadership of our Party in such a manner as to obtain all of the support possible of all opposition strata for the struggle and for *our Party.* (Lenin [1902] n.d.: 103)

Lenin explicitly rejects models of organization based upon trade unions, student circles, and broad democracy. All of these patterns of organization would expose the leadership to being captured by the police and the destruction of its fighting potential at the very time when the decisive battles are to be engaged. Leaders of trade unions are known to the world: they bargain with the opposition. Student circles march "to war like peasants from the plough, snatching up a club" (116). Party organization based upon "broad democracy" is "nothing more than a *useless and harmful* toy" (154). Instead, Lenin argues, "the only serious organizational principle the active workers of our movement can accept is strict secrecy, strict selection of membership and the training of professional revolutionaries" (155). Furthermore, "secrecy is such a necessary condition that all the other conditions must be subordinated to it" (150).

The function of Lenin's revolutionary party is to exercise leadership of a revolutionary movement. The unity of a revolutionary movement depends upon the unity of its leadership. A "dozen professional revolutionaries" centralizing "the secret part of the work" will increase many times over the active participation of the broad masses in the revolutionary struggle. The revolutionary party, thus, is the vanguard of the revolutionary movement performing the secret leadership functions that organize and direct the revolutionary movement as a whole. The basic principles that apply to the party as the vanguard of the revolutionary movement are: (1) strict secrecy, (2) strict selection of membership, (3) strict discipline, and (4) careful training of a small core of professional revolutionaries who exercise leadership of the revolutionary movement. It is such a fighting organization that will lead a revolutionary movement capable of winning "the very fortress of the autocracy."

Lenin's theory of revolution relies upon a command apparatus that is practically a mirror image of the autocracy he sought to destroy. A unified leadership exercises command over a revolutionary movement in much the same way that an autocratic imperial government exercises a unity of power in its command over society. Leadership is exercised by a few professional revolutionaries who in turn select their own membership, in contrast to an imperial tradition based upon patrimonial principles of inheritance. But, in both cases, it is the leadership that exercises command over others in accordance with principles of strict secrecy, strict discipline, strict rules of selection, and professional training to exercise command and control functions.

Once the revolutionary struggle has won the fortress of the autocracy, how is the transformation of society to be achieved so that human beings may be liberated from the circumstances where the few exploit the many? Lenin, in *State and Revolution,* draws upon Karl Marx to make his diagnostic assessment of the basic task to be achieved: the transformation of society that will liberate people from exploitation by the creation of a new socialist society.

Marx's analysis is grounded in the presupposition that private ownership of the modes of production in a capitalist society is the essential element in human exploitation. Those who own the modes of production are capitalists; and they share a class interest in the use of their property to exploit those who are workers. Competitive dynamics yield an increasingly narrow and more powerful class of owners as weaker ones are eliminated and the exploitation of workers intensifies. The state becomes an organ of the capitalist class to maintain its dominance over society through the coercive instrumentalities of the military, the police, and the bureaucracy. Workers become the object of oppression as irreconcilable class antagonisms intensify, yielding a revolutionary potential.

Lenin's theory of revolution is designed to take advantage of this revolutionary potential by seizing the very fortress of the state apparatus. Seizing state power and crushing and destroying the state apparatus are not sufficient, however, to yield a new society free of human exploitation and without class antagonism. New patterns of property relationships need to be established once the oppressed—the proletariat—have seized state power through a dictatorship of the proletariat. The oppressed can use state power to eliminate the oppressors and undertake the reconstruction of society.

The reconstruction of society is achieved by using state power to expropriate private property. The means of production will then be owned by the working class thanks to its control of state power through a dictatorship of the proletariat. The working class as owner of the means of production will then reap the fruits of its own labor, exploitation will be eliminated, and a classless society will exist. The state will no longer have a reason for existence and will wither away. A communist society will come into being and that society will be both classless and stateless. Lenin conceives of the communist party as being the vanguard party exercising leadership on behalf of the dictatorship of the proletariat in achieving a revolutionary transformation where human exploitation will cease to exist.

This same account as offered by Marx and Lenin can be read in a different way. A small core of revolutionaries can be viewed as exercising leadership of a revolutionary movement by control over the secret leadership functions of command and control. Once the fortress of the prevailing leadership of the state is seized, the revolutionary leadership assumes control over the state apparatus, expropriates private property, and establishes command and control over all socialized property. Opposing forces are eliminated and the revolutionary leadership, as the ruling apparatus, exercises command over state power. The revolutionary leadership achieves autocratic control over the state apparatus. A new autocracy replaces the old autocracy and preserves the autocratic principles of governance: strict secrecy, strict discipline, strict selection of membership in the ruling autocracy, and careful training of those who become professional rulers. The more things change, the more they remain the same.

The New Ruling Classes

We have here two contending sets of conjectures. The Marxist-Leninist argument sees a revolutionary struggle culminating in the use of state power to liberate human beings from exploitation and achieve a classless and a stateless society. The Copeland formula sees the use of state power on behalf of a revolutionary movement as achieving the stability necessary for a free world to develop. Both have actually led to a continued effort to consolidate the power of central governments.

Milovan Djilas, a leading figure in the Yugoslav communist movement, describes the results of the Soviet effort.

> Everything happened differently in the USSR and the other Communist countries from what the leaders—even such prominent ones as Lenin, Stalin, Trotsky, and Bukharin—anticipated. They expected that the state would rapidly wither away, that democracy would be strengthened. *The reverse happened.* (Djilas 1957: 37; my emph.)

The state was strengthened and a new ruling class came to dominance, "its power more complete than the power of any other class before in history" (38). In seeking the liberation of people from human exploitation, the communist party has itself created another form of cryptoimperialism.

Much the same observation might be made about the end of imperialism and the blossoming of a free world that was expected to emerge following World War II. Everyone expected that imperialism would rapidly wither away and that democracy would be strengthened. *The reverse has happened.* Cryptoempires are engaging in power struggles that strengthen the repressive capabilities of predatory states and state functionaries to prey upon their own subjects, whose autonomous cultural infrastructures are threatened with destruction without their opportunities for self-governance being increased. American cryptoimperialism may have achieved some measure of short-term stability at the cost of both freedom and long-term stability.

Both the Copeland formula and the Lenin formula rely upon a unity of command to achieve stable forms of control over society. Each relies upon the military, police, and an intelligence apparatus (including the secret police) to deny fundamental human rights and control society. Leadership is exercised by a disciplined elite operating in secrecy. A party apparatus, to mobilize people to support the regime, and censorship, to control public information, are collateral forms of control available to those who exercise leadership prerogatives. Men aspire to be free, as Rousseau long ago explained the human condition, but they are everywhere in chains.

Why do such conditions prevail? This is the subject of the next section.

The Theory of Sovereignty: How the Few Exploit the Many

Basic institutions in human societies are organized to create structures of incentives and deterrents that lead people to behave in predictable and thus ordered ways. There is a type of logic or rationality imbedded in the structure of human institutions. Our effort, then, will be to clarify the logic of state organization and establish why it is that a theory of the state has to provide opportunities for the few to exploit the many. A theory of sovereignty, defined as the authority to govern society, is well elaborated in Thomas Hobbes's *Leviathan* ([1651] 1960) and provides us with a computational logic for the organization of sovereign states.

The problem pertaining to authority to govern arises because human beings order their relationships with one another in societies by references to rules. Rules are linguistic devices that rely upon norms or standards to order choice by distinguishing what is forbidden from what is permitted and required. By interposing limits upon all possible actions, human beings are able to achieve predictability in their relationships with one another and still leave sufficient openness to allow for latitudes of choice. By using a common set of rules of the road, for example, automobile drivers are able to respond to one another in predictable and orderly ways and still have sufficient freedom of choice to proceed by distinguishable and unique routes to unique destinations. Drivers in socialist societies are as dependent upon enforceable rules of the road as drivers in capitalist societies.

The pattern of order in any society depends then upon a body of common rules that enable a multitude of individuals to act with a shared community of understanding. It is a common set of rules that transforms a multitude into an ordered community of relationships. Rules, however, are not self-formulating, self-enforcing, or self-modifying. Instead, they are human creations that depend upon human agents to formulate, enforce, and alter them if there are to be orderly relationships in human societies. It is this complex task of formulating, enforcing, and modifying rules that is the basic function of government. Thus, the authority to govern pertains to what can be referred to as the rule-ruler-ruled relationship.

Without authority to enforce rules, human beings will always be tempted to ignore them and pursue opportunities that are beyond the bounds of lawful relationships. If they do, the resulting conflicts are likely to escalate into violence and destruction. Rule-ordered relationships depend upon some who exercise prerogatives of enforcement in order to make rules binding in human relationships.

A theory of sovereignty—the authority to govern—begins then with a presupposition that law is necessary for ordered social relationships in any society. Further, law is required to have a coherence that can be characterized as a "unity of law." For a unity of law to exist, the further presupposition is made that a "unity of power" is necessary to the peace and concord of society. One single center of authority must exercise the ultimate prerogatives of government. It is this ultimate center of authority that is "sovereign" and has the last say in the governance of a society. A theory of sovereignty presumes a unity of power—a unity of command—where those who exercise sovereignty rule over society (Hobbes [1651] 1960).

This conception, that the unity of law depends upon a unity of power, has been fundamental to organizing the structure of government in most societies throughout recorded history. The character of any such relationship involves deep puzzles and extraordinary tensions for human societies. In order to make rules binding in human relationships and to limit temptations to pursue opportunities that arise from the violation of law, those who exercise the prerogatives of rulership must have access to instruments of coercion to achieve the advantage of rule-ordered relationships. Several implications follow.

One implication is that those who exercise rulership prerogatives in a society achieve positions that are radically unequal to those who are the subject of rules. Rules imply rulers and ruled (subjects). The most radical source of inequalities in human societies is the rule-ruler-ruled relationship. Furthermore, those who exercise the prerogatives of rulership have access to instruments of coercion and force to impose punishment upon those who follow temptation strategies that arise from ignoring or violating law. Rulers have access to instruments of evil (i.e., instruments of punishment) to achieve the advantages that accrue from orderly relationships in human societies.

The rule-ruler-ruled relationship, then, is a Faustian bargain in which human beings have recourse to instruments of evil to do good. These conditions apply alike to the revolutionary who seeks to use state power in order to transform society and eliminate human exploitation; to cryptodiplo-mats who seek to establish stable regimes in a world plagued by coups d'état and revolutionary struggles; and to social reformers who rely upon central governmental authority to undertake measures to advance social welfare. Life in human societies is plagued by radical inequalities in the rule-ruler-ruled relationship and by the circumstance that these inequalities are distinguished by assigning authority to some who can lawfully use instruments of force or coercion to impose deprivation upon others. The presumption that the peace and prosperity of any people depends upon a unity of law, and that the unity of law depends upon a unity of power, further implies that any such center of authority should exercise a *monopoly* over the legitimate use of force in a society. This is the attribute that is used to define the state: in most modern works in the social sciences, the state is the entity that has a monopoly of the legitimate use of force in the governance of society. All instruments of coercive power not controlled by the central authority of the state are presumed to be without legitimacy; they are presumed to be illegal.

Building upon these presuppositions, a theory of sovereignty carries the further implication that those who are sovereign and monopolize the legitimate use of force in a society exercise an authority that is both *unlimited* and *indivisible*. Those who have the ultimate authority to govern, and have a monopoly of the legitimate use of force in a society, exercise an authority to determine all other authority relationships. Sovereigns, then, are the source of law and cannot themselves be held accountable to a rule of law. All others are *subjects* in the presence of a *sovereign;* and sovereigns, not being limited to any enforceable rule of law, stand outside the law, that is, are outlaws in relation to those who are subjects.

Those who are sovereign have access to extraordinary opportunities to use the instrumentalities of governance to dominate the allocation of values in society and exploit others. Sovereigns, and those who act on their behalf, are free to become predators and prey upon others, who are reduced to a position of being relatively defenseless subjects (Levi 1981; Rotberg 1971: see esp. chap. 10). State-building, where the preoccupation is with establishing strong central governments that exercise a monopoly over the legal instrumentalities of coercion in a society, creates unique opportunities for a few to exploit the many. In such circumstances, the exercise of state power can be used to reduce all other potential sources of power to submission. Predatory states created either in the image of American or Soviet cryptoimperialism can be expected to yield impoverishment in the Third World.

Organizing aid to the Third World on a state-to-state basis does not alter the fundamental structures of relationships. Each state, within a world of sovereign states, is presumed to exercise control over its own internal affairs. Military and economic aid, under such circumstances, can be used to enhance the repressive and predatory characteristics of the regime in power. Efforts to modify such tendencies place the contending world powers in the position of relying upon whatever instruments of command are available to the respective heads of state. In the American case, this means that the instrumentalities of cryptodiplomacy are available in the diplomatic, military, and intelligence services. In the Soviet case, these instrumentalities of cryptodiplomacy are reinforced by the command apparatus that is available in the leadership structure of Lenin's revolutionary party. Lenin's vanguard party yields such an advantage in the imperial struggle for domination that the Soviet form of cryptoimperialism can be expected to prevail so long as human freedom and liberation are conceived only with reference to states and state-to-state relationships.

Are There Alternatives?

When we conceive of price as the terms on which alternatives are available, we need not confine our reference to monetary prices. Any effort to "get the prices right" requires a course of inquiry to go beyond market calculations. The possibility of both cryptoimperialism and predatory states implies that market deficiencies cannot always be resolved by turning from markets to states. State officials, or those who control state power, can be as predatory as the most self-serving and avaricious capitalists.

We cannot, however, assume that all heads of state are birds of prey even when some of them view corruption as the lubricant that keeps the machinery of state in motion and consider the modus vivendi of politics as learning how to "steal cleverly" (Hyden 1980: 196). Some heads of state are also motivated by a strong passion to do good rather than prey upon others. But puzzles arise even in these circumstances.

Those who exercise the ultimate authority to govern and simultaneously command the legitimate use of force in a society may, in their passion to do good, seek to eliminate all obstacles that stand in their way. These are the circumstances that yield the most extreme forms of oppression in human societies. Great dangers arise whenever human beings with strong convictions about the rightness of their cause are authorized to use instruments of evil to do good. The results can reach genocidal proportions.

Other circumstances can also prevail where those who exercise the ultimate prerogatives of government are aware of their own limitations as fallible creatures, and seek to use those prerogatives to advance human welfare. Grave difficulties exist even then. I shall draw upon two examples: the emancipation of serfs in Imperial Russia and the emancipation of slaves in the United States.

Tsar Alexander II, after extended inquiry and persistent effort, issued his Edict of Emancipation on February 19, 1861. At that time serfs comprised approximately 80 percent of the population in Imperial Russia. What did an imperial edict accomplish given the immensity of this task? Important changes in the nexus of legal relationships occurred; but as Edward Crankshaw shows in *The Shadow of the Winter Palace,* such a decree could only be a small but important step in the liberation of serfs. Infrastructures in Russian society that might have enabled serfs to achieve freedom and self-governance were tragically lacking. Radical new expectations were formed. In the absence of appropriate institutional arrangements for achieving self-governance, an exceedingly precarious situation was created. Revolutionary disturbances erupted in 1905. The regime itself collapsed in the revolutionary struggle of 1917. Eventually, the regime gave way to one led by Lenin's vanguard party. Whether the collectivization of Soviet agriculture has yielded the liberation of the peasantry or created a new form of serfdom remains an issue some 125 years after the Edict of Emancipation.

Much the same assertion can be made with regard to President Abraham Lincoln's Emancipation Proclamation, issued on September 22, 1862. Putting words on paper was not sufficient to make free men of former slaves. Access to education and the understanding and skills that accrue from education had to be achieved. Among these essential skills were the ones associated with making the legal and political system work to the advantage of the "freed" amid a status quo dominated by their erstwhile oppressors. Blacks could vote with their feet to find a more congenial status quo. But achieving freedom is a long and enduring struggle. Though what Alexander II and Lincoln did were important events in the chronicle of human liberation, the terms on which freedom becomes possible require much more than can be accomplished by heads of state.

A free world, then, depends upon a much more complex configuration of institutional arrangements in human societies. If we human beings are to be free enough to be first and foremost our own governors, we must be prepared to recognize basic human rights and correlative obligations that extend those same rights and obligations to others. Rights to freedom of speech, worship, and assembly; rights to gain access to information and knowledge, to enter into voluntary exchange arrangements, to hold property, and to enter into associated arrangements with others; rights to specify terms and conditions of governance through processes of constitutional choice and to due process of law; all are of fundamental importance if human societies are to be constituted so that freedom may prevail, and people can participate in the governance of society and fashion their own course of development.

The structure of opportunity in a free society allows individuals wide latitude of choice to pursue opportunities consistent with their own aspirations. Freedom of opportunity depends upon the capacity of individuals to relate to others through exchange arrangements and through teamwork. The correlative of exchange arrangements is a lawful right to what is exchanged, that is, to property. The correlative of teamwork is a right to share in the fruits of joint efforts. Freedom cannot exist without constitutionally guaranteed rules of association and property rights.

Problems associated with common-property resources—goods subject to collective use or consumption—and with conflict and conflict resolution require recourse to involuntary patterns of association. But even these can be formulated under terms and conditions that meet the requirements of fairness, and that hold those who exercise extraordinary prerogatives of government accountable to a public trust specifiable under the limits of constitutional law. All such arrangements require that governance occur in an open public realm *(res publica)*, where everyone exercises some basic prerogative of governance and no one exercises unlimited prerogatives of governance.

It follows that a free society depends upon an elaborate structure of institutional arrangements that conform to two basic rules. One is the ancient moral precept, "Do unto others as you would have others do unto you." This precept can be developed into a method of normative inquiry, where human beings take the perspective of others, discount partialities associated with self-love, and strive for impartiality (Kaufmann, Majone, and Ostrom 1986: chap. 11). The other rule is W. R. Ashby's law of requisite variety: To realize specified effects, there must exist as much variety in the strategies available as there is variety in the conditions that obtain (Ashby 1956: 206–13). In short, simple institutional arrangements will not suffice for a complex world.

Adam Smith, in *The Theory of Moral Sentiments,* warns against those who imagine that they can arrange "the different members of a great society with as much ease as the hand that arranges the different pieces on a chessboard" ([1759] n.d.: 380–81). Human societies are, instead, composed of "pieces" that are capable of thinking and acting on their own, for "in the great chess-board of human society, every piece has a principle of motion of its own altogether different than the legislature might choose to impose on it." Only when principles of legislation can be used to fashion institutional arrangements that are consonant with the principles of motion that activate individual human beings can "the game of human society . . . go on easily and harmoniously" and yield results that are "likely to be happy and successful" (381).

Getting the prices right, then, requires more than markets and states. It depends upon appropriate configurations of rule-ordered relationships. Infrastructures are necessary that enable people to have recourse to self-organizing and self-governing institutions appropriate to the pursuit of diverse opportunities. These include the capacity to: (1) organize teamwork and teams of teams in complex patterns of organization appropriate to the task to be accomplished; (2) have access to free-exchange relationships with correlative systems of property rights; (3) undertake communal patterns of organization to arrange roads, schools, waterworks, and other essential communal services and facilities; and (4) have access to governing institutions that operate in accordance with due processes of law.

Many such structures can be fashioned by following Amilcar Cabral's (1973) advice to "return to the source" and to build upon the experiences that are part of the cultural tradition of people in their present circumstances. Every people that has survived to this point in time has acquired some capabilities for teamwork, exchange relationships, and communal organization. These capabilities need to be built upon and extended to meet the opportunities for life in the contemporary world.

It would be naive to assume that people, if left to themselves, will do good. It is possible for human societies to develop where no one trusts anyone else—societies where each is prepared to "do others in or to be done in." If such conditions are to be avoided, the interdependencies of life need to be organized on the basis of reciprocity by "doing unto others as you would have others do unto you." This is the foundation for the common relationships experienced as *res publica*—an open public realm—that is constitutive of democratic, self-governing societies. The task of the analyst concerned with achieving productive potentials in human societies is to "return to the source" as Cabral suggests, understand the conditions that prevail, and develop a self-conscious awareness that alternatives exist and that choices are possible.

The command-and-control structures for fashioning cryptoimperial systems with their predatory states, whether of the American or the Soviet variety, cannot suffice to fashion free societies any more than emancipation proclamations or edicts of emancipation can create free peoples. Instead, the great chessboard of human society must allow for the pieces to move themselves in accordance with rules that facilitate mutually respectful and productive relationships, and afford methods for processing and resolving conflicts so as to maintain a fair game open to the pursuit of diverse opportunities. Freedom can be achieved when the pieces on that chessboard are capable of acting, setting rules, and holding each other to account in accordance with that most basic constitutive rule, "Act in relation to others as you would have others act in relation to you." This is the law of laws that gives unity to self-governing societies. The other condition is to meet the law of requisite variety that is necessary to all forms of artisanship if they are to yield the artifacts that help to sustain human life in meaningful ways. These requirements can be met when people acquire capabilities for self-governance under whatever circumstances.

Copeland's formula for fashioning a cryptoimperialism appropriate to a "Free World" is the antithesis of the principles used in the constitution of American democracy and other systems of democratic governance in the modern world. These principles were reasonably well articulated in studies by Montesquieu, Locke, Rousseau, Hume, Smith, Hamilton, Madison, and Tocqueville, among many others who have contributed to a theory of governance in accordance with rules of constitutional law (V. Ostrom 1987). But these principles cannot prevail in systems of state-to-state relationships grounded in theories of sovereignty. This is why the fashioning of a truly free world depends upon building the fundamental infrastructures that enable different peoples to become self-governing. Otherwise, efforts in the name of the "Free World" or "Peoples Liberation" based upon either the Copeland formula or the Lenin formula will be destructive of human freedom.

The big task in setting the terms on which alternatives are available (i.e., getting the prices right) is to specify principles of human association, as James Madison has suggested, that build upon "the capacity of mankind for self-government" (Hamilton, Jay, and Madison [1788] n.d., no. 39: 243). This is why Tocqueville asserts "A new science of politics is needed for a new world" ([1835] 1945, 1:7). That new science of politics is a science of association that enables peoples to design, create, and maintain systems of governance where they can be self-governing. Such self-governing societies can be conceived as being both classless and stateless societies, for not all systems of governance need be viewed as states that exercise a monopoly of the legitimate use of force in a society. What is nominally viewed as a "state" in the family of "nation-states" need not be ruled by a sovereign. The constitution of a free world cannot be fashioned by theories of sovereignty and cryptoimperialism. Alternatively, federative principles of organization can be used to constitute self-governing societies (V. Ostrom 1987).

Conclusion

It would be irresponsibly cynical to presume that all states are monstrous birds of prey devouring their own subjects. On the other hand, it may also be irresponsibly naive to presume that all states are benevolent creations that can always be relied upon to correct the ills of society and to get the prices right, so to speak. It is essential to address the reality that exists in human societies, and to recognize that the computational logic inherent in the theory of sovereignty, and the associated structures of both American-type and Soviet-type cryptoimperialism, create extraordinary opportunities for a few to exploit the many.

When we begin to recognize the distinct likelihood of predatory states, it may then become possible to mobilize our analytical capabilities to explain the terms on which alternatives become available in human societies. These are the prerequisites for choice; and choice is the prerequisite for a free world. Choice pertaining to the terms and conditions of government is possible; but revolutionary struggles and coups d'état are not effective ways to clarify the terms on which those alternatives are available. Problems of development in the contemporary world can only be clarified in light of: (1) the choice of alternative institutional arrangements and what this implies for the constitutional choices people might make; (2) the collective choices that might be taken, given the terms and conditions that apply to the organiza-tion and conduct of governments; and (3) the great multitudes of operational choices that become available when people can relate to one another through diverse institutional arrangements, organized according to rules that are constitutive of fair games.

REFERENCES

Ashby, W. Ross (1956) *An Introduction to Cybernetics*. New York: Wiley.

Cabral, Amilcar (1973) *Return to the Source: Selected Speeches.* New York and London: Monthly Review Press.

Copeland, Miles (1969) *The Game of Nations: The Amorality of Power Politics.* New York: Simon and Schuster.

Crankshaw, Edward (1986) *The Shadow of the Winter Palace.* London: Papermac.

Djilas, Milovan (1957) *The New Class.* New York: Praeger.

Hamilton, Alexander, John Jay, and James Madison (n.d.) *The Federalist.* Edward Mead Earle, ed. New York: Modern Library. First published in 1788.

Hobbes, Thomas (1960) *Leviathan or the Matter, Forme and Power of a Commonwealth Ecclesiasticall and Civill.* Michael Oakeshott, ed. Oxford: Blackwell. First published in 1651.

Hume, David (1948) *Hume's Moral and Political Philosophy.* Henry D. Aiken, ed. New York: Hafner.

Hyden, Goran (1980) *Beyond Ujamaa in Tanzania: Underdevelopment and an Uncaptured Peasantry.* Berkeley and Los Angeles: University of California Press.

Kaufmann, Franz-Xaver, Giandomenico Majone, and Vincent Ostrom, eds. (1986) *Guidance, Control, and Evaluation in the Public Sector.* Berlin and New York: de Gruyter.

Lenin, V. I. (n.d.) "Where to Begin?" In *Selected Works,* vol. 2. New York: International Publishers, 15–23. First published in 1901.

——— (n.d.) *What Is to Be Done?* In *Selected Works,* vol. 2. New York: International Publishers, 25–192. First published in 1902.

——— (1932) *State and Revolution.* New York: International Publishers.

Levi, Margaret (1981) "The Predatory Theory of Rule." *Politics and Society* 4:431–65.

Locke, John (1952) *The Second Treatise of Government.* Thomas P. Peardon, ed. Indianapolis: Bobbs-Merrill. First published in 1690.

Montesquieu, Charles Louis de Secondat (1966) *The Spirit of the Laws.* New York: Hafner. First published in 1748 as *De l'esprit des loix.*

Ostrom, Vincent (1987) *The Political Theory of a Compound Republic: Designing the American Experiment.* 2d rev. ed. San Francisco: ICS Press.

Rotberg, Robert A. (1971) *Haiti: The Politics of Squalor.* Boston: Houghton Mifflin.

Rousseau, Jean-Jacques (1978) *On the Social Contract.* Roger D. Masters, ed. New York: St. Martin's Press. First published in 1762 as *Du contrat social.*

Smith, Adam (n.d.) *The Theory of Moral Sentiments.* Indianapolis: Liberty Press. First published in 1759.

Tocqueville, Alexis de (1945) *Democracy in America.* 2 vols. Phillips Bradley, ed. New York: Knopf. First published in 1835.

Wicksteed, Philip H. (1933) *The Common Sense of Political Economy.* Lionel Robins, ed. London: Routledge and Kegan Paul.

CHAPTER 9

The Concentration of Authority: Constitutional Creation in the Gold Coast, 1950

Kathryn Firmin-Sellers

In the 30 years since decolonization, scholars have offered a variety of explanations for the concentration of political authority throughout Africa. In the 1960s Aristide Zolberg argued that postcolonial governments concentrated authority to compensate for the weakness of the party organizations that had brought them to power (Zolberg 1966). In his study of West African one-party states, Zolberg catalogued the strategies that postindependence governments used to dismantle the democratic institutions that the colonial powers had installed prior to their departure: opposition parties were repressed; the judiciary's independence was compromised and civil liberties were routinely denied.

More recent literature attributes the concentration of authority not to postcolonial governments, but to the colonial powers themselves. Crawford Young, for example, argues that postcolonial governments inherited the autocratic legacy of the colonial state (Young 1988; see also Wunsch 1990). During the period of colonial rule, hegemonic governments forged few ties between the colonial state and civil society. Consequently, the democratic institutions put in place at independence could not be sustained by independent governments. New rulers were forced to legitimize their hold on power by invoking the paternalistic colonial ideology of trusteeship and by constructing a personalistic network of support (Young 1988: 56–60).

Originally published in *Journal of Theoretical Politics* 7, no. 2 (April 1995): 201–22. Copyright 1995 by Sage Publications Ltd. Reprinted by permission of Sage Publications Ltd. and the author.

Author's note: This is a revised version of an essay presented at the Annual Convention of the Midwest Political Science Association, Chicago, 1992. It has benefited greatly from the comments of Robert Bates, Rick Wilson, Mike McGinnis, Elinor Ostrom, Vincent Ostrom, Patrick Sellers, and participants in the Indiana University Workshop in Political Theory and Policy Analysis. The research was supported by a grant from the National Science Foundation (Grant SES–9108874) and the Fulbright Program.

Though valid, both of these explanations for the concentration of authority are incomplete. The focus on the actions of independence governments highlights the indigenous actors' ability to shape their political environment, but it does not place those actors within a broad historical context. The explanation therefore fails to consider the way in which the indigenous actors' choices were shaped by the history of colonial rule. Conversely, the focus on the colonial state's legacy illuminates the context within which individual decisions were made, but denies the importance of those decisions. This explanation does not specify the ways in which the colonial state shaped indigenous actors' choices and it does not explain why those actors were unable or unwilling to alter their inherited tradition.

In this article, I offer a more complete explanation of the concentration of political authority by looking at the transition to independent government, the period in which new institutions of government were designed and implemented.[1] I argue that a detailed, historical analysis of this period illuminates the linkages between the macro-level structures of the colonial state and the micro-level decisions of indigenous politicians. In so doing, the analysis fills the theoretical gaps outlined above.

This article focuses on a single instance of constitutional creation: the drafting and implementation of the Gold Coast constitution of 1950. The 1950 constitution was the first written by Gold Coast Africans; it was the first to give Africans direct influence over national level policy-making through the creation of a meaningful legislative body. Its creation launched a series of reforms that would culminate in 1957 with independence, an event unprecedented in Sub-Saharan Africa.

Briefly, I argue that the British colonial government did not impose authoritarian institutions upon the Gold Coast Colony (renamed Ghana). Rather, during the original episode of constitutional creation, they adopted procedures that encouraged indigenous actors to use the constitution to pursue narrow, redistributive gains. They adopted procedures that encouraged actors to concentrate authority, deliberately foregoing potential safeguards against arbitrary, authoritarian rule. Thus, the constitution was reduced to a mere parchment barrier, facilitating the subsequent move toward authoritarian rule.

My analysis of these events is divided into four parts. In part I, I introduce the analytical tools necessary for understanding the politics of institutional choice. In part II, I identify the actors who participated in the design of the Gold Coast Constitution of 1950. What goals did these actors pursue, and what power did they wield in pursuit of those goals? In parts III and IV, I examine the drafting and implementation of the constitution. In both these sections, I explore the interaction between British control over procedure and the institutional choices made by indigenous actors.

I. The Politics of Institutional Choice

Scholars of the New Institutionalism have developed many of the analytical tools needed to unravel the politics of institutional design. North defines institutions as the "humanly devised constraints that shape human interaction" (1990: 3).[2] Institutions structure social life, and thus influence social development, by altering the individual citizens' incentives to pursue certain courses of action.

Institutions may promote socially beneficial outcomes by helping actors to resolve "social dilemmas," situations in which individually rational actions aggregate to produce socially irrational outcomes (Bates 1988). Rules governing access to a common pool resource, for example, may promote sustainable use of the resource, and thus help actors to escape Hardin's famed "tragedy of the commons" (Hardin 1968).

Institutions may also promote socially undesirable outcomes. Moe (1990a: 213) argues that institutions are "weapons of coercion and redistribution. They are the structural means by which political winners pursue their own interests, often at the great expense of political losers." Thus, the rules governing access to a common pool resource may promote sustainable use by granting private property rights to a single person, disinheriting all other users.

The question of institutional design is of profound importance. Institutional design determines whether institutions function to promote socially productive ends, benefiting all members of society; or whether they function to promote redistributive ends, benefiting a narrow segment of society, often at the expense of all others.

The consequences of institutional design are greatest within the context of constitution building. Institutions operate at three different levels (Kiser and Ostrom 1982). At the operational level, the individual acts within the framework of fixed institutions and rules. For example, the rules governing use of a commonly held pasture mandate that each farmer may graze two cows on the commons for one hour per day. Each farmer must then decide which of their cattle to graze, and when to exercise their grazing rights. At the level of collective choice, actors work within the framework of existing decision-making institutions to create the rules that structure choice at the operational level: a village assembly or legislature decides how many cows each farmer can graze, or assigns responsibilities for tending the commons. At the constitutional level, actors decide how the decision-making institutions at the level of collective choice will be designed. They determine who will be eligible to participate in collective choice institutions, how their preferences will be weighted and aggregated and what authority actors will have to enforce those decisions. In a very real sense, the choices that actors make at the constitutional level define the most basic rules of politics, the study of who gets what, when and how (qtd. in V. Ostrom 1982: 237; p. 151 of this volume).

Given the fundamental nature of constitutional choice, a number of scholars have adopted the normative stance that actors should create institutions as if they operated under a Rawlsian veil of ignorance (Rawls 1971; see also Buchanan and Tullock 1964). The "veil of ignorance" implies that actors do not know the position that they or their opponents will occupy in any future decision-making institutions. Given that uncertainty, each actor has an incentive to create institutions that will benefit him/her under all circumstances. Each actor is driven to "take a position as a representative participant in a succession of collective choices anticipated. Therefore, he may tend to act from self-interest as if he were choosing the best set of rules for the social group" (Buchanan and Tullock 1964: 96).

In substantive terms, actors operating under a veil of ignorance will create institutions that impede the concentration of political power. For example, actors might divide authority among distinct branches of government, or ensure that local institutions remained vibrant. Through such arrangements, actors can assure themselves that the individuals who ultimately control the new institutions cannot use their position to pursue narrow, redistributive goals to the detriment of those out of power.

Empirically, the conditions under which we observe such outcomes are highly restrictive and rarely met. In most situations, actors develop models about the political environment and about their own place within that environment (North 1981). When actors believe that power is distributed symmetrically, when they believe that they will not control future decision-making institutions, then a veil of ignorance may in fact exist. Actors may "hedge their bets"; they may create institutions that disperse authority such that, regardless of who governs, they will not be severely disadvantaged (Knight 1992: 43–45; see also Przeworski 1991).

When actors believe that power is distributed asymmetrically, when they believe that they will control future decision-making institutions, then the "veil of ignorance" is removed. Actors who believe that they are powerful are likely to choose institutions that concentrate political authority, thereby facilitating their pursuit of redistributive goals (Geddes 1990; Moe 1990a, b).

Clearly, we need to develop a positive theory of constitutional creation that explicitly considers actors' beliefs about the political environment. Rather than assume that actors operate under conditions of extreme uncertainty, as the "veil of ignorance" hypotheses do, we must examine actors' beliefs about the distribution of power and about the position that they might occupy in any future political order. For, as empirical analysis demonstrates, the nature of these beliefs profoundly influences actors' preferences over constitutional design.

A positive theory of constitutional creation must also consider the procedure through which actors' preferences are aggregated. The procedure by which a constitution is created may alter actors' beliefs about the apparent distribution of power. For example, the constitution builders might adopt a procedure that gives weaker actors an equal voice in constitutional negotiations, thus diluting the influence of more powerful actors. Conversely, the constitution builders might decide that powerful actors should be banned from the negotiations, augmenting the power wielded by the remaining participants. In either case, the procedure distorts the perceived distribution of power and may encourage participants to alter their preferences over institutional design.[3]

Procedural choices also determine whether actors retain a coherent view of the constitutional framework. Ostrom (1986: 12) argues that rules operate configurationally. That is, the way in which a single institution functions depends upon the way in which it interacts with other, related institutions.

Ostrom's finding has important implications for constitutional theories. Actors cannot assess how a constitution will structure political life unless they consider the ensemble of collective choice institutions that they are creating: for example, the legislature, the executive, the judiciary and local government. Actors operating under a veil of ignorance cannot construct safeguards against coercive rule, and powerful actors cannot pursue their redistributive, narrowly beneficial goals, unless they are able to view the constitution as a coherent whole.

Actors are more likely to retain a coherent vision of the constitution if the constitution-building procedures allow them to make non-binding decisions during the negotiations. In this way, they are able to reverse past decisions as new choices are made and as the constitution unfolds. Similarly, the procedure encourages cohesion if it forces them at the end to ratify the document as a whole. If these procedural constraints are absent, then actors are more likely to consider each new collective choice institution in isolation, with little regard for its overall impact on political life.

Finally, a positive theory of constitutional creation must consider the path-dependent nature of institutional development (North 1990: 92–98). Individuals possess models of the world, but those models are rarely perfect or complete. Actors cannot predict all future events and they cannot map the precise relationship between their actions and outcomes.

Under these conditions, actors are vulnerable to "surprises." Unforeseen events may alter their models of the world and change their preferences over institutional design. Likewise, the unintended consequences of their actions may prompt actors to reconsider their prior choices. Oftentimes, however, actors do not have the opportunity to act on the basis of this new information. The consequences of random events and mistaken choices become embedded within the institutions, making change difficult if not impossible. Thus, actors may find themselves along a development path which, with hindsight, they might not have wished to follow.

Each of these theoretical considerations—the distribution of power, the procedures for institutional creation and the path-dependent nature of institutional development—is relevant to the analysis of the drafting and ratification of the Gold Coast constitution of 1950. Together, they help us to understand the links between the legacy of the colonial state and the indigenous actors' decision to concentrate political authority. I begin my empirical study, then, by establishing the context within which institutional creation proceeded. Who were the relevant actors, what were their goals and how was power distributed among them?

II. Identifying the Actors

Three sets of actors dominated Gold Coast politics during the period of constitutional reform: British colonial officers in London and in West Africa; the conservative United Gold Coast Convention (UGCC), led by J. B. Danquah; and the more radical Convention People's Party (CPP), led by Kwame Nkrumah.

The British Colonial Officials

British colonial officials conceded the need for immediate constitutional reform in the Gold Coast when, in February 1948, the Colony was rocked by violent rioting. The riots erupted in Accra, the Gold Coast capital, and spread quickly to other urban areas. The protestors targeted European stores and property and besieged the British-run Ussher Fort Prison. Before the violence subsided, 29 people had been killed and 237 more injured (UK 1948: app. 8).

The Accra riots weakened the colonial government. In the wake of the riots, the British officials fell under intense pressure to reform the system of colonial rule in the Gold Coast. The international community, led by the United States, the USSR and the United Nations Trusteeship Council, condemned the violence. In the United Kingdom, the Conservative Party portrayed the riots as proof of the incumbent Labour Party's "unfitness . . . to manage the Empire." At the same time, a radical faction within the Labour Party used the riots to publicize their campaign to dissolve the British Empire (Rathbone 1992: xliii–xliv).

Those inside the Colonial Office feared that the Accra riots could easily balloon into sustained civil unrest. Officials in Accra reported that the riots had been orchestrated by the nationalist United Gold Coast Convention, and expressed their concern that UGCC leaders were communist sympathizers. Officials in London, similarly imbued with a Cold War mind-set, worried that the unrest might spread to neighboring colonies. Citing evidence of communist indoctrination, the British Minister of Defense drew up contingency plans to send military reinforcements to the Gold Coast (Alexander 1948).

In the aftermath of the riots, then, British colonial officials believed their options to be limited. When a commission appointed to investigate the riots (the Watson Commission) called for extensive constitutional revisions, the British consented. Senior officers protested privately, but recognized that it was no longer feasible to deny or delay political reform (Cohen 1948a, 1948b). Thus, in December 1948, the Governor of the Gold Coast Colony appointed a committee composed entirely of Africans to draft a new constitution for the Gold Coast. The committee, convening under the leadership of Justice Henley Coussey, became known as the Coussey Committee.

Although their choices were constrained, British officials continued to wield significant power in the Gold Coast. In appointing the Coussey Committee, British officials determined who would participate in the constitution-building process; and, in deciding the ratification procedures, British officials determined how those actors' preferences would be aggregated. In later sections, I argue that British officials used their power to promote their own interests: they manipulated the constitution-building procedure in an effort to ensure that the "moderate element" in Gold Coast politics (those most sympathetic to the British presence) would govern under the new constitution.

The Indigenous Actors

The United Gold Coast Convention
When the 1950 constitution was drafted, two indigenous groups dominated Gold Coast politics: the United Gold Coast Convention (UGCC) and the Convention People's Party (CPP). The United Gold Coast Convention was formed in 1947 by representatives of the Gold Coast economic elite: wealthy traders, commercial farmers and educated professionals.[4] It was founded to advance members' economic interests and to serve as an umbrella group unifying the diverse political associations in the Colony.

When rioting erupted in 1948, members of the UGCC working committee immediately convened to discuss the best means by which to "take advantage of the day's tragic events." UGCC Vice President J. B. Danquah cabled the Secretary of State in London, decrying the collapse of civil authority in the Gold Coast and volunteering on behalf of the UGCC to assume control of an interim government until a new constitution could be drafted. British officials responded to the offer by arresting six members of the working committee and deporting them to the Northern Territories.[5]

The arrests catapulted the UGCC into national prominence. In the months following the riots, UGCC membership soared. The number of operating branches grew from 13 to 209 by August (Austin 1964: 73). For a time, the UGCC was recognized as the legitimate body speaking for the Gold Coast public.

The Convention People's Party

The UGCC's political prominence was soon challenged by the Convention People's Party (CPP). The Convention People's Party mobilized the Gold Coast's proletariat: urban laborers, market women, unemployed secondary school leavers, artisans and drivers. Its leaders espoused a radical agenda of socialist, state-led development and called for immediate independence from the British. The organization therefore posed a direct threat to the UGCC's conservative constituency and to the British Colonial Office.

Ironically, the CPP's mass membership was first mobilized under a UGCC banner. In December 1947, two months before the riots, the UGCC working committee appointed Kwame Nkrumah, subsequent founder and President of the CPP, to be the General Secretary for the UGCC. From the outset, the relationship between Nkrumah and other members of the UGCC working committee was tense. Working committee members were suspicious of Nkrumah's ties to European socialists, while Nkrumah feared it was "quite useless to associate myself with a movement backed almost entirely by reactionaries, middle class lawyers, and merchants, for my revolutionary background and ideas would make it impossible for me to work with them" (Nkrumah 1957: 62).

For a time, Nkrumah and the UGCC were able to accommodate one another. Nkrumah drew upon the reputation and financial resources of the UGCC, and the UGCC used Nkrumah to gain greater national prominence. But by the close of 1948, when discussions on constitutional reform were underway, it was clear that Nkrumah had developed an independent base of support. In August 1948 the various youth organizations which Nkrumah had helped to mobilize forged the Committee of Youth Organizations (CYO), giving Nkrumah a large and vocal group of supporters. A month later, Nkrumah launched the *Accra Evening News,* a newspaper targeted specifically at his mass-based constituency. The *News'* heavy reliance upon editorial cartoons and sensationalistic articles made it the first publication accessible to a semiliterate population. Virulently anti-British (and later anti-UGCC), the newspaper became an effective means of communicating with, and appealing to, the mass public (Ansah 1991: 88–107). Its success spawned two similar publications, the *Morning Telegraph* in Sekondi and the *Daily Mail* in Cape Coast.

In June 1949, the UGCC working committee tried to rid themselves of Nkrumah by removing him from his powerful post as General Secretary. Hoping to retain the public's support, they agreed to re-appoint Nkrumah to the post of Honorary Treasurer. The gambit failed. At the urging of the CYO, Nkrumah split with the UGCC and forged his own Convention People's Party. He was followed by the bulk of the UGCC's grass roots activists, crippling the UGCC organization (Padmore 1953).

In the months that followed, the CPP organization and membership thrived. By January 1950 Nkrumah had organized a national Positive Action campaign of civil disobedience to demand "self government now." When a labor union's sympathy strike turned violent, Nkrumah and several CPP officials were arrested. Their conviction, writes Apter, gave the CPP "precisely the cap of martyrdom needed by the party" (1966: 172). The CPP became a household name.

The chronology of the CPP's ascendance is important. By the time the Coussey Committee convened, and certainly by the time it finished its work, the CPP had established itself as a viable political force. The CPP's mass-based political following placed it in a position to dominate a future electoral contest and seize control over the new institutions of government.

Given the CPP's strength, and given the antagonism between the CPP and UGCC agendas, we would expect UGCC leaders to agitate for the creation of a constitution that divided political authority. This did not happen. Instead, UGCC leaders, in conjunction with other members of the conservative elite, deliberately chose to concentrate political authority. To understand why, we must examine the procedure by which the constitution was created.

III. The Drafting of the Coussey Constitution

British colonial officials dictated the procedure by which the new constitution would be drafted and later ratified. At both stages, they adopted measures that they believed would promote moderate reform. When they appointed the Coussey Committee, they excluded all CPP sympathizers and members. They failed to appoint a single small farmer, petty trader, urban laborer or CPP official. Instead, they populated the committee with representatives of the old, conservative elite: educated professionals, commercial farmers and a relatively small number of traditional rulers (paramount chiefs) and six members of the UGCC working committee. Significantly, the latter were the only members who voted as a cohesive bloc, a fact that magnified their influence during the committee's deliberations.

The British strategy was intended to encourage moderate reform. It functioned instead to alter the actors' beliefs about the distribution of power in the Gold Coast. The British decision stripped the CPP leaders of their power by denying them the opportunity to influence the constitution's design. The decision also persuaded the UGCC leaders that they, and not the CPP, would govern under the new constitution.

Under these conditions, the members of the Coussey Committee deliberately chose to draft a constitution that centralized authority in national level institutions.[6] Consider, for example, the design of the legislature. Buchanan and Tullock have argued that a bicameral legislature functions to minimize the costs that one actor may impose upon another because it forces two bodies, drawn from two distinct constituencies, to approve a single policy choice (Buchanan and Tullock 1964: 235–36). The Coussey Committee called for the creation of a bicameral legislature and assured that each house would be drawn from different constituencies: one chamber would consist of elected commoners, the other of appointed chiefs and elders. However, the committee sharply restricted the decision-making authority of the second, appointed, chamber. The House of Chiefs would not be allowed to delay legislation longer than one month; it could not prevent the passage of a bill which the House had twice approved; and it exercised no power of initiation (*Coussey Report* 1949: 55–56). In restricting the second body's power, the committee eliminated the potential check on central authority.

In similar fashion, committee members declined to adopt another mechanism by which central authority could be constrained: the preservation of local autonomy (Buchanan and Tullock 1964: 115). In a divided vote, the Coussey Committee recommended the creation of a regional administration to oversee local governments. The regional administrators would act as the "agents of central government": their powers were to be conferred at the discretion of central government officials (*Coussey Report* 1949: 40–41). The arrangement ensured that local administration would be dominated by actors accountable to the center rather than to the local area. It also ensured that the traditional state would no longer be a viable arena for political action. Actors within the traditional state would no longer have the autonomy or authority to initiate or enforce a locally defined property rights system.

The Coussey Committee was willing to concentrate authority because its members believed that they could design a constitution which would nullify Nkrumah's power and thereby perpetuate the advantages conferred upon them by British intervention. In addition to the creation of decision-making institutions, the members of the Coussey Committee were charged with outlining a new electoral system. The committee members sought to use these electoral institutions to disenfranchise Nkrumah's supporters and precipitate his electoral defeat. If the conservative members of the committee could eliminate Nkrumah's power before the election, then they would be certain to wield political authority themselves. Once in power, they could then use that authority to consolidate the already favorable distribution of wealth and power.

The electoral institutions proposed by the Coussey Committee clearly disadvantaged Nkrumah and the Convention People's Party. First, suffrage was to be extended to all registered voters and tax payers over the age of 25. Both the age and tax qualifications assured that some portion of Nkrumah's radical constituency would be ineligible, either because they were too young, or because they lacked the economic resources to pay their taxes.

Second, elections for the rural seats would be conducted on an indirect basis: rural voters would select delegates to sit in an electoral college; these delegates would then elect the rural representatives to the Legislative Assembly. By situating the voters' choice in their local village or town, the local chiefs could influence the outcome directly. Third, electoral constituencies were to be delineated on the basis of each state's population, a move which gave greater representation to the largest (and coincidentally the most prosperous and conservative) states.[7]

UGCC leaders complemented these provisions with an electoral strategy designed to win for them a sizeable portion of votes in the rural areas, where Nkrumah's base was less certain (Ofori Atta 1992). In April 1950 the UGCC working committee issued a blunt statement that, in the face of the CPP's superior organization, the chiefs were the most effective rallying point of sensible opinion left to the party (Austin 1964: 134). The CPP's rhetorical attacks against the chiefs, and against chieftaincy more generally, persuaded the traditional elites to accept the alliance in spite of current tensions.[8]

UGCC leaders believed that the chiefs, acting through their state councils, could "make use of their special machinery of information" to register voters and attract support for the UGCC (Austin 1964: 136). This special machinery of information consisted of the chiefs' ability to influence the citizens of their state or village. Individual citizens would frequently approach a chief, soliciting his opinion on any range of matters. In this way, the chief became something of an "opinion leader" within the area. Political activists believed that this influence could be transferred to the electoral arena. One longtime UGCC and Ghana Congress Party activist explained their logic: "Anytime they went to a village, they approached the chiefs [because] oftentimes, the chief was able to exert an indirect influence. You always knew where the chief stood politically, even when he didn't say anything" (Ofori Atta 1992). The emphasis on village level organization, however, belied the party's heavy reliance upon the paramount chiefs. Party organizers assumed that, if they earned the support of a state's paramount chief, that chief would be able to command the allegiance of those chiefs subordinate to him.[9]

Ultimately, the UGCC gambit failed; the conservative elite could not consolidate their hold on power. In the first elections under the new constitution, the CPP was swept into office. CPP leaders then used the institutions of central government to appropriate the elites' resources for redistribution to their constituents, and to further concentrate political power.

To understand this outcome, we must consider the procedure under which the constitution was ratified and the way in which these unintended outcomes were embedded within the newly forged institutions.

IV. The Passage of the Coussey Constitution

When the Coussey Committee began its deliberations, British officials had not yet decided how the Committee's report would be considered.[10] Both the UGCC and the CPP lobbied the colonial government to adopt a procedure favorable to their party. UGCC members argued that the draft constitution should be considered by a body similar in composition to the Coussey Committee. Nkrumah agitated for the creation of a more broadly representative constituent assembly.

Initially, the Colonial Office had planned to invite a representative delegation of Gold Coast Africans to London to debate the Coussey Report. They believed that such a procedure would demonstrate the British commitment to meaningful change and thus undermine radical criticisms that the reforms were not progressing quickly enough. The procedure would also allow the Colonial Office to continue bolstering political moderates, since British officials would nominate the delegation themselves.

In August 1949, however, just two months before the Coussey Report was published, the Secretary of State expressed reservations about the plan, calling it a "rather novel, and possibly expensive way of considering the report" (Watson 1949). The Governor of the Gold Coast soon added his objections, writing:

> London is clearly no place in which to consider detail and if any great controversy should arise on matters of major importance or of principle it would be extremely difficult to find a representative group of Africans who would be willing to risk the opprobrium which would attach to them if they agreed with our views even as the result of a London Conference. (Arden-Clarke 1949)

Faced with these objections, the Colonial Office abandoned all plans for a conference in London or the Gold Coast. Instead, it decided to send the Coussey Report to the existing Legislative Council. Because the Governor had previously expressed concern that the Legislative Council would reject the document if it were presented in toto, the British also stipulated that the Legislative Council could consider only those clauses related to the Executive and the Legislature. Questions of regional and local government would be determined by the Legislative Assembly which would be formed under the new constitution (Lloyd 1949).

The British decision to send the draft constitution to the Legislative Council was intended to enhance British influence over the constitution-building process. It is ironic, then, that this decision served to strengthen those most hostile to the British presence in the Gold Coast: Kwame Nkrumah and the Convention People's Party.

The decision to send the draft constitution to the Legislative Council profoundly shaped the development path that the Gold Coast would follow. First, the British decision altered the distribution of power among indigenous actors. Where the Coussey Committee had been dominated by conservative, wealthy elites—professionals, merchant traders and members of a landed gentry—the Legislative Council was dominated by paramount chiefs. In addition, while Coussey had effectively denied all representation to the CPP, the CPP did have some allies on the Legislative Council. Kwesi Plange was elected to represent the CPP in a special by-election in Cape Coast, an urban constituency. He assumed his seat in June 1950. In addition, though the chiefs as a group opposed the CPP, several chiefs from the poorer states of the Western Province expressed sympathy with Nkrumah's party. Under these changed circumstances, UGCC leaders could no longer be certain of controlling the constitution's final design; by extension, they could not be sure that they would be able to disenfranchise Nkrumah's supporters and thereby secure their own electoral victory.

Second, the decision to shift debate to the Legislative Council introduced new procedural considerations. In the Coussey meetings, individual actors had constructed a package of institutions which they believed would operate together. In the Legislative Council representatives debated the constitution's component parts; they never considered the constitution as a whole. This procedure encouraged actors to pursue narrow, redistributive gains by manipulating the components, paying little attention to how their actions affected the constitutional "vision" outlined by the Coussey Committee. Equally important, the piecemeal consideration of the constitution meant that some of the constitution's provisions were approved and implemented before others—most importantly the provisions establishing local government and the judiciary—had even been considered.

The Legislative Council convened to deliberate the draft constitution in March 1950. In July 1950 it passed the Coussey Committee's electoral provisions; in December 1950 the new constitution was put into effect through the British Governor's Order in Council.

Over the course of the Legislative Council's debate, members approved a series of amendments to the Coussey proposals. The motivations for each amendment varied: some amendments were sponsored by individuals in pursuit of selective gain at the public expense; other amendments involved a dispute between allies over which institution would produce a mutually agreed-upon goal. Cumulatively, these amendments weakened the already tenuous checks on centralized authority.

Consider, first, the conflict over executive authority. Severe informational constraints helped to fuel a debate among representatives of the conservative intelligentsia as to the proper design of the executive. Danquah championed the Coussey proposal that the majority party in the Legislative Assembly elect a member of the Assembly to serve as Leader of Government Business in the Executive Council (a position akin to that of prime minister). Others, led by the conservative lawyer N. A. Ollennu, preferred that the British Governor appoint a member of the Assembly directly.

The dispute did not stem from the actors' preferences over distributional outcomes; Ollennu was broadly supportive of the more conservative agenda. Rather, the dispute stemmed from the two men's different beliefs about how the institution itself would operate. Ollennu did not believe that party politics would take root in the Gold Coast; therefore, an election within the Legislative Assembly would degenerate into a personality contest, and the best qualified candidate would not be chosen (GC March 21, 1950). Ollennu's view prevailed. When, contrary to expectation, parties formed, the party leader who became the Leader of Government Business was not accountable to the Legislative Assembly.

Other amendments to the Coussey Constitution were passed when new actors in the Legislative Council sought to amend the draft proposal to reflect their interests. Operating for the first time within the formal decision-making institutions, the CPP was able to influence the constitution's design. Kwesi Plange, the newly elected CPP member, introduced an amendment lowering the voting age from 25 to 21. His argument appealed directly to the paramount chiefs. Invoking the democratic principle of "no taxation without representation," Plange warned the chiefs that the youth of the country would not pay their customary tribute until they reached the voting age. The chiefs responded by voting with Plange, lowering the voting age to 21 and enfranchising a large portion of Nkrumah's constituency (Nkrumah 1957: 89).

The battle to secure redistributive gains was most evident in the amendments proposed by the paramount chiefs. A group of paramount chiefs from the Colony, for example, proposed an amendment which would increase the political power wielded by the smaller states at the expense of the larger states. Under the Coussey proposals, elections to the territorial seats were to be conducted on the basis of a state's population, a plan which would have allowed the largest five states in the Colony to dominate the 58 smaller states. A group of Colony chiefs argued that the Joint Provincial Council should serve as an electoral college, a move which would allow the smaller states to dominate.

Both the UGCC and the CPP opposed the amendment on similar grounds. UGCC member Akufo Addo complained that the departure from popular elections threatened the "essential feature of constitutional reform . . . the broadening of the basis of political representation." Kwesi Plange, speaking for the CPP, agreed and condemned the chiefs for trying to force their decisions upon the people (GC July 7, 1950). Their opposition proved unsuccessful. The Colony chiefs, joined by a few non-chiefs who believed that the amendment helped promote national unity, carried enough votes to see the amendment passed.

The paramount chiefs also moved to recapture political power seized by the non-chiefs. The battle was played out over the issue of a bicameral legislature. Recall that, at prior stages, members of the UGCC had advocated institutions which gave the chiefs limited authority in national and local government. At the national level, chiefs were offered seats in a relatively weak second chamber. At the local level, chiefs were made the ceremonial presidents of new local councils, to which they would appoint one-third of the members.

Working through the Legislative Council, the chiefs again sought to increase their future authority. They agitated for their inclusion in a single, unicameral legislature where they would exert the same influence as all elected members.

Shortly before the Legislative Council debates, the Joint Provincial Council (1950) issued a memorandum condemning the Coussey proposal for a bicameral legislature. In the bicameral system, the chiefs would be

> utterly devoid of any power to influence decisions of the Lower House but would be subordinate to the Lower House. . . . It has been suggested and re-echoed by the very people who clamour for Two Houses that Chiefs should not take part in politics. . . . If Chiefs are not to take part in politics, what would be the role of the Chiefs in the Upper House? Would they be there merely for ceremonial purposes? This is a question which has yet to be answered by sponsors of a Bicameral System.

In the Legislative Council, the chiefs proposed the creation of a unicameral body. Their plan provided for the election of 78 representatives to a unicameral Legislative Assembly. Thirty of the 78 were to be elected from rural constituencies, five from urban constituencies; 18 were to be chosen by the three territorial councils. The remaining 19 seats would go to representatives from the Northern Territories.

When the same plan had been considered in the Coussey Committee, none of the Colony chiefs had supported it (Frimpong 1966: 70). Their reversal can be linked to their increased bargaining power: the Coussey proposals were being considered in a body which they dominated, the Legislative Council; and the chiefs were now crucial allies in an upcoming electoral battle. In addition, following the publication of the Coussey Report, British officials had expressed their clear preference for a unicameral legislature (Joint Provincial Council 1950).

Danquah led the opposition within the Legislative Council. The debate which ensued gives life to the strategic bargaining between actors. Danquah clearly perceived the chiefs' proposal as a defection from the UGCC's tacit alliance with the chiefs. In his speech before the Legislative Council, he retaliated by threatening to sanction the chiefs' behavior. First, he warned that the action undermined the basis for future cooperation:

> Do not imagine for one moment that the country is asleep. Do not imagine for one moment that if you insisted and came to the lower house, sold your eldership because you are hungry for power, then the rest of the country . . . is likely to forget what they have purchased from you. (GC March 22, 1950)

He then promised that the action would carry long-term, negative costs. If the chiefs accepted seats in a unicameral legislature now, a "united national party" would form to oppose them; and "when that day comes, you must know that Chieftaincy is finished in this country, and I would be the last to sing a dirge over your mortal remains" (GC March 22, 1950).

Danquah's threats lacked credibility. The UGCC's prior institutional choices had locked them into an electoral strategy in which the chiefs were indispensable allies. Their vote for a unicameral legislature would not cause the UGCC leaders to sanction them. The motion was carried.

Each of these amendments was passed for a unique and unrelated reason. Collectively, however, they served to undermine the coherence and strength of the constitutional design. Ollennu's amendment ensured that, when party politics did emerge, the leader of the Executive Council would not be accountable to the Legislative Assembly as a whole; instead, he would be accountable to a British Governor reluctant to intervene and to his own party organization. The Colony chiefs' amendment ensured that, when Nkrumah moved to vest property rights in the central government, the largest states most harmed by the redistributive policy (and most capable of mounting a defense) were no longer in a position to respond through the formal, institutional structure. Finally, with the move toward the unicameral legislature, even the minimal protection which the bicameral legislature offered against centralized authority was lost. Moreover, the chiefs' refusal to cede authority left them vulnerable to public criticism and potentially weakened their ability to influence voters in the impending elections.

The Elections of 1951

The abrupt shift in the procedure for ratification produced significant changes in the constitution's design and weakened the UGCC's position in the electoral arena. The effect of these institutional changes was exacerbated by the UGCC leaders' miscalculation of their ability to mobilize the voting public. In designing the constitution, UGCC leaders assumed that they could influence rural voters through the intermediation of the chiefs. Their assumption was unfounded. First, CPP activists undermined the effectiveness of the UGCC alliance with the paramount chiefs by appealing directly to the sub-chiefs. CPP leaders manipulated purely local grievances to attract support: if a chief in one village declared support for the UGCC, CPP leaders recruited the chief of a neighboring village to declare support for the CPP. Though neither chief was concerned with the policies of either party, the CPP activists provided valuable resources in contesting stool land or stool disputes.[11] Consequently, when the paramount chief called upon his sub-chiefs to support the UGCC, his appeals often fell on deaf ears (Austin 1964: 144).

Second, CPP activists were often able to sway the delegates sent to the rural electoral colleges. Recall that the rural elections proceeded in two stages: rural voters chose delegates to sit in the electoral college and those delegates selected the rural representatives to the Legislative Assembly. The UGCC belief that the chiefs could influence the first decision-making stage seems to have been accurate. British election observers reported that the majority of seats to the electoral college were uncontested. Delegates were most often chosen according to the "usual custom": village elders, head farmers and the chief jointly agreed upon whom they should send (UK: *Report on the First Elections* 1951). The chiefs' influence, however, was not sustained in the electoral college. There, delegates were subjected to intense campaigning by members of both parties. Austin records that delegates were plied with drink and presents, or locked in a room while the constituency secretary appealed for support for the party candidate (Austin 1964: 140). Election observers concluded that, in the face of such lobbying, "It is not improbable that some voted contrary to instructions" (UK: *Report on the First Elections* 1951).

The combination of circumstances was devastating. As expected, Nkrumah had won all five urban seats outright. In the rural areas, however, the CPP won 29 of 33 seats and polled 72 percent of the vote, an unanticipated outcome. They also gained the support of 19 delegates from the Northern Territories and three delegates from the Territorial Councils. The CPP thus controlled 56 votes in the 84-member Legislative Assembly.

In later years, former UGCC politicians would ally with a new political party to demand constitutional reforms. They agitated for the creation of a federal constitution and for the devolution of power to local and regional governments. Their efforts failed. The choices made during the drafting of the Coussey Constitution were embedded within the nation's institutional structure and could not be dislodged.

Conclusion

My analysis of the drafting and implementation of the Gold Coast constitution of 1950 yields important insights for our theories of constitutional creation and for our understanding of the causes of authoritarian rule in the Gold Coast. The analysis suggests that a positive theory of constitutional creation must examine actors' beliefs about the political environment. When actors believe that power is distributed asymmetrically, and when they believe that they will occupy a prominent place in any future decision-making institutions, then they are quite willing to design a constitution that concentrates political authority, thereby facilitating their pursuit of narrowly beneficial, redistributive goals.

A theory of constitutional creation must also consider the procedure through which the constitution is written and implemented. First, the procedure that actors adopt when creating institutions can amplify or negate perceived power asymmetries, and thus alter the actors' preferences over the constitution's design. In the Gold Coast, British officials adopted a constitution-building procedure that effectively silenced one of the important political powers in the Colony, the Convention People's Party, and artificially inflated the power of a second party, the United Gold Coast Convention. The procedural decision persuaded the UGCC leaders that they would control the new decision-making institutions, and therefore encouraged them to choose institutions that concentrated authority, eschewing measures which would have protected them from a powerful opponent.

Second, procedures affect the actors' ability to draft a coherent constitution. In the Gold Coast, British officials adopted procedures that forced indigenous actors to consider the constitution in a piecemeal fashion. Under these constraints, the debate over the constitution degenerated into a battle to secure narrowly beneficial gains. The coherent vision of the Coussey Committee was lost.

Finally, a theory of constitutional creation must account for the path-dependent nature of institutional development. Rational choice models of individual choice typically are based on the assumption that actors employ true or correct models of the world in which they live (Tsebelis 1990: 7; North 1990: 93). Actors may make an incorrect choice because they have incomplete information, but they quickly receive new information that informs them of the error. They can then act to correct for the mistake.

This essay demonstrates that such an assumption cannot be sustained. Individuals do not necessarily operate with true models of the world. Thus, their choices often yield unanticipated and unintended outcomes. In the Gold Coast UGCC leaders did not anticipate the British decision to send the Coussey Constitution to the Legislative Council. In addition, they grossly misjudged their ability to command votes in an electoral arena. These mistakes were embedded in the constitution when the CPP won the subsequent elections and assumed control over the new decision-making institutions. The UGCC leaders possessed the information necessary to revise their beliefs, but they no longer possessed the political power to amend their prior mistakes.

This more nuanced view of institutional creation allows us to draw linkages between the macro- and micro-level explanations for the concentration of authority in the Gold Coast, and in Africa more generally. British colonialism contributed to the concentration of authority, because it artificially distorted the distribution of power among indigenous actors. Throughout the constitution-building period, officials of the colonial state worked to preserve British influence in the Colony by promoting the "moderate element." They therefore adopted decision-making procedures that lifted the veil of ignorance and gave some actors a false perception of their own political power. In so doing, they encouraged those actors to choose institutions that concentrated political authority.

The subsequent actions of postindependence governments must be understood within this context. Once in office, Kwame Nkrumah used the institutions of central government to repress his opponents and consolidate all political power in the office of the Prime Minister (and later President). But, at each stage of the game, his actions were entirely constitutional. The seeds of Nkrumah's dictatorship lay in the original episode of institutional creation.

This conclusion challenges the conventional view of the Gold Coast elite. Danquah and his UGCC cohorts are remembered as the defenders of the liberal democratic order; and indeed, following Nkrumah's rise to power, Danquah stood as a champion of civil liberties and private property rights in Ghana. He died in detention for his convictions. Nevertheless, the image of the UGCC as conservative democrats is somewhat false; for a close study of the politics of the constitution-building process suggests that these men were quite willing to sacrifice their democratic ideals in the pursuit of self-interest. They deliberately chose institutions which concentrated authority in order to preserve their privileged place in society.

NOTES

1. This historical approach shares some similarities with that endorsed by a growing number of critical theorists (Ashford 1992; Fischer and Forester 1993). They argue that scholars cannot understand individual policy choices unless they (1) situate those choices within their historical context and (2) specify the way in which individual actors perceived both the context and the issue at hand. I am grateful to an anonymous reviewer for bringing this important body of literature to my attention.

2. Institutions can be formal structures of government—legislatures, bureaucracies and the like—or more informal norms of behavior. This essay deals exclusively with the design of formal institutions of government.

3. The procedural issue is hardly trivial. In states making the transition from authoritarian to democratic rule, officials are forced to decide which, if any, of the old parties, politicians, or military authorities will be included in the transition process. Their choice necessarily affects the distribution of power among actors and, by extension, the type of constitution they create.

4. In addition to Grant, the leading members of the Convention were R. S. Blay, J. B. Danquah, R. A. Awoonor Williams, William Ofori Atta, E. O. Akufo Addo, J. W. deGraft Johnson, Obetsebi Lamptey, John Tsiboe and Cobina Kessie. All save Grant, William Ofori Atta and John Tsiboe were lawyers. Ofori Atta was a college professor and Tsiboe owned the conservative newspaper *Ashanti Pioneer*.

5. The "Big Six" were J. B. Danquah, William Ofori Atta, E. O. Akufo Addo, Kwame Nkrumah, Obetsebi Lamptey and Ako Adjei.

6. I was unable to locate the proceedings of the Coussey Committee; thus, the analysis that follows is based largely on the final report. Though this masks the strategic interaction leading to the report, I believe it provides sufficient information to advance the following conclusions.

7. Under the existing constitution, each state in the Southern Colony held one seat on the Joint Provincial Council of Chiefs, regardless of size.

8. In his testimony before the Watson Commission, Nkrumah had dismissed the chiefs as strategic allies, declaring that they would come to the side of whichever party was best organized. In later months, Nkrumah attacked the chiefs more directly: those who did not ally with the CPP would be made to "run away and leave their sandals behind." Since, by custom, a chief's feet could never touch the ground, the statement amounted to a threat of destoolment.

9. My thanks to Kwame Arhin for clarifying this point.

10. Indeed, archival records indicate that the Colonial office did not even begin to

consider these procedural questions until June 1949, six months into the committee's deliberations.

11. Literally, the stool is the seat upon which a chief sits. Metaphorically, the stool is the symbol of the traditional state or village. Because the stool holder was the caretaker of all community owned lands and because the chieftaincy remained an important political office, disputes frequently arose over land ownership and over the legitimacy of a person's tenure in office.

REFERENCES

Secondary Sources

Ansah, P. A. V. (1991) "Kwame Nkrumah and the Mass Media." In Kwame Arhin (ed.) *The Life and Work of Kwame Nkrumah*. Accra, Ghana: Sedco.

Apter, David (1966) *Ghana in Transition*. New York: Atheneum.

Ashford, Douglas (ed.) (1992) *History and Context in Comparative Public Policy*. Pittsburgh and London: University of Pittsburgh Press.

Austin, Dennis (1964) *Politics in Ghana: 1946–1960*. London: Oxford University Press.

Bates, Robert H. (1988) "Contra Contractarianism: Some Reflections on the New Institutionalism." *Politics and Society* 16:387–401.

Buchanan, James, and Gordon Tullock (1964) *The Calculus of Consent: Logical Foundations of Constitutional Democracy*. Ann Arbor: University of Michigan Press.

Fischer, Frank, and John Forester (eds.) (1993) *The Argumentative Turn in Policy Analysis and Planning*. Durham, NC: Duke University Press.

Frimpong, J. H. S. (1966) "The Joint Provincial Council of Chiefs and the Politics of Independence in the Gold Coast (Ghana): 1946–1958." Master's thesis in Political Science, University of Ghana.

Geddes, Barbara (1990) "Democratic Institutions as Bargains among Self-Interested Politicians." MS, University of California, Los Angeles.

——— (1991) "A Game Theoretic Model of Reform in Latin American Democracies." *American Political Science Review* 85:371–92.

Hardin, G. (1968) "The Tragedy of the Commons." *Science* 162:1243–48.

Kiser, L., and Elinor Ostrom (1982) "The Three Worlds of Action: A Metatheoretical Synthesis of Institutional Approaches." In E. Ostrom (ed.) *Strategies of Political Inquiry*. Beverly Hills, CA: Sage. Reprinted in M. D. McGinnis, ed. *Polycentric Games and Institutions* (Ann Arbor: University of Michigan Press, 1999).

Knight, Jack (1992) *Institutions and Social Conflict*. New York: Cambridge University Press.

Moe, Terry (1990a) "Political Institutions: The Neglected Side of the Story." *Journal of Law, Economics, and Organization* 6:213–53.

——— (1990b) "The Politics of Structural Choice: Toward a Theory of Public Bureaucracy." In Oliver Williamson (ed.) *Organization Theory: From Chester*

Barnard to the Present and Beyond. New York: Oxford University Press.

Nkrumah, Kwame (1957) *The Autobiography of Kwame Nkrumah.* London: Nelson.

North, Douglass (1990) *Institutions, Institutional Change and Economic Performance.* Cambridge: Cambridge University Press.

Ostrom, Elinor (1986) "An Agenda for the Study of Institutions." *Public Choice* 48:3–25. Reprinted in M. D. McGinnis, ed. *Polycentric Games and Institutions* (Ann Arbor: University of Michigan Press, 1999).

———— (1990) *Governing the Commons: The Evolution of Institutions for Collective Action.* New York: Cambridge University Press.

Ostrom, Vincent (1982) "A Forgotten Tradition: The Constitutional Level of Analysis." In J. A. Gillespie and D. A. Zinnes (eds.) *Missing Elements in Political Inquiry.* Beverly Hills, CA: Sage. Reprinted as chap. 7 of this volume.

Padmore, George (1953) *Gold Coast Revolution.* London: Dennis Dobson.

Przeworski, Adam (1991) *Democracy and the Market.* New York: Cambridge University Press.

Rathbone, Richard (ed.) (1992) *British Documents on the End of Empire: Ghana.* London: Her Majesty's Stationery Office.

Rawls, John (1971) *A Theory of Justice.* Cambridge, MA: Harvard University Press.

Tsebelis, George (1990) *Nested Games: Political Context, Political Institutions and rationality.* Berkeley: University of California Press.

Weingast, Barry (1992) "The Economic Role of Political Institutions." MS, Stanford University, CA.

Wunsch, James (1990) "Foundations of Centralization: The Colonial Experience." In James Wunsch and Dele Olowu (eds.) *The Failure of the Centralized State.* Boulder, CO: Westview Press.

Young, Crawford (1988) "The African Colonial State and Its Political Legacy." In Donald Rothschild and Naomi Chazan (eds.) *The Precarious Balance: State and Society in Africa.* Boulder, CO: Westview Press.

Zolberg, Aristide (1966) *Creating Political Order: The Party States of West Africa.* Chicago: Rand McNally.

Primary Sources

Alexander (1948) Minute on contingency plans to send military reinforcements to Gold Coast, March 3. PREM 8/924.

Arden-Clarke, C. (1949) Letter to T. Lloyd, September 23. PRO CO 96/800/1, no. 28.

Bradley, K. G. (1947) Report to Creech Jones on the formation of the UGCC, December 12. PRO CO 537/3559, no. 2.

Cohen, A. B. (1948a) Letter to Gerald Creasy, June 14. PRO CO 96/796/5, no. 12.

———— (1948b) Memorandum, June 29. PRO CO 96/796/5, no. 43.

Creech Jones, A., and T. R. O. Mangin (1949) Correspondence, May 12 and 24. PRO CO 4638, nos. 7 and 8.

Danquah, J. B. (1949) Minutes of the Standing Committee of the Joint Provincial Council, November 18. NAG CSO 1119.

Gold Coast [GC] (1950) *Legislative Council Debates,* issue 2–3.

Joint Provincial Council (1950) Minutes of the Standing Committee, January 25–27. NAG CSO 1119.

Listowel, Lord (1949) Letter for Creech Jones to T. R. O. Mangin, April 19. PRO CO 537/4638, no. 4.

Lloyd, T. (1949) Letter to Arden-Clarke, September 23. PRO CO 96/800/ 1, no. 28.

Ofori Atta, Guggisberg, UGCC activist. Interview by author, May 21, 1992, Kyebi.

Scott, R. (1948) Memoranda, March 5. PRO CO 96/795/6, no. 5.

————— (1949) Letter to Creech Jones, March 10. PRO CO 537/4638, no. 1.

UK (1948) *Report of the Commission of Enquiry into Disturbances in the Gold Coast* (the Watson Report). Colonial Office No. 231.

————— (1949) *Report to His Excellency the Governor by the Committee on Constitutional Reform*. Colonial Office No. 248.

————— (1951) *Report on the First Elections to the Legislative Assembly of the Gold Coast.*

Watson, N. D. (1949) Minute for Creech Jones, August 23. PRO CO 537/4635.

Note: The abbreviation PRO refers to the United Kingdom's Public Records Office; CO refers to Colonial Office materials. All PRO references were taken from *British Documents on the End of Empire: Ghana* (London: Her Majesty's Stationery Office, 1992). The abbreviation NAG refers to the National Archives of Ghana. I searched the office of Secretary for Native Affairs (SNA) and Colonial Secretary's Office (CSO) materials as well as the special collections.

CHAPTER 10

Local Organizations and Development: The African Experience

Dele Olowu

Introduction

There has been a renewed interest in the potential contribution of local institutions to the development of countries within the Third World (Esman and Uphoff 1984; *Regional Development Dialogue* 1985; United Nations 1986). Such local institutions might be local governments, cooperatives, local development associations, or some other voluntary organizations. This new interest can be seen as a corollary to the accumulating evidence of the failures and fundamental weaknesses and limitations of statist/centralist approaches for coping with economic crises of the 1970s and 1980s world-wide and in Africa in particular (Conford 1975; World Bank 1981; Wunsch and Olowu 1990). These crises have undermined the capacity of Africa's cash-starved central governments to continue to undertake development projects as in the past, hence their readiness to explore the possibilities of local institutions for self-management and self-financing.

There are other economic, social, and political considerations as well. On economic grounds, participation is deemed as essential not only for mobilizing local people and resources for development but also for ensuring program success and sustainability after the withdrawal of initial external or central government assistance (Cernea 1987). Local institutions are also seen as alternatives to a wasteful public sector and an underdeveloped private sector for the provision of economic and social services especially in Africa's rural areas (Smoke 1988). Moreover, the very complexity of rural

Originally published as "Local Institutes and Development: The African Experience," *Canadian Journal of African Studies* 23, no. 2 (1989): 201–31. Reprinted by permission of the Canadian Association of African Studies (CAAS) and the author.

Author's note: This essay, originally presented at the Dubrovnic Conference on "Advances in Competitive Institutional Analysis," held at Dubrovnic, Yugoslavia, October 19–23, 1987, has benefited from that conference as well as from the detailed comments of Professor Vincent Ostrom of Indiana University and of three anonymous assessors.

development makes it difficult to plan for this in conventional top-down ways, thus requiring much more diverse management capacities.

From the point of view of equity, past centralized development efforts, however well intentioned, were marked by their failure to benefit the rural poor, who constitute the majority in Africa's present circumstances. Finally, the tendency for African governments to treat their own people and indigenous institutions as obstacles to development rather than as contributors to that process is regarded as a major paradox of African development efforts and a veritable explanation of the continent's continued underdevelopment (Cochrane 1983, 1; Uphoff 1985, 43–44; Ake 1987, 1–5).

As a result of some or all of the above considerations, many African countries have embarked on programs of decentralization aimed at involving the local people more effectively in the development process. Unfortunately, most of these decentralization initiatives have ended as failures (Cheema and Rondinelli 1983; Mawhood 1983; Smith 1985).[1] Several attempts have been made to explain such failure. Some scholars have argued that the source of failure is traceable to the inherent weaknesses of local bureaucracies; others trace failure to the absence of managerial capacities in the central government. A few scholars, however, blame the failure of decentralization on the structure of politics in a developing country and the political economy of underdevelopment (Mawhood 1983, 252–54; Smith 1985, 194–99).

While each of these explanations lends some insight into the failure of decentralization, I am going to argue that the source of failure is basically conceptual. I shall penetrate the conceptual confusion surrounding decentralization and development to reveal the fundamental basis for such confusion. *Decentralization* is, generally, a convenient term that hides the true intentions of government officials. This point becomes particularly evident when decentralization is contrasted with local self-governance. I shall show on the basis of past decentralization policies and programs that when African policy-makers speak of decentralization they are actually seeking the extension of the powers and tentacles of the central bureaucracy to control the countryside rather than the promotion of self-governance (Ashford 1967; Nooi 1987; Allen 1987). I intend to argue that decentralization and local self-governance represent different organizational principles—one for control, the other for the stimulation of peoples' creativity to solve their own problems in their own way.

I intend to argue this broad thesis in four parts. First, I shall attempt to clear the conceptual jungle: characterize the two central concepts and trace very briefly their historical evolution in Africa. Second, I shall demonstrate decentralization's failure drawing on the most important cases from Africa. Third, I shall provide, in contrast, examples of successful self-governing institutions across Africa. This latter section seeks only to demonstrate that local peoples in Africa can and do initiate the improvement of themselves and their communities (the presumed goal of development), given the appropriate opportunities. Finally, I shall discuss the dilemma that confronts African policy-makers with respect to decentralization.

Decentralization and Local Self-Governance: Conceptual Clarification and Historical Background

Decentralization

Anyone writing on decentralization has a fairly large body of literature to draw upon, which presents constraints as well as opportunities. As a concept, decentralization evokes different images among policy-makers, administrators, political scientists, and the public. The confusion associated with the concept is perhaps best captured by the following observation:

> Many of the arguments for and against decentralization are as Herbert Simon pointed out "like proverbs; for every principle one can find a contradictory principle. Decentralization promotes efficiency and reduces it. Decentralization enhances national unity and inhibits it." (Lamour and Oale 1985, 1)

It is thus not unusual for decentralization to be sought by opposing groups to achieve contrasting or even contradictory objectives (Conyers 1985, 26–27).

James W. Fesler (1949) is reputed to be the first scholar to cut a fine distinction between administrative and political decentralization, the latter being the one in which the state grants wider latitude of discretionary authority to the decentralized unit.[2] Others, including Henry Maddick (1963), R. E. Wraith (1972), Yves Prats (1973), and P. Mawhood (1983) have followed this tradition in their application of the concepts to Africa. Administrative decentralization is conventionally referred to as "deconcentration" to distinguish it from its political variant, "devolution." For practical purposes, the difference between the two may not be great, and in another work I have suggested that it is possible to find so-called devolved "local governments" that possess the same amount of or even less freedom of discretionary authority than do deconcentrated units (Olowu 1988b, 109). This is why I prefer the twin concepts of decentralization and self-governance here.

The important point about decentralization is that it accepts even by definition that power must first be centralized before it is decentralized to lower-level organizations. Here is the major problem for many protagonists of decentralization in Third World countries with special reference to Africa.

Does it make sense to decentralize power when it is yet to be effectively centralized? Opinions divide rather sharply at this point. Some scholars (especially those of the modernization and political mobilization schools—a rather long list) believe that political decentralization is not feasible until political/economic power has been effectively centralized. Hence, the preference amongst these scholars is for administrative rather than political decentralization (Apter 1965, 357–421; Riggs 1961, 367–96; Rubin and Weinstein 1974, 148–77).

This position often calls on modernizing elites to continue with their programs of modernization without hindrance from the mass of the people who must be cajoled and "mobilized" for "development." The economic variant of the argument emphasizes the need to stimulate economic growth through a program of extraction from agriculture to finance state-sponsored industrialization/modernization programs (Lewis 1955; Rostow 1971). Since this group of scholars is usually called upon to advise on decentralization programs in African countries, the confusion earlier referred to between decentralization and self-governance is further reinforced. In essence, decentralization as used in policy circles in Africa (as well as by several international development agencies) refers to administrative decentralization or deconcentration rather than self-governance.

The problem with decentralization as a concept in Africa is compounded by the early use of the prefectoral model of local administration at the inception of colonial administration. The resulting system christened "indirect rule" in English-speaking Africa was used from about 1900 to the early 1950s in practically all English-speaking African countries. Essentially, indirect rule was rule by central officials through indigenous rulers. Where such local rulers did not exist, as in some parts of Eastern Nigeria and among the Nuer in the Sudan, indigenous potentates were created by warrant. Although some attempt was made to increase the scope of the Native Authorities between the two world wars, they remained largely regulatory, appointive institutions, subject to detailed control from above by the colonising power (Cowan 1958, 12–34; Orewa 1987, 39–41). With the approach of independence, an attempt was made to adopt a more liberal form of local government in many African countries. However, shortly after independence these incipient experiments with self-governance were abandoned. Today, many African countries have abolished their structures of local government and substituted in their place single or fused systems of local administration (Olowu 1988a).

Overall, administrative decentralization (or deconcentration), as an approach to promoting development has been a disastrous failure in Africa, both as policy and in terms of its impact on development. This general point will be substantiated with case studies below. But, first, I will examine the concept of local self-governance and the early attempts made to apply it in Africa.

Local Self-Governance

Local self-governance emphasizes three important attributes: locality, primary accountability to the local people, and the provision of important regulatory, economic, or social services or a combination of all. The direction and control of the affairs of the local community by the people themselves is central to the concept of local self-governance. The detailed structure for local self-governance may differ from one country to the other, but these crucial elements must be present. It is thus possible for decentralized structures to accommodate the self-governing principle. However, post-independent African governments have tended to exclude these elements from their concepts of decentralization.

Not all scholars will of course agree with the above characterization of "local self-governance," especially when the concept is applied to the formal institutions of local government, but most would (Tocqueville [1835] 1969, 62–70; Whalen 1969, 312; Mawhood 1983, 9–10). It is important to point out that my characterization of local self-governance, however, pertains more to basic community or local institutions than to formal structures per se. Generally, many would accept that a positive correlation exists between local self-governance and the practice and advance of democratic life, although it is conceivable that local institutions may be counterproductive in this sense under certain circumstances (Riggs 1961, 373; Selznick 1966, 3; Langrod [1953] 1981; Moulin [1954] 1981). Local self-governing units contribute to the success of democratic life both directly and indirectly. Indirectly, they provide a necessary training in the discipline of democratic association at the local level for all citizens and help to recruit and train local and future national leaders. Directly, effective self-governments can act as a check, under certain circumstances, on the excesses of the central government as well as provide greater opportunities for accountable government. Of course, there have been serious objections to some of these arguments, but they are generally accepted in policy circles as well as among a large number of political scientists and public administration scholars (Feldman 1981, 1–86).

Even though basic community units have played important roles in the development of basic infrastructures in diverse cultures, it is only in relatively recent times that scholarly attention has focused on the economic development potential of local self-governing units in developing countries.

It is generally recognized, for instance, that where a virile system of local self-governing units exists, substantial efforts and resources are usually mobilized by the local people themselves to complement the efforts of the central government.

The major breakthrough with respect to local self-governance in Africa came after the second World War. The increasing restlessness of nationalist political leaders with the indirect rule system coincided with the coming to power of the British Labour Party and its greater commitment to an early political independence for its African colonies. Serious thought was given to the issue of local self-governance. Effective local governments were thought to be essential in preparation for future political and economic development. According to the now famous dispatch of the British Secretary of State for the Colonies in 1947, the key to success in resolving the problems of African administration lay in the development of an efficient and democratic system of local government:

> I wish to emphasize the words: *efficient, democratic and local. Local* because the system of government must be close to the common people and their problems, *efficient* because it must be capable of managing the local services in a way which will help to raise the standard of living, and *democratic* because it must not only find a place for the growing class of educated men, but at the same time command the respect and support of the mass of the people. (Creech-Jones, cited in Hicks 1961, 4)

This new departure in colonial policy in English-speaking Africa at this time has been the subject of much academic controversy (Kasfir 1983, 26–32; Hicks 1961). What needs to be noted at this point, however, is that this new policy constituted a major break with the policy and practice of indirect rule. In addition, the self-governance principle was closer to pre-colonial systems of community governance in most parts of Africa. As a result of this policy change, several experiments in local self-governance were embarked upon in the early 1950s across Africa. The most important contribution of these new institutions was their remarkable success at building basic infrastructure—roads, schools, clinics, bridges, markets, parks, etc.—some of which still exist today. In addition, they were responsible for such other services as water supply, forestry, agricultural extension, and police. Within the few years in which they were allowed to operate, they not only performed creditably but also most of these services were financed from locally generated revenue sources (Hicks 1961). Table 10.1 shows that the new local governments committed a substantial portion of their expenditures to basic health, education, roads, public works, and "others," compared to "administration" or "law and order." The latter constituted the major focus of the native authorities which they replaced.

TABLE 10.1. Main Trends in Recurrent Expenditure of African Local Governments, 1956–57

Country/ Region	British Pounds (1,000s)	Administration (%)	Health (%)	Education (%)	Roads and Works (%)	Other* (%)
Ghana						
Town	1,396	18 (3)	59	10	21	—
Regions	3,358	31 (11)	16	26	17	7
Nigeria						
North	4,797	33 (16)	10	28	16	8
East	1,086	34	14	21	25	2
West	2,169	23	10	37	21	7
Uganda	3,562	30	5	35	16	12
Kenya	943	34 (1)	16	17	23	17

Source: Local Government Accounts and Estimates compiled by Hicks (1961, 271–76).

Note: The budgets are not for all local councils but only for the largest and smallest in each province/division of each country. The data excludes councils in white settled areas and cities. The "Justice" and "Police" components of administration are shown in parentheses.

*The category "Other" includes, for example, housing and natural resources.

Of course, there were problems with these new initiatives. The structure of the British local government system was copied wholesale by emerging nationalist politicians who responded to the metropolitan model as the ideal for their respective countries. For instance, there were problems of adjusting to a multi-tier system of local government as well as the system of "precepting," a method by which one rating authority collected taxes which were shared among several local institutions on the basis of their needs (Wraith and Dent 1988). Recent evidence suggests that some of these problems might have been exaggerated by officials and researchers who doubted the ability of the ordinary people (as opposed to the bureaucratic elite) to govern themselves successfully through their representatives (Gboyega 1987). Also, the fact is often lost on observers that this experiment lasted in most African countries for less than a decade.

Shortly after independence, the pendulum swung to the other extreme in which African governments, confident about the powers and potentials of central government departments to promote and mobilize development and anxious to integrate their polities and to consolidate the positions of the ruling elites through the elimination of all opposition to their administrations, abolished existing local government structures in favour of structures which were usually adorned with management or development committees whose deliberative powers were severely curtailed. Moreover, the size (both in terms of population and area) of the basic units of such institutions was often large. As table 10.2 shows, African local governments have a high population average, a fact that is particularly evident when compared with the average for other countries. These post-independence decentralization experiments have certainly been a greater failure than whatever institutional failures were witnessed by African local governments in the closing years of colonial rule (Mawhood 1983, 5–8; Smith 1995, 188–93; Conyers 1985).

TABLE 10.2. The Size of African Local Governments (1982 Population)

Country	No. of Basic Units	Average Population
Zimbabwe	126	6,000
Central African Republic	68	35,294
Mauritania	43	37,209
Burundi	114	37,719
Ivory Coast	163	54,601
Botswana	14	64,286
Uganda	204	66,177
Guinea	70	81,428
Gambia	8	87,500
Zambia	56	107,143
Mauritius	8	112,600
Kenya	133	136,090
Lesotho	10	140,000
Liberia	13	153,846
Tanzania	119	166,386
Niger	36	168,571
Ghana	65	187,692
Malawi	31	209,677
Cameroon	34	273,629
Nigeria	301	300,957
Mali	19	373,684
Other Countries		
France	37,708	1,320
West Germany	22,510	2,634
United States	79,913	2,756
Italy	8,059	2,717
Canada	4,017	6,372
Netherlands	641	16,170
Sweden	278	29,527
England and Wales	401	122,740

Sources: Olowu (1988a, 47–49); World Bank (1984); Smith (1985, 72); Wright (1982, 10); Bennett (1980, 272).

What is important about local self-governance are those characteristics which give it logic and dynamic: smallness/localness, participation, local accountability, and impact on the peoples' social and economic conditions. These characteristics are re-emphasized here for two reasons. First, several governments in Africa give the nomenclature of "local government" to institutions which do not possess these attributes. Second, a number of institutions have been created by the people themselves to meet their needs that may not be governmental in character but which approximate the characteristics mentioned earlier, and hence have had significant impact on the lives of their members. In some cases, these institutions have been taken over by government with both positive and negative consequences.

Case Studies of Decentralization Programs

Virtually all African countries between the early 1960s and late 1970s embarked on a decentralization program. The consensus of most studies that have attempted to evaluate such decentralization programs is:

1. Decentralization has emphasized administrative rather than political decentralization.
2. Decentralization of responsibilities is carried out with considerable hesitation, and in most cases, little decentralization of decision-making powers or tax and personnel resources is involved.
3. Decentralization often increases the workload of central officials rather than decreasing it as they are called upon to manage more responsibilities directly and indirectly throughout the country. Unfortunately, the required competence is lacking (Rondinelli 1983; Mawhood 1983; Conyers 1985; Smith 1985, 188–91; Nooi 1987; Olowu 1988a).

Decentralization reforms usually follow the same prototype. First, the inherited structures of local government are abolished, and development administration units absorb the responsibilities and finances of these institutions. The new units become extensions of the central administration. Second, a law or decree is passed directing all government activities within a region or district to be coordinated by a very senior political or administrative official, exclusively responsible to the centre. Third, popular committees are created (either elected or selected) that merely advise the regional/district coordinator. Generally, all these units relate to one another hierarchically. District projects must be approved at the regional level and beyond that at the center.

Not all African countries have adopted this model, but many have. A few country-based cases are summarized here:

Zambia

Decentralization measures began with the Local Government Act of 1965, a year after independence, which consolidated and reenacted the various local government laws. Guided by a pseudo-socialist policy of "humanism," President Kaunda announced in 1969 his new initiative on "Decentralization in Centralism." He defined it as:

> a measure whereby through the Party and Government machinery, we will decentralize most of the Party and Government activities while retaining effective control of the Party and Government machinery at the centre in the interest of unity. (Zambia 1986, 13)

Village and Ward Development Committees were set up on the basis of the Village Registration and Development Act of 1971. The essence of this experiment was to decentralize government activities to the localities. These activities were to be run by local officials under the supervision of centrally approved administration officials. As in other African countries, the coordination of these ministerial activities at the local level by a small corps of officials proved an impossible task. Personnel, management, accounting, and policy remained centralized in Lusaka (the capital).

The Local Administration Act of 1980 (which came into effect in the following year) abolished the tripartite local government structures of City/Municipal, Township, and Rural Councils. In their place were now established a single structure of fifty-five districts which were to form the focus of all government and party activities. Each district was headed by a party official, the District Governor assisted by a District Secretary. Above this level was the Province, in which all government activities were carried out by the Provincial Cabinet Minister with the assistance of a Provincial Permanent Secretary. Consultative assemblies were elected/appointed to consider government proposals at each level.

In spite of these arrangements, central government sectoral ministries have been reluctant to decentralize resources and responsibilities to regional departments. Although representation on the councils was strengthened by the 1980 reform, central administrators posted to the district still dominate the local assemblies because they control the budget. The Minister for Decentralization was widely quoted in the *Times of Zambia* (22 September 1986) to the effect that decentralization has not started functioning (cited in Chiculo 1987). In essence, the Zambian reforms seem to have strengthened the central government's control over a wide range of affairs previously regarded as local. Diana Conyers argues that an implicit objective of the Zambian decentralization experiment was the desire to strengthen the nation's single and ruling party at the district and local levels (1985, 29).

Sudan

The objective of the 1971 People's Local Government (PLG) Act was "to achieve maximum participation of citizens in the administration of their local affairs and thus reduce centralization." The Act was followed in 1977 and 1979 by Presidential orders which transferred several executive responsibilities to local governments and made the President of the Republic the patron of all 5,600 local government units in the country. A few ministries were abolished in view of those changes.

At the apex of this decentralization plan is the Provincial Commissioner, a political appointee who presides over the Provincial Executive Council (PEC). Below the PEC are town and rural councils and at the base are the village and "furgan" (nomad) councils. Each council comprises both elected and government officials. The Provincial Commissioner works directly with the President's Office. Responsibilities are decentralized on paper, but the powers of taxation for a wide range of local activities are retained by the central government. Moreover, the People's Executive Council is the only body with budgetary powers. It budgets for all other local governments in each province—villages, towns, and camps. These lower-level councils have no staff of their own and are heavily dependent on central government grants.

One analyst of Sudanese politics suggests that decentralization of responsibilities to local institutions was perceived as the "evading of responsibility by the centre rather than a genuine programme to promote local initiatives" (Norris 1983, 67). Another analyst of decentralization reforms sees it as an article of faith whose tangible benefits are yet to appear (Rondinelli 1983, 98).

Tanzania

Few countries' decentralization efforts have been subjected to as much study and analysis as the Tanzanian decentralization reforms. Perhaps this interest is due to its widely publicized ideology of "self-reliance" or the fact that decentralization was tied to rural development and the basic needs (BN) strategy, nine years before the International Labour Office formally adopted BN as policy.

Having embarked on its now famous *Ujamaa* (villagization) program in 1967, a program of decentralization was initiated in July 1972. Development authorities were established at regional, district, and village levels to coordinate government activities and planning initiatives. Each of these institutional levels was related directly to equivalent hierarchies in the sole political party. Deliberative assemblies were created at all levels, involving both elected representatives and relevant government functionaries at the district and regional levels. Development secretariats were headed by centrally appointed directors both at the district and regional levels in their regions. District budgets were approved at the regional level, and all plan proposals were to be submitted to the Prime Minister's Office for final approval before they could be implemented.

Even though the program of resettling peasants in rural villages was largely successful (attaining ninety percent villagization in 1977), the consensus among all those who have studied Tanzanian decentralization is that it was a failure from the points of view of agricultural productivity, the provision of basic infrastructure, communal production, and administrative management (McHenry 1979, 212; 1981). Even former President Julius Nyerere conceded this recently:

> There are certain things I would not do if I were to start again. One of them is the abolition of local government and the other is the disbanding of the cooperatives. We were impatient and ignorant. . . . We had these two useful instruments of participation and we got rid of them. It is true that the local governments were afraid of taking decisions but instead of helping them we abolished them. Those were our two major mistakes. (1994, 828)

Since 1982, the Tanzanian government has embarked on the revival of the old structures of local government which were once abolished.

In spite of the lessons that Tanzania seems to be learning from the failure of its decentralization experiment, other African countries like Ghana are attempting to implement prototypes of the model that failed in Tanzania (Harris 1983; Akuoko-Frimpong 1987).

Nigeria

The reform of Nigeria's local governments in 1976 was aimed at breaking away from the tradition of deconcentrated/administrative decentralization, which state government-sponsored reforms since independence favoured, toward a genuine allocation of broad responsibilities and resources to local governments. The country's newly created 299 (772 as of 1998) local governments were expected to have their own councils, budgets, and personnel. Traditional revenue sources were revived and new ones added from the national treasury. A new niche was created for local governments as third-tier levels of government in a federation in which federal and state units had been dominant. Local governments were able to put into place an array of social and economic services all over the federation within a short period of time. Most importantly, the reform succeeded in breaking the hold of traditional oligarchs on the local bureaucracy in the northern states (Yahaya 1980). The experiment was successful until 1979, even though from 1978 some of the contradictions of the reform already made themselves evident. Local governments were heavily dependent on grants from the federal government, and since these passed through state governments, considerable opportunity existed for the latter to ensure that the new local governments operated as local administrations, the very model of decentralization that was rejected by the 1976 policy package. Today the local governments are effectively subordinate to state governments rather than to the public. They operate more as extensions of the state bureaucracy than as local self-governing institutions. The councils have been run since 1979 either by selected management committees or senior officials referred to as "sole administrators."[3] The local governments are very large (ranging from 150,000 to over a million population) and are yet to be accepted by the people as their own institutions (Gboyega 1983; Adamolekun 1984; Olowu 1986).

Case Studies of Local Organizations in Africa

With the failure of administrative decentralization programs, diverse African peoples have increasingly embraced, with or without government support, local self-governing organs to fill the gap left by the absence of popular and accepted formal local governments. Local self-governing units include two broad types: first, voluntary local organizations, which can be classified into two subtypes—self-help community associations and cooperative societies; and second, local (self) governments. The literature in respect of these organizations is not as copious as that on decentralization.

Voluntary Local Organizations

The activities of kinship, ethnic, and town unions in Africa are relatively well documented. These associations have contributed immensely through self-help community projects to social and economic development of their respective communities. On Eastern Nigerian ethnic and town unions, Audrey Smock notes:

> Ethnic unions (in Ibo communities) facilitated the accommodation between tradition and modernity by conserving those elements in the traditional political culture [that favoured] development and then by harnessing them on behalf of the development of the primary community. (1971, 243)

Similarly, an ex-colonial officer in the same region notes:

> By the 1950s most unions were planning the development programmes of their communities and taxing both themselves and the rest of their

community to pay for them while the regional government was stimu-
lating these efforts by agreeing to meet half the costs of major construction works (e.g., pipe-borne water supplies) and to staff any secondary
schools or hospitals built by the community. By the 1960s, the more
progressive unions had become the *de facto* government of their
communities. It assumed all the financial duties of government, planning the town's annual budget, deciding how the money was to be
raised, apportioning it between the contributing units, banking it and
controlling its expenditure. (Jones 1979, 60–61)

This form of community government had all the attributes of a local
organization: it was concerned with a defined locality—usually a town or
village—was completely responsible to its membership, and had considerable impact. The bulk of local services was and still is maintained by this
form of government in this area. Its leadership was a novelty in that it
consisted of members of cosmopolitan elites who normally worked/resided
outside the village or town community. Such members of the elite are men
preoccupied with their careers but also with an abiding interest in the
welfare and development of their home towns. Even though they share
offices in the union with the local elites who work and live at home, they are
ready to make heavy financial contributions and to ensure that such resources are used for the purposes that were intended. Analysts of these
institutions generally agree that corruption, which is rife in all governmental
organizations, is almost non-existent in these town unions/community
associations (Jones 1979, 62; Wraith and Simpkins 1963). Peter Ekeh's
(1975) concept of two publics in post-colonial societies thoroughly analyzes
this subject. The activities of ethnic/communal associations in other parts of
Nigeria have also received some attention. Basic educational, health, and
road infrastructures have been built out of the efforts of these types of
organizations in many parts of rural Nigeria, with minimal government
support (McNulty et al. 1984; Akinbode 1977). Moreover, strong informal
community and business networks have been maintained by the various
ethnic groups, most especially by the Hausas in virtually all Nigerian major
cities (Cohen 1973).

The self-help community associations in Kenya are perhaps even more
vigorous than those of southern Nigeria. Dating back to colonial times,
considerable encouragement had been given to the formation of self-help
groups in Kenya on a community basis. These efforts were assisted greatly
by the local government councils from the 1920s onward. At independence,
the country's political leadership, having benefited politically and otherwise
from the self-help movement, gave it considerable impetus. Self-help

schemes in Kenya were valued at US $3.3 million in 1967, and from 1967 to 1972, US $13.9 million were contributed for educational projects alone. Even though a high percentage of these projects focused on education infrastructure, namely the "harambee schools," investment in agriculture, health, social welfare and recreation, water supplies, transport and communications, and fish ponds was also considerable (Wallis 1982). F. Holmquist (1979) also argues that Tanzanian self-help projects compared favourably with those in Kenya until such activities were doused by the central government's top-down rural development initiatives.

Undoubtedly, the African experience with these types of organizations is not limited to these three countries, but they are the best documented cases. A few other experiences have been documented. They include the Sidamo Mahabar Volunteer self-help associations of Ethiopia, which enabled their members to adopt new crops and join cooperative ventures, and guaranteed them access to credit (Hamer 1976). The Malawi self-help water supply committees represent another well-documented case of self-help organizations. Within a decade, these committees, with government assistance for pipes and materials, were able to lay nine hundred miles of water pipes and install two thousand village taps which served 400,000 people in Malawi's rural areas (Liebenow 1981; for other examples see also Esman and Uphoff 1984, 304–42).

Cooperatives

Cooperatives come in different forms as producers', consumers', marketing or credit cooperatives. In most countries, they were established during the colonial era to promote agricultural development. Unfortunately, however, in many countries cooperative societies have not been able to function as the semiautonomous institutions that they are supposed to be. They have been over-bureaucratized. A few African countries have recorded successes through their cooperative societies (Owens and Shaw 1972, 71–104; Seibel 1986). Egypt, Cameroon, and Kenya are all mentioned in the literature, but Nigeria may also be included.

Farmer cooperatives have remained in Nigeria as one of the most crucial institutions for linking small-scale farmers with credit, markets, and innovations. Most of the institutions created by government to provide these services have not been able to relate to the large number of small-scale farmers in the manner in which the cooperative movement does. Cooperative banks have emerged with the assistance of state governments to cater to the special needs of these cooperative societies. The Nigerian cooperative banks have served as key instruments for capital formation in agriculture, using the cooperative movement as its main vehicle. Cooperatives are also involved in food crop and cash crop production, although membership is only about 10 percent of the potential (Osuntogun 1983, 42–43).

The Tanzanian Sukuma Cotton Cooperative is regarded as an outstanding example of a successful producer cooperative. It was established in 1952 by a Sukuma bookkeeper and in spite of initial government reluctance was registered and became a federation cooperative that owned and operated cotton ginneries, which led to a doubling of output and considerable capital formation. A much less known case is the Tiv Farmers Association of Nigeria, even though it is also an outstanding success case (Esman and Uphoff 1984, 336–40). The maiden issue of *African Farmer* (1988, 17–26), a magazine published by the Hunger Project, reports several cases of indigenous peasant farmer organizations (some of them exclusively women's groups) in Kenya, Senegal, Burkina Faso, and Zimbabwe. A number of these benefitted from governmental and international assistance, even though they are founded and directed by peasant farmers.

Perhaps the most interesting documented cases of "cooperative" activities recorded in Africa are those on informal savings mobilization. As much as 8 percent of Ethiopia's national income was estimated to have been handled by savings clubs and associations in the mid-1970s, and this was estimated to be about normal for other African countries. The importance and popularity of these associations in the rural areas and in the urban informal sector arise from the fact that commercial banks in Africa are yet to become effective agents for mobilizing indigenous resources. They are not only few but also remote from the rural people both geographically and socially (Miracle, Miracle, and Cohen 1980, 701–2).

The major problem with all these associations is that their success usually attracts governmental attention which may not always be beneficial. In some cases, it is beneficial as when government recognizes an association and creates better opportunities for its performance. But when government takes it over by appointing its key officials as in the case of the proposed cooperative bank in the Cameroons, the result may be disastrous (Haggblade 1978, 49; Miracle, Miracle, and Cohen 1980, 721).

Local Governments

Even though many countries across Africa have abolished semi-autonomous local governments, some countries have not (Olowu 1988a). Their local government systems are a sharp contrast to the local administration systems earlier described. Such countries have continued with the late colonial model of local government with great dividends. The most outstanding African country in this respect is Zimbabwe, although some other countries have retained elements of this system in the major cities (Kenya is a notable example, Oyugi 1983). Some attention is given to the Zimbabwean system below.

Although a relatively small African country (1986 population of 8.7 million), with an estimated per capita income of US $620, Zimbabwe is one of the most prosperous. In a continent ravished by hunger and drought in 1984, Zimbabwe had a two million ton grain surplus (three times the country's annual consumption). The reasons for this prosperity are diverse—including a relatively substantial industrial base, long-established commercial agricultural enterprise, etc. Nevertheless, analysts of that country have underscored the important role played by farmer organizations in its sustained agricultural productivity (Bratton 1986). To this could be added the contributions of local governments—especially the municipalities and the rural councils in providing basic social and economic infrastructures that support other development activities. Zimbabwean local governments are easily rated as about the most effective on the continent (Olowu 1988a, 74–78; Wekwette 1988).

Zimbabwe has three types of councils: fourteen urban, fifty-six rural, and fifty-five district. The urban and rural councils are by far the more prosperous; the district councils have only been recently reorganized to enable them to serve the majority of peasant farming communities. Each of these councils is filled through multi-party elections. The councils are responsible for a whole range of services both of economic and social types: housing, health, education, social welfare, sewerage, water, refuse collection, and until recently, electricity. They are also involved in business ventures such as the exclusive monopoly of liquor processing, some mining activities, and investment in manufacturing. Most of these responsibilities were once administered by local governments in other African countries but have since been taken over by higher governmental levels.

For finance, Zimbabwean local governments are entitled to the vehicle tax, possess a modern property rating machinery, and charge for a wide range of services they render including water, refuse, and sewerage. The health institutions also levy a charge on the basis of income. Government grants are mainly for councils in the rural areas whereas municipalities receive loans from the government. For instance, the city of Harare had a 1986–87 budget of approximately US $250 million (i.e., a per capita expenditure of approximately $2.5 per annum), only US $4 million of which it received as central government grants for health care services. The average annual per capita expenditure in many African countries is less than $1 million and a substantial number of their tax sources has been either abolished or taken over by the central government (Mawhood 1983,14–18; Smith 1985, 191; Olowu 1988a).

Another important contrast between local governments in Zimbabwe and in other African countries is the relatively smaller size of Zimbabwe's basic local government units. While Zimbabwe's 126 local governing units may be considered a fairly high number for a country of eight million people, it is about a half of the total number of units in Nigeria whose population is estimated at about 100 million. Zimbabwe's average local government (population) size is the smallest in Africa (table 10.2).

It is important to underscore the point that district councils which serve most of the African population in rural Zimbabwe are not as successful as the other two types of councils. They were reorganized in 1980, and some significant progress has been recorded, even though problems not dissimilar to those attending decentralization plans in other African countries have been noted (Mutizwa-Mangiza 1988). The difference between the urban/ rural councils and the district councils is traceable to their colonial origins. The former were established with generous municipal powers existent in Europe to cater for European communities as in other African cities. On the other hand, local government in the African communities was based not on popular rule but on selected chiefs with much more circumscribed local government powers (Home 1983). As in other African countries, these two traditions of local government have persisted beyond the colonial period. As earlier pointed out, a few other African countries (Mauritius, Kenya, Senegal, Côte d'Ivoire, and Botswana) have retained and begun to experiment with vigorous people-based local governments in their urban communities.

The Dilemma of Decentralization for Central Government Officials

Decentralization and local self-governance are not polar concepts. In theory and practice, they ought to be closely related. Decentralization could encompass both administrative and political forms. Some circumstances or particular services require one or the other or a combination of both. The African experience has, however, demonstrated a tendency for decentralization programs to be concerned exclusively with deconcentration—even when the language of local self-governance or devolution is employed. The deconcentrated model is one in which central officials are posted to the regions to coordinate government activities regionally and facilitate communication between people and government. This model has been a universal failure throughout Africa. Even where such decentralization programs succeed as they are reputed to have done in Egypt as a result of both internal (political leadership's) and external (donor) support, the success has been more pronounced with respect to expenditure than to revenue decentralization (Kerr et al. 1983).

Deconcentration in administration is necessary to ensure that central government administration is carried out as expected. All nations operate systems of local administration using different models. However, local administration cannot achieve the objectives of local self-governance: the stimulation of community initiatives, resources, and enthusiasm in the creation of basic infrastructures.

African decentralization programs thus fail for two important reasons. First, the programs place too many demands for coordination and activation of local-level development activities on an administrative system that is "soft" with respect both to executive capacity and integrity. As a result of this and of the fact that the terrain and poor transport and communications networks do not make very many African countries amenable to this style of governance, costly delays and mistakes are made at the local level—the supply of seeds or fertilizers is delayed or the wrong variety is delivered. Second, decentralization programs fail to address the basic social and political issues raised by the strategy: how to create incentives for people to mobilize their own resources in terms of materials and ideas towards the development of their own domain. As has been described above, even when local decentralized units are created, they are denied independent revenue-raising capacities. Moreover, the people's participation in decision making and in ensuring that such structures are locally accountable is substantially circumscribed. As a result, parallel self-governing structures have emerged in several countries of Africa outside of government control.

The crucial question, however, is: why do African government officials behave in this manner? In spite of the rhetoric of central government politicians and officials in favour of decentralization generally, political decentralization or self government poses an embarrassing dilemma. The dilemma is grounded in the following considerations. First, genuine political decentralization, involving a transfer of resources and responsibilities to the local people implies, as with all reforms, that there would be losers and winners resulting from this change. Generally, most policy-makers perceive themselves as losers rather than winners. It must be remembered that African countries are still largely ruled under different styles of autocracy (military or civilian). Political and administrative offices at the local level as well as contracts and other public organizational resources constitute verita-ble sources of spoils to sustain the regime. Moreover, according to Brian Smith, the emerging bourgeoisie is dependent for its growth on national, not municipal, political power. Yet powerful local elites such as traditional chiefs must be appeased. It therefore becomes crucial that the dominant classes offer an appearance of self-determination without its substance (Smith 1985, 194–97).

However, much of the literature assessing decentralization emphasizes the point that the most serious opposition to self-governing decentralization is not from politicians but from senior-level administrators (the bureaucratic elite). It is difficult to argue that the political class in the Sudan, for instance, gave only half-hearted support to decentralization, however misconceived were such decentralization initiatives. Whole ministries were abolished to make way for the government's decentralization policy. But Sudanese senior administrators put up strong resistance to a policy which not only threatened them politically, but which they saw as running against the central values of the "national" bureaucracy.

One explanation for this resistance is that belief in the superiority of hierarchy and centralized planning/management is a carryover from the colonial state and has been reinforced since independence by economic advisers, administrative training institutions, and political leaders obsessed with their political campaigns for realizing their goals of national unity within the shortest possible time. This belief runs deep even among local-level officials. Any talk of reducing the panoply of central controls on local units is viewed with alarm, even though the record of such control to date has been anything but good. Foreign donor preferences (up until the most recent times) as well as the need for centralized planning for national development and the need to reduce intra- and inter-regional differences are other standard arguments used to buttress the case against local self-governance. Some even argue that without close central control, the local democratic processes may be dominated by local oligarchies.

Over the years, some of these arguments have lost their weight. The fear of local oligarchies presumes that the national political system cannot be dominated by oligarchies who strengthen the hands of members of their class at the local level. Planning performance has been dismal in Africa as in most other developing countries which have adopted comprehensive *dirigiste* forms since the late 1950s. A recent review of planning experiences in Third World countries notes that there is no clear association between a high degree of planning efforts and economic growth (Agarwala 1983, 2). The overall effect of continuing central control of local institutions is a negation of the development process, manifested by such evidence as the weakened expenditure and the revenue performance of local administrations and local governments in most parts of the continent, declining social economic infrastructures and the stifling of local initiative. The really serious problem thus turns out to be national officials' perceptions of what constitutes development and what their roles ought to be in that process vis-a-vis the local people.

Development is perceived by central officials very much in the mould of their colonial predecessors as the application of "modern" knowledge and techniques to traditional societies. Given such a mind-set, local people especially in the rural areas are presumed to be ignorant. In the words of one commentator, modernizing elites tend always to presume that poverty and ignorance are causally related without realizing that ignorance is not a special preserve of the poor (Fuglesang 1984). Administrators in Tanzania perceived peasants as "lazy, ignorant, superstitious, devious, and conservative," regarding them as the major obstacles to progress in the rural communities (McHenry 1979, 217).

Drawing on secondary sources, Holmquist has demonstrated an inverse relationship between bureaucratic growth (in numbers and power) and peasant participation in self-help activities in Kenya and Tanzania in the immediate years following political independence, particularly in the latter country. Tanzania's socialist program gave greater prominence to bureaucracy and centralized planning both of which actually undermined the vigour of local people's contributions to their own development in that country. In Kenya, the bureaucracy has not been as successful in totally destroying or displacing the leadership of rural self-help programs (Holmquist 1979, 146–48).

While Africa's bureaucratic classes' contempt for rural peoples' capabilities runs deep and is reinforced by their standard procedures (general rules, financial orders, etc. inherited from the colonial bureaucracy), they are not in a position to countermand openly the political pressure for promoting popular participation by their political leaders—either civilian or military. As a result, they couch their indifference and opposition to such programs in language which seems to tally with the objectives of decentralization but secretly subvert it—by promoting delegation to officials (deconcentration) rather than power-sharing (self-governance). This tendency explains why popular participation in development projects declined with the adoption of decentralization programs in several African countries (Holmquist 1979, 145; Smith 1985, 188–89).

Yet several studies have in fact demonstrated that local people possess much more knowledge concerning their local community than is often appreciated by the experts and officials and that they possess greater organizational skills than is recognized. The cases of successful local organizations cited above with or without governmental support are indicative of the quality of organizational skills possessed by local people across Africa.

As to knowledge, one recent study documents several cases of failed central government projects during and after the colonial period which were embarked upon in spite of the superior knowledge and advice of the local people. Four such commonly cited cases include the decision to treat diseased cocoa with chemicals rather than allowing the land to lie fallow; the "expert" advice in favour of single-cropping as against intercropping on the slopes of Mount Kilimanjaro, the mis-siting of a US $40 million groundnut scheme in Tanzania and the plans for the fish-processing industry in Ghana which ignored the women who had developed an elaborate fish distribution network in that country (Fuglesang 1984). These are only a few of the documented cases, and other cases can be cited to illustrate the same general point. Robert Chambers notes that indigenous agricultural knowledge, generally ignored and overridden by experts, constitutes "the single largest knowledge resource not yet mobilised in the development enterprise" (Chambers 1983; cited by Richards 1985, 14).

One analyst of West African agricultural systems concludes that many of the most successful innovations in crop production over the last fifty years or so have had indigenous roots. This was particularly true of the expansion of groundnut production in Senegal and oil palm production in Sierra Leone and eastern Nigeria; of the later development of cocoa in Ghana, the Ivory Coast, and Western Nigeria; and of groundnut cultivation in northern Nigeria. Major breakthroughs in agricultural innovation took place only when agricultural experts and officials put away their prejudices and listened to the farmers (Richards 1985, 18). This is, of course, part of the general tendency to denigrate unorganized knowledge in contrast to organized or scientific knowledge, particularly among economists and other social scientists, a tendency that has led to fatuous assumptions concerning the extent and possibilities of economic planning (Hayek 1945; Ostrom 1976).

Nevertheless, these findings have immense implications for a reordering of conceptions of development and decentralization in Africa. Unfortunately, however, a lot of these facts are well-known only to specialists. Administrative and policy training schools are unfortunately still wedded to bureaucratic theories and models which exalt "modern" knowledge and technology as well as monocratic administration. The upshot of the above is not to argue that central government activities are irrelevant to local development. The important point being made is the need for complementarities between central and local institutions. Several studies from other parts of the world have noted the fact that no case of successful rural development has occurred in which only one institution was solely responsible for rural development. In every case, "complementarities among institutions were as important as what the institutions themselves did" (Uphoff and Esman 1974, xi–xii). As already noted, central officials need to accord a greater respect to local institutions and local people's capacity for self-management.

Furthermore, most of the basic services by their nature require co-production, that is, the contribution of efforts in terms of cash, knowledge, and organization by both producer and user. This applies to the education, health, agricultural extension and other services connected with infrastructural development (Ostrom and Ostrom 1977; Whitaker 1980). However, co-production is incompatible with top-down development and program administration and with central personnel with little or no incentives for working with local people, etc., as is the case in most African countries.

In order to redress this erroneous conception of development and the appropriate decentralization strategies, comparative research into local institutions is required which will provide additional empirical evidence against the long-established bias of officials against the local people and their capabilities for self-management. Such research must be multidisciplinary and must seek to understand how the different peoples in Africa have utilized and still utilize diverse institutional mechanisms to fulfil their basic human needs. Such understanding will help to render central governments' efforts to build community institutions easier by building on institutions which already exist—rather than the current efforts to build so-called new, development-oriented structures which have proved so far to be unmitigated failures. Where new institutions must be built, they will be constructed on the basis of principles related to popular rule, peoples' self-interest, their capacity for rational choice, ability to search for information and to select what they perceive as a maximizing strategy (including the decision whether or not to create/join an organization) rather than the continued dependency on hierarchy (Ostrom 1989, 48–73). The type of research advocated above will be useful in demonstrating what is possible where there is political will to utilize the principles of self-governance in promoting development and decentralization. Indeed, it is possible to argue that only those countries which are capable of tapping the resources of their basic local organizations for development purposes are likely to surmount the severe economic, social, and environmental problems confronting most nations on the continent.

Conclusion: Lessons of Local Reforms in Other Nations

Indeed, local institutions possess the capability of contributing to African development. The most serious obstacles impeding their wide utilization on the continent are the conceptions of decentralization and development in the minds of development advisers, policy-makers, administrators, and administrative trainers. This problem is situated against the background of the competing economic and social forces in most African countries.

It is important to underscore that the problem of elite bias which this study has tried to highlight is in no way unique to Africa. Up to the late 1960s and early 1970s, conventional wisdom on local government reform and reorganization in Europe and North America was strongly in favour of amalgamation. The presumption was that small local government authorities impeded opportunities for efficient production and delivery of basic community services through hierarchical coordination. It was widely accepted that local governments must be of a minimum size to be financially viable and to satisfy the public as well as its representatives. Small units were not only inefficient in terms of the use of resources, but they were also unprofessional and tended to be parochial in outlook. The fragmentation which they produced in the large metropolitan areas resulted in serious problems of coordination for officials and "presumably overloaded citizens, confused responsibility and frustrated citizens in their efforts to control public policy" (Bish and Ostrom 1973, 8). In particular, small authorities were thought to be unable to engage professional staff of the right number and calibre or to provide reasonable career expectations to those in their employ.

The reform tradition was thus strongly in favour of hierarchy rather than self-governance, and thus in favour of consolidation of local government areas (and where this was not possible some form of federation). In Europe, this reform tradition, aimed at increasing the minimum population size for services, led to major amalgamations in Sweden, the Netherlands, Belgium, West Germany, and the United Kingdom. In Denmark, West Germany, Britain, and Sweden, the reduction in municipal units arising from amalgamation or consolidation was "dramatic" (Council of Europe 1980; Smith 1985). Similarly, in the United States, the Advisory Commission on Intergovernmental Relations (ACIR) describes the fragmented, uncoordinated, and independent local government systems of metropolitan America as "a jungle which must be civilized" by consolidation reform (ACIR 1976, 145). Consolidation reforms especially of school districts were embarked upon in many communities and cities. The total numbers of local government units in the United States declined from 116,694 in 1952 to 79,862 in 1977 (Wright 1982, 10).

However, research since the early 1970s both in the US and Europe indicates that no clear positive relationship exists between local government performance and size. In fact, several studies show that large-sized departments do not perform as efficiently and effectively as small ones. Elinor Ostrom and Roger Parks in a study of eighty metropolitan areas submit with respect to the police service that in no case did large police departments perform more effectively than smaller departments in delivering direct services to citizens in similar neighborhoods (Ostrom and Parks 1987, 13). These studies have been corroborated by other scholars and institutions (including the ACIR) working on other services in the United States. They all show conclusively that to the extent that different services have differing economies of scale, complexity rather than the simplicity of one-unit solutions is more efficient and effective in terms of both the delivery and management of services and of the responsiveness of local government officials to their citizens (Hirsch 1968; Bish and Ostrom 1973; Ostrom and Parks 1987). The research indicators seem to indicate that for a number of critical services—education, police, fire, libraries, public housing, welfare, parks, recreation, refuse collection, and street maintenance—efficiency and effectiveness were enhanced more by small to medium jurisdiction than by larger-sized ones. R. Parks and R. Oakerson summarize the results of several studies conducted in the United States of America when they assert that "more fragmented areas have been found to spend less in the aggregate and often to provide more effective and efficient public services than less fragmented areas" (1987, 2). Even the ACIR had by 1987 come around to a different view, when it stated that a strong case could be made for complexity and that "a significant reduction in the number and variety of local government units . . . could actually reduce the opportunities available to local citizens and officials to increase efficiency and productivity" (ACIR 1987).

Similar research findings are leading to changes in Europe. R. J. Bennett (1980) contends in agreement with others such as L. J. Sharpe (1981, 1986) that there is hardly any firm evidence to support the economies of scale argument in local government services. Brian Smith in a review of European research concludes that the service-efficiency argument is one that carries "so many qualifications and exceptions that it is almost totally useless as a guide to the delimitation of boundaries" (1985, 68). Reformers overlooked several crucial considerations in the vaunted claims for size or consolidation. They underestimated the self-interested role of officials in pushing consolidation reform; they exaggerated the capability of large institutions to gather, process, and utilize information compared to the capability of smaller units; and they presumed that citizen preferences were homogeneous, not heterogenous. Finally and most importantly, they overlooked the possibility of separating service provision from service production and presumed that goods and services supplied by local governments are similar (Bish and Ostrom 1973, 87–91; Paddison 1983, 222–23).

The early reform tradition was informed by the Weberian notions of monocratic administration and unity of command (Ostrom 1972, 479). With time, these decentralization initiatives were packaged under different programs of bilateral and multilateral aid to Africa and other Third World nations (see for instance, United Nations 1975). The African decentralization reforms reviewed above represented different individual nation's efforts to implement these critical aspects of "development administration." The failure of this reform tradition in Africa is thus no different from its failure in Europe and North America. The African situation is, however, compounded by the legacy of colonial rule which was essentially bureaucratic rule; elements of the latter have persisted beyond political independence.

Assuming, as the literature suggests, that there is political will to undertake a genuine program of decentralization in the direction of self-governance in some African countries, research into the actual performance of the different types of local institutions in Africa will go a long way to inform such future policies. Unfortunately, very little research of this nature is currently under way.

In addition, a radically different approach to the training of public officials will be required. Most officials have been exposed to the hierarchical principle as the single most efficient mode for social organization and for promoting development. Few of them are aware of theories and concepts which have become current in recent years in the social sciences which emphasize the limitations of the hierarchical principle, the importance of individual and collective choice, individual rationality and the wisdom of multi-organizational arrangements underpinned by notions of redundancy, overlap, duplication, and public choice (Buchanan and Tullock 1962; Landau 1969; Ostrom 1976, 1989). These concepts are likely to promote genuine self-governance rather than the greater centralization produced by the dubious types of decentralization efforts reviewed above.

Finally, development and donor agencies as well as African governments that are genuinely interested in pursuing long-term development based on mobilizing indigenous resources must give greater attention than they do at present to removing the institutional obstacles to popular participation in the development process. These would demand some structural adjustments of a political rather than a strictly economic nature—the strengthening of local governments, a commitment to popular education, the empowerment of local community groups, cooperatives and other local organizations. This would seem to be the direction of long-term development prospects in Africa, given the fundamental weaknesses of prevailing strategies.

NOTES

1. The cases reviewed in this article are drawn mainly from English-speaking Africa. The author is aware of some decentralization experiments in French-speaking Africa which have been regarded as modest success cases. (See, e.g., Vengroff and Johnston 1997; Koffi 1989.) However, the controversy surrounding the nature of decentralization and decentralization reforms in French-speaking Africa requires a separate treatment. (See Cowan 1958, 35–61, 210–20; Cohen 1980.)

2. Others have examined the issue before Fesler. Tocqueville ([1835] 1969, 87–99) discussed the difference between governmental and administrative central-

ization at length but did not use the same concepts as utilized by Fesler and other English-speaking scholars since 1949.

3. In 1987–88 the Nigerian federal military government took a number of actions aimed at institutionalizing the 1976 decentralization program. Popular elections were held for local governments, direct payments were made as of July 1988 from the federation account to local governments, and the Ministries for Local Government (the State government's main link to local governments) were abolished in all the twenty-one states in October 1988.

REFERENCES

Adamolekun, L. 1994. "The Idea of Local Government as a Third Tier of Government Revisited: Achievements Problems and Prospects." *Quarterly Journal of Administration* 18, nos. 3–4 (April–July): 113–38.
Adamolekun, L., D. Olowu, and O. M. Laleye, eds. 1988. *Local Government in West Africa since Independence*. Lagos: Lagos University Press.
Advisory Commission on Intergovernmental Relations. 1976. *Improving Urban America: A Challenge to Federalism*. Washington, DC: USGPO.
———. 1987. *The Organization of Local Public Economies*. Washington, DC: USGPO.
Agarwala, Ramgopal. 1983. *Planning in Developing Countries: Lessons of Experience*. Washington, DC: World Bank Staff Working Papers No. 576.
Ake, Claude. 1987. "Sustaining Development on the Indigenous." Paper prepared for the Long-Term Perspectives Study, World Bank Special Economic Office, Africa Region.
Akinbode, I. A. 1977. "Participation in Self-Help Project among Rural Inhabitants." *Quarterly Journal of Administration* 11, no. 4: 285–98.
Akuoko-Frimpong, H. 1987. "Decentralized Administration: The Ghanaian Experience." In *Decentralized Administration in West Africa: Cases, Issues and Training Implications*, ed. Dele Olowu. London: Commonwealth Secretariat.
Allen, Hubert J. 1987. "Decentralization for Development: A Point of View." *Planning and Administration* 14, no. 1: 23–30.
Apter, David. 1965. *The Politics of Modernization*. Chicago: University of Chicago Press.
Ashford, Douglas E. 1967. *National Development and Local Reform: Political Participation in Morocco, Tunisia and Pakistan*. Berkeley: University of California Press.
Bennett, R. J. 1980. *The Geography of Public Finance*. London: Methuen.
Bish, R. L., and V. Ostrom. 1973. *Understanding Urban Government: Metropolitan Reform Reconsidered*. Washington, DC: American Enterprise for Public Policy Research.
Bratton, M. 1986. "Farmer Organizations and Food Production in Zimbabwe." *World Development* 14, no. 3: 367–84.
Buchanan, James M., and Gordon Tullock. 1962. *The Calculus of Consent: Logical Foundations of Constitutional Democracy*. Ann Arbor: University of Michigan Press.

Cernea, Michael M. 1987. "Farmer Organizations and Institution Building for Sustainable Development." *Regional Development Dialogue* 8, no. 2: 1–19.

Chambers, Robert. 1983. *Rural Development: Putting the Last First.* London: Longman.

Cheema, G. S., and D. A. Rondinelli, eds. 1983. *Decentralization and Development: Policy Implementation in Developing Countries.* Beverly Hills, CA: Sage.

Chiculo, B. C. 1987. "Mass Participation in Development in Zambia: Problems and Prospects." Yaunde, May 25–27.

Cochrane, Glynn. 1983. *Policies for Strengthening Local Government in Developing Countries.* Washington, DC: World Bank Staff Working Paper No. 582.

Cohen, Abner. 1973. "The Social Organization of Credit in a West African Cattle Market." In *Africa and Change*, ed. C. M. Turnbull, 76–90. New York: Alfred Knopf.

Cohen, M. A. 1980. "Francophone Africa." In *International Handbook on Local Government Reorganization: Contemporary Developments*, ed. D. C. Rowat, 415–24. Westport, CT: Greenwood Press.

Conford, J., ed. 1975. *The Failure of the State: On the Distribution of Political and Economic Power in Europe.* London: Croom Helm.

Conyers, D. 1985. "Decentralization: A Framework for Discussion." In Hye 1985, 22–42.

Council of Europe. 1980. *The Strengthening of Local Structures, with Special Reference to Amalgamation and Cooperation between Municipalities in Council of Europe Member States.* Study Series on Local and Regional Authorities in Europe, no. 10. Strasbourg: Council of Europe.

Cowan, Gray L. 1958. *Local Government in West Africa.* New York: Columbia University Press.

Ekeh, P. 1975. "Colonialism and the Two Publics in Africa: A Theoretical Statement." *Comparative Studies in Society and History* 19, no. 1: 91–112.

Esman, M. J., and N. T. Uphoff. 1994. *Local Organizations: Intermediaries in Rural Development.* Ithaca: Cornell University Press.

Feldman, L. D., ed. 1981. *Politics and Government in Urban Canada.* Toronto: Methuen.

Fesler, J. W. 1949. *Area and Administration.* Montgomery: University of Alabama Press.

Fuglesang, Andreas. 1984. "The Myth of People's Ignorance." *Development Dialogue* 1–2:42–63.

Gboyega, Alex. 1983. "Local Government Reform in Nigeria." In Mawhood 1983, 225–48.

———. 1987. "The Performance of Local Government in Colonial and Post-Colonial Periods." Faculty of Administration, Ile-Ife: University of Ife.

Haggblade, Steve. 1978. "Africanization from Below: The Evolution of Cameroonian Savings Societies into Western-Style Banks." *Rural Africana* 2 (Fall): 35–55.

Hamer, John H. 1976. "Prerequisites and Limitations in the Development of Voluntary Self-Help Associations: A Case-Study and Comparison." *Anthropological Quarterly* 19, no. 2: 107–34.

Harris, D. 1983. "Central Power and Local Reform: Ghana during the 1970s." In Mawhood 1983, 201–24.

Hayek, F. A. 1945. "The Use of Knowledge in Society." *American Economic Review* 35, no. 4: 519–30.

Hicks, U. K. 1961. *Development from Below: Local Government and Finance in Developing Countries of the Commonwealth.* Oxford: Clarendon Press.

Hirsch, W. Z. 1968. "The Supply of Urban Public Services." In *Issues in Urban Economics,* ed. H. S. Perloff and L. Wingo Jr. Baltimore: Johns Hopkins Press.

Holmquist, F. 1979. "Class Structure, Peasant Participation and Rural Self-Help." In *Politics and Public Policy in Kenya and Tanzania,* ed. J. D. Barkan and J. J. Okumu, 129–53. New York: Praeger Publishers.

Home, R. K. 1993. "Town Planning, Segregation and Indirect Rule in Colonial Nigeria." *Third World Planning Review* 5, no. 2: 165–75.

Hye, H. A., ed. 1985. *Decentralization, Local Government and Resource Mobilisation.* Commila: Bangladesh Academy of Rural Development.

Jones, C. J. 1979. "Changing Leadership in Eastern Nigeria: Before, during and after the Colonial Period." In *Politics in Leadership: A Comparative Perspective,* ed. N. A. Shack and P. S. Cohen, 44–64. Oxford: Clarendon Press.

Kasfir, Nelson. 1983. "Designs and Dilemmas: An Overview." In Mawhood 1983, 25–48.

Kerr, G. B., et al. 1993. *The Decentralization of Local Government in Egypt: A Special Assessment for USAID.* Cairo: Office of Local Administration and Development.

Koffi, Attahi. 1988. "Abidjan Ivory Coast—An Assessment of Administrative Decentralization." In *African Cities in Crisis: Managing Rapid Urban Growth,* ed. Richard Stren and Rodney White. Boulder, CO: Westview Press.

Lamour, Peter, and Ropate Oale, eds. 1985. *Decentralization in the South Pacific.* Suva: University of South Pacific.

Landau, M. 1969. "Redundance, Rationality and the Problem of Duplication and Overlap." *Public Administration Review* 29:346–58.

Langrod, C. [1953] 1981. "Local Government and Democracy." In *Politics and Government of Urban Canada: Selected Readings,* 3–13. Toronto: Methuen.

Lewis, A. 1955. *The Theory of Economic Growth.* Homewood: Irwin Ben.

Liebenow, J. Gus. 1981. "Malawi: Clean Water for the Rural Poor." *American Universities Field Staff Reports* Africa No. 40.

Maddick, Henry. 1963. *Democracy, Decentralization and Development.* Bombay: Asia Publishing House.

Mawhood, R., ed. 1983. *Local Government in the Third World: The Experience of Tropical Africa.* Chichester: John Wiley.

McHenry, D. E., Jr. 1979. *Tanzania's Ujamaa Villages.* Berkeley: Institute of International Studies.

———. 1981. *Ujamaa Villages in Tanzania.* Uppsala: Scandinavian Institute of African Studies.

McNulty, M. L., et al. 1984. "Access to Rural Services in Nigeria." In *Rural Public Services: International Comparisons,* ed. R. E. Lonsdale and G. Enyedi, 315–38. Boulder, CO: Westview Press.

Miracle, M. P., D. S. Miracle, and L. Cohen. 1980. "Informal Savings Mobilization in Africa." *Economic Development and Cultural Change* 29, no. 4: 700–724.

Moulin, L. [1954] 1981. "Local Government as a Basin for Democracy: A Further

Comment." In *Politics and Government of Urban Canada*, 19–23. Toronto: Methuen.

Mutizwa-Manziga, N. D. 1988. "Decentralisation in Zimbabwe: The Problems of Planning at the District Level." Department of Rural and Urban Planning, University of Zimbabwe, Harare.

Nigeria. Federal Military Government. 1984. "Local Government." *The Report by the Committee on the Review of Local Government Administration in Nigeria.* Lagos: Supreme Headquarters.

Nooi, P. S. 1987. "Local Self-Government Reform: A Comparative Study of Selected Countries in Africa and South-East Asia." *Planning and Administration* 14, no. 1: 31–38.

Norris, M. W. 1983. "Sudan: Administrative versus Political Priorities." In Mawhood 1983, 49–73.

Nyerere, Julius. 1984. Interview with *Third World Quarterly* 6, no. 4: 815–38.

Olowu, Dele. 1986. "A Decade of Local Government Reform in Nigeria, 1976–86." *International Review of Administrative Sciences* 52–53: 287–99.

———. 1987. *Decentralized Administration in West Africa: Cases, Issues and Training Implications.* London: Commonwealth Secretariat.

———. 1988a. *African Local Governments as Instruments of Economic and Social Development.* The Hague: International Union of Local Authorities.

———. 1988b. "Strategies for Decentralization in Developing Countries: The Nigerian Case." In Adamolekun, Olowu, and Laleye 1988, 109–32.

Orewa, G. O. 1997. "Local Self-Government: Development in Anglophone Africa." *Planning and Administration* 14, no. 1: 39–47.

Ostrom, Elinor. 1972. "Metropolitan Reform: Propositions Derived from Two Traditions." *Social Science Quarterly* 53:474–93.

Ostrom, Elinor, and Roger B. Parks. 1987. "Neither Gargantua nor the Land of Lilliputs: Conjectures on Mixed Systems of Metropolitan Organization." Paper presented at the Midwest Political Science Association Meetings, Chicago, April 9–11. Reprinted in *Polycentricity and Local Public Economies*, ed. M. D. McGinnis. Ann Arbor: University of Michigan Press, 1999.

Ostrom, Vincent. 1976. "Some Paradoxes for Planners: Human Knowledge and its Limitations." In *The Politics of Planning*, ed. L. Chickering, 243–54. San Francisco: Institute for Contemporary Studies.

———. 1989. *The Intellectual Crisis in American Public Administration.* 2d ed. Tuscaloosa: University of Alabama Press.

Ostrom, Vincent, and Elinor Ostrom. 1977. "Public Goods and Public Choices." In *Alternatives for Delivering Public Services: Toward Improved Performance*, ed. E. S. Savas, 7–49. Boulder, CO: Westview Press. Reprinted in *Polycentricity and Local Public Economies*, ed. M. D. McGinnis. Ann Arbor: University of Michigan Press, 1999.

Osuntogun, C. A. 1983. "Cooperatives and Nigeria's Agricultural Development." Ile Ife: University of Ife Inaugural Lecture Series.

Owens, Edgar, and Robert Shaw. 1972. *Development Reconsidered: Bridging the Gap between Government and the People.* Lexington: Lexington Books.

Oyugi, W. O. 1983. "Local Government in Kenya: A Case of Institutional Decline." In Mawhood 1983, 107–40.

Paddison, R. 1983. *The Fragmented State: The Political Geography of Power.* Oxford: Blackwell.

Parks, R., and R. Oakerson. 1987. "Fragmented Local Government: Toward a New Understanding." Workshop in Political Theory and Policy Analysis, Indiana University, Bloomington.

Prats, Yves. 1973. *Decentralization et développement.* Editions Guias. Paris: Bibliotheque de l'Institut International d'Administration Publique.

Regional Development Dialogue. 16, no. 1 (Spring 1995). Special issue on "Role of Community Receiving Mechanisms in Local Development."

Richards, Paul. 1985. *Indigenous Agricultural Revolution: Ecology and Food Production in West Africa.* London: Hutchinson.

Riggs, F. W. 1964. *Administration in Developing Countries: The Theory of Prismatic Society.* Boston: Houghton Mifflin.

Rondinelli, D. A. 1983. "Decentralization of Development Administration in East Africa." In *Decentralization and Development,* ed. G. S. Cheema and D. A. Rondinelli, 77–126. Beverly Hills, CA: Sage.

Rostow, W. W. 1971. *Politics and the Stages of Economic Growth.* Cambridge: Cambridge University Press.

Rubin, L., and B. Weinstein. 1974. *Introduction to African Politics: A Continental Approach.* New York: Praeger.

Seibel, A. H. 1986. "Rural Finance in Africa." *Cooperation and Development* 6:12–14.

Selznick, P. 1966. *TVA and the Grassroots.* New York: Harper and Row.

Sharpe, L. J. 1981. "The Failure of Local Government Modernization in Britain: A Critique of Functionalism." In Feldman 1981, 321–57.

———. 1986. "Intergovernmental Policy-Making: The Limits of Sub-national Autonomy." In *Guidance, Control and Evaluation in the Public Sector,* ed. F. X. Kaufmann, G. Majone, and V. Ostrom, 159–92. Berlin: Walter de Gruyter.

Smith, Brian C. 1985. *Decentralization: The Territorial Dimension of the State.* London: Allen and Unwin.

Smock, Audrey 1971. *Ibo Politics: The Role of Ethnic Unions in Eastern Nigeria.* Cambridge: Harvard University Press.

Smoke, P. 1998. "Reforming Local Government in Developing Countries." Harvard Institute for International Development, Nairobi, Kenya.

Tocqueville, Alexis de. [1835] 1969. *Democracy in America,* trans. George Lawrence. New York: Anchor Books.

United Nations. 1986. *Programme of Action for African Economic Recovery, 1986–1990.* New York: Department of Public Information.

Uphoff, N. T., and M. J. Esman. 1974. *Local Organization for Rural Development: Analysis of Asian Experience.* Ithaca, NY: Rural Development Committee, Cornell University.

Uphoff, Norman. 1985. "Local Institutions and Decentralization for Development." In Hye 1985, 43–78.

Vengroff, R., and A. Johnston. 1987. "Decentralization and the Implementation of Rural Development in Senegal: The Role of Rural Councils." *Public Administration and Development,* no. 3: 273–88.

Wallis, M. A. H. 1992. *Bureaucrats, Politicians, and Rural Communities in Kenya.* Manchester Papers for Development, University of Manchester.

Wekwette, Kamiel. 1988. "The Local Government System in Zimbabwe—Some Perspectives on Change and Development." *Planning and Administration* 15, no. 1: 18–27.

Whalen, H. 1969. "Ideology, Democracy and the Foundations of Local Government." In *Politics and Government of Urban Canada*, ed. L. D. Feldman and M. D. Goldrick, 311–32. Toronto: Methuen.

Whitaker, Gordon P. 1980. "Coproduction: Citizen Participation in Service Delivery." *Public Administration Review* 40, no. 3: 240–46.

World Bank. 1981. *Accelerated Development in Sub-Saharan Africa: An Agenda for Action*. Washington, DC: World Bank.

———. 1984. *World Development Report: 1984*. New York: John Hopkins University Press.

Wright, D. S. 1982. *Understanding Intergovernmental Relations*. Monterey, CA: Brooks/Cole Publishing Co.

Wraith, R. E. 1972. *Local Administration in West Africa*. London: Allen and Unwin.

Wraith, R. E., and M. Dent. 1988. "The British Legacy of Local Self-Government Revisited." In Adamolekun, Olowu, and Laleye 1988, 21–39.

Wraith, R. E., and E. Simpkins. 1963. *Corruption in Developing Countries*. London: Allen and Unwin.

Wunsch, J. S., and Dele Olowu, eds. 1990. The *Failure of the Centralized State: Institutions and Self-Governance in Africa*. Boulder, CO: Westview Press.

Wunsch, J. S. 1986. "Administering Rural Development: Have Goals Outreached Organizational Capacity?" *Public Administration and Development* 6:297–309.

Yahaya, A. D. 1980. *The Native Authority System in Northern Nigeria*. Zaria: Ahmadu Bello University Press.

Zambia. Country Paper. 1986. In *Training for Decentralized Administration in Eastern and Southern Africa*, ed. Commonwealth Secretariat, Harare Workshop. London.

Part III
Development

CHAPTER 11

Institutional Analysis and Decentralization: Developing an Analytical Framework for Effective Third World Administrative Reform

James S. Wunsch

Institutions and Third World Development[*]

There are few defenders and many critics of the centralized, bureaucratic, hierarchical organizational strategy dominant since independence in Third World administration. If one reviews the literature one finds ample criticism at both empirical and theoretical levels, criticism which has nearly reached consensus level on many issues. For example, the centralist hierarchical-bureaucratic organizational modality has been found generally to make administrative coordination among different organizations difficult; shift vast resources to the center from the field; increase coordination and managerial costs; design projects and programs which poorly fit local wants, needs and conditions; reduce flexibility, adaptability, creativity and speed in field services; discourage learning and innovation; continue and even worsen systems of patron-clientage and severe asymmetries in power, wealth and status between center and periphery, and rich and poor; perpetuate the weakness of local governmental units; discourage local dwellers from raising resources to finance public services; at times, destroy existing, effective locally based and managed infrastructure and service systems; perpetuate top-down, authoritarian approaches to problems requiring a genuine partnership between urban-technical and poor and rural people; and, in general, to discourage participation in the development process by poor and rural dwellers (World Bank 1981; Uphoff 1986; Esman 1980; Chambers 1983, 1985; Moris 1981; Hyden 1980, 1983; Wunsch 1983, 1986, 1988; Cheema and Rondinelli 1983a, b; Korten and Alfonso 1983; Rondinelli and Ruddle 1977; Rondinelli 1978; Rondinelli and Cheema

Originally published in *Public Administration and Development* 11, no. 5 (1991): 431–51. Copyright 1991 by John Wiley and Sons Ltd. Reproduced by permission of John Wiley and Sons Ltd. and the author.

*This section summarizes briefly an analysis presented at length in Wunsch 1991.

1984; Wanasinghe 1985; Honadle and Van Sant 1985; Leonard 1977; Leonard and Marshall 1982; Brett 1980; Landau 1969, 1973, 1985, 1986; Landau and Stout 1979; Landau et al. 1980).

Numerous scholarly studies have come to this conclusion: the centralized, hierarchical, bureaucratic administrative model has failed. Indeed, to many it appears to be at best a wasteful enterprise; at worst, it is a primary instrument of an urban/wealthy biased political economy which rests heavily on the rural dwellers and the poor.

By the early 1970s, in part stimulated by the American debacle in Vietnam, serious criticisms were being levelled in several of the "donor" states against this model (Owens and Shaw 1972). Along with this came growing skepticism among scholars as to the wisdom and accuracy of the industrially oriented, top-down development strategy (Adleman and Moris 1973), growing humanitarian concern for the living conditions of the vast majority of the Third World rural poor (Harrington 1977), and evidence from the field that the civil service was simply "not delivering" what was expected of it (Leonard 1977). Indeed, it appeared at times that popular and spontaneous grassroots movements were doing a better job of building infrastructure and delivering services in remote and poor rural areas than was all the power and wealth of the state (Keller 1974; Smock 1971; Hill 1970).

These diverse findings stimulated efforts to change both policies and programs, including the "New Directions" and "Basic Needs" strategies of the United States Congress and USAID, the reorientation to rural and agricultural development of the World Bank, and to a large number of "decentralization" efforts among many Third World governments (World Bank 1981; Mickelwait et al. 1978; Olowu 1995, Honadle and Van Sant 1985; Chambers 1983).

The appeal of decentralization is not difficult to understand. At least in its more substantial forms, where real authority and resources are devolved to autonomous local authorities, decentralization offers opportunities to neutralize some of the commonly accepted problems of centralized, hierarchical and bureaucratic structures. For example, it can encourage: *competition* (directly through privatization, or indirectly among parallel public organizations); *redundancy* (by allowing similar and complimentary functions to be discharged by several organizations in a given area); *accountability to clients* rather than to superiors (by allowing clients to select vendors or officials, to hire and fire personnel, to modify priorities, to change policy, etc.); *learning* (by allowing many units to experiment with policies and programs, and by allowing clients to choose and to live with all the consequences of those choices); *local adaptation* (by eliminating requirements and incentives for functionaries to conform to single, national programs); *simplicity* (by reducing the number of personnel, volume of decisions, amount of tasks, volume of information, number of decisions which centralized bureaucracies have to contend with); and allow utilization *of communal norms of organization* such as reciprocity (by allowing communal units some choice of program and policy).

Decentralization efforts have taken numerous forms. These have included local level planning, enhanced authority for field officials of centrally governed bureaucracies, area development projects ("Integrated Rural Development" projects in particular), efforts to expand participation in specific development projects and programs, management training and expanded resources for local level personnel and, occasionally, some genuine devolution of responsibilities to local governments (Honadle and Van Sant 1985; Olowu 1995; Korten and Alfonso 1983; Uphoff 1986; Wunsch 1988; Conyers 1983a, b; Rondinelli 1981, 1983; Rondinelli and Cheema 1984; Rondinelli and Nellis 1986). Countries with major efforts in these areas have included Kenya, Sri Lanka, Bangladesh, New Guinea, Philippines, Ghana, Nigeria, Zimbabwe and others (Olowu 1995; Conyers 1983b; Cheema and Rondinelli 1983b).

With all these diverse efforts in diverse countries, and good theoretical reasons to expect improved performance through decentralization, it is discouraging and more than a little perplexing that the results so far have been rather dismal. Dennis Rondinelli, a major advocate in the 1970s of decentralization as part of a major reorientation in development policy and practice, observed in 1984, along with G. Shabbir Cheema, that, "Despite its vast scope, decentralization has seldom, if ever, lived up to expectations" (1984, 27). In general, decentralization efforts have not significantly expanded participation, improved project effectiveness or efficiency, increased orientation to rural needs and wants, expanded financial support for local projects and services by rural dwellers, reduced central costs or (much less) redistributed wealth, status or power to the rural areas. Planning systems do not seem any more responsive to rural priorities, local institutions of governance any more viable, and projects any more likely to be sustained after donor and/or central state investments have been completed (Honadle and Van Sant 1985; Wunsch 1988; Rondinelli 1981, 1983; Rondinelli and Cheema 1984; Olowu 1995; Uphoff 1986; Cheema and Rondinelli 1983a, b).

How is the scholar, practitioner or official concerned with Third World development to react to this picture? To this point, it does not seem there is any viable "cure" for the severe underperformance one finds in Third World administration: both "centralization" and "decentralization" appear critically flawed.

In a recent essay (Wunsch 1988), I argue that one avenue to explore in answering this at once perplexing and discouraging situation might be to return to a recurring issue of social analysis: how does one conceptualize the nature of a given problem? Perhaps the failure to reach satisfactory results here grows in part from asking the wrong question? Regarding this, I have argued that administration and administrative performance have been repeatedly misanalyzed as primarily *organizational level* issues, and that this has led to reactions which were ineffective in discerning exactly *why* underperformance occurred and *what* might be done to improve performance (Wunsch 1988).

How does this organizational level focus hinder effective analysis and reform? To begin with, it weakens reform efforts because in its focus on the "organization" it pays little heed to the variations among, and the nature of, the goods and services desired of these organizations. While it may be intuitively obvious to nearly every student of administration that goods and services do indeed vary, developing an analytical framework to make sense of these variations and to show how organizational arrangements might be appropriately varied, has rarely been attempted.

As well as largely ignoring the differences among goods and services desired of organizations, organizational level analysis has tended to approach organizations in a "holistic" way. The question has been phrased, "What is wrong with the Ministry of ????? that it is failing to deliver ?????" Phrased as an organizational level problem, remedies have (not surprisingly) been generally offered at a rather broad organizational level: usually ones of general organizational restructuring (decentralization, privatization, participation, centralization, etc.), or increasing organizational resources (personnel numbers, training, budget size, technology availability). The attraction of decentralization and participation seems in part to grow from this orientation: they offer comprehensive solutions to deal with broadly understood problems. Their implementation certainly has reflected this, with issues of how, when, who, to what extent and the like generally answered at the level of the organization as a whole, or some unit of it. How, why, and when decentralization or participation might make sense given certain goods or services is not really analyzed in any depth or rigor. Finally, organizational level analysis has encouraged analysts and practitioners to overlook regulations, laws and conditions *outside* the organization which can critically affect its likelihood of success. Property rights, taxation provisions, demands and services by *other* organizations, patron-clientage systems, general pricing patterns and the like, are important influences on outcomes achievement of any program or project.

The persistence of the organizational level focus can be seen in the current soul-searching regarding the underperformance of most decentralization-participation efforts. For example, both Cheema and Rondinelli, and Cochrane find there to be critical shortfalls in resources, skills, personnel and national backing for organizations undergoing decentralization. They recommend that these organizational level problems be eased to improve performance (Rondinelli and Cheema 1984; Cochrane 1983; Cheema and Rondinelli 1983a, b). Interestingly enough, there never seem to be enough of these resources to make these experiments work! Equally interesting, one can find numerous examples where extrastate collective action at the local level *has* indeed succeeded quite well in purchasing, managing and sustaining infrastructure and delivering services; all without *any* national political backing, national subventions or subsidies, and with locally available, usually untrained management resources (Smock 1971; Keller 1974; Hill 1970). One wonders why these analysts render the "organization" an abstraction with very little internal consistency or coherence.

A second reason why organizational level analysis has posted particular problems for Third World development administration is because of the dominance of the centralized-hierarchical-bureaucratic model in the Third World. This has meant that the diversity of organizational forms one finds more typically in developed countries is absent. Rather than an organizational "gene pool" available to learn from and experiment with, Third World leaders must consciously design organizational alternatives. An organizational level focus has tended to lead to seemingly dramatic "reforms," which in reality have tended to change little, and which have probably slowed the experimentation with more moderate, appropriate and realistic changes that typically occur quite naturally among the more diverse organizations found in developed societies. An heuristic to help move analysis beyond these limits and effectively guide policy working is surely needed!

Given these problems, what ought the analyst and practitioner do to better understand and improve the performance of Third World administrative systems? This essay joins with several others in recommending what they have called "institutional analysis" as a method of analyzing why organizational arrangements lead to the production (or do not so lead) of specific goods and services. It assumes individuals are "boundedly rational," satisfice, and make choices according to their preferences. Individuals are not assumed a priori to be encapsulated by their organizations, nor to find organizationally rational behavior necessarily consistent with individually rational behavior. They are, furthermore, assumed to have incomplete information on alternatives and consequences before them and, as "satisficers," to be moderately risk-averse (Simon 1965).

These assumptions are important because they direct our attention to the problematic nature of individual choices. As choices are not assumed to be in any way automatic (because of presumed organizational control, complete individual information, or simple personal goal maximization), the diverse factors which affect these variables act to determine the options individuals actually see as possible and desirable: why individuals take the actions they do. This strategy emphasizes the importance of analyzing these factors vis-à-vis key individuals regarding key activities. This is not "reductionistic" in that individuals facing certain behavioral options are understood as located in organizational contexts that critically affect the options the person perceives. As individuals make choices they in turn have consequences for the task or goal at hand, and eventually for the organization.

The analytical frameworks presented below are selected largely because in other work they have appeared to lend insight into important determinants of the conditions that affect individual choices. The very need for these analytical frameworks is because, I believe, earlier research and practice assumed individual choice and behavior "out" of the model. Because individual choices and behaviors were not automatic, and organizations did not behave holistically, however, much earlier research and practice did not lead to fruitful field design.

In this model, therefore, individuals are regarded as the driving force of an organization, making choices and taking actions which are affected by the "institutional arrangements" within that organization. The latter are the many working rules which allocate (or fail to allocate) authority, information and resources; structure decision-making; allocate accountability; create property rights and the like within any organization, and vis-à-vis its environment (E. Ostrom 1986a, b; V. Ostrom 1985, 1986a, b).

Institutional analysis thus focuses on *goods and services, individuals, institutional arrangements,* and how these interrelate to lead to some behaviors and not to others. In this framework, the recurrent question is—how do given *institutional arrangements* encourage and discourage *individuals* to produce given goods or services? Put another way, given certain goods or services, what sort of institutional arrangements create incentives which will be likely to lead individuals to produce them?

Having established "Simonian" assumptions regarding individuals, to do institutional analysis one must engage in three complementary analytical steps:

1. What individuals are key to the production and fruitful use of a given good or service?
2. What characteristics of given goods or services (and their production processes) create incentives and disincentives for the production, use, abuse, maintenance, financing, etc. of those goods or services?
3. What sorts of institutional arrangements, given the characteristics of the goods and services, will encourage the key individuals to take those actions necessary to produce, maintain, fruitfully use and finance given goods or services?

In this analytical strategy *a given good or services production process* is the *level* of analysis; and the *individuals* taking or not taking actions to produce those goods or services are the *unit* of analysis. *Organizational arrangements,* among other factors, become variables important in predicting/explaining why certain outcomes are reached or not (Gregg 1974; E. Ostrom 1986a, b).

Having analyzed given goods or services along these lines, practitioners and scholars ought to be able to pursue far more subtle and refined strategies of organizational reform, where at times incremental and modest changes in location of responsibility, authority, resources, accountability, financial responsibility, prerequisites to action, public information and the like, may be what is necessary to incline individuals to produce (maintain, finance, sustain, etc.) given goods or services. Finally, this analysis can help analysts to determine when broad, comprehensive organizational change is likely to work (and when not), given the important characteristics of the goods or services under consideration.

The remainder of this essay will do two things. First it will explore, in an introductory way, how desired goods and services might be analyzed to explain and predict the incentive structures, *ceteris paribus,* they present to producers and users. Then it will explore how various organizational arrangements might be expected to modify those incentive structures in ways which encourage more desirable outcomes. To do this I will present an analytical framework composed of eight variables that can be used to analyze a given good or service, and explain the incentives and disincentives unique to it that will encourage and discourage individuals from using/abusing/producing/financing it. Finally, I will explore several variations of institutional arrangements and explain how they neutralize or reinforce the incentives and disincentives unique to the various goods and services.

Analyzing Goods and Designing Institutions

It should be clear to any student of public services that not all public services are "cut from the same cloth." Education differs in immediately apparent ways from repairing and maintaining streets, from policing, and from health services. Indeed, within a single category, such as health services, such component functions as mass inoculations, public health education, clinical medical services, and the training of personnel are quite different from one another. The key question is not whether or not these are different, but through what conceptual tools can the analyst or policy maker categorize these differences and discern their implications for institutional design? This would include the matter of finance and financial institutions. While I would agree there are *no doubt* others of relevance and importance, I would like briefly to discuss eight conceptual tools in this section in order to suggest how rational choices may be made among varying institutional structures. These questions or "analytical" frameworks do not provide a simple "formula" to make these decisions, but help practitioners determine what the implications are for various organizational alternatives, given the nature of the goods or public service desired.

Excludability

To what extent can a producer or provider of goods or a service exclude consumers from its consumption (Ostrom and Ostrom 1977)? When the producer of goods is able to do so, then the private market can function to produce the goods concerned. In this circumstance, producers can deny consumers the goods until consumers have paid for the unit of consumption they desire. A properly operating free market may be expected under these circumstances to provide optimal flows of resources at efficiency prices. Otherwise, however, when goods are not excludable, entrepreneurs cannot recoup their investments in resources, capital or labor through the market because of the problem of free-riding (Olson 1965). The market will fail to provide the goods, and governmental provision may be necessary in order to require all who consume the goods to share in its production costs.

There are a variety of organizational arrangements by which this might be done. For example, government organizations can act to collect taxes and produce the goods. Alternatively, they can collect taxes, specify the amounts and distribution of the goods desired, and contract to private parties for the actual *production* of the goods. This has the advantage of maximizing competition and (in some cases) improving economic efficiency (Oakerson 1987). In either case, centralized control is not particularly advantageous. It is the capacity to authoritatively raise revenue (to tax) which is critical, and it is necessary that the taxing authority is proportionate to the service delivered (Schroeder 1989). For example, physical infrastructure in general is often characterized by non-excludability. Thus, its management and maintenance are usually a challenge. This challenge is intensified in the Third World because central governments have been overloaded, distant from the field, and reluctant to share authority with other organizations (Thomson 1981; Moris 1981). Mixed institutional arrangements can help solve this problem.

Problems of non-excludability may be resolved by a variety of governmental arrangements, and at any of several levels of government. The key is raising revenue by levy to overcome the problems of non-excludability, and organizing production at a level that is sensible given the goods being produced and the people consuming it.

Jointness of Consumption

In some situations, goods and services may be consumed "jointly" by varying numbers of people (Ostrom and Ostrom 1977). Under these conditions additional consumers do not detract from the supply of the goods nor raise its production cost. When these goods are also non-excludable, there is great incentive to provide such goods and services to very large numbers of people to obtain economies of scale. National defense is a good example of such goods. Others might be a regional flood control project, irrigation system maintenance and management, agricultural research on improved seed varieties, or improved curricula for schools. It is very important, however, in maximizing efficient and effective production, that these goods be produced so that they correspond to their clientele's needs and preferences. Thus, seed variety production must be organized with reference to regional and climatic conditions, school curricula to relevant cultural needs and perspectives, and flood control to relevant physical areas. This is particularly clear when "coproduction" is involved (i.e., when clients must actively work with producers to achieve outcomes; discussed below), for if culturally, practically or otherwise offensive or inappropriate joint goods are produced, one can expect at least withdrawal from coproduction, if not overt resistance and hostility (Parks et al. 1982; Kiser and Ostrom 1982). In either case, production flags and costs rise.

Thus, joint non-excludable goods ought to be carefully evaluated on the possible need for decentralization to correspond to local public preferences and conditions. This is particularly the case when some joint "goods" are regarded as "bads" by others. For example, downstream pollution is a public "bad" characterized by joint consumption (Buchanan 1970). Here, decentralization strategies may need to be balanced by rules that require local intergovernmental agreements and/or the assent of regional or national organizations to ensure that such "bads" are jointly consumed only by those who choose to live with them, for whatever reasons they might have for doing so (V. Ostrom 1985). Intergovernmental financing rules can have an important impact on how such questions are resolved, for better and for worse (Schroeder 1987, 1989).

However, when consumption of the goods concerned is not joint (i.e., a unit consumed by one individual may not be consumed by a second), but goods remain non-excludable (infeasible to exclude users) a new set of production and organizational challenges arise. With these, often called "common pool resources" (CPRs), problems of overuse appear paramount, as well as questions of disruptive or polluting uses and competition for consumption which can disrupt productive use, efficient use, and equitable distribution of the resource (E. Ostrom 1987). In these cases, organizational implications can be mixed. For example, relatively small common pool resource systems, with few "spillovers," complex and changing internal features (i.e., valued resources that move about, vary in quality and location from year to year, and cannot be predicted), with relatively non-conflictual relationships among users, may be good candidates for local self-government. Among other advantages local self-government may bring is the possible enhancement of social pressure as a regulating device, something particularly useful when enforcement is problematic and conditions are changeable, as they usually are in the case of common pool resource systems (E. Ostrom 1987).

However, when use of a CPR is fraught with the danger of costly spillovers that could impact upon other CPRs or persons, or when several conflicting uses are made by groups with no common institutional framework, then administration may be called for at a more inclusive level. In either circumstance, taxes or some other form of general levy may be called for to raise funds for CPR management, because of the problem of exclusion (E. Ostrom 1989). For "toll goods" (joint but excludable), if there is resolution of equity concerns, "user fees" can be used. Either levy can be imposed by any level of government, although each would make sense at the level of the unit concerned with the largest share of administration of the resource. This is because such arrangements might link cost and benefit in the user's mind (easing revenue raising costs) and avoid revenue "leakage" to other, unrelated units and services (Ostrom and Ostrom 1977; Schroeder 1987, 1989). Obviously, close attention to local finance systems may be necessary to help reinforce the effectiveness of these arrangements. Questions of location of authority, local decision-making capability, "fitting" administrative systems to local abilities and traditions, and the like, are critical issues here.

Spillovers and Externalities

Some goods and services can easily contain the costs and benefits of their production process within an area defined by their "consumer." Some, like elementary education, public safety or public services, tend to spread positive spillovers across broad areas, as the improvements generated by, or for, some persons in increased productivity or freedom tend to benefit others as well. Similarly, pollution of water or air, or erosion of land and siltation of a watershed, etc., are "negative" spillovers that are caused by the production of some public goods and services (Buchanan 1970). "Capturing" the externalities is a serious challenge in either case. In the case of positive spillovers, the case can be made for general revenue contributions to localized service systems, with or without proportionate allocation of administrative control to those wider constituencies (depending upon other questions). This is to encourage optimal levels of production, which may not be met by local resources or perceptions of desirable production levels alone. In the case of negative spillovers, one must still internalize the externalities. This might be accomplished via the implementation of general performance bonds or regulation established at the level of the broader constituency for the "industry" concerned, by taxes, or charges levied on those producing the spillover sufficient to repair any damage, etc. In either positive or negative spillovers, sufficient authority needs to be allocated to an administrative unit to provide for these problems, although its authority over the activity usually need not be all-inclusive (E. Ostrom 1987, 1989). The link among diverse aspects of institutional arrangements is particularly clear here: tax and revenue institutions, for example, can be critical mechanisms to regulate and/or compensate for thorny management problems such as spillovers and externalities.

Technical Certainty

When optimal (or even feasible) technologies for production of desired goods or services are not known or are uncertain, then decentralization to local governments or even to private markets may be a beneficial strategy. This avoids premature programming and over-investment in a single, problematic strategy, and encourages a diversity of experiments which may bring forth more effective technologies, refine them, and allow their comparative evaluation (Landau 1969; Landau and Stout 1979). Most service delivery and management systems have uncertain technologies, making them vulnerable to "fads" that can seriously set back production if uncritically and too widely accepted. Alternatively, well known and reliable technologies can be encouraged in a variety of ways, including centralized training for several personnel, centrally based technical assistance capacities or, when necessary, through central mandate.

Measurability and Specifiability of Outputs or Inputs

Some goods and services, the amount wanted, and their specific characteristics can be clearly defined; similarly, the nature of the outputs, their conformity to specifications, their timeliness, volume and effectiveness can be clearly measured. Improved seed development may be an example of such goods, as might be transporting a given volume of agricultural commodities between certain points on a certain schedule.

However, some services such as "local development," "health services," or "education" can be less clearly specified a priori, and are often debatable with regard to measuring output: either in agreement as to what constitutes the desired output, or in measuring the outputs themselves. For example, individuals may not be technically well enough versed to specify exactly what inputs they need to improve local public health or elementary education, or the optimal technology may be as yet uncertain. Similarly, at the point of evaluating performance one might question whether a successful public health field service is one which records high incidence of disease and public health problems, because that indicates great energy and activity on its part, or if such data indicate poor performance, because they suggest there are serious field problems? Often, as well, quality of performance (e.g., what a public health nurse actually does on community rounds) is difficult to evaluate by his/her superiors. The issue can be interpreted in a variety of ways, and distant, "objective" evaluation systems tend to operate poorly. To note that such ambiguities can be "settled" by fiat before a service is commenced is really to miss the point: supervisors cannot closely observe actual field performance, there often exists no obviously agreed upon and valid and reliable indicator of performance, and *any* a priori choice by a single purchasing entity is going to bias organizational performance towards one or another interpretation of the nature of the service desired (the problem of "teaching for the test" in contemporary American society is a good example of this, as U.S. states impose single tests on all potential graduates). Bureaucratic goal displacement and performance rigidity are encouraged by formal measures of performance, when performance is hard to measure.

Another example of measurement and specification difficulty can be seen in road and irrigation system maintenance. In irrigation systems, for example, the sometimes vast areas covered, the large number of persons using the systems, the relative inaccessibility of much of the system, and the idiosyncratic patterns of flow, maintenance needs, etc., mean that the information and transaction costs involved in central management of maintenance are large. Trying to manage and maintain a system from the center through a hierarchical bureaucracy would call for immense amounts of information which are likely to be prohibitively expensive. Even though in theory these could be measured and specified, the cost of gathering the data to do so means that, in fact, they cannot. Using smaller units which have greater access to local data and can use existing social organization for enforcement is one alternative.

When there is great ambiguity in specifying desired inputs or outputs or measuring their attainment, radically decentralizing public services may be a reasonable strategy to provide services, all other aspects held constant (Oakerson, Parks, and Bell 1987). Under this form of "decentralization" citizens may renew or cancel contracts for services strictly on the basis of their satisfaction with performance. When ambiguity is a problem and goods are non-excludable (such as irrigation and road systems), the difficulty in specifying contract terms, evaluating contract compliance and the desirability of facilitating quick and continuous feedback between consumers and producers suggests that decentralized, local *community* units (when they exist and are effective, formal local governments) may be the best providers and producers of the goods (Oakerson 1987). However, a complete analysis of optimal strategy would also depend on the effectiveness of the local accountability system for government, coproduction, size of the relevant local community, and scale of operation related to average cost, etc. Given the combined answer to these questions, the location of the authority to decide upon, deliver, fund, and evaluate services may vary greatly.

Importance of Co-Production

When service goals require citizens to actively work to "coproduce" desired goods (such as is often the case in public health, agricultural extension, irrigation system maintenance and education), close cooperation between professional and citizen is imperative (Ostrom and Ostrom 1977; Parks et al. 1982). Smaller units to organize and supervise such services may have an advantage in achieving economical and effective production. They can be more closely tailored to consumer desires and local needs. More informal contact between professional and official has generally been associated with smaller units of production as well, and might be expected to encourage coproduction. Depending on such questions as jointness and excludability, either governmental or private mechanisms might be chosen to produce such goods. In either case, goods and services characterized by coproduction are excellent candidates for production through smaller organizational units of one variety or another.

Coproduction in areas such as health, infrastructure maintenance, policing, and renewable resource management can involve several tactics (Whitaker 1980). These might range from citizen informal assistance with road maintenance, to upkeep of tertiary irrigation canals by organized user maintenance groups, to policing of village forest areas or control of overgrazing on pastures. Parental involvement in primary education may be critical, as in provision of family health services as well. The key question is—what form of structure provides for enough genuine client input to make their investment of time and resources worthwhile?

Scale of Operation Regarding Average Unit Cost

The idea of economies and diseconomies of scale is not a new one, but is nonetheless one which deserves close attention in regards to Third World administration. Third World governments have tended to overemphasize the centralized, bureaucratic organization. And institutional arrangements have tended to eliminate or preclude all alternative organizations (e.g., lack of authority of local governments; restrictions on rights of private property and contract, state monopolies in multiple enterprises, state control of capital; central planning of all investments, etc.). This has led to overemphasis on state monopolies in all areas, and to diseconomies of scale in many public services and programs.

The question of economies and diseconomies of scale addresses these problems, challenging the tendency to organize and manage most public services and programs in the Third World from the center. It emphasizes instead the need to design institutions which are generally more flexible and appropriate to any organization's multiple responsibilities. For example, routine road maintenance may best be carried on at a far smaller scale than it currently is, perhaps by local governments, traditional social units, or even individuals. However, road building in general may require a larger scale operation. Indeed, road building will itself vary in optimal scale by the type of road desired: dirt, gravel, improved, concrete, etc. Thus, one item of goods or service produced by what has usually been a single ministry can be broken down to several subordinate goods or services.

Indeed, as the analyst explores these several areas, they break out to additional subordinate areas (network planning, route choice, surveying, design, construction, maintenance, policing, finance, etc.), each of which has its *own* scale of optimal operation. The complexity and variability among these "sub-sub-areas" brings us to the need to consider the multitude of institutional arrangements (i.e., rules) that encourage and discourage alternative organizations from developing to perform these activities.

In asking these questions, the analyst must remember that generally no single analytical framework alone is likely to lead him/her to an optimal solution. For example, if one finds that the goods or services in question are characterized by excludability, it is possible to allocate this production to the private sector, when non-excludability and jointness of consumption both obtain, then government at a regional or national level may be the best provider of the goods. Critical coproduction issues, however, as well as the question of degree of choice by users, may suggest some form of local control be built into the structure (Ostrom and Ostrom 1977).

Degree of Choice by Users

Goods provided in an area may or may not allow for choice among users. Clean air is there for all to breathe, regardless of their preference for other forms of air, just as are safe streets, fire protection, etc. As these are generally desired goods, this poses no problem, except in so far as how they are paid for (as our discussion of excludability suggests). However, when public goods become public "bads," such as congested streets, economic inflation, dysfunctional irrigation systems—or even where different groups value some goods as positive and others as negative (such as religious observances in schools)—diverse and difficult organizational issues abound (Ostrom and Ostrom 1977).

In some cases, degree of choice may be enhanced by shrinking administrative size, so that varying subgroups may adapt services to their own demands and tastes. However, such strategies must be wary of creating the possibility of new negative spillovers *among* separate administrative units, allowing some to benefit from the positive spillovers of others whose costs they no longer pay (as in the case of wealthy suburbs benefiting from an urban-industrial economy, but sharing none of the social welfare costs of the casualties of that economy if they are confined to the older city), general equity concerns, and the possibility that new "policy-minority" groups will be created in the new administrative units. Some of these problems may never be solvable, leading as they do to an almost infinite regression of minority preferences. Nevertheless, the existence of a cross-cutting, judicial structure with the authority to direct compliance with certain basic personnel rights can help resolve these dilemmas (E. Ostrom 1989; Ostrom and Ostrom 1977).

This section of the essay has attempted to demonstrate eight "analytical frameworks" and show how they pose questions regarding programs and projects which can help practitioners determine what sort of organizational arrangements fit what outcomes. These frameworks have proved their usefulness in public policy and program analysis already. They are, however, not the only ones that might be used in field exercises, as research and work in these areas is currently continuing.

Institutional Alternatives to Improve Performance

One of the great tragedies of the post independence experience of the Third World has been the paucity of institutional forms utilized by their governments. Drawing from the hierarchical and bureaucratic repertoires left by the colonial era, and probably overly influenced by the technocratic faith then dominant in both West and East (Packenham 1973), the new states adopted virtually only a single institutional form as their development tool (Owens and Shaw 1972). While there is certainly variation among the many Third World countries, in general they distrusted market-driven economies, saw traditional, locally based governments as anarchic and ineffective, and distrusted modernized systems of genuine local government as potentially wasteful and as sources of potential political opposition to them (Olowu

1995). Thus, the hierarchical, bureaucratic system was adopted throughout the Third World as the developmental norm. It was guided by a national plan, directed by leaders in the capital, and rationalized as the most effective, efficient and modern system (Hyden 1983).

As many have now come to agree, its record of performance has been disappointing. Responsible analysts must ask, however, "what else is there?" In fact, there are many ways by which development efforts can be organized. Depending upon the "nature of the goods" concerned (as discussed) and the outcomes desired, a government might responsibly choose from among the following:

- "public service" industries
- private sector / market provision
- contemporary local government units
- indigenously or "traditionally" based social-political units
- hierarchical bureaucracies
- a mixture of these

I will now discuss some of these alternatives.

Public Service Industries

The possibility of what some have called "public service industries" becomes clear when one realizes one can distinguish between the "provision" and "production" of goods and services (Oakerson 1987; E. Ostrom 1983). If provision is understood to be the funding and planning for goods and services, the concern of many that these functions remain under the influence of government makes good sense. In the case of public goods (access to which cannot be easily regulated by a producer; see above), provision by government units of one sort or another is probably essential. Unless someone (or some organization) has the authority and ability to levy compulsory fees upon users or a general population (a "tax"), it will be difficult to ensure that the goods or services are paid for. Similarly, where substantial spillovers of either a positive or negative nature are associated with goods or services, governmental involvement in their planning and general management can also be seen as necessary. Thus, in order to assure equity and effective service levels, and to avoid displacing costs on third parties, the authority of government may be required.

However, provision can be separated from "production," if we understand the second to be the actual physical delivery of the service or production of the goods. With planning decisions made by government and financed by revenues raised by government, then multiple, private entities can be contracted to deliver/produce the service/goods. This approach has several advantages.

When superior technologies of production are not clearly known, separating production from provision facilitates multiple producers which can experiment among alternative technologies, generating a database for public choices later on. Similarly, when production is characterized by diseconomies of scale at or below the size of the appropriate *provisioning* unit, multiple producing units can avoid these diseconomies. Multiple production units can also encourage consumer differentiation, when people within a provisioning area have tastes and preferences about the amount of, or manner in which, goods or services are delivered. Finally, the provisioning unit of government is in an effective position to evaluate the relative performance of production units, and encourage cheaper and better performance through general regulation.

Competition to encourage minimum unit cost can also be encouraged by "public service industries." Certainly, one of the accepted propositions of modern economics, and a critical lesson learned in contemporary public administration, is the inefficiency of monopolies, private *and* public (Lowi 1969; E. Ostrom 1983; Lindblom 1977). The coupling of monopoly with political power has proved to be a recipe for inefficiency, stagnation, waste, inflexibility and poor responsiveness to consumers. These perverse incentives, not just incidentally, are cited in several studies of the unwillingness of the public to finance public services, in the Third World and elsewhere (Schroeder 1985, 1987, 1989; Dahl and Lindblom 1953; Lindblom 1977; Lowi 1969). "Public service industries" can help overcome these problems.

Infrastructure construction and maintenance are excellent candidates for "public service industries." Activities could be divided by area and/or by task to take advantage of the above characteristics. The requirements of governmental planning and funding (*provision*) can be combined with the potential flexibility, innovation, lower cost and local responsiveness of private and small units of *production*. Such a solution to infrastructure maintenance problems might require institutional redesign in such areas as tax law, procedures for private incorporation, property rights of private persons, corporation law, bidding regulations, authority of local governmental units, discretion by bureaucrats, etc. Many of these would be "decentralizing." Others might have the opposite effect in some respects, and be equally needed.

Private Markets

Some have oversold the value of fully privatized service/goods delivery/ production systems, while others have refused completely to consider their potential value. These appear at times suspiciously like ideological battles rather than analytical choices. The point to be made here is that objective, identifiable characteristics of discrete service/goods systems ought to be the issues on which these choices turn. For example, where goods are *not* "public" goods, are not "common pool" resources, lack significant positive and negative spillovers, allow quality evaluation fairly easily by potential consumers, and pose no significant equity issues (i.e., such as are posed by such questions as access to health care), then private markets may be an efficient and effective way to produce such goods.

Recent research on management, the costs of performing it from the center, and the problem of doing it at all when technologies are unknown and environments are severe, suggest that externalizing management functions to the private sector is a strategy Third World leaders might seriously consider (Landau et al. 1980; Wunsch 1986). Centralizing management, under these conditions, is costly, likely to become trapped in premature programming and cost-ineffective technologies, and at times leads to politically explosive battles. Finally, by training, temperament, and bureaucratic regulations, administrative careerists are often ill-suited for the ambiguous and necessarily innovative tasks which development administration requires (Downs 1966). It would seem better to externalize these situations to individuals outside government, where self-selection will tend to encourage better managers and innovators to provide the services.

Good cases in point for this argument are the usually flourishing transport sector in most Third World cities, and the traditional medical services sector. While municipal and state transport companies regularly operate at substantial losses and with marginal effectiveness, the private transport sector literally teems with providers (Linn 1983). A strong user sector can be critical to the long-term viability of infrastructure (Schroeder 1987, 1989). First, it can be a source of revenues to maintain and manage the infrastructure. Minimizing managerial costs, using the cheapest capital and most flexible labor supply, it can provide economically productive transport, help people earn a living, and produce an economic surplus that can be captured to fund roads maintenance. Rather than operating as a double "black hole" in the economy (soaking up state subsidies to operate and paying nothing for infrastructure maintenance), it can provide a double *benefit* instead. Similarly, organizations of private producers who benefit from infrastructure have a critical interest/incentive in seeing that the investment continues in a healthy state. They thus have a potential to help governments police abusive use of the infrastructure. Similarly, while the state medical services have largely collapsed in rural areas, traditional healers and midwives, often without any formal training, carry on as the sole source of health care (Chambers 1983).

Modern Local Government Units

Many aspects of both "public service industries" and the market require formal units of local government to assist and regulate them. They also need it to link them to other services and goods necessary for their effective operation. For example, the taxing function necessary to sustain public service industries presumes government. And, national levels of government may be too distant, too preoccupied with other issues, or present too great diseconomies of scale to effectively tax localities for local goods and services (Schroeder 1987, 1989). Similarly, when use has erosive consequences for infrastructure (and of course most use does), government authority is probably necessary to control who, with what technologies, under what conditions, and at what density, is allowed to use the infrastructure. Once again, national levels of government may not be well suited to that task. It might be better devolved to local governments, particularly if actual users of the infrastructure have a voice in local government (Uphoff 1986).

How this task would be performed could blend several organizational forms. For example, private operators may be effective policing agents, once use parameters are set. However, their temptation to "consume" a larger share of the infrastructure in order to maximize their profit may require government-set regulations if it is to be controlled. Then, aware that abusive users are the exception rather than the norm, and with government sanction backing them up, local users or their associations may be effective police agents.

A similar logic applies to potential "producers" under a public service industry system. Local government may be needed to regulate entry to the market and assure overall field performance (bonding producers, supervising technologies used and standards of production).

Indigenous or "Traditional" Social Political Units

When maintenance and management are highly coproductive, when abusive use methods are not particularly obvious, when goods or a service, such as much infrastructure, is a "common pool" resource (i.e., both non-excludable and used simultaneously by multiple users), when technologies are both simple and with few economies of scale, and when there are few spillovers, then small, cohesive social-political units can be effective agents for both maintenance and management of infrastructure. The cohesion of indigenous communities, the high level of mutual awareness often found among their members, and the existence of institutions which can make and enforce decisions can increase the likelihood of infrastructure's survival. While such units are not appropriate for all types of goods and services under these circumstances, they might be rather effective. Like the "private market," however, they must not be oversold. Spillovers, systems larger than localities, and damaged traditional institutions are common, and limit the effectiveness of these institutions in this task (Leonard and Marshall 1982).

National Bureaucracies

Using the logic of analysis already developed, certain functions ought to continue at the national level. Financing projects and programs with major positive economic spillovers ought to involve national revenue bases, or such projects will be suboptimally produced. Also, planning major infrastructure projects to link regions or major natural resources (river basins, ports, railroads, etc.) also probably requires a large national role.

Projects and programs with large economies of scale, and where technologies are well known, easily observed and complex, also can benefit from national, hierarchical control. Where in fact the goods to be produced are effectively national "public goods" or a national "common pool resource" (perhaps a national heavy duty highway, or a national river basin development project such as contemplated in Bangladesh), then national funding and management may be necessary. However, as the following section will argue, such national efforts are usually best operated with a mix of the other institutional forms discussed here.

Mixed Institutional Arrangements

As may be clear from the preceding discussion, rarely will a single institutional form be an effective way to deliver a given service or sustain an infrastructure. For example, while *local governments* and *indigenous-traditional, political-social units* may be highly useful in some site decisions for infrastructure, linking them to regional and national systems will involve *national decision-making institutions* as well. The same logic would apply to managing service personnel on the one hand, and training them on the other. Or, while *public service industries* may be effective for some aspects of construction and maintenance of infrastructure, *national* organizations may have key roles to play in quality control of certain inputs, *local governments* may be key managers and fund raisers, and *indigenous-traditional units* may be key actors to provide routine maintenance and police abuse uses of infrastructures. Similarly, while *private market* systems may be superb management devices to organize use, raise finance, and perhaps assist in managing service delivery and in policing of infrastructure, *modern local governments* may be needed to set and enforce general standards of training and appropriate and sustainable use methods, and to develop and manage revenue systems which effectively link users with the infrastructure and services.

When one looks at any service area or any infrastructure, one will probably find certain activities characterized by great economies of scale, with easily supervised and well accepted technologies, and done easily on a regular schedule. These might be best done by national bureaucracies, while other activities with smaller economies of scale, less clear technologies, requiring closer supervision, and on a rapid-response basis, might benefit from a more decentralized approach. The latter might include local government, public service industries or even traditional local institutions. These could easily coexist, and offer the same goods or service the advantage of multiple-institutional forms, each of which best fits the *particular* tasks needed. The key point here is that certain types of goods or services require certain types of actions (or behaviors) to be done well, and the various institutional forms provide varying incentives for varying actions. Fitting the three together (good or service, behavior/actions, appropriate incentive structure through institutions) is the issue at hand.

Conclusions

In a recent major paper, Rondinelli and Cheema suggested that support for or opposition to decentralization was becoming essentially an "ideological" position (1984). I have tried to show in this essay that with an appropriate analytical framework, decentralization (and, by implication, other administrative modalities) can at times be justified as far more than that. Once one abandons the organization level approach of most administrative analysis, and seeks patterns of incentives and disincentives in the context of given goods and services, one can explain the poor performance of most centralized *and* many decentralized administrative structures in the less developed countries (LDCs).

In moving beyond analysis and in applying this strategy to the real world, the analyst must pay heed to the general political context. Some conditions may dramatically affect choice structures, but be well beyond the control of the practitioner. An administrative environment in which individual choice-sets cannot reasonably be presumed to be influenced by organizational arrangements and incentives is certainly one. For example, an imploding political economy such as that which Ghana experienced from the mid-1970s to the 1980s is probably a factor beyond the reach of the analyst: that is, this approach can help explain its impact on public programs, but it probably lacks the political "leverage" to affect that impact. Severe ethnic conflict along the lines of contemporary Sri Lanka or the Punjab of India may also be a situation where the real influence of the administrative analyst is likely to pale before overwhelming socioeconomic conflict. The break-down of all impartial application of law along the lines of Zaire; the dominance of patron-clientage system in such countries as Bangladesh; and the apparent complete permeation of organizations by radical, amoral individual goal-seeking by civil servants as described by Richard Joseph and Peter Koehn in Nigeria, would also be difficult environments for this strategy to be pursued (Joseph 1987; Koehn 1990). It is probably countries somewhat more economically and socially stabilized, with some ongoing institutional cohesion, such as Egypt, Morocco, Kenya, Zimbabwe, Thailand or Mexico that provide the best opportunity for this strategy in the field actually to lead to fruitful changes.

Having noted this as a final concern, this essay suggests that frameworks of analysis can be developed which can help scholars and officials choose when, where and how to pursue organizational reforms more likely to succeed. In this regard the real challenge will not be "winning" ideologically laden battles between "decentralization" and "centralization" but one of developing complex, mixed administrative systems that define institutional arrangements that produce incentive/disincentive structures appropriate to completion of the task at hand.

REFERENCES

Adleman, Irma, and Cynthia Moris (1973) *Economic Growth and Social Equity in Developing Societies.* Stanford, CA: Stanford University Press.

Brett, E. A. (1980) "State Power and Economic Inefficiency: Explaining Political Failure in Africa." *Institute of Development Studies* 17:22–29.

Buchanan, James M. (1970) "Public Goods and Public Bads." In John P. Crecine (ed.), *Financing the Metropolis,* 51–71. Beverly Hills, CA: Sage Publications.

Chambers, Robert (1983) *Rural Development: Putting the Last First.* London: Longman House.

——— (1985) *Managing Rural Development: Ideas and Experience from East Africa.* West Hartford, CT: Kumarian Press.

Cheema, G. Shabbir, and Dennis A. Rondinelli (1983a) *Implementing Decentralization Programmes in Asia: Local Capacity for Rural Development.* Nagoya: United Nations Centre for Regional Development.

——— (1983b) *Decentralisation and Development: Policy Implementation in Developing Countries.* Beverly Hills, CA: Sage Publications.

Cochrane, Glynn (1983) *Policies for Strengthening Local Government in Developing Countries.* Washington, DC: World Bank.

Conyers, Diana (1983a) "Decentralization: The Latest Fad in Development Administration?" *Public Administration and Development* 3:97–109.

——— (1983b) "Decentralization and Development: A Review of the Literature." *Public Administration and Development* 4:187–97.

Dahl, Robert A., and Charles E. Lindblom (1953) *Politics, Economics and Welfare.* New York: Harper and Brothers.

Downs, Anthony (1966) *Inside Bureaucracy.* Boston: Little, Brown.

Esman, Milton (1980) "Development Assistance in Public Administration: Requiem or Renewal." *Public Administration Review* 40, no. 5: 426–31.

Gregg, Philip M. (1974) "Units and Levels of Analysis: A Problem of Policy Analysis in Federal Systems." *Publius* 4:59–86.

Harrington, Michael (1977) *The Vast Majority: A Journey to the World's Poor.* New York: Touchstone.

Hill, Polly (1970) *Rural Capitalism in West Africa.* Cambridge: Cambridge University Press.

Honadle, George, and Jerry Van Sant (1985) *Implementation for Sustainability: Lessons from Integrated Rural Development.* West Hartford, CT: Kumarian Press.

Hyden, Goran (1980) *Beyond Ujamaa in Tanzania: Underdevelopment and an Uncaptured Peasantry.* Berkeley: University of California Press.

——— (1983) *No Shortcuts to Progress: African Development Management in Perspective.* Berkeley: University of California Press.

Joseph, Richard A. (1987) *Democracy and Prebendal Politics in Nigeria: The Rise and Fall of the Second Republic.* Cambridge: Cambridge University Press.

Keller, Edmund (1974) "Harambeel: Educational Policy and the Political Economy of Rural Community Organization in Kenya." Paper presented at the African Studies Association, Chicago.

Kiser, Larry, and Elinor Ostrom (1982) "The Three Worlds of Action: A Metatheoretical Synthesis of Institutional Approaches." In Elinor Ostrom (ed.), *Strategies of Political Inquiry,* 179–222. Beverly Hills, CA: Sage Publications. Reprinted in M. D. McGinnis, ed. *Polycentric Games and Institutions* (Ann Arbor: University of Michigan Press, 1999).

Koehn, Peter (1990) *Public Policy and Administration in Africa.* Boulder, CO: Westview Press.

Korten, David, and Felipe B. Alfonso (1983) *Bureaucracy and the Poor: Closing the Gap.* West Hartford, CT: Kumarian Press.

Landau, Martin (1969) "Redundancy, Rationality, and the Problem of Duplication and Overlap." *Public Administration Review* 29:346–58.

——— (1973) "Federalism, Redundancy and System Reliability." *Publius* 3:173–96.

——— (1985). *On Multi-Organizational Systems in the Public Administration.* Berkeley: University of California Press.

——— (1986) "On Decision Strategies and Management Structures: With Special Reference to Experimentation." For presentation to ISARD-FORD Workshop on "The Contribution of Management Science to Irrigation Systems," Colorado State University, Fort Collins, April 15–18.

Landau, Martin, and Russell Stout Jr. (1979) "To Manage Is Not to Control: Or the Folly of Type II Errors." *Public Administration Review* 39:148–56.

Landau, Martin, Suchitra Punyaratabandhu-Bhakdi, Ledivina Carino, Rolando Tungpalan, and James Wunsch (1980) *Final Report: Provincial Development Assistance Programme—Philippines.* Berkeley: Institute of International Studies, University of California.

266   Polycentric Governance and Development

Leonard, David (1977) *Reaching the Peasant Farmer: Organization Theory and Practice in Kenya*. Chicago: University of Chicago Press.

Leonard, David, and Dale Rogers Marshall (1982) *Institutions of Rural Development for the Poor*. Berkeley: University of California Press.

Lindblom, Charles E. (1977) *Politics and Markets: The World's Political-Economic System*. New York: Basic Books.

Linn, Johannes (1983) *Cities in the Developing World: Policies for Their Equitable and Efficient Growth*. New York: Oxford University Press.

Lowi, Theodore (1969) *The End of Liberalism*. New York: Norton.

Mickelwait, Donald et al. (1978) *The "New Directions" Mandate: Studies in Project Design, Approval and Implementation* (revised). Washington, DC: Development Alternatives, Inc.

Moris, Jon R. (1981) *Managing Induced Rural Development*. Bloomington, IN: International Development Institute, Indiana University.

Oakerson, Ronald J. (1987) "Local Public Economies: Provision, Production and Governance." *Intergovernmental Perspective* 13 (Summer–Fall): 20–25.

Oakerson, Ronald J., Roger B. Parks, and Aaron Bell (1987) "How Fragmentation Works—St. Louis Style." Paper presented at the Midwest Political Science Association meetings, Chicago.

Olowu, Dele (1995) "The Failure of Current Decentralization Programs in Africa." In J. Wunsch and D. Olowu (eds.), *The Failure of the Centralized State: Institutions and Self-Governance in Africa*, 1–22. San Francisco: ICS Press.

Olson, Mancur (1965) *The Logic of Collective Action: Public Goods and the Theory of Groups*. Cambridge: Harvard University Press.

Ostrom, Elinor (1983) "A Public Service Industry Approach to the Study of Local Government Structure and Performance." *Policy and Politics* 11, no. 3: 313–41.

——— (1986a) "Multiorganizational Arrangements and Coordination: An Application of Institutional Analysis." In F. X. Kaufmann, G. Majone, and V. Ostrom (eds.), *Guidance, Control, and Evaluation in the Public Sector*, 495–510. Berlin and New York: Walter de Gruyter.

——— (1986b) "A Method of Institutional Analysis." In F. X. Kaufmann, G. Majone, and V. Ostrom (eds.), *Guidance, Control, and Evaluation in the Public Sector*, 459–75. Berlin and New York: Walter de Gruyter.

——— (1987) "Institutional Arrangements for Resolving the Commons Dilemma: Some Contending Approaches." In B. J. McCay and J. M. Acheson (eds.), *The Question of the Commons: The Culture and Ecology of Communal Resources*, 250–65. Tucson: University of Arizona Press.

——— (1989). "Microconstitutional Change in a Multiconstitutional Political System." *Rationality and Society* 1, no. 1 (July): 11–50.

Ostrom, Vincent (1985) "Multiorganizational Arrangements in the Governance of Unitary and Federal Political Systems." In Kenneth Hanf and Theo A.J. Toonen (eds.), *Policy Implementation in Federal and Unitary Systems*, 1–16. Dordrecht: Martinus Nijhoff Publishers.

——— (1986a) "A Fallabilist's Approach to Norms and Criteria of Choice." In F. X. Kaufmann, G. Majone, and V. Ostrom (eds.), *Guidance, Control, and Evaluation in the Public Sector*, 229–49. Berlin and New York: Walter de Gruyter.

—— (1986b) "Constitutional Considerations with Particular Reference to Federal Systems." In F. X. Kaufmann, G. Majone, and V. Ostrom (eds.), *Guidance, Control, and Evaluation in the Public Sector,* 111–25. Berlin and New York: Walter de Gruyter.

Ostrom, Vincent, and Elinor Ostrom (1977) "Public Goods and Public Choices." In E. S. Savas (ed.), *Alternatives for Delivering Public Services: Toward Improved Performance,* 7–49. Boulder, CO: Westview Press. Reprinted in M. D. McGinnis, ed. *Polycentric Games and Institutions* (Ann Arbor: University of Michigan Press, 1999).

Owens, Edgar, and Robert Shaw (1972) *Development Reconsidered.* Lexington, MA: Lexington Press.

Packenham, Robert A. (1973) *Liberal America and the Third World.* Princeton, NJ: Princeton University Press.

Parks, Roger B., Paula C. Baker, Larry Kiser, Ronald Oakerson, Elinor Ostrom, Vincent Ostrom, Stephen L. Percy, Martha Vandivort, Gordon P. Whitaker, and Rick Wilson (1982) "Coproduction of Public Services." In Richard C. Rich (ed.), *Analyzing Urban-Service Distributions,* 185–99. Lexington, MA: Lexington Books. Alternative version reprinted in M. D. McGinnis, ed. *Polycentricity and Local Public Economies* (Ann Arbor: University of Michigan Press, 1999).

Rondinelli, Dennis A. (1978) "National Investment Planning and Equity Policy in Developing Countries: The Challenge of Decentralized Administration." *Policy Sciences* 10:45–74.

—— (1981) "Government Decentralization in Comparative Perspective: Theory and Practice in Developing Countries." *International Review of Administration* 47:133–45.

—— (1982) "The Dilemma of Development Administration: Complexity and Uncertainty in Control-Oriented Bureaucracies." *World Politics* 35:43–72.

—— (1983) "Implementing Decentralization Programmes in Asia: A Comparative Analysis." *Public Administration and Development* 3:181–207.

Rondinelli, Dennis A., and G. Shabbir Cheema (1984) *Decentralization in Developing Countries: A Review of Recent Experience.* Washington, DC: World Bank.

Rondinelli, Dennis A., and Kenneth Ruddle (1977) "Local Organization of Integrated Rural Development: Implementing Equity Policy in Developing Countries." *International Review of Administrative Sciences* 43:20–30.

Schroeder, Larry (1985) "Bangladesh: Urban Government Finance and Management Issues and Opportunities." Report No. 5790, Urban and Water Supply Division, South Asia Projects Department. Washington, DC: World Bank.

—— (1987) *Rural Development Grants to Local Governments in Asia.* New York: Syracuse University, Metropolitan Studies Program, Monograph No. 19.

—— (1989) "Research in Local Government Finance and Administration: Final Report of the Local Revenue Administration Project." Occasional Paper No. 132, Maxwell School, Syracuse University, New York.

Simon, Herbert A. (1965) *Administrative Behavior: A Study of Decision-Making Processes in Administrative Organization.* New York: Free Press.

Smock, Audrey (1971) *Ibo Politics: The Role of Ethnic Unions in Eastern Nigeria.* Cambridge: Harvard University Press.

Thomson, James T. (1981) "Public Choice Analysis of Institutional Constraints: Firewood Production Strategies in the West African Sahel." In C. S. Russell and N. K. Nicholson (eds.), *Public Choice and Rural Development*, 119–52. Washington, DC: Resources for the Future.

Uphoff, Norman (1986) *Local Institutional Development: An Analytical Sourcebook With Cases*. West Hartford, CT: Kumarian Press.

Wanasinghe, S. (1985) "Decentralization for Rural Development: The Sri Lankan Experience." In G. S. Cheema (ed.), *Rural Development in Asia: Case Studies on Programme Implementation*, 236–64. New Delhi: Sterling Publishers.

Whitaker, Gordon P. (1980) "Coproduction: Citizen Participation in Service Delivery." *Public Administration Review* 40, no. 3 (May–June): 240–46.

World Bank (1981) *Accelerated Development in Sub-Saharan Africa: An Agenda for Action*. Washington, DC: World Bank.

Wunsch, James (1983) "Strengthening Rural Development Management through International Assistance Projects." *Public Administration and Development* 3:239–63.

————— (1986) "Administering Rural Development: Have Goals Outreached Organizational Capacity?" *Public Administration and Development* 6:287–308.

————— (1988) *Rural Development, Decentralization and Administrative Reform: Toward a New Analytical Framework*. Washington, DC: National Association of Schools of Public Affairs and Administration.

————— (1991) "Sustaining Third World Infrastructure Investments: Decentralization and Other Strategies." *Public Administration and Development* 11, no. 1: 5–24.

CHAPTER 12

Improving the Performance of Small-Scale Irrigation Systems: The Effects of Technological Investments and Governance Structure on Irrigation Performance in Nepal

Wai Fung Lam

1. Introduction

During the past decade in Asia, the focus of irrigation development in many less-developed countries (LDCs) has been shifted from a strategy that emphasizes constructing large-scale irrigation systems to one that helps existing small-scale irrigation systems to improve their performance. A major factor that prompted such a reorientation was the disappointing results of the past irrigation development strategy. Despite the investment of billions of dollars by national governments and international donor agencies, a majority of large-scale irrigation systems constructed in Asia during the past several decades have performed inadequately. Large-scale irrigation systems continue to be among the infrastructure projects that have the lowest levels of performance in the developing world (World Bank 1994). Moreover, as good locations for irrigation have already been developed, the construction costs for new large-scale irrigation systems have been increasing. The construction of new systems might not be as economically feasible as investing in improving the operation of existing systems (Johnson 1991; Gill 1991; Bottrall 1981).

Small-scale irrigation systems always play an extremely important role in agricultural development in Asia.[1] As of 1991, it was estimated that around half of the irrigated land in South and Southeast Asia fell under small-scale irrigation (Gill 1991). These systems are the lifeline to a large number of poor farmers in the Asian continent whose livelihoods depend on

Originally published in *World Development* 24, no. 8 (August 1996): 1301–15. Reprinted by permission of Elsevier Science and the author.

Author's note: The author would like to thank Elinor Ostrom, Vincent Ostrom, Roger Parks, James Perry, John Williams, and two anonymous reviewers, for their helpful comments and suggestions.

subsistence farming (Chambers 1988). Recent research has found that small-scale irrigation systems frequently achieve higher levels of performance when compared to many large-scale systems constructed and managed by a government bureaucracy (E. Ostrom 1992; Tang 1992; P. Pradhan 1989a, b; E. Ostrom, Lam, and Lee 1994). While these findings point to the potential of small-scale irrigation systems, one should not overlook the disparity in performance among them. Many of these systems do not operate as well as they should; room for improvement is substantial. The question, then, turns to how effective intervention efforts can be designed to enhance their operation and performance. This essay addresses the question by examining how engineering infrastructure and governance structure might affect the performance of small-scale irrigation systems in Nepal.

This essay is organized into nine sections. In the following section, I begin by discussing some of the intervention experiences in Nepal and other Asian countries that have brought about counterintentional and counterintuitive outcomes. In sections 3 and 4, I lay out the logic of a policy recommendation that emphasizes technological fixes as a major policy tool to improve irrigation performance, and present empirical evidence that might challenge the validity of that logic. In section 5, I present theoretical arguments and evidence that explicates the possible effects of technological investments on incentives facing individuals using and/or managing the irrigation systems. In section 6, I turn to a discussion of the possible effects of a farmer-managed and an agency-managed governance structure on the incentives facing farmers in Nepal. Empirical evidence that substantiates some of the arguments is presented in section 7. This is followed by a discussion of a successful intervention experience in Nepal. The implications of the findings on designing effective intervention to small-scale systems are discussed in the last section.

2. Past Experiences of Helping Small-Scale Irrigation Systems in Nepal and Other Asian Countries: Issues and Puzzles

In Nepal where agriculture is the major economic activity, irrigation systems are an important resource.[2] As the scope to increase agricultural production by bringing more area under cultivation is limited,[3] irrigation will play a key role to increase Nepal's agricultural productivity in the coming decades (Satyal 1991). Until the 1950s, irrigation development in Nepal was largely a concern of local communities.[4] As of 1988, there were more than 16,000 farmer-managed irrigation systems (FMIS) in the country, irrigating a cultivated area of approximately 714,000 hectares, which was about 67% of the country's total irrigable land (P. Pradhan 1989b, 2). Most of these FMIS are small in scale,[5] reflecting the small size of agricultural holdings in Nepal (Agarwal 1991).

Active government involvement in irrigation development began in the early 1950s, which focused largely on the construction of large-scale agency-managed irrigation systems (AMIS). Small-scale irrigation has since been given little attention (Benjamin et al. 1994). In recent years, prompted by the disappointing performance of many of these large-scale AMIS, the Department of Irrigation (DOI) in Nepal has reoriented its approach to irrigation development. Designing interventions which would help those small-scale systems that are facing difficulties has become a major policy concern. Experiences on which lessons for designing effective intervention can be drawn, however, are rather limited. Although different intervention strategies have been tried out in the country by various agencies, both governmental and nongovernmental, knowledge about what can be done to help the small-scale systems is still sparse and far from conclusive (Shivakoti 1992; WECS/IIMI 1990). The intervention experience in the Kodku Irrigation System in the Lalitpur District, however, is typical.

The Kodku Irrigation System was constructed by local farmers a long time ago.[6] As of 1988, the service area of the system was estimated to be about 560 hectares. The system had a temporary headworks built of mud and tree branches, and unlined canals. The source of the system, Khotku Khola, had a varying water flow; its course changed frequently. In order to keep the system operable, farmers on the system had to repair the temporary headworks regularly. Since its inception, the system had been operated and maintained by local farmers. A number of *Si Guthis*, the traditional organizations of Newar communities for the funeral and cremation functions, were able to coordinate and mobilize local farmers to operate and maintain the system.

In 1965, the Department of Irrigation, Hydrology, and Meteorology (DIHM) of Nepal (the predecessor of DOI), undertook an intervention seeking to improve the operation and performance of the Kodku Irrigation System. That intervention effort included replacing the temporary headworks with a permanent one, and lining a portion of the main canal in the system. After the construction works, the DIHM, and later the DOI, took over responsibilities of operating and maintaining the system. Presumably, the better infrastructure would free the farmers from the arduous tasks of maintenance, and officials from the DOI would be able to do a better job in system operation. Such a happy scenario, however, did not happen. Since the construction of the new structures, the level of water in the system has been decreasing. Farmers at the middle and the tail end of the system found themselves having to work very hard to get adequate irrigation water. Furthermore, the working relationships among farmers with regard to irrigation operation and maintenance have deteriorated ever since the construction of the new structures. On one hand, the farmers tended to defy the water allocation "order" as stipulated by the DOI officials; on the other, they became unwilling to contribute their efforts to operation and maintenance activities.

The intervention experience in the Kodku Irrigation System is by no means unique; many case studies have documented similar experiences in disparate locations in Nepal (see, e.g., Curtis 1991; Hilton 1990; Shrestha 1988; U. Pradhan 1988; Peabody 1983). Nor is such a disappointing experience unique to Nepal. While technological fixes continue to be practiced in most Asian countries as a tool of intervention, their effects on irrigation performance have been mixed. Notwithstanding successful experiences (see, e.g., Hafid and Hayami 1978; Gupta, Singh, and George 1973), cumulative evidence from different Asian countries such as Thailand, Indonesia, India, and Malaysia, suggests that technological fixes and government management do not necessarily offer benefits to small-scale irrigation systems as expected (Miranda and Levine 1978; Wickham and Valera 1978; Taylor 1978, 1981; Tan-Kim-Yong 1983; Pant 1984; Bhuiyan 1987; Rosegrant et al. 1987; Ambler 1993). The typical diagnosis is that farmers are not yet ready to organize themselves for the operation of the newly constructed engineering structures, or to develop effective working relationships with irrigation officials. Little attention has been given to why the lack of organizing capability could happen to farmers who have had years of experience of working with one another to manage irrigation and many other activities effectively. When a policy recommendation is acted upon and leads to counterintentional policy outcomes, it suggests that (1) the recommendation may be mis-specified and its underlying logic needs to be critically assessed, and (2) more empirical evidence needs to be collected and examined to gain a better understanding of the relevant phenomena.

3. Technological Fixes as a Policy Tool to Improve Irrigation Performance

Technological investments can potentially improve the technical capacity for water diversion and water delivery that, in turn, affects the effectiveness of an irrigation system. In Nepal where most of the irrigation systems are of the run-of-the-river type, the structure of headworks and the condition of canal lining are the two most important physical attributes that affect the technical efficacy and the maintenance requirements of an irrigation system.

In many irrigation systems in Nepal, headworks are temporary and made out of simple materials such as boulders and leaves. Although these temporary headworks may operate relatively well, many of them are prone to damage by floods and various natural disasters. They may be washed out once a year if not more frequently and require frequent maintenance. Moreover, these temporary headworks typically do not have water adjustment devices such as water gates. Adjusting water flow must be done with less elegant methods including mud and timber walls. These methods are labor intensive and, during the monsoon season, ineffective. A low level of flexibility in water control is a likely consequence.

A permanent headworks with concrete dams, weirs, and control structures is often considered to be a prerequisite to effective irrigation (Ascher and Healy 1990). From an irrigation engineering point of view, a properly constructed permanent headworks has a higher level of water diversion capacity in comparison to a temporary one. In many instances, such a capacity is further complemented by the presence of water gates at the headworks, which give farmers or irrigation managers better control of the timing and amounts of water entering the system. Since permanent headworks are constructed with concrete materials, they presumably require less maintenance effort.

Once water is diverted into a system, how much of it can reach the service areas depends significantly upon the conditions of canals in the system. Other conditions being similar, canals that are lined are more likely to have lower levels of water seepage than the ones that are partially lined or not lined. A higher level of water delivery efficiency of lined canals not only makes more water available to farmers, but also helps alleviate water scarcity at the tail end.

Based upon this policy logic, two major hypotheses regarding the effects of technological investments can be derived:

Hypothesis I: Technological investments such as constructing permanent headworks and lining canals can reduce maintenance costs. In irrigation systems in Nepal, the reduced maintenance costs are reflected in lower levels of labor mobilization for routine maintenance.

Hypothesis II: Technological investments, by reducing maintenance costs and improving the technical capacity of an irrigation system, can bring about higher levels of performance in terms of the condition of physical structure, water delivery effectiveness, and agricultural productivity.

The validity of these hypotheses pertains to the viability of a conventional irrigation policy that emphasizes technological fixes as a solution to inadequate maintenance. So far, most of the empirical evidence available has come from a literature of case studies. The authors of these case studies, however, have concentrated on only a small number of irrigation systems due to the labor-intensive nature of case study research. The small number of cases used in these studies means not only a thin empirical base, but also limited leverage for researchers to make causal inference (Lieberson 1985; King, Keohane, and Verba 1994).

As an effort to establish a solid empirical foundation for the study of how various institutional, physical, and sociocultural factors affect irrigation performance in Nepal, colleagues associated with the Workshop in Political Theory and Policy Analysis at Indiana University and the Institute of Agriculture and Animal Science (IAAS), Chitwan, Nepal, have established the Nepal Irrigation Institutions and Systems (NIIS) database that contains information about 150 irrigation systems in the country.[7] Of these 150 systems, 136 can be classified as small- to medium-sized irrigation systems in accordance with the classificatory scheme used by the DOI.[8] The availability of information about a large number of irrigation systems provides an excellent opportunity to examine empirically the effects of technological investments and governance structure on the performance of small-scale systems, and to offer insights for a better understanding of the relevant phenomena.

TABLE 12.1. Classification Scheme for System Size

System Classification	Non-*terai* Areas	*Terai* Area
Small systems	Less than 50 hectares	Less than 500 hectares
Medium systems	50 to 500 hectares	500 to 5,000 hectares
Large systems	More than 500 hectares	More than 5,000 hectares

Source: *Irrigation Policy* (HMG/N, 1992).
Note: The terai is the flat plains in southern Nepal adjacent to India.

4. Assessing the Hypotheses

Headworks and canals work closely with each other in affecting the technical efficacy of an irrigation system; together they constitute an environment in which individuals operate and manage irrigation. Using the variables of *Headworks* (coded as 0 for temporary headworks, 1 for permanent headworks) and *Lining* (coded as 0 for unlined canals, 1 for partially or completely lined canals) as dimensions, systems in the NIIS database for which relevant information is available are classified into a categorization of infrastructural environment (IE) (table 12.2). Systems in IE I have the lowest level of technological investments, those in IE II the medium level, and those in III the highest level.

TABLE 12.2. Distribution of Systems in Infrastructural Environments

	Number of Systems
IE I	
Systems without lining and without permanent headworks	37
	28%
IE II	
Systems with at least partial lining and without permanent headworks	42
	31%
IE III	
Systems with permanent headworks	55
	41%
Total	134
	100%

In most of the irrigation systems in Nepal, a decrease in maintenance costs means a smaller amount of labor devoted to routine maintenance. As shown in table 12.3, while systems with temporary headworks and unlined canals have the highest level of labor mobilization for routine maintenance, systems with permanent headworks require the least amount of labor. This pattern corroborates Hypothesis I that more sophisticated engineering infrastructures are likely to spare farmers from much of the hard work of fixing and rebuilding the physical structures in their system. The question, then, turns to whether a decrease in labor requirements will bring about higher levels of performance.

Irrigation performance is notoriously ambiguous and difficult to conceptualize and measure (Wade and Seckler 1990). In an effort to accurately measure the performance of irrigation systems, a measurement model has been developed for evaluating irrigation performance (Lam 1998). In this model, three dimensions of irrigation performance have been identified:

1. Physical: the condition of the physical structure of irrigation systems,
2. Delivery: the water delivery effectiveness,
3. Productivity: the agricultural productivity of the systems.

On the basis of the measurement model, a factor score is calculated to measure each of these three dimensions of performance for each of the systems in the NIIS database. Each of these factor scores integrates information from multiple variables.[9] Complete information on all three dimensions is available for 100 cases in the NIIS database (table 12.4).

TABLE 12.3. Labor Days by Infrastructural Environments

	Total Labor Days	Labor Days per Household	Labor Days per Hectare
IE I			
Systems without lining and without	1447.28	8.48	10.61
permanent headworks	[2735.49]	[11.25]	[15.39]
	(25)	(25)	(25)
IE II			
Systems with at least partial lining	965.79	5.33	10.46
and without permanent headworks	[1981.44]	[7.83]	[13.83]
	(29)	(28)	(29)
IE III			
Systems with permanent headworks	719.19	2.2	3.94
	[1132.3]	[2.58]	[5.49]
	(37)	(36)	(43)
	F = 1.04	F = 5.14	F = 3.45
	p = 0.36	p = 0.01	p = 0.04

Note: Standard deviations are in brackets.

TABLE 12.4. Summary of Dimensions of Performance

	Mean	Std. Dev.	Min.	Max.	N
Physical condition	3.44	0.72	1.42	4.75	100
Delivery	3.39	0.83	1.69	5.04	100
Productivity	4.06	0.99	1.83	5.51	100

The mean scores of the three performance dimensions in different IEs are arrayed in table 12.5. Different IEs do make a difference in irrigation performance; systems in different IEs have different average scores in all three dimensions. While the existence of strong effects of IEs is consistent with what many irrigation officials and specialists might have expected, the direction of the effects would appear to them counterintuitive. Systems with permanent headworks are shown to have the lowest scores in all three dimensions compared to other systems, systems with temporary headworks and at least partially lined canals are shown to outperform other systems in terms of the physical condition of systems and the effectiveness of water delivery. In terms of agricultural productivity, systems that do not have lining nor permanent headworks achieve the best performance.

TABLE 12.5. Dimensions of Performance by Infrastructural Environments

	Physical Condition	Delivery	Productivity
IE I			
Systems without lining and without	3.65	3.63	4.60
permanent headworks	(26)	(26)	(26)
IE II			
Systems with at least partial lining	3.81	3.87	4.31
and without permanent headworks	(32)	(32)	(32)
IE III			
Systems with permanent headworks	3.04	2.9	3.5
	(41)	(41)	(41)
	p = 0	p = 0	p = 0

5. Understanding the Effects of Engineering Infrastructure

Part of the reason why more sophisticated physical structures have not brought about the expected improvements in performance is that many modern engineering infrastructures in Nepal were not appropriately constructed to fit in the local environment. For instance, it is not uncommon to find a modern engineering infrastructure idle soon after its construction because the source of water that the infrastructure was supposed to capture has changed its course. Furthermore, many engineering infrastructures are of sophisticated design and are therefore difficult to operate and maintain. Works that require electricity to operate, for example, are stymied by frequent power outages. In such a situation, ineffective maintenance is by no means surprising.

The lack of complementarity between engineering infrastructure and the local environment, however, is not the only reason for the counterintuitive outcomes of technological investments. In many instances, the working orders among farmers begin to unravel shortly after the construction of sophisticated engineering structures. To understand the effects of technological investments, one has to pay attention to why farmers become unwilling to contribute their efforts in maintenance when the technical efficacy of their systems have been improved.

(a) Asymmetries in Irrigation Systems

Since water in a canal flows from head end to tail end, farmers whose fields are located near the head end of the canal (headenders) frequently have natural priorities over farmers near the tail end (tailenders) in water appropriation. Perceiving that water is "easily available," headenders have a tendency to take more water than their crops really need and pay less attention to the prevention of water wastage. In many instances, headenders are not aware of the possible adverse effect on scarcity for tailenders caused by their actions. But even if a headender sees the problem, he[10] is not likely to refrain from taking more water because he would think his doing so would not make much difference unless other headenders also refrained. In fact, there are very few, if any, intrinsic incentives for headenders to engage in collective action in regard to the regulation of water allocation.

Suppose that there is a small leak at the head end of a canal that results in water seepage. Such a small amount of water loss may not seriously affect the amount of water available to the farmers near the head end. Headenders are frequently unable to comprehend the significance of their seemingly trivial efforts, such as fixing a small leak on a canal, on overall water delivery efficiency.

As water flows further down canal, however, small amounts of water loss are compounded. When farmers along the reach do not do proper maintenance work due to an inability to perceive the problem, the cumulative water loss may become a serious water scarcity for tailenders (Sparling 1990).

Asymmetries between headenders and tailenders exacerbate the difficulty in organizing collective action in irrigation. Unless the amount of labor needed by headenders to get water is greater than they can provide on their own, headenders have the tendency to take advantage of their comparatively advantageous position at the expense of tailenders. When such an asymmetry is not coped with by effective institutional arrangements and the active organizing efforts of individuals managing the systems, poor performance is a likely result.

(b) Technological Investments and Asymmetries

As discussed above, the construction of permanent headworks can result in a substantial drop in the amount of labor allocated to system maintenance. Such a decrease in labor mobilization could free farmers from tedious maintenance work. A significant drop in the amount of labor for maintenance, however, could also have serious impacts on the balance of bargaining power among farmers in a system, as well as on the farmers' perception of the need to work with one another in irrigation management. In particular, contributing one's labor to system maintenance is a major way for a farmer in FMIS, where de jure water rights often do not exist, to establish his de facto claim to a portion of water from the system (Ambler 1990; E.

Ostrom and Gardner 1993; E. Ostrom 1994). For farmers at the tail end of a system, being able to make such a claim is especially important because a reliable supply of irrigation water for them largely depends upon headenders allowing adequate water to flow down the canal.

Headenders are more likely to agree to the water claims of tailenders when the labor contribution of tailenders is essential to keeping the system operable. The necessity of organizing for routine maintenance is, to a large extent, an equalizer which prevents headenders from exploiting their strategic physical position at the expense of tailenders. With lower maintenance costs brought by the construction of permanent headworks, headenders might find themselves able to bear the costs of routine maintenance all by themselves. When the labor contribution of tailenders is not needed, headenders are not likely to feel the need to give attention to the well-being of tailenders.

Furthermore, headenders can enjoy the comparatively advantageous position only after water is diverted into the system. To deal with such an uncertainty, headenders often found it necessary to work with tailenders in fixing and operating their temporary headworks to make sure that adequate water would be diverted into the system. When tailenders and headenders were working with one another, their interdependency became most obvious to them. Maintenance activities became a collective endeavor for mutual interests. Once a permanent headworks is built using external funds with no requirement to pay back, however, headenders find themselves better assured of a water supply without the labor contribution of tailenders. With the more reliable water supply, headenders no longer see the necessity of working with tailenders.

Unlike headworks, lining the canals is less likely to exacerbate the asymmetries among farmers on an irrigation system. As indicated in table 12.3, even after canals are lined, farmers still have to work with one another to carry out various maintenance activities such as cleaning the canals and fixing the headworks. In fact, having canals lined may actually bring about a positive effect of helping farmers get water to the tail end. As the benefits of better maintenance and water delivery brought by lining tend to offset the asymmetries between headenders and tailenders, lining the canals is more likely to improve irrigation performance.

Evidence in the NIIS database corroborates the argument. In the database, information about water availability at the head end and at the tail end of an irrigation system is available. By subtracting the scores of water availability achieved at the tail end of a system from the scores achieved at the head end across three seasons, a score of difference in water availability to headenders and tailenders is calculated. For the purpose of analysis, the score is transformed into a dichotomous variable by coding 0 for systems that have no difference in water availability to headenders and tailenders, and 1 for systems that have a difference in water availability of various degrees. In table 12.6, this dichotomous variable is arrayed by the three IEs. IE III has a larger percentage of systems that have a difference in water availability to headenders and to tailenders than the other two IEs. On the other hand, IE II has the lowest percentage of systems that have a difference. The pattern of relationships in table 12.6, when interpreted with reference to the relationship between IEs and labor for maintenance (table 12.3), attests to the argument that a drastic decrease in labor input for maintenance resulted from the construction of permanent headworks is likely to bring about a higher level of asymmetries between headenders and tailenders. Table 12.7 further indicates that in each of the three dimensions of performance, systems that do not have a difference in water availability have outperformed systems that have a difference in water availability.

TABLE 12.6. The Relationship of Difference in Water Availability and Infrastructural Environments (systems for which the performance data are available)

Difference in Water Availability between Head End and Tail End	IE I Systems without Lining and without Permanent Headworks	IE II Systems with at Least Partial Lining and without Permanent Headworks	IE III Systems with Permanent Headworks
No	15 58%	22 69%	15 37%
Yes	11 42%	10 31%	26 63%
Total	26 100%	32 100%	41 100%

Note: Chi^2 = 7.83
p = 0.02

TABLE 12.7. The Relationship of Difference in Water Availability and Irrigation Performance

	Difference in Water Availability Does Not Exist (53)	Difference in Water Availability Exists (47)	F	p
Physical condition	3.63	3.23	8.31	0
Delivery	3.65	3.11	11.7	0
Productivity	4.35	3.73	10.45	0

6. Governance Structure and Irrigation Performance

Some policy makers and irrigation specialists assume that assigning a corps of professional officials to manage irrigation is a most effective way to resolve problems of collective action in irrigation. In particular, it is often argued that when an irrigation system becomes larger and the tasks become more complicated, a government irrigation agency that commands the necessary resources, expertise, and authority, is required for effective irrigation management. Evidence in the NIIS database, however, does not support such an argument. In table 12.8, the three dimensions of performance are arrayed by governance structure. The information suggests that AMIS have a lower average score than FMIS in all three dimensions of performance.[11]

TABLE 12.8. The Relationship of Governance Structure with Dimensions of Performance

	N	FMIS (70)	AMIS (30)	F	p
Physical condition	(100)	3.73	2.78	57.14	0
Delivery	(100)	3.73	2.60	62.73	0
Productivity	(100)	4.38	3.35	27.13	0

While larger size and higher degrees of complexity do give rise to the need for a higher degree of organization,[12] organization is not necessarily equivalent to management by a government agency. Recent studies have indicated that farmers in many large-scale irrigation systems in Nepal have been able to design sophisticated institutions to govern and manage their systems (Yoder 1994). Research on common-pool resource management further shows the viability of nested institutional arrangements in managing large-scale resource systems (E. Ostrom 1990; E. Ostrom, Gardner, and Walker 1994).

Furthermore, the presence of irrigation officials does not automatically mean that the problems of collective action are resolved. Earlier research has found that Nepali irrigation officials who are assigned the task of managing AMIS are given very few incentives to do a conscientious job or to establish long-term productive relationships with farmers (Benjamin et al. 1994; E. Ostrom, Lam, and Lee 1994). Consequently, like FMIS farmers, AMIS farmers' ability to organize themselves to cope with problems in irrigation is an important variable explaining performance. Factors affecting farmers' capabilities and willingness to engage in collective action are complex and vary from one system to the next depending on specific contexts. The structure of governance, however, is a major source of incentives affecting the farmers' behavior.

(a) Incentives Facing Farmers in AMIS

In many AMIS in Nepal, irrigation officials are the de jure governors who formulate and enforce rules for water allocation and labor mobilization for maintenance. Working in a bureaucracy, these officials have incentives to design rules so that they are easy to administer. As a result, rules used in AMIS tend to be uniform in scope and in their application to different parts of the systems. Rules that are designed solely upon the premise of easy implementation are likely to be less flexible and less compatible with local situations. As farmers perceive that the chance of having the rigid rules changed is slim, and that complying with the rules might mean a serious crop loss for themselves, breaking the rules frequently appears to be the only alternative.

In some AMIS, farmers do try to take up the task of designing rules for themselves to resolve problems involved in irrigation management. A fundamental problem, however, is that irrigation officials are the de jure rule-makers. They might assert their power to govern whenever they choose to, and declare farmers' self-organizing efforts "illegal." Such a possibility poses to farmers a high level of uncertainty concerning the payoffs of their costly self-organizing efforts. This uncertainty frequently makes farmers hesitate to invest in self-governing activities.

In the process of intervention, it is commonplace that irrigation officials do not give recognition to the prior property rights, institutions, and the common understandings developed by local farmers (Curtis 1991). These rules and common understandings often define the terms and conditions of cooperation upon which farmers relate to one another (Yoder 1994; E. Ostrom 1994; P. Pradhan 1989b). When these are declared invalid, farmers become uncertain about whether their contributions to irrigation operation and maintenance will pay off or if they do contribute, who will enjoy the benefits. The resulting uncertainty often drives farmers to pursue their short-term self-interests at the expense of the interests of the others. Furthermore, the introduction of irrigation officials as the managers of irrigation systems, if not handled appropriately, often destroys social capital by changing farmers' habits of heart and mind. When farmers perceive that the operation and maintenance activities are the responsibility of irrigation officials, they see no obligation to contribute their efforts.

(b) Incentives Facing Farmers in FMIS

A major characteristic of FMIS is that farmers can engage in rule-crafting activities from time to time to restructure day-to-day situations. The incentives to prey upon others in irrigation do not simply disappear when farmers participate in irrigation management. The establishment and maintenance of a viable and effective working order relies upon farmers being able to craft continuously effective rules that counteract perverse incentives, and provide positive incentives for cooperation. It is more likely to be attained if farmers are given opportunities to change the situations they face.

There is nothing automatic about the self-organizing process among farmers in FMIS. For FMIS farmers, however, the very existence and availability of the means to change their situations opens up possibilities of problem-solving that are literally denied to AMIS farmers. When farmers perceive that there are opportunities for them to do something to improve their well-being, they are likely to give it a try. These opportunities to act upon conceptions and ideas of joint and individual benefits are a prerequisite to the unleashing of their social energy and productivity. When a presumably resourceful government is not there to help, FMIS farmers are likely to have a higher level of awareness of their interdependency. Consequently, they tend to be more willing to invest their resources in self-organizing activities, and to communicate, discuss, and compromise with one another. Such willingness to reason with one another, in the long run, is a building block of farmers' problem-solving capability.

Rules that are made by farmers are likely to take information and knowledge about the local situation into consideration (Freeman 1990). Rules that are designed with close reference to the problems that they are intended to resolve are likely to be more effective than those designed at some distance. Furthermore, rules that incorporate local knowledge about the physical and socioinstitutional characteristics of a community are likely to be more suitable to particular local situations (E. Ostrom 1990, 1992).

Irrigation staff in FMIS, if they exist, are usually chosen and hired by farmers. In many instances, irrigation staff are themselves farmers in the systems. They not only know the systems well, but also have incentives to work to satisfy the farmers in order to keep their jobs. In many FMIS where the staff's salary is dependent on how well they carry out their assigned tasks, the staff are given positive incentives to contribute their best efforts. In addition, as the staff themselves are from the community, they can work closely with farmers in operating and maintaining the systems. Such a close working relationship also increases the effectiveness of staff monitoring.

7. Governance, Patterns of Interaction, and Irrigation Performance

Rules that are crafted by farmers who live and work in an irrigation system for years are more likely to be followed than rules imposed by irrigation officials who seldom visit the system. Among farmers of the 100 systems in the NIIS database about which information is available, almost 60 percent of the FMIS achieve a high level of rule-following while less than 30 percent of the AMIS are able to do so (table 12.9).

TABLE 12.9. The Relationship of Rule-Following and Governance Structure

Level of Rule Following among Appropriators	FMIS	AMIS
Low/Moderate	29	21
	41%	72%
High	41	8
	59%	28%
Total	70	29
	100%	100%

Note: Chi² = 7.88
      p = 0.01

The existence of rules alone does not guarantee that they will be followed by individuals automatically. Whether monitoring and sanctioning arrangements are in place significantly affects the level of rule conformance and also the effectiveness of rules (North 1990; Weissing and E. Ostrom 1991, 1993). To measure the extent to which monitoring and sanctioning is in place in irrigation systems, I identify five institutional variables in the NIIS database that are concerned with rules in regard to (1) information on water appropriation, (2) information on individual farmers' contributions to maintenance, (3) penalty for rule violations, (4) monitoring rule conformance in daily interactions, and (5) variations in levels of sanctioning. For each of these variables, a 1 is assigned if the particular rule exists in a system, and a 0 is assigned if it does not. An index of monitoring and sanctioning is then created by adding up the values of these five variables. For the purpose of analysis, I classify irrigation systems into two groups by the score of the index, one for the systems with a score of less than 4 in the index, and the other for those with a score of at least 4. In table 12.10, I arrayed these two groups by the type of governance structure. Table 12.10 provides strong evidence that FMIS are more likely to have a large array of monitoring and sanctioning arrangements in place than AMIS.

Rules that are well-designed, monitored, and followed allow farmers to establish stable expectations of one another. Such expectations provide the basis for collective action. Table 12.11 shows the relationship between the type of governance structure and the level of mutual trust among farmers on a system. Consistent with what one would expect, farmers in FMIS, when compared with their counterparts in AMIS, are more likely to have developed a high level of mutual trust with one another.

TABLE 12.10. The Relationship of Monitoring and Sanctioning and Governance Structure

Index of Monitoring and Sanctioning	FMIS	AMIS
Scored less than 4	22 39%	17 74%
Scored at least 4	34 61%	6 26%
Total	56 100%	23 100%

Note: $Chi^2 = 7.82$
   $p = 0.001$

TABLE 12.11. The Relationship of Mutual Trust and Governance Structure

Level of Mutual Trust among Appropriators	FMIS	AMIS
Low	26 38%	21 70%
High	43 62%	9 30%
Total	69 100%	30 100%

Note: $Chi^2 = 8.78$
   $p = 0.00$

The patterns of interaction associated with the governance structure of FMIS are more conducive to cooperative activities among individuals, and are a major factor contributing to their generally high levels of performance. Table 12.12 suggests that systems in which farmers enforce rules so as to attain a high level of rule conformance and a high level of trust are more likely to have a better physical condition of systems, more effective water delivery, and higher levels of agricultural productivity than those in which rules are less well developed and are largely not followed.

8. Institutional Arrangements and Technological Investments: An Example of Organizing Effective Intervention

That the construction of engineering infrastructure might increase the asymmetries between headenders and tailenders does not mean that technological investments are doomed to fail. Possibilities exist that institutional arrangements can be crafted to cope with the asymmetries. Furthermore, that an agency-managed governance structure may suffer from flaws in its institutional design does not mean that government involvement is necessarily futile. Improving irrigation management involves many complex tasks that farmers alone might not have adequate capability and resources to handle (E. Ostrom 1992; Tang 1992; Lam 1995). Instead of trying to eliminate government involvement, it would be more useful to examine how government intervention can be designed so that it complements and enhances the working relationships among farmers. Recent research has shown that the design of government interventions to irrigation systems, including technical assistance, significantly affects the probability of success of the efforts (Ambler 1990; E. Ostrom 1994; Lam, Lee, and E. Ostrom 1994).

TABLE 12.12. Relationships of Patterns of Interaction and Irrigation Performance

Scores of Index of Monitoring and Sanctioning

	Less than 4 ($N = 39$)	At least 4 ($N = 40$)	F	p
Physical condition	3.22	3.64	6.93	0.01
Delivery	3.11	3.62	7.92	0.01
Productivity	3.75	4.60	15.99	0

Level of Rule Following among Appropriators

	Low/Medium ($N = 50$)	High ($N = 49$)	F	p
Physical condition	3.29	3.60	4.88	0.03
Delivery	3.22	3.58	4.80	0.03
Productivity	3.80	4.35	8.20	0.01

Level of Mutual Trust among Appropriators

	Low ($N = 47$)	High ($N = 52$)	F	p
Physical condition	3.15	3.71	16.81	0
Delivery	3.05	3.71	17.88	0
Productivity	3.65	4.44	18.22	0

While the details of how institutional arrangements can be crafted to cope with the possible asymmetries brought by technological investments vary from one instance to the next, an intervention effort conducted by the Ford Foundation, the Water and Energy Commission / Secretariat of Nepal (WECS), and the International Irrigation Management Institute in Nepal (IIMI) illustrates the possible complementarity between technological investments and institutional arrangements, and offers insights into how such complementarity can be attained.

The major goal of this intervention project was to enhance the agricultural productivity of a number of small-scale, farmer-managed irrigation systems through a simultaneous improvement of physical structures and the organizational capability of farmers on the systems. Under this project, 20 irrigation systems in the Sindhu Palchok District of Nepal that had shown the potential to benefit from better physical structures were first identified. The farmers in these systems were offered assistance to improve their physical structures if they agreed to:

1. cooperate with the engineers sent to help improve the physical structures by showing them how their systems operated and what could be done to improve the operation of the systems,
2. help to rank the desired infrastructure improvements in their system,
3. make contributions of labor for the new construction,
4. attend a farmer-to-farmer training program that would enable them to learn from the organization experiences of more successful irrigation systems, and
5. keep records of their expenditures and decisions made at meetings. (WECS/IIMI 1990)

Various studies have shown that the intervention effort has been a success (WECS/IIMI 1990; Lam and Shivakoti 1992). This effort not only brought about higher levels of agricultural productivity in the systems, but also generally enhanced their productive capability. Several principles that underlie the design of the intervention effort might account for the success of this effort, and might be drawn upon when technological investments are designed. First, while external agencies provided necessary resources, technical advice, and guidance, farmers were encouraged to be actively involved in the process of improving the physical structures of their systems. An advantage of getting farmers actively involved is that farmers' knowledge about their systems can be integrated in the design of the new construction. Another advantage is that, through actively working with one another, farmers are constantly reminded of their interdependence. Such an awareness of interdependency can counteract the asymmetries that might possibly be brought about by the new construction.

Second, farmers were given incentives to make effective use of the assistance they received. Farmers were asked to rank all of the desired infrastructure improvements into a priority list. The project only provided funds to cover the cost of first-priority improvements. Farmers were informed, however, that if they could save money on first-priority infrastructure improvements, they would be able to use the money saved for the improvements of lower priority. Given such a rule, farmers could see the benefit of evaluating their needs seriously and of carrying out the improvement works effectively. Moreover, the accounts were open to farmers' inspection. Such transparency allows farmers to monitor the progress of the project, as well as possible opportunistic behavior of one another.

Third, institutional development was made a coherent part of the process of improving the physical structures of the systems. By moving back and forth between designing new construction and crafting institutional arrangements, a high degree of complementary between physical capital in terms of technological investments and social capital in terms of effective rule-ordered working relationships is more likely to develop.

9. Conclusion

Contrary to what many irrigation specialists expect, sophisticated engineering infrastructure does not necessarily bring about better irrigation performance. A pitfall of the construction of a permanent headworks in a system is an increase in inequality of water availability to farmers located at the head end and tail end which, in turn, might dampen headenders' incentives to work with tailenders. Furthermore, the institutional design of the agency-managed governance structure in Nepal gives irrigation officials very few incentives to do a conscientious job, and tends to discourage farmers from contributing to operation and maintenance efforts.

The findings of this study shed light on why many attempts by government agencies or international donor agencies to help improve small-scale irrigation have had limited success, or in some cases, brought about negative outcomes. Although modern engineering infrastructure can potentially enhance the water delivery capability of a system, the extent to which the potential can be realized depends upon whether effective institutions exist that provide social capital in terms of managerial capability and productive working relationships to support the maintenance of the infrastructure.

The construction of physical capital and the development of social capital are intricately related, and should not be considered as two isolated domains. Attention should be paid to the questions of how institutions should be developed and designed to support the maintenance of engineering infrastructure, and of how the social capital that has already existed in the local community can be better utilized. Engineering infrastructure could be designed in a way that it complements local institutions and water rights to the extent possible. Furthermore, given that the process of institutional development is often difficult, an analyst should not presume that the establishment of institutional arrangements necessarily comes after the construction of physical infrastructure. Instead of asking what kinds of institutions are needed to cope with a new engineering infrastructure, the analyst should make a critical assessment on the local situation before an engineering infrastructure is constructed. Such an assessment then, can serve as a reference with which a more manageable engineering infrastructure can be constructed. For example, in systems where farmers have not been able to organize themselves effectively, or where officials have difficulty mobilizing necessary resources for maintenance works, projects should consider constructing a technologically less sophisticated infrastructure instead of a more sophisticated one.

The findings of the analysis above on the effects of governance structure might lead one to conclude that a farmer-managed governance structure is necessarily better than an agency-managed one. Yet caution is warranted before drawing such a conclusion. Instead of relying upon simplified dichotomous notions such as "agency-managed versus farmer-managed governance structures" for the solution, it would be more useful to understand the underlying principles and mechanisms of institutional design that provide positive incentives to farmers and officials to work with one another. Principles such as allowing farmers to engage in rule-crafting activities, designing rules that are enforceable and easy to monitor, and relating benefits and costs in a coherent manner, can all be applied when an intervention project is designed. To recognize that there are diverse ways of putting institutional arrangements together to complement the physical and sociocultural attributes of a particular situation, hence, to attain productive patterns of relationships, is a prerequisite for successful intervention.

NOTES

1. There are different types of small-scale irrigation systems. The important ones include pump systems, river diversion systems, and tank schemes. While all these types of systems are important, this essay focuses only on river diversion systems, which are most common in Nepal.

2. Agriculture accounts for more than 60 percent of Nepal's GDP and over 80 percent of the country's export earnings.

3. The total area of Nepal is 147,000 square kilometers. The topography is mountainous, and Khadka (1993) reports that only about 20 percent of total land in Nepal is cultivable.

4. In the seventeenth century, King Ram Shah issued an edict proclaiming that "trivial disputes" related to irrigation would not be heard in court but would be resolved in the local community (Riccardi 1977). This edict laid the foundation for local organization of irrigation in Nepal.

5. The definition of *small-scale irrigation systems* varies, depending on the way that specific countries define it. In Nepal, the classification of irrigation systems is based upon both size and geographic terrains (see table 12.1).

6. The information about the Kodku Irrigation System used in this essay is based upon the work of Shrestha, Tiwari, and Shrestha 1988; and Shrestha 1987.

7. The data for this study was collected through the Nepal Irrigation Institutions and Systems (NIIS) project conducted by a research team associated with the Workshop in Political Theory and Policy Analysis at Indiana University. To establish an empirical foundation for the study of irrigation management in Nepal, the NIIS research team designed a set of structured coding forms as the instrument to record information on various aspects of irrigation systems in Nepal at a particular time (NIIS Research Team 1993). The focus of the forms was put on identifying and measuring various attributes that might affect the incentive structures faced by individuals and the patterns of outcomes. A large number of case studies of irrigation systems in Nepal from prior research were identified and coded with the structured forms. The information was then entered into a database. As information from these case studies was secondary data, it was a major concern that the data obtained from these case studies was of good quality. Such a concern prompted the NIIS team to conduct fieldwork in Nepal during 1991 and 1992 to verify the data. During the fieldwork, the accuracy of the data was checked, missing variables filled out, and some new cases added. The initial NIIS database contains information about 127 systems, and was the basis for a series of studies (Lam, Lee, and E. Ostrom 1994; E. Ostrom, Lam, and Lee 1994; E. Ostrom and Gardner 1993; Lam and Shivakoti 1992). During 1993, the NIIS team conducted another round of data collection in Nepal in an effort to strengthen the initial NIIS database. Information about 23 new cases, and missing information for four old cases, was added to the initial NIIS database. This expanded NIIS database with 150 cases is the empirical base for this article. For more detailed discussion about the NIIS database, see Benjamin et al. 1994. Effort to increase the number of cases in the database continues.

8. The classification scheme for system size used by the Department of Irrigation of Nepal is shown in table 12.1.

9. The variables that constitute the three dimensions of performance are as follows:

Physical: 1. The condition of the physical structure of the system.
              2. Short-run economic technical efficiency.
Delivery: 1. Water adequacy.
              2. Equity in water distribution.
              3. Reliability of water supply.
Productivity: 1. The number of metric tons of agricultural product per hectare per year.
              2. Cropping intensity at the head end.
              3. Cropping intensity at the tail end.

10. Although women actively participate in agricultural activities in Nepal, major decisions in a farming household related to irrigation are usually made by the head of the household who is almost always a man. Women are only infrequently involved in the physical work of maintaining an irrigation system or in the governance activities. For simplification, I use *he* to refer to a farmer in this article.

11. Note that only small-and medium-sized systems are included in the analysis. Thus, the effect of the large size of AMIS is, to a certain extent, controlled. Of course, it is recognized that even among these small-and medium-sized systems, AMIS generally are larger than FMIS. . . .

12. The term *organization* is used to refer not to the "formal" structures of a collective, but to the patterns of actions and interactions of individuals within a collective as a result of an organizing process, which is defined as changing the situation from one in which individuals act independently to one in which they act in a coordinated manner in an effort to accomplish collective goals (E. Ostrom 1990; Miller 1992).

REFERENCES

Agarwal, Madan Lal (1991) "A country paper: Nepal." In Asian Productivity Organization (ed.), *Management Irrigation Facilities in Asia and the Pacific*, 256–73. Tokyo: Asian Productivity Organization.

Ambler, John S. (1990) "The influence of farmer water rights on the design of water-proportioning devices." In Robert Yoder and Juanita Thurston (eds.), *Design Issues in Farmer-Managed Irrigation Systems*, 37–52. Colombo, Sri Lanka: International Irrigation Management Institute.

——— (1993) "Performance indicators: A case of a newly developed FMIS in Bali, Indonesia." In Shaul Manor and Jorge Chambouleyron (eds.), *Performance Measurement in Farmer-Managed Irrigation Systems: Proceedings of an International Workshop of the Farmer-Managed Irrigation Systems Network*, 3–12. Colombo, Sri Lanka: International Irrigation Management Institute.

Ascher, William, and Robert Healy (1990) *Natural Resource Policy Making in Developing Countries*. Durham, NC: Duke University Press.

Benjamin, Paul, Wai Fung Lam, Elinor Ostrom, and Ganesh Shivakoti (1994) "Institutions, incentives, and irrigation in Nepal." Decentralization: Finance and Management Project Report. Burlington, VT: Associates in Rural Development.

Bhuiyan, Sadiqul I. (1987) "Irrigation technology for food production: Expectations and realities in South and Southeast Asia." In Wayne R. Jordan (ed.), *Water and Water Policy in World Food Supplies: Proceedings of the Conference May 26–30, 1985, at Texas A&M University, College Station, Texas*, 325–35. College Station: Texas A&M University Press.

Bottrall, Anthony F. (1981) "Comparative study of the management and organization of irrigation projects." World Bank Staff Working Paper, No. 458. Washington, DC: World Bank.

Chambers, Robert (1988) *Managing Canal Irrigation: Practical Analysis from South Asia*. Cambridge: Cambridge University Press.

Curtis, Donald (1991) *Beyond Government: Organizations for Common Benefit.* London: Macmillan.

Freeman, David M. (1990) "Designing local irrigation organizations for linking water demand with supply." In R. K. Sampath and Robert A. Young (eds.), *Social, Economic, and Institutional Issues in Third World Irrigation Management,* 111–40. Boulder, CO: Westview Press.

Gill, Mushtaq Ahmed (1991) "Farm-level water management systems (public and private)." In Asian Productivity Organization (ed.), *Farm-Level Irrigation Water Management, Report of a Study Meeting in Lahore, Pakistan,* 79–87. Tokyo: Asian Productivity Organization.

Gupta, D. D., A. Singh, and M. V. George (1973) "Water management practices in sandy arid zones." *Agriculture and Agro-Industries Journal* 6, no. 6: 34–38.

Hafid, Answar, and Y. Hayami (1978) "Mobilizing local resources for irrigation development: The subsidi desa case of Indonesia." *Irrigation Policy and Management in Southeast Asia,* 123–33. Los Banos: International Rice Research Institute.

Hilton, Rita (1990) *Case Studies—Cost Recovery and Local Resource Mobilization: An Examination of Incentives in Irrigation Systems in Nepal.* Burlington, VT: Associates in Rural Development.

HMG/N (His Majesty's Government, Nepal) (1992) *Irrigation Policy.* Kathmandu, Nepal: Ministry of Water Resources.

Johnson, Sam H., III (1991) "Status and progress of irrigation development: Policy and programmes." In Asian Productivity Organization (ed.), *Farm-Level Irrigation Water Management, Report of a Study Meeting in Lahore, Pakistan,* 79–87. Tokyo: Asian Productivity Organization.

Khadka, Narayan (1993) "Institutional reforms in Nepal's agricultural sector." *Asian Profile* 21, no. 2: 145–63.

King, Gary, Robert O. Keohane, and Sidney Verba (1994) *Designing Social Inquiry: Scientific Inference in Qualitative Research.* Princeton, NJ: Princeton University Press.

Lam, Wai Fung (1995) "Institutional design and collective actions: A study of irrigation associations in Taiwan." Paper presented at a conference on Government Action, Social Capital Formation, and Third World Development, Cambridge, MA, American Academy of Arts and Sciences, May 5–6. A subsequent version of this paper is reprinted as chap. 13 of this volume.

——— (1998) *Governing Irrigation Systems in Nepal: Institutions, Infrastructure, and Collective Action.* Oakland, CA: ICS Press.

Lam, Wai Fung, and Ganesh Shivakoti (1992) "A before and after analysis of the effect of farmer-to-farmer training as an intervention strategy." Technical Report. Bloomington: Indiana University, Workshop in Political Theory and Policy Analysis.

Lam, Wai Fung, Myungsuk Lee, and Elinor Ostrom (1994) "An institutional analysis approach: Findings from the NIIS on irrigation performance." In Jennifer Sowerwine, Ganesh Shivakoti, Ujjwal Pradhan, Ashutosh Shukla, and Elinor Ostrom (eds.), *From Farmers' Fields to Data Fields and Back: A Synthesis of Participatory Information Systems for Irrigation and Other Resources,* 69–93.

Colombo, Sri Lanka: International Irrigation Management Institute, and Rampur, Nepal: Institute of Agriculture and Animal Science.

Lee, Myungsuk (1994) "Institutional analysis, public policy, and the possibility of collective action in common pool resources: A dynamic game approach." Ph.D. diss., Indiana University.

Lieberson, Stanley (1985) *Making It Count: The Improvement of Social Research and Theory*. Berkeley: University of California Press.

Miller, Gary J. (1992) *Managerial Dilemmas: The Political Economy of Hierarchy*. Cambridge: Cambridge University Press.

Miranda, S. M., and G. Levine (1978) "Effects of physical control parameters in lowland irrigation management." *Irrigation Policy and Management in Southeast Asia*, 77–91. Los Banos: International Rice Research Institute.

NIIS (Nepal Irrigation Institutions and Systems) Research Team (1993) *Common Property Resources Project: Nepal Irrigation Institutions and Systems Database Coding Sheets and Forms*. Bloomington: Indiana University, Workshop in Political Theory and Policy Analysis.

North, Douglass C. (1990) *Institutions, Institutional Change, and Economic Performance*. Cambridge: Cambridge University Press.

Ostrom, Elinor (1990) *Governing the Commons: The Evolution of Institutions for Collective Action*. New York: Cambridge University Press.

——— (1992) *Crafting Institutions for Self-Governing Irrigation Systems*. San Francisco, CA: ICS Press.

——— (1994) "Constituting social capital and collective action." *Journal of Theoretical Politics* 6, no. 4 (October): 527–62.

Ostrom, Elinor, and Roy Gardner (1993) "Coping with asymmetries in the commons: Self-governing irrigation systems can work." *Journal of Economic Perspectives* 7, no. 4 (Fall): 93–112. Reprinted in M. D. McGinnis, ed. *Polycentric Games and Institutions* (Ann Arbor: University of Michigan Press, 1999).

Ostrom, Elinor, Roy Gardner, and James Walker (1994) *Rules, Games, and Common-Pool Resources*. Ann Arbor: University of Michigan Press.

Ostrom, Elinor, Wai Fung Lam, and Myungsuk Lee (1994) "The Performance of self-governing irrigation systems in Nepal." *Human Systems Management* 13, no. 3: 197–207.

Pant, Niranjan, ed. (1984) *Productivity and Equity in Irrigation Systems*. New Delhi: Ashish Publishing House.

Peabody, N. S., III (1983) "Labdu-Dhikure-Sera Irrigation Project." Project Component Analysis, vol. 3. Kathmandu, Nepal: Rasuwa/Nuwakot Rural Development Project, Socioeconomic Unit, Project Coordinator's Office.

Pradhan, Prachanda (1989a) *Increasing Agricultural Production in Nepal: Role of Low-Cost Irrigation Development Through Farmer Participation*. Kathmandu, Nepal: International Irrigation Management Institute.

——— (1989b) *Patterns of Irrigation Organization: A Comparative Study of 21 Farmer-Managed Irrigation Systems*. Colombo, Sri Lanka: International Irrigation Management Institute.

Pradhan, Ujjwal (1988) "Local resource mobilization and government intervention in hill irrigation systems in Nepal." Working paper prepared for the Water Management Synthesis Project. Ithaca, NY: Cornell University.

Repetto, Robert (1986) "Skimming the water: Rent-seeking and the performance of public irrigation systems." Research Report, No. 4. Washington, DC: World Resources Institute.

Riccardi, Theodore (1977) *The Royal Edicts of Ram Saha of Gorkha, Kailash: A Journal of Himalayan Studies*. Kathmandu, Nepal: Ratna Pustak Bhandar.

Rosegrant, M., F. Kasryno, L. Gonzales, C. Rasahan, and Y. Saefudin (1987) *Price and Investment Policies in the Indonesian Food Crop Sector*. Washington, DC: International Food Policy Research Institute.

Satyal, Ram Prasad (1991) "Country reports: Nepal." In Asian Productivity Organization (ed.), *Farm-Level Irrigation Water Management, Report of a Study Meeting in Lohore, Pakistan*, 79–87. Hong Kong: Nordica International Ltd.

Shivakoti, Ganesh (1992) "Variations in intervention, variations in result: Assisting FMIS in Nepal." Irrigation Management Network Paper, No. 11. London: Overseas Development Institute, Irrigation Management Network.

Shrestha, S. P. (1987) "Multifunctional, nonresidential irrigation organization: A case study of the Kodku Irrigation System of the Kathmandu Valley." Lalitpur, Nepal: Development Research Group.

———— (1988) "Helping a farmers' organization: An experience with Chiregad Irrigation Project." Kathmandu, Nepal: International Irrigation Management Institute.

Shrestha, S. P., D. N. Tiwari, and M. Shrestha (1988) *Kodku Irrigation System: Study in the Growth of Organization to Manage the System*. Lalitpur, Nepal: Development Research Group.

Sparling, Edward W. (1990) "Asymmetry of incentives and information: The problem of watercourse maintenance." In R. K. Sampath and Robert A. Young (eds.), *Social, Economic, and Institutional Issues in Third World Irrigation Management*, 195–213. Boulder, CO: Westview Press.

Tan-Kim-Yong, Uraivan (1983) "Resource mobilization in traditional irrigation systems of Northern Thailand: A comparison between the lowland and upland irrigation communities." Ph.D. diss., Cornell University.

Tang, Shui-Yan (1992) *Institutions and Collective Action: Self-Governance in Irrigation*. San Francisco, CA: ICS Press.

Taylor, D. C. (1978) "Financing irrigation services in the Pekalen Sampean Irrigation Project, East Java, Indonesia." *Irrigation Policy and Management in Southeast Asia*, 111–22. Los Banos: International Rice Research Institute.

———— (1981) *The Economics of Malaysian Paddy Production and Irrigation*. Bangkok, Thailand: Agricultural Development Council.

Wade, Robert, and David Seckler (1990) "Priority issues in the management of irrigation systems." In R. K. Sampath and Robert A. Young (eds.), *Social, Economic, and Institutional Issues in Third World Irrigation Management*, 13–30. Boulder, CO: Westview Press.

WECS/IIMI (Water and Energy Commission Secretariat, Nepal, and International Irrigation Management Institute) (1990) *Assistance to Farmer-Managed Irrigation Systems: Results, Lessons, and Recommendations from an Action-Research Project*. Colombo, Sri Lanka: IIMI.

Weissing, Franz J., and Elinor Ostrom (1991) "Crime and punishment: Further reflections on the counterintuitive results of mixed equilibria games." *Journal of Theoretical Politics* 3, no. 3 (July): 343–50.

———— (1993) "Irrigation institutions and the games irrigators play: Rule enforcement on government-and farmer-managed systems." In Fritz W. Scharpf (ed.), *Games in Hierarchies and Networks: Analytical and Empirical Approaches to the Study of Governance Institutions*, 387–428. Frankfurt am Main: Campus Verlag; Boulder, CO: Westview Press. Reprinted in M. D. McGinnis, ed. *Polycentric Games and Institutions* (Ann Arbor: University of Michigan Press, 1999).

Wickham, T. H., and A. Valera (1978) "Practices and accountability for better irrigation management." *Irrigation Policy and Management in Southeast Asia*, 61–75. Los Banos: International Rice Research Institute.

World Bank (1994) *World Development Report 1994: Infrastructure for Development*. Washington, DC: World Bank.

Yoder, Robert (1986) "The performance of farmer-managed irrigation systems in the hills of Nepal." Ph.D. diss., Cornell University.

———— (1994) *Locally Managed Irrigation Systems*. Colombo, Sri Lanka: International Irrigation Management Institute.

CHAPTER 13

Institutional Design of Public Agencies and Coproduction: A Study of Irrigation Associations in Taiwan

Wai Fung Lam

1. Introduction

Taiwan's irrigation systems are reportedly among the most effective in the world. In a study comparing the water delivery efficiency in different rice-growing systems in Asia, Levine (1977) estimated that the basic water requirement per crop in Taiwan was 1,000 mm, as compared to 2,500 mm in the Philippines and 1,400 mm in Malaysia. In the Tou Liu system in Taiwan (currently part of the Yunlin Irrigation Association), the requirement was even as low as 650 mm. The effectiveness, however, is not confined to the high levels of efficiency in water delivery. Water delivery and distribution in Taiwan's irrigation systems are generally organized in an orderly manner, and the physical structures are kept in relatively good condition (Moore 1983, 1989).[1]

Originally published in *World Development* 24, no. 6 (June 1996): 1039–54. Reprinted by permission of Elsevier Science and the author.

Author's note: The full research report on which this essay is based is available through the Workshop in Political Theory and Policy Analysis, Indiana University or by contacting the author directly. A preliminary version was presented at a conference on "Government Action, Social Capital Formation, and Third World Development," sponsored by the Economic Development Working Group, Social Capital and Public Affairs Project, at the American Academy of Arts and Sciences, Cambridge, MA, May 5–6, 1995. The author appreciates the support of the Social Capital Project, which enabled him to make one more field trip to Taiwan during December of 1994. The author would like to thank Peter Evans, Mick Moore, Elinor Ostrom, and Judith Tendler for their helpful comments and suggestions. I am also grateful to Li-Jen Wen, Yung-Teh Lin, Ming-Hua Tsai, Ching-Ho Kuo, and Wen-Jung Hu at the Council of Agriculture, who assisted in planning my fieldwork in Taiwan. I am also appreciative of the help offered by many IA officials who generously shared their ideas with me during my fieldwork. In particular, Jin-Shi Hsu, Yung-Tang Chou, Yun Cheng, Ming-Dao Wang, Hui-Yuan Chang, Yung-Hsing Lai, and Jiunn-Ji Yu deserve special thanks. None of these people bear any responsibility for the findings, interpretations, and conclusions expressed in this essay; those are the author's alone.

One might be tempted to attribute this effectiveness to the heavy investment made by the Taiwanese government in irrigation development and to the sophisticated engineering infrastructure that is commonplace in Taiwan. A high level of infrastructural investment, however, does not tell the whole story. Even the most sophisticated structures must be operated by individuals. How these individuals work with one another significantly affects irrigation performance (Coward and Levine 1987; E. Ostrom 1992; Ambler 1993; Lam 1998; Lam, Lee, and E. Ostrom 1997).

Productive patterns of relationships, however, do not just exist; they are constituted and sustained by a large array of rules relating individuals to each other. Some of these rules are considered formal in the sense that they are created and enforced by governmental authority, others are considered informal in that they are sustained by "private" actions of individuals. Some of these rules are crafted by conscious efforts; others evolve slowly through human interaction. How these rules work together to allow individuals to realize their productive potential is a question of importance in resource management in particular, and public administration in general. This essay addresses this question by studying the successful experience of irrigation management in Taiwan.

Taiwan's successful experience in irrigation management is of major policy relevance, not simply because it is in sharp contrast to the experience of irrigation development in much of the developing world where many high-cost and sophisticated irrigation systems have been nonsustainable due to inadequate operation and maintenance (Ascher and Healy 1990; Chambers 1988; E. Ostrom, Schroeder, and Wynne 1993). The persistent underperformance of irrigation agencies in much of the developing world in the last several decades has raised serious doubts about the usefulness and feasibility of relying on government officials to manage irrigation and other public services. The viability of government agencies serving as the agent for development has come under serious challenge. Taiwan's experience, however, represents a rare case where irrigation agencies work.

Numerous calls for reforming the governance structure for development have been made (Israel 1992; Kessides 1993; World Bank 1994). Research findings suggest that self-governance can work and, in many instances, outperform government agencies in the management of an infrastructure and resources such as irrigation systems (Ostrom, Schroeder, and Wynne 1993; E. Ostrom 1990, 1992; Tang 1992; Lam 1998). Unfortunately, that self-governance can work (in some instances) has been used by some policy makers and researchers in developing countries as the justification for a policy recommendation that aims at downsizing, if not getting rid of, the government. Parallel to such a bias in the policy circle is the prevalence in current development literature of studies that focus solely on why government agencies do not work; the question of what can be done to make agencies work better has largely receded to the background (Tendler and Freedheim 1994; Uphoff 1994). Yet as many scholars have cautioned, local organization alone is no panacea. The administration of public affairs often involves complex tasks that citizens alone might not have adequate capability and resources to handle. Moreover, the survival and operation of self-governing local organizations are usually nested within, and conditioned by, a broader institutional setting (E. Ostrom 1992; Tang 1992; Lam 1998). A high degree of complementarity between officials and farmers is necessary for the effective provision and production of many public goods and services. Thus, instead of trying to get rid of government agencies, it would be more useful to study how government agencies can be designed to perform effectively, and complement citizens' efforts in broader institutional settings, in conducting public affairs. This study addresses these issues from a microperspective, examining the mechanisms by which a large array of institutions enables irrigation officials and farmers in Taiwan to conduct irrigation operation and maintenance in an effective manner.

2. The Setting

(a) Physical Environment

Although rainfall in Taiwan is abundant, its distribution is uneven in both space and time. While the annual average rainfall in the northeastern part of the country is about 6,500 mm, it is only 1,000 mm on the west coast where most of the cultivated land is located. Moreover, more than 80 percent of the total rainfall falls between June and October. In other months of the year, the monthly average rainfall is rarely more than 100 mm. During the winter season, areas on the west coast commonly have no rainfall. Thus, effective irrigation management is a major factor affecting the extent of agricultural potential that can be realized.[2] The physical environment in Taiwan is hostile to irrigation. Rivers are short and with high gradients. This, together with the high concentration of rainfall in the rainy season, results in a high level of run-off flowing into the sea (Kuo 1986).

(b) Socioeconomic Context

Perhaps the most important event that fundamentally shaped the social landscape of Taiwan's rural areas was the Land Reforms conducted in the early 1950s.[3] As a result of the Reforms, large landlords in Taiwan virtually disappeared. Since then, the country's agricultural sector has mainly comprised small family-owned farms. In 1952, the average farm size in Taiwan was 1.29 hectares. It dropped to 1.12 hectares in 1984, and to 1.1 hectares in 1992 (COA 1993). Given the small size of farm households, effective irrigation management involves the collective action of a large number of irrigators that, in turn, requires a high degree of coordination and organization. A more intensive mode of irrigation management was deemed necessary. In addition, without large landlords who usually assume the traditional leadership role in the rural areas, farmers tend to organize themselves around scattered small groups. Such small group centricity, to a certain extent, explains why farmers in Taiwan do not stand out as having unusual levels of trust and solidarity. Earlier research indicates that farmers in Taiwan did not hesitate to engage in water theft when water was scarce (VanderMeer 1971).

(c) Institutional Overview

The primary irrigation institutional arrangements in the country are the 17 Irrigation Associations (IAs), which have the responsibility of operating and maintaining irrigation systems located within one or more hydraulic regions.[4] These IAs are parastatal agencies that are legally owned and formed by farmers and supervised by governments at higher levels. Their legal status as juristic entities entitles them to a high degree of de jure autonomy and also certain public authorities to levy water fees.

The activities of the IAs are primarily confined to main-system management. The IA staff at headquarters diverts water to a system and allocates water to different regions. Within a region, a management station coordinates water allocation to different areas. A working station is in place in each area to deliver water to various irrigation districts.[5] Within an irrigation district, the tasks of operation and maintenance are presumably coordinated by a network of irrigation groups (IGs). The structure and operation of IGs vary, depending on specific local environment. Usually, an irrigation district is further divided into several irrigation blocks; in each of these blocks, farmers are presumably organized into irrigation teams (ITs) to carry out the tasks of operation and maintenance. While IGs and ITs are said to be farmers' self-organizing units, they appear in organizational charts as subsidiaries to the IAs.

Government agencies at various jurisdictional levels are also involved in the governance and management of irrigation. At the local level, the interaction between the IAs and local organizations, such as the county governments, conditions the ways that irrigation systems are governed and managed.[6] At the provincial level, the Provincial Water Conservancy Bureau is in place to formulate and implement water resource policies. The Bureau is also responsible for supervising the IAs. Every year, each IA is required to submit a report with details on every aspect of its operation during the last year to the Bureau for review; in addition, every year the Bureau sends a working team to the IAs to evaluate their operation and performance, and to audit their budgets. At the national level, the Council of Agriculture is the lead agency that formulates policies concerning irrigation in general and the operation of the IAs in particular.

3. Team Production, Coproduction, and Governance

An irrigation system is a common-pool resource (CPR) where the cost of excluding potential beneficiaries is nontrivial and benefits are subtractable (Gardner, Ostrom, and Walker 1990). If any farmer can take water from a system whether or not he or she has contributed to the operation and maintenance of the system, he or she sees few incentives to contribute. Furthermore, when the water supply is scarce and unpredictable, allocation of water is necessary to ensure that water is distributed equitably and used productively. The need to allocate water, however, implies that farmers are likely to obtain a smaller amount of water than they desire. Farmers usually want enough water to attain the highest possible returns by working their land to its full potential, they also want more water as insurance against risk and unexpected exigencies. Given the threat of a substantial crop loss, there are usually temptations for farmers to take more water than allowed or to take water out of turn.

(a) Team Production and Coproduction

The concept of team production is central to the understanding of the problem of motivation in irrigation agencies. Organization[7] enables individuals to reap the benefits of team production. Many complex tasks in the public sector cannot be accomplished unless individuals put their efforts and resources together and work as a team. Team production, however, is rarely a simple process of pooling the efforts and resources of individuals. It is a process through which individual efforts and resources are structured in complementary ways that yield a higher level of joint productivity (Lachmann 1978). This is why, in a team production process, the marginal productivity of an individual is a function of the efforts of the others (Alchian and Demsetz 1972).

Coproduction is a form of team production. In a coproduction process, the efforts of the irrigation officials (the regular producers) and those of the farmers (the consumer producers) are largely interdependent; neither can totally substitute for the other (Parks et al. 1982). In the irrigation process, while officials might possess "scientific" knowledge concerning some physical aspects of irrigation systems, the farmers possess time-specific and place-specific local knowledge of the systems upon which their livelihood depends (Freeman 1990). Only when both kinds of knowledge are utilized can effective operation and maintenance be attained.

The interdependence of efforts may give rise to the problem of shirking similar to the setting of team production. In many large-scale irrigation systems, irrigation officials assume that water allocation and maintenance are the responsibilities of the farmers because farmers are directly affected by the performance of operation and maintenance. From the farmers' perspective, the irrigation officials are presumably specialists who have the responsibility of managing the system. Because the officials are the "managers," they are the ones who "should" be doing the operation and maintenance. Since both farmers and officials think that managing the system is the responsibility of the other, it is possible that neither of them invests much effort in irrigation management activities. If no one maintains the systems, they begin to operate less effectively. Such a problem is often exacerbated by the blurred boundary between those who constitute the members of the coproduction team.

For a coproduction process to succeed, incentives must be in place so that regular producers (the irrigation officials) are motivated to serve the interests of consumer producers (the farmers). If the payoffs to irrigation officials are somewhat dependent on how well they serve the farmers, the officials are more likely to take the interests of the farmers into consideration. Unfortunately, there are usually few intrinsic incentives in irrigation that could motivate irrigation officials to serve the interests of farmers. Irrigation officials are usually not the ones who have a stake in the efficient operation of the irrigation systems in which they work. Whether the officials take the interests of the farmers into consideration depends on how the relationships between the officials and the farmers are understood and structured in particular societies.

(b) Governance

Unlike irrigation construction that deals with the delivery of tangible goods such as dams and canals, irrigation management is mainly concerned with the provision of a less tangible good: rule-ordered relationships among farmers. This puts irrigation management in the policy domain where the patterns of relationships between individuals, as a way of life, are part of the situation that the agencies are meant to deal with. Policy outcomes, that is, the degree to which these problems are resolved, are inherently linked to how well individuals can work with one another.

In irrigation, effective water delivery largely hinges upon farmers following water allocation rules, taking care of their system in daily exigencies, and contributing their efforts to the maintenance of the structures whenever necessary. While these patterns of relationships are a major part of the outcomes of irrigation management, they cannot be "produced" directly by irrigation officials. Thus, assigning an irrigation agency to handle irrigation does not automatically solve the problems of collective action among farmers involved in irrigation operation and maintenance. What is essential is to design the governance structure in the way that rules are crafted, monitored, and enforced, so that they enable farmers to establish productive working relationships with one another. How the agencies can fit in the governance structure is a question of major import in institutional design.

The problems of team production, coproduction, and governance can serve as the point of departure for understanding the operation and performance of irrigation institutions in Taiwan. In the following sections, I examine the design of Taiwan's irrigation institutions, and the mechanisms through which these institutions enable individuals to cope with the problems. The analysis proceeds from three angles: (1) the structures and incentives within the IA; (2) the ways that water delivery is carried out in the field; and (3) the interactions between farmers and officials.

4. Inside the Bureaucracy: The Structure and Procedures

Like a typical government agency in Taiwan, the structure of an IA is highly bureaucratic and centralized, and designed upon the principles of division of labor and hierarchical control. At the top of the bureaucracy is a chairman who, until 1994, was elected by farmer representatives who were in turn elected by farmers. The chairman appoints a general manager and a chief engineer, who assist the chairman in overseeing the operation of the association. The day-to-day operation is carried out by various divisions responsible for specialized functions.[8] Within a particular division, the tasks are further divided and assigned to several sections.

The centralized image is also reflected in the relationships between the IA headquarters and its field offices (management stations and working stations). The field offices are perceived as the implementation arms of the headquarters. They collect information necessary for irrigation planning, and manage the implementation of irrigation plans and other tasks assigned by the headquarters. While the working stations assist the headquarters in making decisions concerning irrigation management, they do not participate in the decision-making process.

(a) Flexibility

The bureaucratic characteristics of the IAs in Taiwan seem to contradict the image portrayed by prior research. It is particularly interesting that while observers have often likened the IAs to street-level bureaucracies where coordination, discretion, and responsiveness are emphasized, officials in both the central government and the IAs have always emphasized the importance of hierarchy and control in the associations.[9] The puzzle, then, is how the two seemingly contradictory images can be reconciled and geared toward enhancing the performance of the associations.

A possible answer to the puzzle is that the headquarters and the working stations operate on quite different principles, which allow them to deal with problems of different scopes and nature at different levels. The formal organization of the working stations is based upon the bureaucratic image of the headquarters. A station chief is assigned to oversee the operation of a station, and the station staff members are assigned to various sections with specific functions such as engineering and irrigation management. Unlike at the headquarters, however, the size of the working station staff is usually very small, with an average of eight persons. The small staff makes the division of labor by functions more a formality than a meaningful organizational feature. That every one of the staff sits in an open office space further shortens their social distance.

Instead of a division of labor by functions, the small size of the staff makes it necessary to have division of labor by irrigated areas. Each official at the working station, including the station chief, is assigned the responsibility of overseeing the irrigation management of a certain number of IGs and their irrigated areas. The official, then, serves as the contact person between the working station and farmers in particular areas. This type of division of labor facilitates communication between the IA officials and farmers, but more important, it affects the dynamic of interaction among officials within a working station.

First, a division of labor by irrigated areas, to a certain extent, enables individual officials to monopolize information on their particular areas. This area-specific information becomes a unique asset of individual officials. Since every piece of such area-specific information is essential to the effective operation of the working station, each official holds a key to the overall success of the station. Officials who feel they have something important to contribute to their organization are more likely to perceive their work as meaningful and to do a conscientious job. Moreover, since effective irrigation management in a particular area usually requires complementary actions of officials managing the adjacent areas, horizontal coordination among officials becomes necessary. Thus the working station staff is put in an interdependent situation of which they are well aware. Such awareness not only helps create collective identity among the staff but also signifies to them the importance of cooperation.

Second, assigning individual officials areas for which they are responsible implicitly holds them accountable to what might happen in the assigned areas. An official is likely to face much pressure from others in the station if his or her area faces persistent problems. In fact, assigning responsibilities in this way also applies to the working stations as a whole. By assigning each working station to oversee the irrigation management of a particular area, officials at the station are held collectively responsible for what might happen in the area. Such collective responsibility creates a sense of collective identity among officials, which transcends hierarchical relationships among them.

While work at the headquarters is basically a nine-to-five routine, work at the working stations requires much more flexibility. The need for such flexibility is well known, and has been consciously promoted through various institutional arrangements. A standard working station is a two-storied building. While the ground floor is used for office space, the upper floor is an apartment where the station chief[10] and his family live. Living in the station, the chief is expected to stay alert 24 hours a day. This arrangement allows the working station to better deal with emergencies.

When emergencies come up, the chief alone is unlikely to be able to deal with them. Extra effort from other officials at the station is needed. These other officials, however, are not paid to make the extra effort. For these officials, giving their help to the chief in case of an emergency is doing the chief a favor; it would not be difficult for them to avoid making the extra effort if they chose. The subordinates' ability to do the chief a favor gives them bargaining power that, in turn, affects the way in which they interact with each other, vis-à-vis the chief. As a station chief succinctly puts it, "there will be many occasions when extra effort of the staff is required, whether the staff will offer the extra effort is purely a matter of goodwill. How can I offend them?" Under such a situation, the chief would find that command and control is unlikely to be an effective way to get things done.

Given that irrigation management involves many uncertainties, irrigation managers in almost every system in the world are expected to contribute extra effort when emergencies arise. What is special in the Taiwanese case, however, is that the station chief is locked into the task of dealing with emergencies by various kinds of institutional arrangements. He is targeted as the one who is given incentives and responsibilities to mobilize and coordinate necessary efforts for dealing with emergencies. Now compare this situation to that in many South Asian countries such as India and Nepal where irrigation officials managing the systems are also expected to deal with emergencies. There, with strict hierarchical control in place, subordinates do not have incentives to take any action before they are ordered to. Infringing on the authority of superiors could be extremely detrimental to an official's career. Ironically, the requirement that the subordinates consult their superiors before they act provides a legitimate excuse for the subordinates to do nothing. So while every official knows that they, the officials as a whole, are expected to deal with emergencies effectively, which officials should be doing the job is not clear.

(b) Autonomy

A more organic mode of organization at the working stations is possible only when the headquarters refrains from intervening. The low level of intervention, ironically, is made possible by the bureaucratic principle of strict division of labor across units at different levels. The headquarters is responsible for the overall planning, larger scale maintenance work, management of water sources, and water delivery at the system level. Once the water flows into laterals, it is the responsibility of the management stations to allocate water to different areas managed by different working stations. Usually the management stations only deal with the working station chiefs, but not farmers directly. It is clearly understood that the working stations are where the distribution of water to farmers' fields occurs, and where farmers interact with irrigation officials. Such an understanding is essential. It gives the working station chiefs leverage to make necessary adjustments in dealing with water allocation at the local level.

Such local autonomy is further enhanced in that the working stations are given the responsibility of facilitating, and communicating with, the IGs. Although the IGs are shown on the organizational chart as subsidiary units to the IAs, neither IA officials nor farmers see them as part of the associations. Irrigation officials often cite the respect for local democracy as a reason for their unwillingness to be involved in the IGs. But such a reason seems unlikely to be true, given that irrigation officials have never hesitated to intervene when necessary. Instead, several reasons might explain the officials' hesitancy. First, the IA staff see themselves largely as government agents (although they do not have civil service status) and irrigation professionals (even though most of them do not have professional qualifications). Organizing farmers in irrigation operations is not the kind of task that they see themselves fit to do. Second, the ambiguous nature of the IAs as parastatal organizations does not give the IA staff the legitimacy to intervene. While farmers as a whole might not actually play an active role in supervising the IAs, the image that farmers are the boss of the IAs is very clear in the mind of IA officials.

Third, from the perspective of the IA officials, being involved in the mushy business of water allocation at the field level is the last thing they want. It is especially the case in the areas where local factions do not get along with one another. Since it is clearly stipulated in regulations that water allocation at the field level is a responsibility of farmers, irrigation officials are glad to oblige. Finally, until very recently, the farmers' extra contributions (other than the water fees they were required to pay) in terms of voluntary labor and monetary chip-in were an important source of resources for irrigation management at the local level. These extra contributions were largely based upon farmers' goodwill as well as the calculus that they might enjoy payoffs from these contributions. Too much intervention from the IA could offend farmers and damage local goodwill. An unhappy farmer is unlikely to be willing to offer extra contributions.

Since the IAs do not see themselves in the position to be actively involved in the operation of the IGs, the headquarters maintains only limited formal interactions with the groups. The limited involvement of the headquarters in the IGs leaves a vacuum between the IA and farmers that the working stations are in the position to fill. Irrigation operation and maintenance at the local level requires cooperation and coordination between IA staff and farmers. As the officials at the working stations must deal with farmers in their work whether they want to or not, they must have de facto autonomy in dealing with the IGs. Such autonomy allows the working station staff and IGs to develop arrangements to cope with the local situations. For example, in systems where water mainly comes from natural springs and rivers, a water shortage might render rotation within an irrigation block necessary. The order of rotation is therefore arranged normally by farmers themselves. In many instances, farmers draw lots to determine the rotation order. Such an arrangement can be maintained, however, only when the working station is able to adjust water delivery to complement the agreed-upon order.

Earlier irrigation literature has pointed out the importance of a handover point between officials and farmers in irrigation management (Wade 1987; Chambers 1988). Yet the mere existence of a handover may not be enough, because whether the handover can be designed in a complementary manner depends on whether the two teams of individuals at the hand-over point are given liberty to work things out. The high degree of autonomy enjoyed by the working stations in dealing with irrigation groups has facilitated coordination between the two teams.

5. Working Together: The Organization of Water Delivery

While effective irrigation management involves close cooperation between officials and farmers, such cooperation cannot be taken for granted. A large array of rules must be in place to specify the division of work, to create positive incentives for the parties to contribute their efforts, and to help the parties maintain stable mutual expectations of each other. In this section, I decipher the "nuts and bolts" of the institutional arrangements in Taiwanese irrigation systems that relate the efforts of officials and farmers by examining the organization of water delivery—an activity that requires high levels of continual cooperation.

Given the diverse physical characteristics in disparate locations in the country, there are diverse means by which water delivery is conducted. The following discussion deals mainly with water delivery in the Tainan area of the Chianan IA[11] where the major water source for irrigation is two connected large-scale reservoirs, the Tsengwen Reservoir and the Wushantou Reservoir. These reservoirs make the practice of rotation irrigation possible.

(a) The Formulation of the Irrigation Plan

The practice of rotation irrigation requires a relatively accurate and comprehensive irrigation plan. The process of working out the irrigation plan starts at the working stations. Every year before the first planting season, irrigation officials at the working station convene a meeting of IG leaders in the area to plan irrigation operations in the coming year. A major concern of discussion, of course, is the level of water demand for irrigation in the coming season.

Two factors are the basis upon which the water demand in a particular irrigation block is calculated. The first factor is the physical characteristics of the fields. These include soil type, the topography of the land, the rate of seepage of the soil, and the distance of the land from the gate to where water is diverted into the block. Information about all these physical characteristics is meticulously recorded and integrated in a formula used for the calculation of the amount and timing of water flow to particular fields. The second factor is the expected cropping patterns of the irrigated land.[12]

It is obvious that variations in these two factors across time are minimal. On the one hand, the physical characteristics of the land are unlikely to change dramatically in the short run. The major source of change in physical characteristics is reduction in the size of irrigated areas due to changes in the patterns of land use. On the other hand, the expected cropping patterns are fixed and rarely adjusted. In fact, broad cropping categories such as "paddy" and "miscellaneous crops" used in the irrigation plan are meant to serve more as a yardstick in determining the amounts of water delivered to a particular area than to control what farmers grow in their fields. In other words, the so-called water demand is defined mainly with reference to the amount of water that a farmer is entitled to receive in a particular season.

Information on water demands provided by the IGs is gathered by the working station staff. The staff checks to see whether the information is reasonable, based upon the past records, and makes necessary adjustments. The information is then submitted to the headquarters. There, the management division staff first checks out the expected amount of water available in the coming year, based upon information about past years and weather forecasts. This estimate of water supplies is the most important variable that basically sets the constraints on the irrigation plan. If water is adequate to meet all the water demands, the management division staff can satisfy the demands (after making sure that the water demands are reasonable). If the expected water supply is inadequate, the management division decides which areas will receive water. Usually, areas that have the lowest rate of conveyance loss are given priority. In other words, upstream areas are usually given water during the period of water shortage. Areas that are not given water are left fallow. The central government (not the IA) will compensate farmers who own cultivated land in the fallow areas at a rate of NT 20,000 per hectare per season. Such an amount is about 50 percent of the revenue that would have been made had cultivation been possible. The IA's freedom to decide how much land it is going to irrigate allows it to better balance water demand and water supply and, hence, to avoid overstretching its managerial capacity.

(b) Flexibility Amid Rigidity

The irrigation plan has a strong flavor of centralized control. Outside observers are frequently amazed, if not stunned, by how detailed the irrigation plan appears to be. The irrigation plan literally specifies the amount and the timing of water delivered to the fields of individual farmers; recently, such detailed calculation has been further facilitated by the use of computers. Obviously, if such a plan was strictly adhered to, it would require a very high level of managerial inputs on one hand, and would severely limit the flexibility of farmers on the other.

Such a possible pitfall of rigidity is coped with by the rule that water delivery within each irrigation block (i.e., below sublaterals) is taken care of by IGs organized by farmers themselves. Such an arrangement combines reliability and flexibility. On the one hand, farmers in a particular irrigation block, as a collective, are assured that they will receive a certain amount of irrigation water for the block. On the other hand, they are given much liberty in adjusting the distribution of water at the field level. In such a situation, the irrigation plan can serve three functions. First, it constitutes an implicit contract between IA officials and farmers—water demands are seen as entitlements of farmers rather than needs. Ironically, because these demands are fixed and rather stable, arbitrary actions on the part of officials are less likely. Such an implicit contract not only supports the farmers' expectations of the reliability of water supplies, but also represents a plan of action, or a focal point, with reference to which farmers and officials work together.

Second, the plan can serve as a yardstick by which farmers evaluate officials' performance. If farmers in an irrigation block have not received the amount of water to which they are entitled, the IA officials are held responsible. Note that it is the IA who, based upon the expected water supplies, decides the size of area that will be delivered water. It would be impossible for them to blame the possible inefficiency in water delivery on the excessive demands of farmers.

Third, while the irrigation plan is not strictly implemented below the level of sublaterals, it does provide a framework with which water distribution among farmers is carried out. So while adjustments within an irrigation block are possible, outright inequality is likely to be prevented. It is a de jure right of a farmer who is not given the amount of water entitled to him to take the case to the working station for resolution. Furthermore, the entitlement nature of the irrigation plan implicitly creates water rights for farmers, which allow them to deal with one another more effectively.

As each farmer is entitled to receive a certain amount of water, each working station, then, has a claim for the amount of water equal to the summation of the amounts of water entitled to individual farmers in the area under its jurisdiction. Water claims at different levels set up a dynamic of backward monitoring in the process of water delivery. For an IG leader,[13] being able to deliver the amount of water to which the farmers in his group are entitled requires that he insist on, if not fight for, their water allotment. By the same token, in order to have adequate water for irrigation groups in its jurisdiction, the working station also has the incentive to stick to its water claim. In other words, a unit at a particular level has the incentive to hold the unit from which it receives water accountable; or it will face problems from the unit to which it delivers water. Such a dynamic greatly enhances the mutual accountability between different units in the water delivery process.

(c) Water Allocation at the Field Level

Prior research has noted that while the water distribution effort within an irrigation block is supposed to be organized by farmers, and rotation irrigation is supposed to be practiced, little is known about how it is actually carried out. The IT is supposed to be the farmers' organization that deals with water distribution within an irrigation block, but whether such an organization exists at all has been questioned by researchers. Since the IA has neither formal authority nor responsibility to manage water distribution within an irrigation block, farmers in different locales have been able to develop their own ways of coping with the problems.

IG and IT are most active in areas where rotation is seriously practiced and the amount and timing of water flows are specified. Neither IG nor IT exists in that their names suggest. Since farmers who are served by the IA are automatically members of the IG and IT, they have a right (or an obligation) to participate in the IG meetings before the planting seasons, and a right to vote in the election of the IG leader every four years (IT leaders are appointed by IG leaders). Yet unlike what many Taiwanese officials and earlier research have suggested, farmers in general are not actively involved in water delivery. In most instances, the IG leader and a few IT leaders are the only farmers involved in the operation of irrigation in particular areas.

The IG leaders, however, perform many important functions in facilitating irrigation management in Taiwan. One of these functions is to hire water guards to carry out water distribution as well as minor repair works. Usually, one to two water guards will be hired for each irrigation block. These are part-time positions and the salaries are paid by the IG. Water guards are the ones who actually operate the system and allocate water to individual farmers' fields. Conflict resolution is another function of IG leaders. As many of them are local notables who have many local social and political ties, they are respected by both farmers and IA officials. Thus, on one hand, their reputations give them "moral power" to serve as arbiters in resolving conflicts. On the other, their political and social resources enable them to interact with IA officials effectively.

Water guards are supposed to allocate water based upon the irrigation plan. In reality, however, they have a relatively high degree of autonomy in making necessary adjustments. Their high degree of autonomy generally comes from two sources. The first is their seniority in the local community. The water guards are usually local farmers. Obviously, as they are members of the local community, any acts that are perceived by farmers as unfair might place them under pressure of social ostracism. Second, a majority of the water guards are elderly men who have been serving as water guards for many years. As both IA officials and farmers are well aware, the task of allocating the water is not easy by any means. One has to know the physical as well as social landscapes really well to carry out the task effectively. Such knowledge cannot be taught but has to be learned by doing. The experience and local knowledge of water guards allows them to establish authority on matters concerning water allocation, and to gain confidence from farmers.

Since the experience and local knowledge is highly specific, water guards cannot be easily replaced. As a result, threatening to quit becomes an effective leverage for the water guards to deal with farmers and IA officials. Such a threat is made even more credible by the low salary received by the guards. Although the salary varies across different IGs, it is normally about NT 400-500 per day. For many water guards, giving up such a small amount of money, if necessary, is not a hard choice to make. From the perspective of many irrigation officials and farmers, the job of the water guards is more like a community service than a way of earning money. By taking up the job, the water guards actually are doing the community a big favor. So unlike patrollers in many irrigation systems in South Asia who command no respect either from their superiors or from farmers, water guards in Taiwan are seen as individuals who not only know irrigation and the local situation well, but are also willing to contribute to the local community.

6. Interaction between IA Officials and Farmers

Discussion in the last section suggests that farmers and IA officials are able to develop complementary relationships in water delivery. While it is generally agreed that such complementary relationships are embedded in the broader pattern of cooperative relationships, how such a pattern of relationships is maintained is subject to less agreement. Earlier research argued that elections and water fee payments are the two major mechanisms that sustain the cooperative relationships. Recent research disputed the importance of these mechanisms and focused on the more subtle means that farmers use to hold IA officials accountable, such as signaling their dissatisfaction by delaying payments and social ostracism.

(a) Elections, Water Fees, and Social Embeddedness

Interviews with officials and farmers indicate that the elected farmer representatives have never played an important role in controlling the IA. These representatives might give some suggestions concerning the budget of the IA at the annual meeting, or stop by the headquarters once in a while to convey farmers' concerns, and that is the extent of their involvement. Given that farmers in Taiwan are generally subservient and many of them are part-time farmers, it is not surprising that the representatives did not exercise effective control over the IA. More important, the election of farmer representatives was more of an extension of local politics than irrigation politics per se. The representatives were unlikely to pay as much attention to irrigation as warranted.

To most IA officials and farmers, water fees were similar to taxes that farmers had to pay. The government was effective in enforcing fee payment. Defaults in water fee payments happened from time to time, but in most of these instances, it was only because farmers did not receive water at all. Withholding payment of water fees was rarely used by the farmers as leverage to have their voices heard. In fact, the water fees have long ceased to be essential to the survival of the IAs. In most IAs, the water fees are not even enough to pay for the salaries of the IA officials. That the central government has been paying water fees on the farmers' behalf since the early 1990s further breaks the link between the water fee payments and control by farmers.

While these formal mechanisms might not have carried the control functions that they were supposed to, they were not totally irrelevant. First of all, as some officials and farmers eagerly pointed out, the process of collecting water fees provided opportunities for officials to talk to farmers. These conversations were not necessarily about irrigation only, but also issues concerning the local community. In other words, these conversations were not formal communication between officials and farmers, but casual discussions between acquaintances. Such conversations might not help improve irrigation management directly, but they allow farmers and officials to gain a better understanding of each other's views.

Second, the officials at the working stations were responsible for collecting water fees. Given the small size of the station staff, the help from the IG leaders was extremely important.[14] As mentioned earlier, the IG leaders are mostly local notables who are respected by the local community; many of them are also representatives to various local government functionaries. Their help could make the process of water fee collection much easier and create incentives for the officials at the local level to maintain a close relationship with the IG leaders. To a large extent, it was just such a close relationship between the working station staff and the IG leaders that mediated the interaction between the IAs and farmers.

Third, although the farmer representatives did not perform the control functions that they were supposed to, their existence was essential to constituting the farmers' perception of their relationship with the IA. As long as farmers saw their representatives in place to supervise the IA, they felt it was legitimate to speak out when they faced problems. According to IA officials, a result of the recent reform that replaced the elected representatives with appointed committee members has been a decrease in the number of farmers' complaints. While such a decrease could be due to a better job done by the appointed members, it could also be due to a change in the farmers' perception on their relationship with the IAs.

Recent research has argued that the embeddedness of local IA officials in the local community is a more important reason for the close relationship between officials and farmers. Irrigation officials are frequently residents of the local community. Their daily interactions with local people in the community can provide them with information on different issues concerning irrigation as well as the community. Since they are part of the community, any wrongdoing on their part that causes harm to the local community could put them under much social pressure or even social ostracism. Moreover, irrigation officials serving at the working stations tend to serve in particular working stations for a long period of time. Knowing that they will have to deal with the same group of local farmers for a long time makes building a good relationship with them a good strategy.

(b) Local Politics and Social Embeddedness

While IA staffs, farmers, and officials at the central government are fond of referring to the IAs as organizations owned by, and representing, farmers and local communities, they generally take a dim view of local politics and tend to downplay its importance in the operation of the IAs. The ambiguous attitude toward local politics is reflected in the continual debate on the importance of elections, compared with control and guidance from the central government, in the operation of the IAs. There is no doubt that some IA officials play an active role in the elections of local public offices, and that local factions are to a certain extent involved in the elections of IA offices. To examine the effects of activities on the IAs, however, requires a detailed analysis of Taiwan's local politics, which is beyond the scope of this essay. Several observations and conjectures on the way that local politics plays out, however, might shed light on how cooperative relationships between farmers and officials are sustained.

Many researchers and government officials have tended to understand the linkage between local politics and the IAs by focusing on the formal arenas such as the election of the farmer representatives and the IA chairman. They have thus often come to the conclusion that, notwithstanding the potential for rent-seeking activities, local politics has only minimal direct effects on the IAs' day-to-day operations. What has not been given as much attention is the possibility that local politics might be instrumental in sustaining, if not facilitating, the embeddedness of the IAs in the local community. Space constraints, however, do not allow a detailed discussion of local politics in the country.[15]

To understand how the embeddedness works out, however, several features of Taiwan's local factional politics, as laid out by Bosco (1992), might be relevant: (1) In all local elections, factions provide the core of support to particular candidates. On average about two-thirds of the voters are estimated to be divided between two factions and the remaining one-third are the free voters to whom the factions try to appeal. (2) Taiwan's local factions are held together not by common ideology or class but by social ties such as kinship, patron-client relations, friendship, etc. They arose because although power and authority are concentrated in the hands of the Kuomintang (KMT) in which mainlanders dominate, the central authorities have to deal with local Taiwanese politicians in order to keep local order. (3) Factions are usually visible only during elections. Outside of elections, most villagers maintain social relationships without consideration for faction.

The existence of local political factions, to a certain extent, provides essential glue to the rural society where the multitude of small farmers could have made any organizing efforts difficult. The competition among the factions, with their emphasis on bringing favors to constituents as an appeal to voters, can bring the farmers' attention to public interests that pertain to their well-being. The competition, then, serves an interest-articulation purpose in a political system where, until the last several years, there was only one political party.[16] Moreover, the factions that do not control the IAs have the incentive to monitor the ones who do. This creates a system of checks and balances in the operation of the IAs. As the factions usually overlap with various social ties at different levels, such a checks-and-balances mechanism has a rather comprehensive scope. It is the mutual reinforcement between local factions and social ties that makes embeddedness possible.

The competition between factions does not necessarily operate in a benign way. Yet the fluid structure of factions, the limited scope of factional activities, the need to appeal to the middle votes, and the overlap between factions and various social ties, all prevent the competition from getting out of hand. Furthermore, in maneuvering to keep factions under control, the ruling KMT has always tried to keep the balance between rival factions, and to confine their activities to the local level. By doing so, KMT government not only gears the operation of factional activities toward enhancing local governance, but also uses factions to help it control the countryside in which mainlanders have few social or political ties.

7. The Role of the Central Government in Irrigation Governance

Political economists that are interested in the developmental state of Taiwan and other East Asian newly industrializing countries (NICs) often wonder at the seemingly paradoxical coexistence of an authoritarian state on the one hand, and space for self-organized activities in the society on the other. An important question, then, is what is the role of the central government in creating, or sustaining, the patterns of relationships described above. In particular, how do the actions of the government allow, or encourage, irrigation officials to make adjustments and to acquiesce to some self-organized activities by farmers?

(a) Government as Epistemic Leader

The central government plays an important role in setting the tone of what irrigation management is supposed to be and how it should be conducted. By advocating ideas such as "serving the farmers comes first," the government serves as an epistemic leader. The government not only promulgates ideas but actively carries out activities that promote and sustain them. For example, model IG leaders are selected and honored by the president of Taiwan every year; there is also an irrigation festival every year that highlights the importance of irrigation.

These ideas are extremely important in the governance of irrigation in Taiwan. First, they help constitute motivations faced by officials and farmers. A chance at being honored by the president, for example, has been a primary motivating force for many IG leaders to take up their jobs. Second, these ideas constitute the major part of the conceptualization of farmer-IA relationships commonly shared by farmers and officials. The way individuals see the game significantly affects how they are to play the game. Third, the activities that enhance these ideas can serve to signal the government's commitment to irrigation development that is essential to backing the bargaining power of farmers vis-à-vis IA officials.

(b) Government as Arbiter

The shadow of the government also poses the fundamental constraints within which IA officials and farmers interact. Maintaining effective coproductive relationships requires a certain degree of reciprocity between officials and farmers. The sustenance of reciprocity involves, among other things, a relatively symmetric relationship, complementarity, and credibility. Government actions might help create and sustain these elements.

The farmers' contribution to operating and maintaining field-level channels is substantial. IAs have neither the necessary resources nor the capability to micromanage water allocation and maintain farm-ditches. How much and how well farmers organize themselves and mobilize adequate resources for operation and maintenance affects the overall performance of irrigation systems. Note that those ultimately affected most by the overall performance are farmers themselves. IA officials have few intrinsic incentives to see to it that a certain level of performance is attained. Under such a situation, the interests of officials and farmers are in an asymmetric relationship.

Such asymmetry can be somewhat ameliorated if payoffs to officials are linked to the performance of the irrigation systems. If the government, which is able to reward and punish the IA, is committed to satisfying the irrigation needs of farmers, farmers' complaints represent a credible threat to IA officials. The dynamic of the situation changes in that the contributions of farmers are essential for officials to get their jobs done. It implies not only that officials would be more sensitive to farmers' needs, but that fostering the self-organization of farmers is also in the interests of the officials. Government commitment, in other words, reduces the asymmetry on the one hand, and turns farmers self-organization into a complementary activity on the other.

(c) Government as a Source of Finance

Another of the central government's roles is as the major source of financial resources for the IAs. This was the case even before the government started paying water fees on behalf of farmers in the 1990s. The amount of financial support and the way that it is channeled to the IAs affect the capability as well as the management practices of the IAs.

The amount of financial support poses a constraint with which the IAs have to cope. Before the reform in recent years, for example, the government mainly provided financial support to engineering work, but not to the operation of the systems. It created a need for IAs to try to extract resources from farmers for operation and maintenance activities. Such a need may have had positive effects on the overall provision of irrigation services, for officials had incentives to maintain good relationships with farmers to make sure that the farmers' contribution was forthcoming.

As the IAs are receiving a large amount of financial support from the government, their relations with the government have been a contentious issue. The core concern is that while the IAs are spending government money, government control is minimal. How to make sure that the IAs spend the money in a responsible manner has become an important concern. Government subsidies, however, do not necessarily imply direct government control. While the government's control at the constitutional level is significant, its involvement in collective-choice rules is minimal. This is where the IAs can exercise their autonomy in deciding how they operate, and how to raise and spend their money. The reason for the government's restraint from intervening too much at this level is unclear. Given that the government has never hesitated to change the structure of the IAs when necessary, it is unlikely that the government avoids intervening simply to uphold local democracy. A more plausible reason is that the government finds itself incapable of micromanaging. But no matter what the reasons are, the government's restraint allows the IAs to formulate policies and management practices that fit local situations.

8. Conclusion: Institutional Design and Irrigation Governance

The provision and production of many public goods and services involve the joint effort of government officials and citizen-users. This essay examines the successful experience of irrigation governance and management in Taiwan as a way of understanding how joint efforts can be established and sustained through institutional arrangements. Cognizant of a large array of institutions involved, I have focused in this essay on the institutional design and operation of irrigation associations (IAs) in Taiwan, and on the mechanisms by which institutions create incentives to irrigation officials to do a conscientious job and to relate their efforts to farmers.

Several features of the institutional design of IAs are instrumental in coping with these problems. One of them is the multiple arenas at different levels of the IAs in which farmers can work things out, communicate with one another, and resolve conflicts. These arenas provide public space where the "benign" activities can be played out. Moreover, to reduce the cost of participation to farmers and the potential for conflicts due to excessive participation, the scope of farmers' participation is carefully defined. While generally farmers' participation is encouraged, conducting the "technical" tasks such as formulating water plans and conducting major maintenance work is the responsibility of the IAs. Note that these "technical" tasks often set the parameters within which the farmers' participation operates. For instance, while farmers have much leverage in deciding water allocation within an irrigation block, the amounts of water allocated to particular blocks are determined by the IAs. The effectiveness of the IAs in conducting these "technical" tasks can reduce the farmers' need for active participation. Furthermore, monitoring mechanisms are in place that reduce the possibility of rent-seeking activities. For instance, while IGs might decide on what maintenance works are to be done, the signature of the working station chief is required for payments made to the contractors, even though the farmers raise the money themselves.

Various rules are in place that enhance the complementarity of interests between individuals. At the most general level is the relationship between the IAs and farmers. Institutional arrangements, such as farmer representatives, the payment of water fees, and the status of IAs as juristic entities formed and owned by farmer members, all help create and sustain a conceptualization that emphasizes the mutually dependent relationship between the IAs and the farmers. Such conceptualization provides the basis upon which the officials and farmers develop productive relationships.

A high degree of complementarity of interests can also be found among the IA officials. The prevalence of lifetime careers, as a result of the IAs personnel system, for example, aligns the careers (not only jobs) of the officials with the fate of the association as a whole. Stable membership of the organization allows the officials to adopt a longer time horizon in their relationships with each other. The resultant low discount rates of officials are more conducive to their investing time and effort in developing productive relationships with each other. Such an awareness of mutual dependence and low discount rates are further reinforced by the signaling of the IA that emphasizes the close relationship between the officials and the association. The practice of delivering an annual bonus is one of the ways by which the IAs signal their commitment and goodwill to their staffs. Although, some IAs are currently facing serious financial problems, they still manage to deliver the bonus. The emphasis on mutual interests and long-term cooperation is consistent with the observation of prior research that many incentives in the IAs are designed to be "group-oriented" (Wade 1982, 1987).

Like irrigation bureaucracies in other Asian countries, authority is an essential component in the institutional design of the IAs. Through a structure of hierarchy, and also a tight control process in irrigation planning, authority is used rather extensively in the operation of the bureaucracy as well as in the process of water delivery. While authority might enhance coordination, reduce transaction costs associated with negotiating the terms of cooperation in spot markets, and extract contributions from individuals by metering and sanctioning (Coase 1937; Alchian and Demsetz 1972; Williamson 1985), it comes with many potential disadvantages (e.g., Lindblom 1977; V. Ostrom 1989; Tullock 1987; Nicholson 1994). Among these potential disadvantages the most serious is the asymmetries of interests and power between those who exercise authority and who are supposed to obey. Such asymmetries potentially provide opportunities and incentives for the abuse of authority, and might also hinder communication and learning. More important, they dampen the incentives of those in the subordinate position.

What is peculiar about the institutional design of the IAs in Taiwan is its ability to cope with the possible asymmetries brought by the use of authority. First, authority is closely aligned with responsibility. For instance, while a working station chief has much authority in handling water allocation within the areas under his jurisdiction, he is also responsible for what might happen in the areas. Saying that the alignment of authority and responsibility is important is a truism, is it not a major design principle of irrigation bureaucracies in many other countries? What makes the Taiwanese case different, however, is that the alignment is supported not simply by bureaucratic rules but also by norms and social sanctions. As mentioned earlier, while a working station official has much discretion in managing the irrigated areas assigned to him, he is likely to be subject to much pressure from colleagues if his areas are facing problems persistently. Similarly, while the working station has a relatively high degree of discretion in handling water delivery and irrigation maintenance, the lengthy stay of station officials in the local community ensures that they will be held responsible for their actions.

Second, institutions are designed so that authority is checked and balanced. Perhaps the most obvious check-and-balance designs can be found in the personnel system. The loose alignment between the rank system and the position system, and the frequent reshuffling of leadership positions, make it less likely that those in leadership positions will abuse their authority. Less conspicuous designs involve the establishment of symbiotic relationships among individuals in which each possesses resources that are essential to the well-being of the others. For example, while the working station staff is evaluated by whether irrigation in the areas assigned to them is well managed, the staff alone usually does not have adequate resources to handle water delivery and system maintenance. Farmers' contributions are essential to the staff to do the job. It is especially the case in systems where rotation irrigation is seriously practiced.

Another major characteristic of the institutional design of the IAs is the various domains of autonomy. Such autonomy is essential for individuals at different levels to exercise their problem-solving capabilities. Within the IA, for example, the working stations are given the liberty of working out arrangements of water delivery and distribution with local farmers. At the field level, the irrigation groups (IGs) also retain a certain level of autonomy in deciding how water delivery is conducted within irrigation blocks. In systems where rotation irrigation is seriously practiced and, hence, farmers' efforts are even more essential, the IGs are given the liberty of deciding how to finance the operation and maintenance activities at the local level. In terms of water delivery, perhaps the most important autonomy is that given to the water guards. As noted by prior researchers, the water guards, rather than the working station staff, are the ones who make decisions about, and actually conduct, the allocation of water to farmers' fields (Moore 1983). The water guards' autonomy is the lubricant between the rigid irrigation plans and the diverse local environments.

The domains of autonomy allow individuals in different settings to develop (informal) rules to cope with various problems that they might face. Autonomy, however, is not equivalent to a hands-off mode of management.

Instead, the exercise of autonomy at different domains is supported and facilitated by various mechanisms. First, the boundary of the autonomy is clearly understood. The autonomy of units at different levels within the IAs is based upon the bureaucratic principle of the vertical division of labor; the autonomy of IGs from the IAs, on the other hand, is supported by the understanding, strongly fostered by the national government, that emphasizes the dominant position of farmers vis-à-vis the IAs. Second, the autonomy at lower levels is nested within institutions at higher levels, that is, institutions at higher levels can serve various supportive functions. Prior research, for example, notes that the operation of the IAs, or more generally of irrigation management, is in a default upward mode, in which those problems which cannot be handled effectively at the lower level are transmitted to the next higher level (Levine 1978b; Moore 1983). Thus, while individuals at different levels are given opportunities to exercise problem-solving capabilities, they are provided with backup by higher levels.

In sum, Taiwan's Irrigation Associations are not only examples of efficient water delivery, they also illustrate a number of interesting features of organizational design that should have broad relevance to other public sector organizations. In this analysis of the IAs, I identified several important principles for designing effective institutions. In particular, I highlighted the problems of team production and coproduction involved in irrigation management and analyzed how these problems can be coped with by various institutional mechanisms. As many goods and services provided or produced in the public sector share similar characteristics of irrigation systems, lessons learned from the experience of irrigation management in Taiwan can be drawn upon to inform institutional reforms in other public sector contexts.

NOTES

1. My observations during my fieldtrips to Taiwan in 1993 and 1994 were largely consistent with what had been said about the good working order of water delivery and well-maintained infrastructures in irrigation systems in the country.

2. Earlier research has suggested that the high potentials of irrigation might be a reason why the governments in Taiwan, the colonial government before 1945 and the Nationalist government afterward, have made significant investments in irrigation development. It might also explain why irrigation institutions and management procedures have been developed into a high level of sophistication (Levine 1977, 1978a, b).

3. For more detailed discussion of the Land Reform in Taiwan, see Kuo, Ranis, and Fei 1981; Kuo 1983; Gold 1986.

4. Note that, unlike in irrigation agencies in many South Asian countries such as India and Nepal, the construction of irrigation facilities is not a responsibility of the IAs. The limited scope of responsibilities of the IAs might avoid the tension between

the engineering-oriented function of construction, and the management-oriented function of operation and maintenance often observed in South Asian irrigation bureaucracy (Wade 1987; Chambers 1988).

5. Only IAs with a large service area have the management stations. On smaller IAs, the working stations report to the headquarters directly.

6. The county or city governments, for example, can determine the amount of water earmarked for domestic uses. As irrigation is given relatively low priority in water uses, IAs frequently have to adjust their irrigation plans to cope with the demands from these governments.

7. In this study, the term *irrigation agency* is used to denote an aggregate of irrigation staff who are given a set of tasks pertaining to the governance and management of irrigation systems. The term *organization* is used to refer not to the "formal" structures of an agency, but to the patterns of actions and interactions of individuals within an agency as a result of an organizing process, which is defined as changing the situation from one in which individuals act independently to one in which they act in a coordinated manner in an effort to accomplish collective benefits (E. Ostrom 1990; Miller 1992).

8. A typical IA includes: an engineering division, a management division, a finance division, an administrative division, an accounting division, a personnel division, and a security division.

9. When I mentioned to senior IA officials during interviews that many observers had found rather equitable patterns of relationships among IA officials, the officials were eager to explain to me, somewhat apologetically, why such a "leakage of authority" had happened. To them, the IA should operate like a bureaucracy in which authority is respected. The equitable relationships were viewed very negatively.

10. Although there are female staff working in the IAs, and some of them are in leadership positions, the posts of working station chief are almost always taken by a male staff member. For simplification, I use *he* to refer to a working station chief in this study.

11. The irrigated area managed by the Chianan IA is in the western part of Taiwan, located within Chiayi City, Chiayi County, Tainan City, and Tainan County. As of 1994, the total irrigated area is about 78,113 hectares. The climate of the area is subtropical with an average temperature of 21-24 degrees Celsius and annual average rainfall of 1,600 mm.

About 80 percent of the rainfall occurs in the wet season from May to September. Paddy rice and sugarcane are the two major crops in the area.

The major source of water is from reservoirs. There are a total of 33 reservoirs of various sizes. The largest are the Tsengwen and Wushantou reservoirs that provide water to a service area of more than 57,000 hectares. Besides reservoirs, surface water from rivers, springs, and urban sewage systems are other major sources of water. Generally speaking, cultivated lands located in the Chiayi area rely mainly on surface water, whereas those in the Tainan area rely on reservoirs. While the construction of the large-scale reservoirs has significantly expanded the area of cultivation, water is still so scarce that crop rotation is practiced in most of the Tainan area. In addition, rotation irrigation is encouraged at the field level. Although rotation irrigation is supposedly practiced in most of the irrigated lands in the Chianan area, it is seriously practiced only in the Tainan areas where reservoirs are the major source of irrigation water.

The Chianan IA is the largest IA in Taiwan in terms of the size of irrigated area, budget size, and the number of officials. As of 1993, the Chianan IA had 678 employees, more than 20 percent of the total number of IA officials in Taiwan. About 30 percent of the staff work at the headquarters, and the other 70 percent at the field offices. Chianan IA is said to be one of the best managed IAs in Taiwan.

12. Of the total irrigated area of 78,113 hectares the distribution of irrigated areas under various patterns of cropping is as follows: three years-two crops district: 36,534 hectares; double rice crop district: 23,276 hectares; single rice crop district: 9,515; simple rotation district: 360 hectares; and sugarcane district: 8,428 hectares.

13. Although women actively participate in agricultural activities in many places in Taiwan, major decisions in a farming household related to irrigation are usually made by the head of the household, who is almost always a man. As a result, irrigation group leaders are almost always men. In this essay I use *he* to refer to an irrigation group leader.

14. In some areas in the Pingtung IA where abundant underground water makes irrigation organization less necessary, the only function of the irrigation groups is to help the IA collect irrigation fees.

15. For a more detailed discussion of local politics in Taiwan, see Bosco 1992; Stavis 1994; and Gallin 1966.

16. Presently the chairmen of all 17 IAs in Taiwan are members of the KMT.

REFERENCES

Abel, Martin E. (1975) "Irrigation systems in Taiwan: Management of a decentralized public enterprise." Development of Agricultural and Applied Economics, Staff Paper. Minneapolis: University of Minnesota.

Alchian, Armen A., and Harold Demsetz (1972) "Production, information and economic organization." *American Economic Review* 62, no. 5: 777–95.

Ambler, John S. (1993) "Performance indicators: A case of a newly developed FMIS in Bali, Indonesia." In Shaul Manor and Jorge Chambouleyron (eds.), *Performance Measurement in Farmer-Managed Irrigation Systems: Proceedings of an International Workshop of the Former-Managed Irrigation Systems Network*, 3–12. Colombo, Sri Lanka: International Irrigation Management Institute.

Ascher, William, and Robert Healy (1990) *Natural Resource Policy Making in Developing Countries*. Durham, NC: Duke University Press.

Bosco, Joseph (1992) "Taiwan factions: Guanxi, patronage, and the state in local politics." *Ethnology* 31, no. 2: 157–83.

Bottrall, Anthony F. (1977) "Evolution of Irrigation Associations in Taiwan." *Agricultural Administration* 4:245–50.

—— (1981) "Comparative study of the management and organization of irrigation projects." World Bank Working Paper, No. 458. Washington, DC: World Bank.

Chambers, Robert (1988) *Managing Canal Irrigation: Practical Analysis from South Asia*. Cambridge, MA: Cambridge University Press.

Chianan Irrigation Association (n.d.) *Brief Introduction of Chianan I.A.* Tainan: Chianan Irrigation Association. (In Chinese.)

—— (1994) *Statistical Data of the Chianan I.A., 1993*. Tainan: Chianan Irrigation Association. (In Chinese.)

Coase, Ronald H. (1937) "The nature of the firm." *Economica* 4:386–405.

Council of Agriculture (1989) *Report on the Improvement of Irrigation Associations.* Taipei: Council of Agriculture, Executive Yuan, Republic of China.

——— (1993) *Basic Agricultural Statistics, Republic of China.* Taipei: Council of Agriculture, Executive Yuan, Republic of China.

Council for Economic Planning and Development (1994) *Taiwan Statistical Data Book 1994.* Taipei: Council for Economic Planning and Development, R.O.C.

Coward, E. Walter, Jr., and Gilbert Levine (1987) "Studies of farmer-managed irrigation systems: Ten years of cumulative knowledge and changing research priorities." In IIMI/WECS/Government of Nepal (ed.), *Public Intervention in Farmer-Managed Irrigation Systems,* 1–31. Colombo, Sri Lanka: International Irrigation Management Institute.

Freeman, David M. (1990) "Designing local irrigation organizations for linking water demand with supply." In R. K. Sampath and Robert A. Young (ed.), *Social, Economic, and Institutional Issues in Third World Irrigation Management,* 111–40. Boulder, CO: Westview Press.

Gallin, Bernard (1966) *Hsin Hsing, Taiwan: A Chinese Village in Changes.* Berkeley: University of California Press.

Gardner, Roy, Elinor Ostrom, and James Walker (1990) "The nature of common-pool resource problems." *Rationality and Society* 2, no. 3 (July): 335–58.

Gold, Thomas (1986) *State and Society in the Taiwan Miracle.* Armonk, NY: M. E. Sharpe.

Israel, Arturo (1992) *Issues for Infrastructure Management in the 1990s.* Washington, DC: World Bank.

Kessides, Christine (1993) *Institutional Options for the Provision of Infrastructure.* Washington, DC: World Bank.

Kuo, Ching Ho (1986) "Irrigation management in Taiwan, ROC." Working Paper. Taipei: Council of Agriculture, Executive Yuan.

Kuo, Shirley W. Y. (1983) *The Taiwan Economy in Transition.* Boulder, CO: Westview Press.

Kuo, Shirley W. Y., Gustav Ranis, and John C. H. Fei (1981) *The Taiwan Success Story: Rapid Growth with improved Distribution in the Republic of China, 1952–1979.* Boulder, CO: Westview Press.

Lachmann, Ludwig M. (1978) *Capital and Its Structure.* Kansas City: Sheed Andrews and McMeel.

Lam, Wai Fung (1998) *Governing Irrigation Systems in Nepal: Institutions, Infrastructure, and Collective Action.* Oakland, CA: ICS Press.

Lam, Wai Fung, Myungsuk Lee, and Elinor Ostrom (1997) "The institutional analysis and development framework: Application to irrigation policy in Nepal." In Derick W. Brinkerhoff (ed.), *Policy Studies and Developing Nations: An Institutional and Implementation Focus,* vol. 5, 53–85. Greenwich, CT: JAI Press.

Levine, Gilbert (1977) "Management components in irrigation system design and operation." *Agricultural Administration* 4 :37–48.

——— (1978a) "Notes on the experience with the reorganization of irrigation associations in Taiwan." MS, Cornell University.

——— (1978b) "Irrigation association response to severe water shortage—The case of the Yun-Lin Irrigation Association, Taiwan." MS, Cornell University.

Lindblom, Charles E. (1977) *Politics and Market.* New York: Basic Books.

Miller, Gary J. (1992) *Managerial Dilemmas: The Political Economy of Hierarchy.* Cambridge: Cambridge University Press.

Moe, Terry M. (1990) "Political institutions: The neglected side of the story." *Journal of Law, Economics, and Organization*, special issue, 6:213–53.

Moore, M. P. (1983) "Irrigation management in Taiwan." MS, Institute of Development Studies.

———— (1989) "The fruits and fallacies of neoliberalism: The case of irrigation policy." *World Development* 17, no. 11: 1733–50.

———— (1993) "Economic structure and the politics of sectoral bias: East Asian and other cases." *Journal of Development Studies* 29, no. 4: 79–128.

Nicholson, Norman K. (1994) "Advantages and disadvantages of hierarchy: Exploring the limits of bureaucratic reorientation and reform." In Norman Uphoff (ed.), *Puzzles of Productivity in Public Organizations*, 167–97. San Francisco: ICS Press.

Ostrom, Elinor (1990) *Governing the Commons: The Evolution of Institutions for Collective Action.* New York: Cambridge University Press.

———— (1992) *Crafting Institutions for Self-Governing Irrigation Systems.* San Francisco: ICS Press.

———— (1993) "Institutional arrangements and the commons dilemma." In Vincent Ostrom, David Feeny, and Hartmut Picht (eds.), *Rethinking Institutional Analysis and Development: Issues, Alternatives, and Choices*, 101–39. San Francisco: ICS Press.

Ostrom, Elinor, Larry Schroeder, and Susan Wynne (1993) *Institutional Incentives and Sustainable Development: Infrastructure Policies in Perspective.* Boulder, CO: Westview Press.

Ostrom, Vincent (1989) *The Intellectual Crisis in American Public Administration*, 2d ed. Tuscaloosa: University of Alabama Press.

Parks, Roger B., Paula C., Baker, Larry L. Kiser, Ronald Oakerson, Elinor Ostrom, Vincent Ostrom, Stephen L. Percy, Martha B. Vandivort, Gordon P. Whitaker, and Rick Wilson (1982) "Coproduction of Public Services." In Richard C. Rich (ed.), *Analyzing Urban-Service Distributions*, 185–99. Lexington, MA: Lexington Books. Alternative version reprinted in M. D. McGinnis, ed. *Polycentricity and Local Public Economies* (Ann Arbor: University of Michigan Press, 1999).

Pingtung Irrigation Association (n.d.) *Brief Introduction to Pingtung Irrigation Association.* Pingtung: Pingtung Irrigation Association. (In Chinese.)

Rabushka, Alvin (1987) *The New China: Comparative Economic Development in Mainland China, Taiwan and Hong Kong.* Boulder, CO: Westview Press.

Speare, Alden, Jr. (1992) "Taiwan's rural populace: Brought in or left out of the economic miracle?" In Dennis Fred Simon and Michael Y. M. Kau (eds.), *Taiwan: Beyond the Economic Miracle*, 211–33. Armonk, NY: M. E. Sharpe.

Stavis, B. (1994) *Rural Local Governance and Agricultural Development in Taiwan.* Ithaca, NY: Cornell University.

Taiwan Joint Irrigation Association (1992) *Introduction to Water Conservancy and Irrigation in Taiwan, Republic of China.* Taipei: Taiwan Joint Irrigation Association, R.O.C.

Tang, Shui-Yan (1992) *Institutions and Collective Action: Self-Governance in Irrigation.* San Francisco: ICS Press.

Taoyuan Irrigation Association (n.d.) *Brief Introduction to Taoyuan Irrigation Association.* Taoyuan: Taoyuan Irrigation Association. (In Chinese.)

Tendler, Judith, and Sara Freedheim (1994) "Trust in a rent-seeking world: Health and government transformed in Northeast Brazil." *World Development* 22, no. 12: 1771–91.

Tullock, Gordon (1987) *The Politics of Bureaucracy.* Lanham, MD: University Press of America.

Uphoff, Norman, ed. (1994) *Puzzles of Productivity in Public Organizations.* San Francisco: ICS Press.

VanderMeer, Canute (1971) "Water thievery in a rice irrigation system in Taiwan." *Annals of the Association of American Geographers* 61:156–79.

Wade, Robert (1982) *Irrigation and Agricultural Politics in South Korea.* Boulder, CO: Westview Press.

——— (1987) "Managing water managers: Deterring expropriation or equity as a control mechanism." In W. R. Jordan (ed.), *Water and Water Policy in World Food Supplies,* 177–83. College Station, TX: Texas A & M University Press.

——— (1988) "Management of irrigation systems: How to evoke trust and avoid prisoners' dilemma." *World Development* 16, no. 4: 489–500.

Wade, Robert, and David Seckler (1990) "Priority issues in the management of irrigation systems." In R. K. Sampath and Robert A. Young (eds.), *Social, Economic, and Institutional Issues in Third World Irrigation Management,* 13–30. Boulder, CO: Westview Press.

Wen, Li-Jen (1981) "Improvement of irrigation systems and water management in Taiwan." Proceedings of the 11th Congress on Irrigation and Drainage, question 36, pt. 1, 117–42. New Delhi: ICID.

——— (1991) *Reorganization of Irrigation Associations for Irrigation and Drainage Systems Management in Taiwan R.O.C.* Taipei: Council of Agriculture, Executive Yuan.

Williams, Jack F. (1994) "Vulnerability and change in Taiwan's agriculture." In Murray A. Rubinstein (ed.), *The Other Taiwan: 1945 to the Present,* 215–33. Armonk, NY: M. E. Sharpe.

Williamson, Oliver E. (1985) *The Economic Institutions of Capitalism.* New York: Free Press.

World Bank (1994) *World Development Report.* New York: Oxford University Press.

Wu, Chian Min (n.d.) *Management of Water Resources in an Island Nation: The Taiwan Experience.* Taipei: Water Resources Planning Commission MOEA.

Yunlin Irrigation Association (1990) *Brief Introduction to Yun-Lin Irrigation Association.* Touliu: Yunlin Irrigation Association. (In Chinese.)

CHAPTER 14

Informal Credit Markets and Economic Development in Taiwan

Shui-Yan Tang

1. Introduction

Recent debates about the East Asian Newly Industrialized Countries (NICs) center around the relative importance of state guidance versus market mechanisms in economic development. An emerging theme from these debates is that governments in these countries have been actively involved in governing and directing markets and, by so doing, have contributed to their rapid economic growth (Amsden 1989; Islam 1992; Wade 1990). The achievement of these NIC governments contrasts with the failure of many Latin American governments whose economic policies were strongly influenced by rent-seeking activities of various interest groups (Haggard 1990; Gereffi and Wyman 1990). A major focus of the recent literature has been to examine the institutional, political, and historical factors that enabled and motivated government leaders in the East Asian NICs to adopt measures that enhanced capital accumulation, efficient resource allocation, and productivity change (Amsden 1994; World Bank 1993).

While much of this literature focuses on the part of an economy that is directly regulated by government legislation and policies, relatively little of it systematically examines the informal sector's contributions to the development process.[1] Such neglect contradicts conventional wisdom about the region. In a recent issue of *The Economist*, for example, a Taiwanese banker

Originally published in *World Development* 23, no. 5 (1995): 845–55. Reprinted by permission of Elsevier Science and the author.

Author's note: Numerous individuals and organizations have helped me in preparing this essay. While it is impossible to mention all their names here, I wish to acknowledge, in particular, the help by Vivian Chen, Anita Chou, Richard Chou, Li-Chun Chiang, Jen-Hui Hsu, Jong-Huh Huang, Thomas Huang, Jia-Dong Shea and Yung-Nane Yang. Gerald Caiden, Ami Doshi, Don Fuller, Peter Robertson, Robert Stallings, and two anonymous reviewers provided useful comments on an earlier version, which was presented at the Workshop on the 20th Anniversary of the Workshop in Political Theory and Policy Analysis, Bloomington, Indiana, June 1994. Financial support from the Pacific Cultural Foundation is gratefully acknowledged.

was quoted as saying that "Taiwan's economic miracle is built on illegal businesses."[2] One form of such "illegal" or "extra-legal" businesses is Taiwan's informal credit markets, which are estimated to have provided more than one-third of the total amount of loans to private enterprises in the country. Is there any validity to the conventional wisdom about the informal sector? If so, how can it be reconciled with scholarly concentration on formal political and economic institutions?

Although not prominently featured in the East Asian development literature, the informal sector has recently gained increased recognition in the general literature on development (Chickering and Salahdine 1991; Jenkins 1988; Roemer and Jones 1991). Among the most prominent is de Soto's *The Other Path* (1989), in which he argued that numerous business transactions in Peru had been conducted outside the formal legal framework. The informal sector played an important role in supporting a wide variety of economic activities, including housing, commerce, transport, and industrial production. Some 39% of the 1984 GDP in Peru was produced and 61% of all work hours were spent in the informal sector (de Soto 1988). The informal sector has become an important source of entrepreneurship in Peru. Its pervasiveness, according to de Soto, had mostly resulted from the inefficiency of the larger legal and political institutions. The informal sector had compensated for the inadequacy and restrictiveness of the formal sector.

The Peruvian experience poses an interesting question about the role of the informal sector in East Asian development. Since government institutions and policies in the East Asian NICs are considered by many scholars as relatively efficient and supportive of productive business transactions, is the sizable informal sector in these countries performing essential functions that cannot be adequately handled through formal institutional channels? Or are some aspects of the formal institutions in these countries less efficient than are generally assumed, and, as a result, the informal sector plays an important role in compensating for the formal sector's inadequacy? This essay examines some of these issues by studying Taiwan's informal credit markets whose sizes and operations are relatively well documented, especially in Chinese sources.[3] Defined as credit transactions that operate outside government control and regulation, as in contrast to the regulated money market and the formal banking system, informal credit markets exist in various forms—rotating credit associations, trade credit, indigenous banking, etc. The essay first explores several general issues about the economic role of informal credit markets in developing countries. Then it looks closer at some salient features of the informal credit markets in Taiwan and how they are affected by various government regulations and policies. It concludes by discussing the theoretical and practical implications of Taiwan's experience.

2. The Economic Role of Informal Credit Markets

A major economic problem in developing countries is financial intermediation—the mobilization of capital from one group (savers/lenders) and its simultaneous allocation to meet the needs of another group (borrowers/ entrepreneurs) (Christensen 1993). Critical for efficient capital mobilization and allocation, financial intermediation can be performed through various forms of instruments, the three most important ones being equities (stocks), long-term loans (bonds), and short-term loans (credit) (Stiglitz 1989b). In most developing countries, because of the relative underdevelopment of the first two forms of instruments, credit markets for short-term loans become the major means of financial intermediation.

The capital mobilization function of credit markets is, however, constrained by several factors. First, when there is a lack of macroeconomic and monetary stabilities, as experienced by many Latin American countries during the 1970s and 1980s, people prefer to invest in fixed assets—real estate, jewelry, etc.—or to save in foreign currencies overseas, instead of depositing local currencies in domestic institutions. Second, savers are willing to deposit money in a saving institution only if they believe that they will be able to withdraw the money according to prespecified terms. The risk of bank closure and the availability of deposit insurance become important considerations for potential depositors. In many countries, governments establish banking regulations such as capital and reserve requirements to ensure the ability of banks to meet withdrawal demands. Third, government regulation creates opportunities for political abuses. In some developing countries, for example, the formal banking system is tightly controlled by government officials who see it as a convenient source of cheap credit for their own expenditure projects and their favored political clients (Hanke and Walters 1991). Offering mostly negative real interest rates to depositors, the banking system is not an attractive saving avenue for most people (Fry 1988; McKinnon 1973). The limitation of the formal banking system may be compensated by informal credit arrangements that offer higher returns for depositors, but these informal arrangements are usually limited in scale and lack legal protection for depositors.

In addition to overcoming obstacles for capital mobilization, credit markets need to overcome information problems associated with credit allocation (Stiglitz 1989b). First, because of the potential for default, lenders need to solve the selection problem—screening loan applications based not just on how much interest they are willing to pay, but on their probability of default. Second, enforcement problems concern the ability of lenders to ensure that principals and interests will actually be repaid by borrowers at specified times. Third, loan contracts need to include a variety of provisions other than interest rates. Nonprice terms such as collateral and other kinds of restrictive covenants, such as market interlinkage,[4] are often needed to create appropriate incentives for loan repayment.

Various forms of credit markets tackle these problems differently. Faced with a wide array of potential borrowers, the formal banking system tends to tackle the selection and enforcement problems by making these borrowers homogeneous, for example, by imposing stringent collateral requirements or by requiring borrowers to provide carefully documented evidence showing their intention and ability for repayment (Floro and Yotopoulos 1991). The efficiency of the formal banking system in credit allocation is enhanced if the legal framework makes collateral agreements enforceable at low costs. Other institutional infrastructures such as reliable public accounting systems and credit reporting services can also make credit allocation through the banking system more efficient. The efficiency of the formal banking system in many developing countries can be improved by strengthening these basic legal and institutional infrastructures.

No matter how efficient the legal infrastructures, the formal banking system can only cater to the needs of a limited portion of the population, that is, enterprises or individuals who can provide collateral or documented credit references. Credit needs of the poor and many small entrepreneurs will remain unsatisfied through the formal banking system. These people mostly are unable to provide collateral, or the loans they need are so small that administrative costs for lenders outweigh expected returns. While small borrowers generally encounter difficulties in obtaining credit from formal financial institutions in developed economies, those in developing economies face even greater obstacles because banking systems in these economies tend to be more rigid and small firms generally lack accounting records.

This characteristic of credit markets creates serious problems for policy makers in countries in which small enterprises play an important role in economic development. A common prescription in many developing countries has been for governments to develop concessional credit programs to help farmers, small enterprises, and start-up companies. These programs, however, are faced with formidable problems in solvency due to high default rates, failure to deliver credit to targeted groups, administrative inefficiency, etc. (Adams and Pischke 1992; Braverman and Guasch 1993).

Many of the attempts by governments and international donors to increase the supply of finance to the noncorporate sector have focused on providing access to affordable credit. They have foundered because they did not take into account the true costs and risks of lending to the sector. (World Bank 1990, 100)

In many developing countries, informal credit markets play an important role in solving allocation problems associated with individuals, farmers, and small enterprises. Because of the absence of direct government regulations, informal credit markets are usually characterized by flexibility of operation. Various arrangements are developed by participants to deal with specific information problems associated with different transactions (Adams and Fitchett 1992; Floro and Yotopoulos 1991). By utilizing such mechanisms as social networks and market interlinkage, informal credit arrangements can reduce many selection, enforcement, and incentive problems inherent in credit transactions which, otherwise, may not be effectively handled in formal financial institutions. It is well documented, for example, that informal moneylenders, who utilize personal ties to facilitate contract enforcement, can potentially provide an important service to rural people who lack tangible collateral for securing loans from the banking system (Adams and Fitchett 1992). In both rural and urban areas, trade credit is based on market interlinkage, in which credit is linked to borrowers' behaviors in other transactions. Such interlinkage increases lenders' ability to monitor borrowers' behaviors; it also motivates borrowers to repay loans by making other transactions contingent upon loan repayment. Trade credit is critical for the survival of many small and medium enterprises in developing countries (Ghate 1992).

While informal credit markets play an essential financial intermediation function in many developing countries, they are also subject to various limitations. Participants in informal credit markets frequently operate illegally and are subject to severe penalties. The operation of these markets tends to be limited and secretive and sometimes involves bribes and kickbacks to government officials (Hanke and Walters 1991). These markets tend to be highly segmented, with participants limited to only those with personal relations with one another. Since transactions are mostly undertaken without legal protection, participants are vulnerable to potential losses and abuses. With transactions confined mostly to specific social circles, risk diversification is often limited. To reduce default risk in the absence of tangible collateral, informal loans tend to be small and short term. This raises the transaction costs. Because loans usually come from lenders' equity instead of third-party deposits, the money creation function of the informal credit market is limited (Christensen 1993). In transitional societies where old social relations and networks have broken down before new institutions are established, no effective informal credit market may exist.

Despite the recognition of both the potential and limitations of informal credit markets in developing countries, many policy issues remain unsolved. Among the most important is how government policies affect the operation of informal credit arrangements. Should a government try to support or to eliminate informal credit markets? How would financial sector reform affect the role of informal credit markets in financial intermediation? Many scholars argue that some informal credit markets may be locally efficient, and ill-conceived government interventions may undermine an otherwise efficient local market (Floro and Yotopoulos 1991). In developed and developing economies alike, private money lenders face problems of contract enforcement and of screening and monitoring borrowers. If government intervenes, it will face the same problems, though maybe in slightly different forms than would the private moneylender. While government interventions may help to reduce enforcement problems in credit transactions, these options need to be used selectively. Adverse selection and monitoring difficulties, for example, may undermine a government's attempt to provide subsidized credit to poor farmers through direct administrative means. As argued by Stiglitz (1989a, 202):

> It may be foolhardy for the government to go where the private market fears to tread: credit rationing in private capital markets does not necessarily suggest a role for government providing credit. It may, indeed, be at a disadvantageous position both in screening applicants and monitoring loans (ignoring the obvious political economy problems to which government loan programs can give rise, particularly in highly inflationary situations).

Under certain circumstances, informal credit arrangements may be more effective in solving selection, enforcement, and incentive problems in credit transactions.

Although not directly sanctioned by government, informal credit transactions are not undertaken in an institutional vacuum. Most of these transactions are governed by customary rules among participants. If effectively enforced, these rules facilitate transactions by reducing selection, enforcement, and incentive problems among participants. While some of these rules are parts of traditional social practices and conventions, others are adaptations or reactions to existing legal, political, and economic constraints. As argued by Chandavarkar (1992), it is useful to distinguish between two components of the informal financial sector—the "autonomous" and the "reactive" components. The former refers to traditional financial arrangements that predated the formal sector in modern times (e.g., indigenous banking and rotating credit associations). The latter refers to informal financial arrangements that developed in response to the restrictions, or deficiencies, inherent in the formal sector (e.g., underground finance companies). This "reactive" component often expands and contracts in response to cycles of repression and liberalization in the formal financial sector. While, in reality, many informal credit arrangements consist of both of these components, Chandavarkar's argument underscores the multiple factors that affect the development of these arrangements.

3. Informal Credit Markets in Taiwan

Taiwan is a case of how informal credit markets help to compensate for the limitations of the formal financial system, especially in regard to satisfying the credit needs of small enterprises. Instead of competing directly with each other, the formal and informal sectors have largely complemented each other in solving crucial financial intermediation problems in Taiwan's development process. The experience of Taiwan also illustrates that informal credit markets do not operate in an institutional vacuum; government regulations and policies affect the way participants in informal credit markets solve problems in selection, enforcement, and incentive. Furthermore, recent changes in Taiwan demonstrate the continued resilience and relevance of informal credit markets during a process of financial liberalization.

(a) Complementarity between Formal and Informal Credit Markets

In Taiwan, small and medium enterprises play an important role in its export-driven development strategy. In 1985, for example, small and medium enterprises (those with fewer than 300 employees) contributed about 50% of value added and employed 62% of the workforce in Taiwan. These enterprises also produced 65% of total export value in the same year (Biggs 1991, 169). These small and medium firms form extensive subcontracting networks among themselves and with larger enterprises. Such an industrial structure enables the economy to compete internationally by focusing on exporting products based on intermediate technology (such as electronics components for machinery) that is characterized by high volatility and the need for rapid adaptation to change.

The banking system in Taiwan, which until recently has been mostly government owned, mainly serves the needs of public enterprises and large-scale private enterprises. The government-controlled banking system has supported export-oriented industries by providing large companies in those industries with additional and concessional credit (Wade 1990). The banking system, however, has been unresponsive to the credit needs of small and medium enterprises. By examining the distribution of loans from formal financial institutions, Shea and Kuo (1984) and Shea (1990) found that productivity, profitability, and growth potential of industries had little effect on credit rationing decisions. During 1965–82, five times more bank credit per dollar of sales went to large firms than small ones, and four times more credit per unit of value added went to large firms (Shea and Kuo 1984). According to annual surveys conducted by the Central Bank during 1964–90, private enterprises borrowed an average of 35% from outside formal financial institutions (Shea 1992, 3). Among private enterprises, the smaller their scale, the larger the proportion of their loans came from informal credit markets. According to a survey conducted by the Central Bank in 1983, private firms with assets of one to five million NT dollars received 68.9% of their domestic borrowings from informal credit markets; those with 40–100 million received 39.7%; and those over 1,000 million received 10.3% (Shea 1992).

The informal credit market from which enterprises obtain their loans exists in many forms. One of them is trade credit. As a popular form of informal credit in many countries, trade credit utilizes information links between parties that have developed over time through contracting arrangements or commodity transactions (Ghate 1992, 31). In Taiwan, trade credit between enterprises mostly exists in the form of "supplier's credit," that is, loans from supplying firms to buying firms (Wade 1990). It also exists in the form of "upstream" firms providing loans to "downstream" contractors (Biggs 1991). In many cases, larger firms obtain funds from the formal banking system, and then extend loans at substantially higher interest rates to smaller firms with which they have ongoing business relationships.[5]

While relying heavily on external debt financing, private enterprises also rely on internal sources, which accounted for around 45–55% of total private enterprise investment in the past three decades. Internal financing was even higher among smaller firms, amounting to 60–65% (Biggs 1991, 178). Although it is difficult to estimate how much of these internal sources came from personal or family savings, it is likely that a good portion came from rotating credit associations among relatives and friends. While these associations vary in format, the general principle is similar. For example, a group of, say, 10 individuals makes an agreement that each individual contributes a sum of money to form a pool every month. Each month, through a bidding process, one individual receives the pool. In this way, those who need money more than others can receive a pool of money and promise to pay a certain interest on a monthly basis. The same process goes on for another nine months, and each month those who have yet to receive a pool of money earlier in the process and those who do not need it can wait until later in the process and earn interest from others in the group.[6] Two general household surveys conducted around 1980 indicated high participation rates in these associations, one indicating 85% and the other 68% (Peng and Chang 1985, 188). According to a recent survey, the participation rate among business people was even higher, at 95% (Chen 1993, 37). Furthermore, based on two household surveys in 1978 and 1981 respectively, it is estimated that the volume of funds that were processed through rotating credit associations fell within the range of 2.7 to 6.8% of GNP annually (Peng and Chang 1985, 188). Rotating credit associations appear to have been a major means of raising capital to start a small business.

Besides trade credit and rotating credit associations, there is a wide array of other informal credit arrangements. One major form is underground bankers who conduct bank-like businesses including deposit-taking and lending, but without a proper license. Such underground bankers offer loans at higher interest rates (usually several times regular bank rates). Although charging higher interest rates, these bankers serve a useful function by providing short-term loans to most people in a speedy manner (Huang et al. 1983). Another form of informal credit arrangement involves firms accepting deposits from their own employees. Such deposits serve as a form of liquid capital for the firm and are considered as a personal loan from employees to firm. Since the late 1970s, there has emerged an increasing number of leasing companies that financed the purchase or leasing of heavy equipment and machinery by small and medium firms. The total amount of financing through these companies increased from 0.7 billion NT dollars in 1977 to 17.7 billion in 1983 (Peng and Chang 1985). Many of these companies were associated with large manufacturing firms and their capital was mostly borrowed from banks. These companies served as a financial conduit between the banking system and small and medium firms.[7]

Taiwan's experience with informal credit markets is not unique. As indicated in many recent studies, formal and informal credit systems coexist in most countries worldwide (Ghate 1992; Adams and Fitchett 1992; Hoff, Braverman, and Stiglitz 1993). In Taiwan, maybe more than many other developing countries, the formal and informal credit markets complement each other in solving crucial development problems. As argued by Wade (1990), the highly regulated financial system has enabled the Taiwanese government to limit private economic power, to channel funds to industrial production, and to implement conservative monetary policy and inflation control. Rigid government regulations, together with the inherent information problems associated with small-scale credit transactions, made it difficult for innovative, small enterprises to secure loans from the formal banking system. Informal credit markets compensate for this limitation of the formal sector by catering to the credit needs of these small companies.[8]

While informal credit markets contribute to financial intermediation, it is also necessary to understand their limitations and potential problems. In fact, most of the Chinese sources on the subject emphasize problems associated with informal credit markets. There are frequently reports of innocent people being victimized by malpractice in informal credit markets.

In the early 1980s, for example, there were a number of well-known cases in which organizers of rotating credit associations defaulted on members for millions of dollars (Chen 1993; Lin et al. 1991; Shen 1984). Government authorities were, on occasion, under social pressure to deal with manifest problems or abuses in the informal credit market. While serving an important financial function, informal credit markets are not foolproof.

(b) Government Regulations and Informal Credit Markets

The Taiwanese government's attitude toward informal credit markets can be characterized as a form of benign neglect. While some forms of informal credit arrangements such as underground banking are outlawed, the government appears to be neutral about other forms such as rotating credit associations. Transactions in rotating credit associations have been considered to be based on private contracts among participants. Such contracts have not been prohibited by the law. Indeed, the government has recently initiated legislative change to the Civil Code to include provisions about the rights and duties of participants in rotating credit associations (Chen 1993, 37). For the outlawed component of the informal market, the Ministry of Finance and the Bureau of Investigation in the Ministry of Justice are responsible for investigating and prosecuting illegal operations. Except during periods in which financial scams became major public concerns, as in the late 1980s, these agencies appeared to lack the resolve to clamp down on illegal financial practices. Court action was taken mostly to deal with open grievances from the parties involved (Lin et al. 1991; Shen 1984). It is also interesting to note that the Economic Research Department of the Central Bank publishes interest rates in informal credit markets on a monthly basis. Usually two or three times the regular bank rates, these informal interest rates are used by Central Bank officials as a reference for setting official interest rates. The Economic Research Department of the Central Bank also includes in its annual survey of *Flow of Funds in Taiwan District* the volume of informal financial transactions. Furthermore, multiple pages of classified advertisements on informal credit appear daily on major newspapers and are tolerated by government authorities.

The Negotiable Instruments Law enacted in the 1950s has facilitated formal credit transactions. According to the Law, it is a criminal offense to fail to honor postdated checks. The legal liability is shared by both the issuer and all additional endorsers. Banks are legally obligated to report violations to the authorities. Because of this law, banks limited the number of blank checks available to customers. Such legal protection enabled the postdated check to become a widely used credit instrument in the informal credit market. When a person borrows from an underground banker and lacks sufficient real estate, stocks, or other valuables as collateral, a common practice is to have the person write three checks—the first posting the loan amount plus interest, the second posting two to three times of the loan amount, and the third blank. If the lender is unable to cash the first check on the specified date, he or she could submit the second one or the third one with any amount he or she writes in. The issuer is liable for criminal prosecution after three bounced checks. Because of the legal sanction associated with the postdated check, it is known that underground bankers often preferred it to such collateral as real estate and stocks which may require complicated legal procedures to process (Shen 1984).

The postdated check is also a major instrument in trade credit transactions. A common method is for purchasers to issue a postdated check (posting the product price plus interest and the payment date) in favor of suppliers (Biggs 1991, 184–85). When suppliers have accumulated large numbers of postdated checks and need cash, they can endorse the check and use it as collateral to secure a loan from another party. A discounting market for postdated checks, similar to the regulated money market, has emerged. Sometimes a postdated check can be endorsed by several people and discounted many times. Because of the information costs involved, the market for postdated checks is highly segmented—checks are traded mostly among people in the same industry who know one another well.

The postdated check system has become so important to business transactions that the government has, on occasion, intervened to maintain its stability. In 1985, for example, the government initiated a temporary program that allowed major industries and enterprises a six-month grace period for redeeming bad checks without criminal prosecution (Biggs 1991).

While the legal status of postdated checks has facilitated informal credit transactions, it has also been criticized (Effros 1971). One major criticism is that the enforcement of the Negotiable Instruments Law had preoccupied much of the criminal justice system. According to Biggs (1991, 182), the majority of the criminal cases that went through the court system in the 1970s were related to that particular law. There are also well-known cases in which underground bankers used potential criminal prosecution to threaten and extract additional compensation from borrowers who had used postdated checks as collateral. In these cases, a legal means is employed to support illegal and unfair practices (see Shen 1984, 18). Sometimes, innocent people were penalized and the crooks fled as in cases when a husband had used his wife's name chop to write bad checks and left her behind to face criminal prosecution (Wade 1990, 163).[9] All these problems had exerted pressure on the government to reform the Negotiable Instruments Law. After substantial efforts in building a regulated money market from the late 1970s (Emery

1991), the government finally abolished the criminal penalty associated with postdated checks in 1987. While this legislative change helps to prevent some of the problems mentioned earlier, postdated checks remain a common instrument in informal credit transactions. Bad checks are still subject to sanctions by individual banks. In the *Financial Statistics Monthly* published by the Central Bank, market interest rates for unsecured loans are still listed separately from those that are backed by postdated checks. Yet interest rate differentials between the two types of loans have become minimal. In February 1993, for instance, the average monthly interest rate in Taipei for loans against postdated checks was 1.95 as compared with 2.00 for unsecured loans.

Besides specific policies toward informal credit transactions, other policies also have indirect effects on the informal financial market. As mentioned earlier, the banking system in Taiwan has been unresponsive to the credit needs of small firms. This is partly due to the inherent difficulties for banks in overcoming the selection, enforcement, and incentive problems associated with lending to borrowers who lack collateral and accounting records. The tendency to be unresponsive to small firms is exacerbated by an institutional feature of the banking system. Until 1992, the government of Taiwan directly owned and managed most of the domestic banks. These banks are subject to numerous accounting, budgeting, personnel, and auditing restrictions characteristic of government bureaucracies. State-owned banks are under the supervision of 15 agencies in the central and provincial governments (Cheng 1993, 80). Loans from these banks are treated as government assets by auditing agencies which are reluctant to write off bad loans. Because they may be legally liable for loan defaults, bank officials emphasize collateral as the major criterion for loan decisions (Shea 1992).

Lax disclosure regulations and practices in Taiwan also make it difficult for banks to collect information about medium and small firms. Most companies, especially medium and small, lack accurate financial statements, a practice encouraged by the tax code that allows companies without complete accounting records to use the average rate of the specific industry as a base to calculate taxes. Even though it is legally required, about 72% of all registered companies in 1980 failed to file financial statements with the Ministry of Economic Affairs (Chen 1993, 81). The public accounting system is generally considered unreliable. These conditions make it extremely difficult for banks to determine the creditworthiness of most companies that lack tangible collateral. These, together with the conservative orientation of bank officials, have made the informal credit market more important in satisfying credit needs of small enterprises.

Finally, Taiwan's relatively stable fiscal environment has contributed to the strength of informal credit markets. One major political-economic problem confronting many developing countries, especially those in Latin America, has been the national government's inability to create a stable fiscal environment. With unstable price levels and often negative real interest rates in the formal banking system, individuals want to invest primarily in nonproductive assets such as precious metals and real estate, or to divert their wealth abroad. In Taiwan, throughout most of the postwar period, the national government has maintained restrictions on citizens transferring money abroad, restrictions on land speculation, and conservative government spending and fiscal policies (Ranis and Mahmood 1992; Wade 1990). These policies have helped to create a favorable macroeconomic structure that encourages citizens to save in the nation's own monetary units. While the formal banking system offers lower interest rates than the informal sector, deposits are virtually guaranteed because of the public ownership of most banks. For people who seek a higher return on their savings, the informal credit market offers a riskier but viable alternative. All these factors have provided a supportive environment for people to invest in the informal credit market.

(c) Financial Sector Reform and Informal Credit Markets

While the limitation of the formal financial system has partly been compensated by the flexibility of informal credit markets, major pressures have built up since the 1980s for the Taiwanese government to reform its formal financial system. First, internationalization of finance has become a major trend worldwide since the mid-1980s (*Economist* 1992). It has become more and more counterproductive for countries to try to limit the flow of international capital. In response, the Taiwanese government has considerably lessened restrictions on capital flow in and out of the country in recent years. Unless Taiwan can develop a competitive financial system that can efficiently handle large capital transactions, its economy will be disadvantaged in the international market.

Second, the rapid economic growth and conservative government spending policies in the past few decades have enabled the central government to accumulate large amounts of cash reserve. It has become increasingly evident that the rigid financial system has encountered difficulties in allocating excess capital to productive uses. It is, for example, estimated that 40% of bank deposits remained idle in 1987 (Cheng 1993, 90).

Third, the underdeveloped financial and capital markets appear to be incapable of satisfying the investment needs of people who have accumulated increasing amounts of wealth. One result is an increasing number of scandals associated with underground investment companies during the second half of the 1980s. During this period, instead of being satisfied with putting money in the banking system or such traditional credit arrangements as rotating credit associations, increasing numbers of people put money into underground investment companies that emerged after 1985. Promising investors unrealistically high rates of return, these companies were engaged in real estate and stock market speculations and varieties of financial scam (Lin et al. 1991). These companies mostly operated in violation of government securities laws and were engaged in financial transactions beyond what is usually considered part of the informal credit market. According to one estimate, these companies had attracted around NT $200–300 billion of investment by 1989, which was 15–23% of the year's national budget (Cheng 1993, 85). The subsequent failure of an increasing number of these companies finally compelled the government to close them down in 1989. Such an episode further confirmed the need to reform the financial system.

Fourth, a rigid financial system was used by Kuomintang, the ruling party, as a means to prevent large concentrations of capital in the hands of individuals or groups who might turn out to challenge the party's authority, as was the case during the 1930s and 1940s in mainland China (Hamilton and Biggart 1988). With the increasing democratization of the political system, such a consideration has become less important for the political leadership. The leadership has become more willing to embrace financial liberalization.

The question nowadays is no longer whether to reform the financial system or not, but how to reform it. Experience in Taiwan shows that informal credit markets play a critical role in the reform process. Since the late 1970s, the government has begun to encourage the development of a regulated money market. Such an effort seems to have decreased enterprises' credit demand on the informal credit market. The share of private enterprises borrowing from the informal market decreased from around 36% in 1978 to around 30% in 1984. The share, however, went up in 1985 and 1986 (at 35 and 40%, respectively), until it began to go down again after 1987 reaching 24% in 1990.[10] Some scholars attribute the temporary jump in 1985 and 1986 to the government's effort to lift restrictions on bank interest rates starting in the early 1980s (Shea 1992; Shea and Yen 1991). In 1985, the government further broadened the range in which banks could set their lending rates. This change, however, was implemented at a time when most banks were still government owned and run according to rigid bureaucratic guidelines. A combination of higher interest rates and continuing conservatism of the banking system might have turned more enterprises from the formal banking system to the informal credit market during the period.

It is likely that the introduction of 15 new private banks in 1992 and subsequent privatization of government-owned banks will eventually make the formal financial system more competitive and responsive to the needs of small and medium enterprises. Nevertheless, it is unlikely that the reformed financial system will totally eliminate the function of the informal credit market, which is likely to remain a viable source of credit for individuals and smaller firms that need short-term credit but lack collateral and credit records. At present, major newspapers are still filled with pages of advertisements for informal loans. In 1991, the informal credit market still constituted about 25% of all financial transactions.[11] Interest rate differentials between informal loans and bank loans remain substantial. In February 1993, for instance, the average annual interest rate for informal loans against postdated checks was 26.08 as compared with the prime rates charged by domestic banks that ranged from 7.875 to 10.500.[12] Yet current differentials have slightly decreased in comparison with those in the mid-1970s and early 1980s, during which interest rate differentials between general (short-term) bank loans and informal loans against postdated checks averaged about 20% (Biggs 1991).

4. Discussion and Conclusion

Formal credit markets in both developed and developing countries tend to favor large firms in credit allocation. Such a phenomenon is especially pronounced in Taiwan where public enterprises and large private firms receive the lion's share of credit from the formal sector, and medium and small firms obtain most of their credit from the informal sector. Such market segmentation was interpreted by some scholars as evidence of "financial repression" in which governments impose unnecessarily restrictive regulations on the formal financial sector. While valid to a certain extent, such a view neglects the transaction costs associated with the allocation of credit. From the transaction-cost perspective, credit allocation is subject to various selection, enforcement, and incentive problems. In catering to the credit needs of smaller firms that lack collateral and a documented credit record, the informal sector may have a comparative advantage over the formal sector by virtue of its ability to utilize social networks and market interlinkage to solve various transaction problems. In Taiwan, the informal sector performs a complementary function by filling the gap left by credit rationing in the formal sector. This complementary function of informal credit is especially important given Taiwan's heavy reliance on small and medium enterprises as a major engine of economic growth.

While informal credit can help to fill the gap left by the formal sector, it does not mean that informal credit is foolproof. Informal financial transactions are subject to various limitations and potential abuses. Taiwan's recent experience with underground investment companies, for example, demonstrates the need for governments to help provide reliable institutional channels for investment once people have accumulated substantial wealth. The challenge facing Taiwan and many other developing countries nowadays is to develop enabling legal frameworks that facilitate efficient transactions in both the formal and informal sectors.

Indeed, Taiwan's own experience shows that legal rules and other public institutions affect credit transactions in both sectors. The Negotiable Instruments Law, for example, had for many years facilitated the operation of informal credit markets. The government's failure to help develop a reliable public accounting system has made it difficult for formal credit institutions to collect information about medium and small firms, and such a failure has indirectly encouraged the use of informal credit among those firms. To strengthen the role of the formal sector in financial intermediation in Taiwan, it is insufficient just to lift restrictions on interest rates and to allow for the opening of new private banks. The development of institutional infrastructure that facilitates information flow and contract enforcement is needed to help the formal sector overcome various credit transaction problems. In this regard, a more credible public accounting system is one form of institutional infrastructure Taiwan needs to develop.

This article supplements the recent political economy literature on the East Asian NICs which emphasizes government's leadership in economic development. While government policies in Taiwan have had major impacts on informal credit markets' mode of operation, these markets also operate in ways that are beyond direct government control. This shows that important social and economic institutions are not only those that are sanctioned by government authorities. Many informal social and economic arrangements play an important role in facilitating economic transactions. The comparative advantage of a nation involves not just human and natural resources, but also the "social capital" (Coleman 1993) embedded in these informal institutions. By complementing formal institutions, the informal sector can play a significant role in economic development. Instead of viewing the informal sector as purely a symptom of underdevelopment, future research on East Asia needs to examine how different configurations of formal and informal institutions affect developmental processes, how government regulations and policies affect the operation of the informal sector, and how the informal sector responds to economic reform processes.

NOTES

1. As pointed out by a reviewer, some studies exist on the empirical level for almost every country in the region, but the informal sector is largely ignored in the

general analysis of East Asian development. This is partly due to the statist orientation of that literature. Another issue concerning the study of the informal sector is definitions. Two general types of definitions exist—one focusing on functional attributes (e.g., small sizes and labor-intensive operations) and the other focusing on the extralegal status of the informal sector. In this study, I adopt the latter focus and refer the informal sector to economic activities that operate outside formal legal and financial institutions. According to this view, sizes and degrees of complexity are not defining characteristics of the informal sector. For general discussions about definitions, see Chickering and Salahdine 1991; Jenkins 1988; and Rakowski 1994.

2. *Economist,* November 6, 1993, 37.

3. See Lin et al. 1991, for an extensive bibliography on Chinese sources.

4. Market interlinkage refers to arrangements in which two parties are involved in two or more market exchanges simultaneously (see Floro and Yotopoulos 1991).

5. As will be discussed in the next section, most trade credit transactions are facilitated by the use of postdated checks.

6. For further details about various forms of rotating credit associations, see Huang et al. 1983; and Shen 1984.

7. For further details about the operation and scale of these and other informal credit arrangements, see Biggs 1991; and Peng and Chang 1985.

8. The Taiwanese government has attempted to solve the problem partly from within the formal sector by establishing banks specialized in serving small and medium enterprises and various loan guarantee programs. As indicated in several studies, these efforts have reached only a small number of the targeted firms (Yang and Hsio 1993).

9. It is customary in Taiwan to use one's personal name chop, instead of signature, to endorse checks.

10. See Shea 1992, table 2. The data are based on annual surveys conducted by the Central Bank of China. Borrowings from informal credit markets include those from other enterprises and households.

11. Central Bank of China, *Flow of Funds in Taiwan District, The Republic of China (1965–1991).*

12. Central Bank of China, *Financial Statistics Monthly: Taiwan District, The Republic of China (March 1993).*

REFERENCES

Adams, Dale W., and Delbert A. Fitchett, eds. (1992) *Informal Finance in Low-Income Countries.* Boulder, CO: Westview Press.

Adams, Dale W., and J. D. Von Pischke (1992) "Microenterprise credit programs: Deja vu." *World Development* 20, no. 10: 1463–470.

Amsden, Alice M. (1989) *Asia's Next Giant: South Korea and Late Industrialization.* New York: Oxford University Press.

———, ed. (1994) "Special section on the World Bank's *The East Asian miracle: Economic growth and public policy.*" *World Development* 22, no. 4: 615–70.

Biggs, Tyler S. (1991) "Heterogeneous firms and efficient financial intermediation in Taiwan." In Michael Roemer and Christine Jones (eds.), *Markets in Developing Countries: Parallel, Fragmented, and Black.* San Francisco: ICS Press.

Braverman, Avishay, and J. Luis Guasch (1993) "Administrative failures in rural credit programs." In Karla Hoff, Avishay Braverman, and Joseph E. Stiglitz (eds.), *The Economics of Rural Organization: Theory, Practice, and Policy.* New York: Oxford University Press.

Central Bank of China (Various years) "Financial statistics monthly." Taipei: Economic Research Dept., Central Bank of China.

————— (Various years) "Flow of funds in Taiwan District." Taipei: Economic Research Dept., Central Bank of China.

Chandavarkar, Anand (1992) "Of finance and development: Neglected and unsettled questions." *World Development* 20, no. 1: 133–42.

Chen, Elaine (1993) "The Chinese road to riches: Rotating credit association." *Sinorama* (Sept.): 36–43.

Cheng, Tun-jen (1993) "Guarding the commanding heights: The state as banker in Taiwan." In Stephen Haggard, Chung H. Lee, and Sylvia Maxfield (eds.), *The Politics of Finance in Developing Countries.* Ithaca, NY: Cornell University Press.

Chickering, A. Lawrence, and Mohamed Salahdine, eds. (1991) *The Silent Revolution: The Informal Sector in Five Asian and Near Eastern Countries.* San Francisco: ICS Press.

Christensen, Garry (1993) "The limits to informal financial intermediation." *World Development* 21, no. 5: 721–31.

Coleman, James S. (1993) "The rational reconstruction of society." *American Sociological Review* 58, no. 1: 1–15.

de Soto, Hernando (1988) "Constraints on people: The origins of underground economies and limits to their growth." In Jerry Jenkins (ed.), *Beyond the Informal Sector: Including the Excluded in Developing Countries.* San Francisco: ICS Press.

————— (1989) *The Other Path: The Invisible Revolution in the Third World.* New York: Harper and Row.

Economist (1992) "Fear of finance: A survey of the world economy." Sept. 19.

Effros, Robert C. (1971) "The problem of postdated checks in the Republic of China." *International Monetary Fund Staff Papers* 18, no. 1: 113–35.

Emery, Robert F. (1991) *The Money Markets of Developing East Asia.* New York: Praeger.

Floro, Sagrario L., and Pan A. Yotopoulos (1991) *Informal Credit Markets and the New Institutional Economics: The Case of Philippine Agriculture.* Boulder, CO: Westview Press.

Fry, Maxwell J. (1988) *Money, Interest and Banking in Economic Development.* Baltimore: Johns Hopkins University Press.

Gereffi, Gary, and Donald L. Wyman, eds. (1990) *Manufacturing Miracles: Paths of Industrialization in Latin America and East Asia.* Princeton, NJ: Princeton University Press.

Ghate, Prabhu (1992) *Informal Finance: Some Findings from Asia.* New York: Oxford University Press.

Haggard, Stephan (1990) *Pathways from the Periphery: The Politics of Growth in the Newly Industrializing Countries.* Ithaca, NY: Cornell University Press.

Hamilton, Gary G., and Nicole Woolsey Biggart (1988) "Market, culture, and authority: A comparative analysis of management and organization in the Far East." *American Journal of Sociology* 94, supp., S52–S94.

Hanke, Steve H., and Alan A. Walters (1991) "Financial and capital markets in developing countries." In Steve H. Hanke and Alan A. Walters (eds.), *Capital Markets and Development*. San Francisco: ICS Press.

Hoff, Karla, Avishay Braverman, and Joseph E. Stiglitz, eds. (1993) *The Economics of Rural Organization: Theory, Practice, and Policy*. New York: Oxford University Press.

Hoff, Karla, and Joseph E. Stiglitz (1993) "Imperfect information and rural credit markets: Puzzles and policy perspectives." In Karla Hoff, Avishay Braverman, and Joseph E. Stiglitz (eds.), *The Economics of Rural Organization: Theory, Practice, and Policy*. New York: Oxford University Press.

Huang, Yung-Jen et al. (1983) *Problems of Underground Finance in Taiwan*. Taichung: Center for Research and Training on Local Finance. (In Chinese.)

Islam, Iyanatul (1992) "Political Economy and East Asia Economic Development." *Asian-Pacific Economic Literature* 6, no. 2: 69–101.

Jenkins, Jerry, ed. (1988) *Beyond the Informal Sector: Including the Excluded in Developing Countries*. San Francisco: ICS Press.

Lin, Chung-Hsiung et al. (1991) *A Study on Preventing and Controlling Underground Financial Activities*. Taipei: Research, Development, and Evaluation Committee, Executive Yuan. (In Chinese.)

McKinnon, Ronald I. (1973) *Money and Capital in Economic Development*. Washington, DC: Brookings Institution.

Peng, Pai-Hsien, and S. H. Chang (1985) "Financial channels for informal finance in Taiwan." *Bank of Taiwan Quarterly* 36, no. 3: 165–205. (In Chinese.)

Rakowski, Cathy A. (1994) "Convergence and divergence in the informal sector debate: A focus on Latin America, 1984–92." *World Development* 22, no. 4: 501–16.

Ranis, Gustav, and Syed Akhtar Mahmood (1992) *The Political Economy of Development Policy Change*. Oxford: Blackwell.

Roemer, Michael, and Christine Jones (1991) *Markets in Developing Countries: Parallel, Fragmented, and Black*. San Francisco: ICS Press.

Shea, Jia-Dong (1990) "Financial development in Taiwan: A macro analysis." Paper presented at the Conference on Financial Development in Japan, Korea and Taiwan. Taipei: Institute of Economics, Academia Sinica.

——— (1992) "The welfare effects of financial liberalization under market segmentation—With special reference to Taiwan." Discussion paper. Taipei: Institute of Economics, Academia Sinica.

Shea, Jia-Dong, and Ping-Sing Kuo (1984) "The allocative efficiency of banks' loanable funds in Taiwan." In *Proceedings of the Conference on Financial Development in Taiwan*. Taipei: Institute of Economics, Academia Sinica. (In Chinese.)

Shea, Jia-Dong, and Tzung-Ta Yen (1991) "Comparative experience of financial reforms in Taiwan and Korea: Implications for mainland China." Discussion paper. Taipei: Institute of Economics, Academia Sinica.

Shen, Ying-Ming (1984) *A Study of Underground Finance*. Taipei: Ministry of Finance. (In Chinese.)

Stiglitz, Joseph E. (1989a) "Markets, market failures, and development." *American Economic Review* 79, no. 2: 197–203.

———— (1989b) "Financial markets and development." *Oxford Review of Economic Policy* 5, no. 4: 55–68.

Stiglitz, Joseph E., and Andrew Weiss (1981) "Credit rationing in markets with imperfect information." *American Economic Review* 73, no. 5: 912–27.

Wade, Robert (1990) *Governing the Market: Economic Theory and the Role of Government in East Asia Industrialization.* Princeton, NJ: Princeton University Press.

World Bank (1990) *Financial Systems and Development.* Washington, DC: World Bank.

———— (1993) *The East Asian Miracle: Economic Growth and Public Policy.* New York: Oxford University Press.

Yang, Ya-Hui, and Hsuan I. I. Hsio (1993) "An analysis of financial intermediation of medium and small enterprises." *Taiwan: Community Financial Journal* 26 (March): 101–44. (In Chinese.)

CHAPTER 15

Crossing the Great Divide: Coproduction, Synergy, and Development

Elinor Ostrom

1. The Hypothetical Divide

Peter Evans identifies a strong divide between "a market-based logic of development and traditional theories of public administration." He identifies Judith Tendler's concept of blurred public-private boundaries and my work on coproduction as "radical" and potentially offending to "everyone's sense of propriety."

> Public Administration purists see it as threatening the insulation necessary for clearheaded decisions that are in the public interest. Market advocates see it as hopelessly muddying the logic of individual incentives and rational resource allocation. (Evans 1996)

Since I think the great divide between the Market and the State or between Government and Civil Society is a conceptual trap arising from overly rigid disciplinary walls surrounding the study of human institutions, I am delighted to be considered a radical. If trying to remove artificial walls surrounding disciplines is offensive, I regret assailing individual senses of propriety. I proceed on the assumption that contrived walls separating analysis of potentially synergetic phenomena into separate parts miss the

Originally published in *World Development* 24, no. 6 (1996): 1073–87. Reprinted by permission of Elsevier Science and the author.

Author's note: The author wishes to thank Robert Putnam for his energetic intellectual, and entrepreneurial leadership of the Social Capital and Public Affairs Project and Peter Evans for his similarly skilled leadership of the Economic Development Working Group and for his comments on the first draft of this paper. The author is appreciative of the materials made available by, and useful comments of, N. Vijay Jagannathan of the World Bank, about condominial systems and other water user organizations; and of the time and generous help extended by many public officials and local villagers while the author was in Nigeria during the summer of 1991. Mark Granovetter and Michael Lipsky provided insightful and useful comments on earlier papers. George Varughese and Patty Dalecki both greatly improved the readability of this manuscript. Financial support from the Ford Foundation (Grant 920–0701) is gratefully acknowledged.

potential for synergy (see V. Ostrom 1997). By developing more fully the theory of coproduction and its relevance to the study of synergy and development, I hope to change the views of social scientists toward the hypothetical "Great Divide."[1]

My own approach to breaching the great divide utilizes the concept of "coproduction." By coproduction, I mean the process through which inputs used to produce a good or service are contributed by individuals who are not "in" the same organization. The "regular" producer of education, health, or infrastructure services is most frequently a government agency. Whether the regular producer is the only producer of these goods and services depends both on the nature of the good or service itself and on the incentives that encourage the active participation of others. All public goods and services are potentially produced by the regular producer and by those who are frequently referred to as the client. The term *client* is a passive term. Clients are acted upon. Coproduction implies that citizens can play an active role in producing public goods and services of consequence to them.

To provide grist for the discussion of coproduction in section 3, I discuss two experiences with coproduction in developing countries. One is based on excellent, detailed case materials by other scholars, and the second is based on my own and colleagues' fieldwork. In both cases, public officials play a major role: in the first case, public officials actively encourage an unusually high level of citizen input to the production of public goods. In the second case, the actions of public officials discourage citizen contributions. The first occurs in a somewhat unlikely sector: peri-urban water and sanitation. The second occurs in a sector where one would hope to find relatively high levels of coproduction: primary education.[2] In section 3 of this essay, I present a brief overview of the theory of coproduction and use it to explain some of the patterns of relationships discussed in section 2. In the last section of the essay, I address the implications of coproduction for the study of synergy and development.

2. Empirical Cases

(a) Activating Coproduction of Urban Infrastructures in Brazil

Constructing major infrastructures, especially water and sanitation works in urban and peri-urban areas, is not where one would first look to find important, replicable examples of effective coproduction in developing countries.[3] Because of the technical expertise needed to design effective public works, the considerable economies of scale present in large-scale construction projects, and the difficult legal problems of acquiring rights-of-way across private lands, most analyses of infrastructure have presumed that the provision of infrastructure was best performed in the public sector (but see World Bank 1994; and E. Ostrom, Schroeder, and Wynne 1993). The actual construction of infrastructure facilities has usually been undertaken by public agencies themselves or arranged for by these agencies through contracts with large-scale, private for-profit contractors. The opportunities for illegal side payments in this form of provision and production are substantial.

This system has not, however, been successful in providing safe water and adequate sanitation to citizens living in developing countries even after a decade (1981–90) devoted by the international donor community to enhancement of drinking water supply and sanitation. While the percentage of urban dwellers receiving water and sanitation increased during 1980–90, the absolute number of urban dwellers without adequate sanitation rose by about 70 million people (Briscoe and Garn 1994, 3). In a few large cities in developing countries, such as Karachi and Christy Nagar in Pakistan, and in Brasilia, Recife, Natal, and several smaller urban areas in Brazil, the number of housing units connected to a low-cost waterborne sanitation system has, however, been growing steadily throughout the 1980s (Watson 1995, 10–12). In Brazil alone, more than 75,000 connections serving 370,000 residents have been made to this type of "condominial system"—so called since it is like a system that might be designed for a co-owned apartment building. The living units exist on a horizontal plane, however, rather than in vertical relationships to one another.

The Recife-based Brazilian engineer, Jose Carlos de Melo, identified in the 1980s a number of institutional factors which, he argued, exacerbated the problems of developing countries already facing extreme financial constraints. First, centralizing infrastructure provision at the national level kept municipalities from access to decision-making responsibilities and resources in this area. Second, excessively high engineering standards set in a capital city were inappropriate, de Melo argued, for bringing better service to poorer regions and neighborhoods. Third, citizens were themselves helpless to do anything about squalid conditions even though they possessed skills and time that could be applied toward solving aspects of the problems they faced. While the proportion of Brazilian urban population receiving water had increased from 55% to 83% during the decade of the 1980s, the percentage connected to sewerage services rose from only 22% to 37% (Watson 1995, 13). Moreover, most of those served were in the wealthier neighborhoods.

The reform plan initiated by de Melo combined an innovative approach to the design of engineering works combined with an active role for citizens.[4] Instead of designing all sanitation systems with large cast-iron pipes sunk deep under urban streets at high per household costs, de Melo proposed much smaller feeder lines that can run through urban blocks either in the back yards, front yards, or sidewalks of those being served. By placing these feeder lines away from heavy traffic, the costs of constructing the feeder section are about one-fourth that of conventional designs. Local residents have the skills needed to dig and maintain the feeder lines. The condominial feeder lines are then connected to larger trunk lines that are constructed to regular engineering standards, located under urban streets, and leading to treatment plants.

A key part of this program is the activation of local citizens to participate from the very start in the planning of their own condominial systems. To accomplish this goal, project teams first set up a series of neighborhood meetings where a general overview of the process, opportunities, and costs of a condominial system is presented. Then, meetings are held in *each* block where detailed discussions center on the choices that residents will have to make, their implications in regard to cost and in regard to the maintenance of the system. Block meetings are called off if half of the households on a block are not in attendance to ensure that there is wide availability of relevant information and good discussion among those living on a block.

All of this effort to involve citizens is directed, however, toward facilitating their making real decisions in a process of negotiation among neighbors and with project personnel. Residents decide on the layout of the system they want, which affects the cost of the system and the charges that they will pay. Arriving at these decisions can take considerable time if some neighbors want the less expensive (but more intrusive) backyard layout while others want the more expensive (and less intrusive) front yard or sidewalk options. Much of the costs of determining and achieving rights-of-way agreements are borne by residents themselves. Residents also develop a plan for constructing the feeder lines, thus allowing for common agreement to be achieved about how diverse participants would contribute to maintenance. Before construction begins, residents sign a formal petition requesting a condominial system and committing themselves to the payment of the fee agreed upon during negotiations. The first blocks in an area may take from four to six months to gain the needed agreement, but these serve as demonstration projects for others to see and understand the process. The process speeds up once residents can see how alternative designs work and talk with others who have successfully obtained services. Condominial project planners have learned that they cannot restrict the planning process to only those issues that planners think should be on the agenda. Residents in each city have raised different issues that were crucial to them. As Watson concludes:

The evolution of what is negotiated and what is not reflects both project planners' refinements of the process of providing residents with choices, and the ability of residents and neighborhood associations to push for their concerns with service providers. The lesson is that there is no "right" way to approach projects, but that each project's design, implementation strategy, and management arrangements evolve during the course of give-and-take negotiations between the project team and residents. (1995, 23)

The overall performance of these systems has varied from project to project and depends both on the success of the negotiation process to achieve a plan that neighbors can really implement and on the construction of high quality trunk lines arranged for by public agencies. Watson (1995) reports that medium-sized local firms who contract with a municipal- or state-level water agency built better performing trunk systems. A reputation for high-quality work is important to a local contractor and may be of little concern to a large firm (with political connections to national leaders) who may never return to that locality.

Studies of the performance of condominial systems point to difficulties in all stages of providing, producing, and maintaining these systems. Some systems perform at low levels.[5] The extensive involvement of citizens requires time and effort on the part of public officials. Some neighborhood groups need more effort from facilitators than others to help them learn how to keep up their commitments. In addition, the problems of monitoring the performance of those who construct trunk lines do not disappear even though the length of the trunk lines is substantially reduced. On the other hand, many of these systems have been successful, and have dramatically increased the availability of lower cost, essential urban services to the poorest neighborhoods of Brazilian cities. Similar systems are now completed or under construction in Kenya, Paraguay, and Indonesia (Watson and Jagannathan 1995).

While the results are impressive and similar efforts to encourage coproduction are being established in other parts of the world, the condominial system depends on three difficult challenges: (1) the organization of citizens and their fulfillment of promises to undertake collective action (what Judith Tendler [1995] refers to as social capital *outside* the government), (2) good teamwork within a public agency (what Tendler calls social capital *within* the government), and (3) effective coordination between citizens and an agency. In many regards, the citizens in a condominial system face a similar set of problems to those of any group of potential beneficiaries facing the problem of producing a collective benefit. The rich literature on successful and unsuccessful efforts to organize to produce public goods or common-pool resources focuses on closely related problems.[6] Similarly, the literature on principal-agent relationships and on team production focuses on the second task.[7] Less attention has been paid, given the gulf perceived between public and private spheres, to the problem of relating citizen and official inputs.[8] Watson stresses the possibility that what citizens do improves the performance of what agencies can do.

> Good agency performance results not from "strengthening" public sector agencies, but from increasing their responsiveness to customers. . . . The condominial system activates residents by engaging them during project implementation when service level, layout, maintenance arrangements, and cost recovery mechanisms are negotiated. This fosters an active, vocal constituency that puts in motion the accountability mechanisms needed for good agency performance. (1995, 49)

Making these systems work effectively over the long run requires as much change in the attitude and operational routines of public agencies as it requires input from residents in all phases of the project.[9]

(b) Thwarting Coproduction of Primary Education in Nigeria

A marked contrast exists between the condominial systems in Brazil and what frequently happens in other developing countries. To provide a more typical example of how the actions of public officials at the heads of state agencies and national governments discourage effective participation of citizens, even in those sectors where such participation could be most efficacious, I draw on fieldwork conducted in 1991 in Nigeria.[10] We visited schools and health clinics in four Local Government Authorities (LGAs) in western, eastern, central, and northern Nigeria, talked with many school teachers and health workers, and dug into as many records as we could find about the provision and production of these services. Here I limit my focus to a review of our findings related to the coproduction of primary education.

Until the colonial period ended in Nigeria, primary schools were largely provided by missionary and philanthropic organizations. Schools were normally constructed by local villages and run by a religious organization. Local villagers frequently provided housing and food for the teachers at a local school and considered it to be "their" school. They usually had some voice in decisions about the retention of teachers based on their views of teacher effectiveness. During the 1970s, in an era of centralized military rule, all mission schools throughout the country became public schools even though they continued to carry their original names.

In 1976, in a dramatic move, the Federal Military Government launched an ambitious nationwide program of universal primary education. Formal enrollment in primary schools leapt from 6.2 million students in 1975 to 8.1 million students the next year and continued to grow rapidly until 14.7 million students were formally enrolled in 1983. Formal enroll- ment then fell for four years in a row until it reached 11.5 million in 1987 (estimated to be 77% of the school-age population). In 1990, enrollment was up to 13.6 million students, still not at the level it had been seven years previously (Ayo et al. 1992, table 5.1, 30–31). The national government provided full grants to finance education during 1976–78.

The first oil shocks led the national government to demand that state governments begin to shoulder part of the cost of education. The national government stopped funding primary education in 1981. The World Bank estimated that per-pupil expenditures dropped from $92 in 1970, to $60 in 1974; $48 in 1981; and $55 in 1983 (Word Bank 1988, table A-17, 141, in constant 1983 dollars). The first year that structural adjustment policies would have been felt was 1987, when expenditures on public education fell from $848 million in 1986 to $680 million. In 1988, the national govern- ment assumed responsibility for funding a portion of expenditures on primary education. In a sudden turnaround in 1991, it announced a decen- tralization program making local governments fully responsible for financ- ing and managing local schools.

Thus, throughout the 1970s and 1980s, turbulent change characterized national, state, and LGA policies related to the organization of primary education. Early claims were made that neither local nor state governments were capable of providing and producing adequate levels of education, and that a massive infusion of funds from the national level was essential. As the costs of carrying out such policies became apparent, however, diverse strategies were adopted to shift the costs through changes in funding formulae. Changes in financial responsibility carried with them dramatic changes in who hired teachers; what standards were to be used in retaining, transferring, or promoting teachers; and exactly how teachers were to be paid. At several junctures, teachers waited for long periods of time to receive their paychecks. Parents were told at one point that they should not have to pay for education only to have school fees reestablished a short time thereafter. Free books were provided in one period but not in the next. Teachers had very little input to such decisions and local villagers even less. All policy switches appeared in a top-down proclamation by the national government, acting alone, or after some consultation with State governments.

In all of the villages we visited, informal associations of villagers were actively engaged in community projects such as the maintenance of a road, the repair of a school building, and/or the construction of a community center. In many cases, the successful "sons and daughters" of the village returned each year to participate in general planning of improvements that could be made and they sent funds to purchase supplies that were needed to undertake the project. Some projects would take many years to complete because of limited resources, but all of the villagers were proud to tell us of the projects they had undertaken. In all of the villages, therefore, it was possible to mobilize citizen effort for community affairs and the coproduction of goods and services.

In each of the villages we found teachers wanting to increase the skills and knowledge of their students but facing immense problems in trying to create an effective learning environment. All of the schools suffered from a paucity of books and teaching materials. Most of the teachers had the minimal certification necessary for teaching at a primary school, but many of them hoped they could find ways of obtaining further training or higher educational degrees themselves. Most of them, however, did not feel that they had any voice in making decisions either about how they could improve education in the school to which they were assigned, or about their own career development. They all faced immensely difficult financial constraints exacerbated by the recent and major devaluation of their currency on top of their need to pay for their own housing and to try to find land where they could grow some of their own food.

While differences always exist among administrative structures, all four of the LGAs we visited were relatively similar in regard to the type of top-down decision making that characterized them. Officials in the LGA headquarters worked in isolation from what was going on in the villages. While vehicles were parked in the LGA lot, funds were not available for gas and maintenance. Traveling to the villages was a rare adventure for LGA officials. Since decisions from the State and National government came arbitrarily, issuing the same kind of top-down orders to local schools was the accepted way of handling key decisions. Village administration is not considered part of the formal structure of governance even though substantial activities are organized within each village and carried out by the villagers themselves. The four villages included in our study varied substantially in the support they provided to primary education even though we could find no evidence of major difference at the LGA level.

Let us first discuss two villages located in the western and eastern parts of Nigeria where villagers provided a higher level of support to their primary schools than the two villages located in the central and northern regions. The two schools in Itagunmodi village located in the Atakunmosa LGA in Oyo State[11] were in the best condition of all of the schools we visited during our study. The teachers also had the highest morale. Itagunmodi, a village of about 200 households, is located on a barely motorable road about 40 minutes from Osu, which was the headquarters of the LGA. Parents-Teachers Associations had remained active at each school since 1970 when the formerly missionary schools became public schools. The buildings themselves were in good repair. While in the lower grades, two or three students shared a desk, there were desks in all classrooms, and upper-grade students each had their own desk to use. Teachers at both schools indicated that all eligible students attended primary school and that parents did not try to keep children at home. School records were available showing the number of students completing sixth grade and the rate of success in passing the state-administered Primary School Leaving Certificate. Since 1979, 85% of the students at the Methodist School and 82% of those at the Nawarudine School had obtained their Certificates.

This excellent record was achieved in a setting where few parents were able to purchase books for their children. Most classrooms had no more than three or four books per classroom for classes that averaged 17 pupils in Nawarundine and 28 pupils in the Methodist School. The problem of unavailable textbooks was greatly exacerbated by the fact that the list of textbooks authorized by the Ministry of Education changed every year. Students from one class could not, therefore, pass books onto the next class to allow for a slow accumulation of books for each class. Further, teachers were confronted with new books to master every year. Given the limited teaching materials, teachers found that they had to dig into their own diminishing salaries to provide essential charts and other teaching supplies.

Illustrative of the formal administrative structure that teachers faced is their lack of control over where they would be assigned to teach. The Headmaster of the Nawarudine School traced his career path for us since he graduated from Teachers College in 1979. During these 11 years he had taught at seven different schools, never staying at one school more than two years at a time. With one exception, the transfers were all initiated by his superiors. He had most recently been shifted from being a teacher at the Methodist School to become Headmaster at Nawarudine, where he had never taught previously.

The second village included in our study where we found higher levels of coproduction was Ofemilli, located in the Oji River LGA in Anambra State about 32 kilometers from Enugu, the state capital. The school in Ofemilli village had been built by the community in 1945 and staffed by the Roman Catholic Church until it became a public school after the civil war. The building, while small, was in reasonable physical condition. All four classes were conducted in the same large, rectangular classroom. As many as 120 children and their teachers used the same room simultaneously. Only a few benches were available at each of the major blackboards. Again, only a few children in each class had textbooks.

Parents in this village were highly supportive of primary education and the local school. They had decided upon several projects that would improve the physical structure and sanitary conditions of the school. One project was building a new pit latrine for the school. All work on this project was on hold, however, waiting for permission from the state government authorities. Attendance rates were high. The headmaster proudly told us that 32 out of 34 students passed the school-leaving examination in the prior year (94%) and one with distinction. A local progressive union awards scholarships to at least three students from the village to attend secondary school.

The LGA Educational Authority was in a similar situation to the LGA authorities visited elsewhere. During 1983–88, teacher paychecks had been issued irregularly as various changes had occurred in the financial responsibility for the payment of teachers. Some years, books arrived from the State government late in the year and sometimes never arrived. Getting the books out to the schools was not, however, a high priority for LGA officials as we stumbled over crates of books in the office of the Director of the LGA Education Authority.

The two villages that members of our team visited in Plateau and Sokoto States were a distinct contrast. Plateau State is located roughly in the center of Nigeria. We focused on Wereng Village in the Barakin Ladi LGA located about 50 kilometers southeast of Jos, the state capital. This area had been a tin mining area, but the larger commercial firms had all left the region during the mid-1960s when the tin mines no longer produced sufficiently for commercial mining. During the tin mining era, considerable investment had been made in the construction of all-season roads and other public facilities including schools and health clinics.

The maintenance of school buildings in the area was generally deficient. In a relatively rich village that we visited, Foron, the primary school was in a deplorable state of repair and had virtually no classroom furniture. In Wereng, the roof blew off one section of the primary school in 1988 and a second section in 1989. Members of the community replaced one section of roofing not long before we arrived after giving up hope of getting the LGA to do the repair.[12] This classroom, however, had not yet been returned to use for classes as the community had also hired a carpenter to repair broken furniture and he was using this classroom for that purpose. Thus, only about half of the students attended school at one time and classes were divided between a morning and afternoon session. The number of books available in any one classroom varied from a low of zero books (in one of the Grade 5 classrooms) to a high of 21 books (for the 32 students in the second Grade 5 classroom). Overall, an average of just under one-third of the students had the textbooks assigned for their class.

The proportion of students in Wereng who received a full six years of education is lower than the average for Barakin Ladi. Further, many children enter school after the first grade for a year or so before dropping out. For example, 53 boys and 66 girls started first grade in 1986 and 84 boys and 88 girls showed up for second grade. The problem was even greater in 1987 when more than half of the students in the second grade had not attended first grade. Tracing students through five years revealed that only about one-fourth of the girls and boys in the first or second grade in 1985 or 1986 were in fifth or sixth grade in 1990. Many erratic changes had occurred in class size during the interim period, and very few students attended classes during the rainy season where their labor was needed by their families. Few students continue education after the sixth grade. No data were available regarding the proportion of students obtaining a school-leaving certificate.

Teacher morale was obviously low in this setting. Besides the problems of overcrowded and short sessions, they all mentioned the lack of teaching materials in the classroom. In the words of the teachers themselves:

- I don't like to teach in a school where the students don't attend.
- I would like to go somewhere where parents can give us more of the cooperation we need.
- The atmosphere here is very bad for teaching. No roof. No textbooks. No writing paper. No teaching aids. No uniforms. Lots of students drop out.
- The government should not neglect the plight of the teacher. The problem is nationwide, not just Barakin Ladi. Barakin Ladi is a relatively good teaching assignment compared to some places.

In Sokoto State in the northern part of Nigeria, we included the Bodinga LGA and Darhela village in our study. The school in Darhela was constructed by the State Government in 1970 and was in a state of bad repair. The roof of one of the three blocks had blown off in early 1990 and remained off. Birds had invaded several of the classrooms and several had no windows or outside doors. None of the 53 students officially enrolled in Class I by the Headmaster had attended school from January through July of 1991. Only one-third of the 36 students who completed sixth grade passed the entrance examination to secondary school. A girl was the only student to actually enter secondary school, located 50 kilometers from the village.[13]

In each village, the capability to devote greater inputs into the educational process was demonstrated by the diversity of community projects in progress. In two of the villages, where parents valued education highly, this ability was focused on the primary schools and enhanced what the teachers could do. In these villages, most children of school age obtained at least six years of primary education and 85% or more of them passed their school-leaving examination. In the other two villages, parents did not value education highly and contributed little to the local primary schools. Without parental support, the teachers were incapacitated and demoralized. In these villages, children obtained a scattered education, if at all, and only a few successfully passed their school-level examination. The number of children from these villages going on to secondary education was also smaller.

When coproduction is discouraged by taking over schools that villagers had perceived as being "their" schools, by creating chaotic changes in who was responsible for funding and running a primary school system, and by top-down administrative command as the style for all decision making, only the most determined citizens will persist in coproductive activities. In Brazil, many urban neighborhoods that had never undertaken collective action were empowered by the action of government officials to make real decisions and coproduce an urban service that was highly valued. In Nigeria, villages that had demonstrated their capabilities to engage in collective action were discouraged by government officials from active engagement in the education of village children.

3. Coproduction

The concept of coproduction was initially developed by colleagues associated with the Workshop in Political Theory and Policy Analysis during the late 1970s as we struggled with the dominant theories of urban governance underlying policy recommendations of massive centralization.[14] Consolidation of all governments serving metropolitan areas was proposed in many urban areas. Scholars and public officials argued that citizens as clients would receive more effective and efficient services delivered by a professional staff employed by a large, bureaucratic agency (see E. Ostrom 1972). After studying police services in metropolitan areas, however, we had not found a single instance where a large, centralized police department was able to provide better direct service, more equitably delivered, or at a lower cost to neighborhoods inside the central city when these were carefully matched to similar neighborhoods located in surrounding jurisdictions.[15] Our findings were replicated by us and other scholars repeatedly over a 15-year period. A study recently conducted by Parks (1995) replicated the earliest findings in Indianapolis after the passage of a quarter of a century.

In our efforts to understand these strong empirical results, we came to recognize that several myths adversely affected how scholars viewed service production. First, there was the notion of a single producer responsible for urban services within each jurisdiction. We found, instead, many public agencies (e.g., municipalities and counties) as well as private firms (e.g., security services) producing immediate response services. Turning to intermediate police services, we found even more variety. Forensic laboratory analysis was frequently produced in a public or private hospital. Training was often produced in a local community or private college. We were dealing with a public-private industry rather than with the bureaucratic apparatus of a single government (V. Ostrom and E. Ostrom 1965; E. Ostrom, Parks, and Whitaker 1974, 1978).

Second, drawing on the work of Lipsky (1973), we recognized that street-level bureaucrats were not simply the pawns of a central bureaucratic machine that would do whatever their supervisors commanded. Riding eight hour shifts with police officers enables one to see their job more as they do and recognize how much discretion they have in how they spend their time. A motivated officer uses time in many ways that enhance the safety of a beat. An officer who is not motivated finds many ways to escape the summons of the police radio and get some sleep.

Third, we realized that the production of a service, as contrasted to a good, was difficult without the active participation of those supposedly receiving the service. If students are not actively engaged in their own education, encouraged and supported by their family and friends, what teachers do may make little difference in the skills students acquire. If citizens do not report suspicious events rapidly to a police department, there is little that a department can do to reduce crime in an area or solve the crimes that occur. We developed the term *coproduction* to describe the potential relationships that could exist between the "regular" producer (street-level police officers, schoolteachers, or health workers) and "clients" who want to be transformed by the service into safer, better-educated, or healthier persons. Coproduction is one way that synergy can occur between what a government does and what citizens do.

All production involves the transformation of some set of inputs into outputs—or a production function. In the conventional way of thinking of production, a principal, such as an entrepreneur or a bureau chief, organizes factors of production (traditionally, land, labor, and capital) to produce varying levels of output. All relevant aspects of these factors are under the command of the principal who decides how much of any one factor will be combined with other inputs based on relative costs and capabilities. Production functions array the tradeoffs that a principal faces in making combinatorial decisions in order to get the most out of one set of inputs given their relative costs and the production technology in use and amount of other inputs allocated to this process.

In some important production processes, however, not all of the inputs that could potentially be used to produce an output are under full control of a single, public-sector principal. In constructing infrastructure facilities, for example, the labor used to construct a facility could all be employed by a public utility, it could all be contributed by citizens, or some of the labor could come from both sources. Whether a production process would best be organized entirely in the public sphere, entirely in the private sphere, or coproduced by both depends primarily on the shape of the production function. The relative role of public or private sector depends on the relative costs of the inputs contributed by these sources of potentially productive labor (and, as we discuss below, the likelihood of motivating either public employees, private citizens, or both).

In analyzing coproduction, we also use production functions. Production functions may involve strictly substitutable processes. If inputs are strictly substitutable, no potential for synergy exists. In figure 15.1, for example, Q_1, Q_2 and Q_3 represent three levels of output that could be achieved from a combination of inputs from citizens and from government. Inputs by public officials are completely substitutable for the inputs of citizen-producers. In such a situation, no advantage exists to finding ways of coproducing a good using both sources of input. Rather, the decision to produce the good in the public sector (e.g., sending a public truck on a regular route to collect garbage or recyclable materials) or to have citizens produce the good (e.g., require that citizens take garbage or recyclables to a designated location) depends on the wage rate paid to public officials as compared to the opportunity costs facing citizens for spending their time in transport.[16] If the wage rate of public officials is lower than the opportunity cost of citizens—as illustrated by budget constraint B_2—then the most efficient form of production is located entirely in the public sector. The most output, Q_2, could be produced entirely by the public agency assuming that public officials are fully motivated to work up to their capacity. Alternatively, if the opportunity costs of citizens were comparably lower than the wage rate of public officials, as illustrated by B_1, the most output could be entirely produced by citizens alone, again assuming full motivation to perform to capacity.

When the inputs from a government and citizen are complementary, as shown in figure 15.2, output is best produced by some combination of input from both sources. Now, a potential for synergy exists. With such production functions, it would be possible to achieve the same level of output with many combinations of input from a government agency and from citizens. A combination of inputs, however, is needed rather than reliance on only citizens or only officials. If the opportunity costs of contributing are high for citizens, as compared to the wage rate of public officials, as shown in B_1, the least cost combination would be for C_1 inputs from citizens and A_2 from a government agency. The same quantity of output, Q_1 could also be produced by C_2 from citizens and A_3 from an agency, and this would be the least cost combination if the relative costs were reflected as in the B_2 budget constraint.

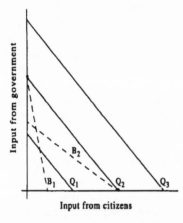

Input from citizens

Fig. 15.1. Substitutable contributions from government and citizens to output

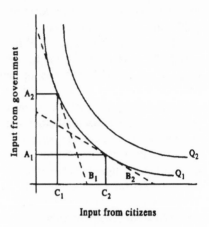

Input from citizens

Fig. 15.2. Complementary contributions from government and citizens to output

Analytically, the possibilities of coproduction are clear and of particular relevance in a developing country context. In many developing countries, the shape of a budget constraint is closer to that of B_2 in figure 15.2 than to B_1. Many poor regions and neighborhoods are characterized by severe underutilization of the knowledge, skills, and time of residents—which means the opportunity costs of devoting these inputs to the creation of valued public outputs are low. Obtaining better infrastructure and services generates very high benefits.

Designing institutional arrangements that help induce successful coproductive strategies is far more daunting than demonstrating their theoretical existence. Part of the problem stems from the nature of the goods and services typically produced in the public sector. It is notoriously difficult to specify a clear production technology for education, health, and police services (Wilson 1989). While production technologies for constructing infrastructure are better known, how to regulate their use and keep them well maintained is a substantial technological puzzle. In addition, as discussed below, part of the innovative aspects of the condominial systems was changing the professionally proscribed production technologies themselves. Public sectors typically rely on incentive systems that send very weak signals about performance to staff who are employed on long-term, low-paying contracts with few legal opportunities for advancement. The signals encouraging citizen inputs are even more feeble.

The operational challenge exists in both developed and developing countries, but the severity of the problems involved is greater in many sectors of developing countries where the importance of central control and direction has dominated official thinking since the end of colonialism. The situation in many cases is illustrated by figure 15.3, where the technically achievable production function for combinations of inputs from government and from citizens is shown as Q, while the current output at X is far from the frontier of what is feasible given budget constraints. Much less is being generated from both sources of inputs than could be produced if everyone were motivated to exert more effort.

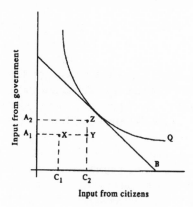

Fig. 15.3. Output below feasible level

In such a situation, substantial problems need to be addressed in enhancing the productivity of inputs from the public sector itself, let alone finding ways of more effectively motivating citizens and coordinating the efforts of diverse inputs not subject to the command of a single principal. In both the Brazilian and Nigerian cases, public servants receive relatively low wages. In Nigeria, after the devaluation of the naira during the late 1980s, the value of teachers' salaries plummeted. Earlier, they lost the food and housing that local communities used to provide. Now, teachers had to devote even more time to finding affordable housing and in tending their own gardens to provide food for their families. Arbitrary assignments and transfers, little chance for promotion, unkept promises by national and state governments regarding the support of primary education, and frequent top-down changes of relative responsibilities of national, state, and local authority over education, generate few incentives for highly motivated teaching. In villages where parents are relatively uninterested in primary education, who send only a small proportion of their children to school, and where school buildings are left without roofs, neither teachers nor citizens are actively putting effort into the production of primary education. In villages where parents are more supportive of primary education, for example, contributing C_2 of effort in figure 15.3 rather than C_1, output levels of Y rather than X could be achieved even without any increase in the effort of teachers. If teachers were to respond positively to increased support by parents and students, and themselves move from A_1 to A_2, output would increase still further to Z. The much higher proportion of students attending school and graduating after six years, and passing external examinations in the villages where parents supported primary schools, is evidence consistent with a change such as the one from X to Y (and, perhaps Y to Z) in figure 15.3.

At any one point in time, it is useful for analytical purposes to conceptualize production functions as a fixed technology. Entrepreneurs in both the private and public sectors can change the shape and components of production functions over time. Creative entrepreneurship is itself more likely in environments that encourage innovation and allow for a wide array of options in the organization of public service production. The innovative condominial program in the Brazilian case brought together several crucial ideas that expanded the level of services made available to poorer residents of Brazilian towns and cities. First, the idea to split sanitation systems into two linked systems—large-scale public works and small-scale community works—allowed for the separation of what had been one production function into two component parts. The effectiveness of the public sector inputs in the construction of systems requiring deep trenches and large pipes is considerable. This advantage disappears in the construction of shallow trenches and small pipes. Further, the opportunity costs of organizing residents to construct condominial systems in one neighborhood are much lower than trying to coordinate residential work teams for a citywide project. The money saved by minimizing the length of trunk lines to serve any one system could then be applied to the construction of trunks in other neighborhoods as well as to pay for staff to work with communities in the time-consuming process of negotiating local contracts.

Another innovation of the condominial system is the intensive involvement of citizens in the initial design and continuing maintenance of these systems. This changed the *shape* of these production functions so that what citizens did made the efforts of public officials more efficacious and vice versa. Developing new production functions and changing the shape of others was indeed a major breakthrough for the condominial systems. Even more important, however, is motivating both public officials and citizens to work effectively together in settings where coproduction has rarely occurred and considerable distrust exists. This has been accomplished in the more successful systems by a slow building of citizen organization that, in turn, has affected the incentives of officials in a positive direction. Officials designing and operating infrastructure projects are usually supported by large construction firms interested in receiving more contracts. The incentives of this system are well known and do not lead to quality construction, good monitoring, or effective operation (E. Ostrom, Schroeder, and Wynne 1993).

The condominial systems depend more on satisfied users to mobilize political support to construct still more condominial systems. Those systems performing at higher levels have solved some of the difficult problems of operating and maintaining these systems over time. According to Watson (1995, 41), the key elements of successful operation of these systems are "(1) staff continuity between the construction and operations phases; (2) a specialized condominial maintenance crew; (3) face-to-face contact with residents; and (4) ongoing network monitoring and repairs and customer education." These elements change the nature of information available as well as the incentives of participants. It also generated social capital in the form of urban residents learning how to work with each other and with public agencies. This social capital is then a potential asset to be drawn on to obtain other kinds of urban goods and services.

Coproduction is not, of course, universally advantageous. Nor, is it a process that will occur spontaneously simply because substantial benefits could be achieved. Several conditions heighten the probability that coproduction is an improvement over regular government production or citizen production alone. First, the technologies in use must generate a complimentary production possibility frontier (such as in figs. 15.2 or 15.3) rather than merely a substitutive one (as in fig. 15.1).[17] When coproductive inputs are legally owned by diverse entities and complements, synergy can occur. Each has something the other needs. In the condominial systems, citizens had information, skills, time, and other resources essential to constructing the condominial works. Officials had the capabilities for constructing the public works and connecting the feeder lines to the trunk lines and treatment plants. By obtaining a modest cash contribution from the community, they are more motivated to make sure the system works.

Second, legal options must be available to both parties. In centralized systems, many potentially productive options are restricted. Teachers are not authorized to change a curriculum to make it more relevant for their students. Headmasters do not have the authority to change the timing of the school year so that school is open when children are not essential for the agricultural activities of their families. Parents who must wait many months to obtain permission before building a school latrine are hindered by such restrictions in their efforts to make their children's school a healthier place. The condominial system broke through such restrictions to open up a much wider set of options for both officials and citizens.

Third, participants need to be able to build a credible commitment to one another so that if one side increases input, the other will continue at the same or higher levels. Clear and enforceable contracts between government agencies and citizens enhance that credibility. The complementarity of their inputs is analytically similar to the production of a local, public good that is jointly enhanced if either side increases its inputs. In the condominial system, residents signed a formal contract outlining what they were willing to do in order to obtain a connection to a major trunk line. In the Brazilian cities where this petition was fully recognized as a dual commitment (at least after experience with the system over time), higher performance levels were achieved than where citizens did their part only to find that the trunk lines were shoddily constructed and poorly maintained. It is also important to make a credible commitment not to undertake actions. If citizens come to believe that a government agency will bail them out if they do not perform according to their side of an agreement, citizens will be more likely to break the promises they make.

Fourth, incentives help to encourage inputs from both officials and citizens. Such incentives may be little more than the opportunity for officials to get to know citizens and vice versa in an open and regular forum. Teachers who are feted when the children they teach excel in competitions are more motivated than those who are ignored no matter what their students do. One lesson from the Nigerian cases is that coproduction will be quite uneven when it is officially discouraged.

The last three of these conditions are more likely to be met in a polycentric political system than in a monocentric (or, highly centralized) political system. A polycentric polity offers citizens opportunities to organize not one, but many, governing authorities (see V. Ostrom, Tiebout, and Warren 1961; V. Ostrom 1987, 1991). Each unit in a polycentric system exercises independent authority to make and enforce rules within a specified area for particular policy areas. A condominial system is one example of a polycentric system. In this case, the smallest unit of the system is only one or two blocks in size. It is nested in a municipal, state, and national regime that can complement the activities of citizens organized in these mini-polities (see E. Ostrom, Schroeder, and Wynne 1993, chap. 9).

In a polycentric system, rules at a large-system level can be written in a general form that can then be tailored to local circumstances. In regard to the school year, for example, a large unit can specify the number of days that schools must be open while smaller units can specify the particular dates to fit the local agricultural seasons. A larger unit can specify a series of textbooks that are authorized for a decade or so at a time. Then, smaller units can pick those books that have examples of most relevance to the students in the smaller units. In other words, many more actions tailored to local arenas can be authorized in a polycentric system than in a monocentric system that tries to establish uniform rules for all settings. Incentives that encourage coproduction are easier to design when some of the units in a polycentric system are relatively small and encourage more meaningful contact among officials and citizens.[18] The overlap of governmental units could perform the oversight needed to reduce the threat of arrangements that are "too cozy" in a smaller unit.

4. Implication of Coproduction for Synergy and Development

Let me be more radical than Peter Evans expects and suggest that coproduction of many goods and services normally considered to be public goods by government agencies and citizens organized into polycentric systems is crucial for achieving higher levels of welfare in developing countries, particularly for those who are poor. Prior efforts directed at improving the training and capacity of public officials have frequently had disappointing results. Efforts directed at increasing citizen "participation" in petitioning others to provide goods for them have also proved disappointing. Efforts directed at increasing the potential complementarities between official and citizen production or problem-solving activities may require more time at the initial stage of a process, but promise a much higher, long-term return.[19]

In regard to physical infrastructure, the potential complementarities may be great, especially when those facilities involve major "trunk" lines and "feeder" lines. This is the case for highway systems, water and sanitation systems, and most communication systems. Planning the location and specification of the major trunk lines is a task requiring the input of larger agencies in a polycentric system because of the economies of scale, the need to raise large sums of monetary resources, and the capability of larger units to deal with externalities. When the construction and maintenance of feeder lines is then planned by a smaller unit in a polycentric system to meet reasonable general standards, but also local needs and capabilities, the large and small polycentric units complement each other. Each perform tasks the other cannot perform well. Small units cannot effectively plan the backbone of a large network. Large units do not have the relevant information about local time and place information.

As long as public officials and citizens in developing countries continue to see a great divide between them, however, potential synergies will remain mere potentialities. Contemporary textbooks contribute to this artificial wall. Many textbooks on public administration stress managerial skills within the bureaucracy itself and few discuss the skills needed to work effectively in problem-solving activities with citizens. Economics textbooks that address problems of market failure assert that "the" government must provide in those cases where the market fails.[20] Textbooks in political science tend, in recent times, to focus on the formal aspects of national governments, on how party systems work, and on struggles to achieve dominance in a legislative body. They seldom discuss how services are produced and delivered, or how agencies work at levels below that of national government. The role of citizens is depicted as casting ballots and watching the action. Even books comparing local government in Nigeria and the United States focus entirely on the formal structure of authority in both countries (Aborisade and Mund 1995).[21] No mention is made of village governance, which is the only governance that has an impact on the lives of most Nigerians. Textbooks that focus on local governance tend to posit the presence of a large number of local units of government as evidence of fragmentation and overlap of authority (and thus a detriment to good governance) rather than as the existence of organization on many different scales (and thus an asset for good governance).

One reason given for creating a divide between public and private sectors is controlling corruption. Corruption is a threat to the effectiveness, fairness, and growth of all polities and economies (Wade 1984, 1985). Other forms of opportunistic behavior—including free-riding, shirking, deception, and untrustworthy behavior—are also threats. If the remedy to corruption is seen as the creation of a strict bureaucratic structure to separate the servants of the public from the public, it is likely that behind the closed doors of a centralized system corrupt practices can flourish without much fear of exposure (Klitgaard 1988). The efforts to control corruption by creating a gulf between polity and society may encourage other forms of opportunistic behavior to proliferate along with corruption. When public officials and the citizens they are supposed to serve work together in diverse sets of open, nested arenas, productivity can be higher and all forms of opportunistic behavior are more likely to be exposed, but never totally eliminated.[22]

The experience of success of coproduction also encourages citizens to develop other horizontal relationships and social capital (Putnam 1993). Those working with condominial systems report that local activism through coproduction rapidly spills over to other areas. Alert citizens are able to increase the quality of services they obtain from multiple government agencies and not just the initial project.

Thus, let me recommend that the bridging of the gulf between the analysis of private activities apart from those of government agencies needs to be high on the agenda of development theorists and activists. No market can survive without extensive public goods provided by governmental agencies. No government can be efficient and equitable without considerable input from citizens. Synergetic outcomes can be fostered to a much greater extent than our academic barriers have let us contemplate.

NOTES

1. Tendler and I are, of course, not alone in bridging this gulf. See also Klitgaard 1991; Bates 1987; D. Korten 1980; F. Korten 1982, 1985; Levine 1980; and Evans 1995.

2. Bates (1976) stresses the investment of Zambian parents in their children's education as a rational strategy to ensure income when the parents are no longer able to provide for themselves.

3. Jon Van Til (1982) stressed the importance of coproduction of energy by citizens in conjunction with public and private energy producers—a field that also requires major investment in infrastructure facilities.

4. It appears that several fortuitous circumstances came together to support this program over the hurdles that would normally prevent it from ever moving from paper to practice. Natal is where the first systems were developed. A World Bank loan to support the effort of the state water company CAERN to provide sanitation services to poor neighborhoods made the funds available. de Melo obtained the enthusiastic support of the President of CAERN and a small group of entrepreneurial and social-minded engineers in his division. "The team had considerable autonomy of action: they developed their own work plans, ordered materials without going through lengthy procurement procedures, and hired consultants as they saw fit. It was mission-oriented and composed of young, eager engineers, who saw their work as providing previously excluded groups access to critical social benefits" (Watson 1995, 19).

5. See Watson 1995, for an analysis of the difference between the high- and low-performing systems. See Tendler and Freedheim 1994; and Tendler 1997 for other positive developments in the tropics.

6. Relevant books include: McCay and Acheson 1987; Fortmann and Bruce 1988; Wade 1994; Berkes 1989; Pinkerton 1989; E. Ostrom 1990; Sengupta 1991, 1993; Blomquist 1992; Bromley et al. 1992; Tang 1992; Martin 1989/92; Thomson 1992; Dasgupta and Mäler 1992; V. Ostrom, Feeny, and Picht 1993; Netting 1993; E. Ostrom, Gardner, and Walker 1994; Keohane and Ostrom 1995.

7. See in particular Milgrom and Roberts 1992; Alchian and Demsetz 1972; and Marshak and Radner 1972.

8. But see Lam 1995 and the literature cited therein; WECS/IIMI 1990; and the works cited in section 3.

9. Implementation teams have frequently involved both engineers and social workers and over time have involved a larger number of paraprofessionals so as to keep the costs of these time-intensive activities lower (see Watson 1995, 23).

10. The fieldwork was part of the Decentralization: Finance and Management project, which was jointly conducted by Associates in Rural Development, Syracuse University, and Indiana University and funded by the Research and Development Bureau of the Agency for International Development (DHR-5446-Z-00-7033-00). I was the team leader for a Nigerian-American team composed of Dele Ayo, Kenneth Hubbell, Dele Olowu, and Tina West. I am deeply appreciative of the good fortune of working with such talented and productive colleagues. Parallel studies were conducted in Ghana (Fiadjoe et al. 1992), Ivory Coast (Garnier et al. 1992b), and a synthesis report comparing experiences in all three countries (Garnier et al. 1992a). See also Green 1994.

11. After our study, Oyo State was further divided into two states and Atakun-mosa ended up in Osun State.

12. That the community could repair the roof is evidence that they had the skills and capability of doing so. The community had also built a public health clinic. When the supply of medicine and facilities to that health clinic turned out to be inadequate, the community was able to attract a private pharmacist to the area who ran a very successful private clinic. The community, and our research team, was also fortunate to have an action-research team from the University of Durham and the University of Jos in the area helping collect relevant information and providing useful input to community problem-solving skills. That the community was waiting for the Government to repair the roof is a reflection of the perception that the Government had taken over the school in relatively good repair and promised them to provide higher quality education than they had had previously.

13. The problem of getting good data in the field, especially for an adequate managerial picture of what is happening, is illustrated by the following description of our team's effort to obtain data in this school:

> The data on enrollment had to be fished out from enrollment registers which were thrown in different classrooms and were in tattered shape. In spite of the spirited assistance of the teachers and the Headmaster, we were not able to establish enrollment data for any year besides 1990 and 1991. Diaries, school record books, files and ten copies each of textbooks supplied by the Federal Ministry of Education through the State Ministry of Education (for English Language, Mathematics, Social Studies, and Hausa) were found in various cupboards in the Headmaster's office. (Ayo et al. 1992, 124)

14. See Parks et al. 1982; Kiser and Percy 1980; Percy 1978; Rich 1979, 1981; and Whitaker 1980.

15. See E. Ostrom and Whitaker 1973; E. Ostrom and Parks 1973; E. Ostrom, Parks, and Whitaker 1974; Parks and Ostrom 1981; and Parks 1984.

16. An example of "own production" of major infrastructures is that of farmer-constructed irrigation systems where the farmers design, finance, construct, operate, and maintain an irrigation system (see E. Ostrom, Lam, and Lee 1994; E. Ostrom 1996).

17. There is, of course, still a further logical possibility of a concave relationship where one source of inputs interferes with the inputs of the other. There was, after all, an era in the history of U.S. education when parents were told not to "interfere" with their children's learning. The consistent finding in study after study is that parents' SES is strongly associated with children's educational performance (see Hanushek 1986, for a review of this literature). This leads one to conclude that this relationship operates in practice via the type of encouragement given to students in middle-class families and the help extended to children in such families who are having difficulty with some subject at school. If some process did have a concave production relationship, coproduction would be inefficient rather than synergistic at any level.

18. Even though Nigeria is formally a federal nation, the control of the national government over state governments, and of state governments over LGAs has been

so extensive that little effective polycentricity exists other than in the village setting where what goes on is largely ignored by the formal units of government.

19. Recent efforts to rethink management, training, and institutional development congruent with local cultures led by Mamadou Dia at the World Bank reflect the general effort to rethink development processes that bridge previously defined gulfs. See Serageldin and Taboroff 1994; and Bryant 1994. See also Dia 1993, for an application to the reform of civil service systems in Africa.

20. As Sugden (1986, 3) indicates: "Most modern economic theory describes a world presided over by a *government* (not, significantly, by governments), and sees this world through the government's eyes."

21. For a completely different and important approach to the importance of indigenous as well as governmental governance structures, see Wunsch and Olowu 1995; and Olowu and Erero 1995.

22. Most game-theoretical analyses of complex opportunistic behavior agree that such behaviors are never completely eliminated in social dilemmas or games of trust (see, e.g., Weissing and Ostrom 1991, 1993; Güth and Kliemt 1995; and Laffont and Tirole 1993).

REFERENCES

Aborisade, Oladimeji, and Robert J. Mundt, eds. (1995) *Local Government in Nigeria and the United States: Learning from Comparison.* Ile-Ife, Nigeria: Obafemi Awolowo University, Department of Local Government Studies, Local Government Publication Series.

Alchian, Armen A., and Harold Demsetz (1972) "Production, information costs, and economic organization." *American Economic Review* 62, no. 5 (Dec.): 777–95.

Ayo, Dele, Kenneth Hubbell, Dele Olowu, Elinor Ostrom, and Tina West (1992) *The Experience in Nigeria with Decentralization Approaches to Local Delivery of Primary Education and Primary Health Services.* Decentralization: Finance and Management Project Report. Burlington, VT: Associates in Rural Development.

Bates, Robert H. (1976) *Rural Responses to Industrialization. A Study of Village Zambia.* New Haven, CT: Yale University Press.

——— (1987) *Essays on the Political Economy of Rural Africa.* Berkeley: University of California Press.

Berkes, Fikret, ed. (1989) *Common Property Resources: Ecology and Community-Based Sustainable Development.* London: Belhaven Press.

Blomquist, William (1992) *Dividing the Waters: Governing Groundwater in Southern California.* San Francisco: ICS Press.

Briscoe, John, and Mike Garn (1994) *Financing Agenda 21: Freshwater.* Washington, DC: World Bank, Transportation, Water, and Urban Development Department.

Bromley, Daniel W., et al., eds. (1992) *Making the Commons Work: Theory, Practice, and Policy.* San Francisco: ICS Press.

Bryant, Coralie (1994) "Culture, management, and institutional assessment." In Ismail Serageldin and June Taboroff (eds.), *Culture and Development in Africa,* 447–64. Washington, DC: World Bank.

Dia, Mamadou (1993) *A Governance Approach to Civil Service Reform in Sub-Saharan Africa*. Washington, DC: World Bank.

Dasgupta, Partha, and Karl Göran Mäler (1992) *The Economics of Transnational Commons*. Oxford: Clarendon Press.

Evans, Peter (1995) *Embedded Autonomy: States and Industrial Transformation*. Princeton, NJ: Princeton University Press.

────── (1996) "Government action, social capital and development: Reviewing the evidence on synergy." *World Development* 24, no. 6: 1119–32.

Fiadjoe, F., David Green, Charles Schwabe, and Tina West (1992) "Decentralization: Improving governance in Sub-Saharan Africa—Ghana case study." Decentralization: Finance and Management Project Report. Burlington, VT: Associates in Rural Development.

Fortmann, Louise, and John W. Bruce, eds. (1988) *Whose Trees? Proprietary Dimensions of Forestry*. Boulder, CO: Westview Press.

Garnier, Maurice, David Green, Elinor Ostrom, Charles Schwabe, James Thomson, and Tina West (1992a) "Decentralization: Improving governance in Sub-Saharan Africa—Synthesis report." Decentralization: Finance and Management Project Report. Burlington, VT: Associates in Rural Development.

Garnier, Maurice, A. B. Noel, Charles Schwabe, and James Thomson (1992b) "The experience in Ivory Coast with decentralized approaches to local delivery of primary education and primary health services." Decentralization: Finance and Management Project Report. Burlington, VT: Associates in Rural Development.

Green, David B. (1994) "Decentralized public service provision in Sub-Saharan Africa—A false start. Lessons from the DFM project." Decentralization: Finance and Management Project Report. Burlington, VT: Associates in Rural Development.

Güth, Werner, and Hartmut Kliemt (1995) "Competition or cooperation: On the evolutionary economics of trust, exploitation and moral attitudes." Working paper. Berlin: Humboldt University.

Hanushek, E. A. (1986) "The economics of schooling: Production and efficiency in public schools." *Journal of Economic Literature* 24: 1141–77.

Keohane, Robert O., and Elinor Ostrom, eds. (1995) *Local Commons and Global Interdependence: Heterogeneity and Cooperation in Two Domains*. London: Sage Publications.

Kiser, Larry L., and Stephen L. Percy (1980) "The concept of coproduction and its prospects for public service delivery." Working paper. Bloomington: Indiana University, Workshop in Political Theory and Policy Analysis.

Klitgaard, Robert (1988) *Controlling Corruption*. Berkeley: University of California Press.

────── (1991) *Adjusting to Reality: Beyond "State vs. Market" in Economic Development*. San Francisco: ICS Press.

Korten, David C. (1980) "Community organization and rural development: A learning process approach." *Public Administration Review* 40, no. 5 (Sept.–Oct.): 480–511.

Korten, Frances F. (1982) "Building national capacity to develop water users' associations: Experience from the Philippines." Staff Working Paper No. 528. Washington, DC: World Bank, Agricultural and Rural Development Department.

———— (1985) "A participatory approach to irrigation development in the Philippines." In Jean Claude Garcia-Zamor (ed.), *Public Participation in Development Planning and Management: Cases from Africa and Asia*, 179–86. Boulder, CO: Westview Press.

Laffont, J. J., and Jean Tirole (1993) *A Theory of Incentives in Procurement and Regulation*. Cambridge, MA: MIT Press.

Lam, Wai Fung (1996) "Institutional design of public agencies and coproduction: A study of irrigation associations in Taiwan." *World Development* 24, no. 6: 1039–54. Reprinted as chap. 13 of this volume.

Levine, Gilbert (1980) "The relationship of design, operation, and management." In E. Walter Coward, Jr. (ed.), *Irrigation and Agricultural Development in Asia: Perspectives from the Social Sciences*, 51–64. Ithaca, NY: Cornell University Press.

Lipsky, Michael (1973) "Street level bureaucracy and the analysis of urban reform." In George Frederickson (ed.), *Neighborhood Control in the 1970s*. New York: Chandler Publishing Co.

Marshak, Jacob, and Roy Radner (1972) *Economic Theory of Teams*. New Haven, CT: Yale University Press.

Martin, Fenton (1989/1992) *Common-Pool Resources and Collective Action: A Bibliography*, vols. 1 and 2. Bloomington: Indiana University, Workshop in Political Theory and Policy Analysis.

McCay, Bonnie J., and James M. Acheson (1987) *The Question of the Commons: The Culture and Ecology of Communal Resources*. Tucson: University of Arizona Press.

Milgrom, Paul, and John Roberts (1992) *Economics, Organization and Management*. Englewood Cliffs, NJ: Prentice-Hall.

Netting, Robert McC. (1993) *Smallholders, Householders: Farm Families and the Ecology of Intensive, Sustainable Agriculture*. Stanford, CA: Stanford University Press.

Olowu, Dele, and John Erero (1995) "Governance of Nigeria's villages and cities through indigenous institutions." Working paper. Ile-Ife, Nigeria: Obafemi Awolowo University.

Ostrom, Elinor (1972) "Metropolitan reform: Propositions derived from two traditions." *Social Science Quarterly* 53 (Dec.): 474–93. Reprinted in M. D. McGinnis, ed. *Polycentricity and Local Public Economies* (Ann Arbor: University of Michigan Press, 1999).

———— (1990) *Governing the Commons: The Evolution of Institutions for Collective Action*. New York: Cambridge University Press.

———— (1996) "Incentives, rules of the game, and development." In *Proceedings of the World Bank Annual Conference on Development Economics 1995*, 207–34. Washington, DC: World Bank.

Ostrom, Elinor, and Roger B. Parks (1973) "Suburban police departments: Too many and too small?" In Louis H. Masotti and Jeffrey K. Hadden (eds.), *The Urbanization of the Suburbs. Urban Affairs Annual Reviews* 7: 367–402. Beverly Hills, CA: Sage Publications.

Ostrom, Elinor, and Gordon P. Whitaker (1973) "Does local community control of police make a difference? Some preliminary findings." *American Journal of*

Political Science 17, no. 1 (Feb.): 48–76. Reprinted in M. D. McGinnis, ed. *Polycentricity and Local Public Economies* (Ann Arbor: University of Michigan Press, 1999).

Ostrom, Elinor, Roy Gardner, and James Walker (1994) *Rules, Games, and Common-Pool Resources*. Ann Arbor: University of Michigan Press.

Ostrom, Elinor, Wai Fung Lam, and Myungsuk Lee (1994) "The performance of self-governing irrigation systems in Nepal." *Human Systems Management* 13, no. 3: 197–207.

Ostrom, Elinor, Roger B. Parks, and Gordon P. Whitaker (1974) "Defining and measuring structural variations in interorganizational arrangements." *Publius* 4, no. 4 (Fall): 87–108. Reprinted in M. D. McGinnis, ed. *Polycentricity and Local Public Economies* (Ann Arbor: University of Michigan Press, 1999).

——— (1978) *Patterns of Metropolitan Policing*. Cambridge, MA: Ballinger.

Ostrom, Elinor, Larry Schroeder, and Susan Wynne (1993) *Institutional Incentives and Sustainable Development: Infrastructure Policies in Perspective*. Boulder, CO: Westview Press.

Ostrom, Vincent (1987) *The Political Theory of a Compound Republic: Designing the American Experiment*. 2d rev. ed. San Francisco: ICS Press.

——— (1991) *The Meaning of American Federalism: Constituting a Self-Governing Society*. San Francisco: ICS Press.

——— (1997) *The Meaning of Democracy and the Vulnerability of Democracies: A Response to Tocqueville's Challenge*. Ann Arbor: University of Michigan Press.

Ostrom, Vincent, and Elinor Ostrom (1965) "A behavioral approach to the study of intergovernmental relations." *Annals of the American Academy of Political and Social Science* 359 (May): 137–46. Reprinted in M. D. McGinnis, ed. *Polycentricity and Local Public Economies* (Ann Arbor: University of Michigan Press, 1999).

Ostrom, Vincent, David Feeny, and Hartmut Picht, eds. (1993) *Rethinking Institutional Analysis and Development: Issues, Alternatives, and Choices*. 2d ed. San Francisco: ICS Press.

Ostrom, Vincent, Charles M. Tiebout, and Robert Warren (1961) "The organization of government in metropolitan areas: A theoretical inquiry." *American Political Science Review* 55 (Dec.): 831–42. Reprinted in M. D. McGinnis, ed. *Polycentricity and Local Public Economies* (Ann Arbor: University of Michigan Press, 1999).

Parks, Roger B. (1984) "Linking objective and subjective measures of performance." *Public Administration Review* 44, no. 2 (March–April): 118–27.

——— (1995) "Do we really want to consolidate urban areas?" *Polycentric Circles Newsletter* 1, no. 2 (Indiana University, Workshop in Political Theory and Policy Analysis, June). Reprinted in M. D. McGinnis, ed. *Polycentricity and Local Public Economies* (Ann Arbor: University of Michigan Press, 1999).

Parks, Roger B., and Elinor Ostrom (1981) "Complex models of urban service systems." In Terry N. Clark (ed.), *Urban Policy Analysis: Directions for Future Research. Urban Affairs Annual Reviews*, vol. 21, 171–99. Beverly Hills, CA: Sage Publications. Reprinted in M. D. McGinnis, ed. *Polycentricity and Local Public Economies* (Ann Arbor: University of Michigan Press, 1999).

Parks, Roger B., Paula Baker, Larry Kiser, Ronald Oakerson, Elinor Ostrom, Vincent Ostrom, Stephen Percy, Martha Vandivort, Gordon Whitaker, and Rick Wilson (1982) "Coproduction of public services." In Richard C. Rich (ed.), *Analyzing Urban-Service Distributions,* 185–99. Lexington, MA: Lexington Books. Alternative version reprinted in M. D. McGinnis, ed. *Polycentricity and Local Public Economies* (Ann Arbor: University of Michigan Press, 1999).

Percy, Stephen L. (1978) "Conceptualizing and measuring citizen coproduction of community safety." *Policy Studies Journal* 7: special issue, 486–93.

Pinkerton, Evelyn (1989) *Cooperative Management of Local Fisheries. New Directions for Improved Management and Community Development.* Vancouver: University of British Columbia Press.

Putnam, Robert (1993) "The prosperous community: Social capital and public life." *American Prospect* 13 (Spring): 35–42.

Rich, Richard C. (1979) "The roles of neighborhood organizations in urban service delivery." *Urban Affairs Papers* 1 (Fall): 81–93.

—— (1981) "Municipal service and the interaction of the voluntary and government sectors." *Administration and Society* 13 (May): 59–76.

Sengupta, Nirmal (1991) *Managing Common Property: Irrigation in India and the Philippines.* London: Sage Publications.

—— (1993) *User-Friendly Irrigation Designs.* New Delhi: Sage Publications.

Serageldin, Ismail, and June Taboroff, eds. (1994) *Culture and Development in Africa.* Washington, DC: World Bank.

Sugden, Richard (1986) *The Economics of Rights, Cooperation, and Welfare.* Oxford: Basil Blackwell.

Tang, Shui-Yan (1992) *Institutions and Collective Action: Self-Governance in Irrigation.* San Francisco: ICS Press.

Tendler, Judith (1995) "Social capital and the public sector: The blurred boundaries between private and public." Paper presented at the Conference of the Economic Development Working Group, Social Capital and Public Affairs Project, American Academy of Arts and Sciences, Cambridge, MA, May.

—— (1997) *Good Government in the Tropics.* Baltimore: Johns Hopkins University Press.

Tendler, Judith, and Sara Freedheim (1994) "Trust in a rent-seeking world: Health and government transformed in Northeast Brazil." *World Development* 22, no. 12: 1771–92.

Thomson, James T. (1992) *A Framework for Analyzing Institutional Incentives in Community Forestry.* Rome: Food and Agriculture Organization of the United Nations.

Van Til, Jon (1982) *Living with Energy Shortfall. A Future for American Towns and Cities.* Boulder, CO: Westview Press.

Wade, Robert (1984) "The system of administrative and political corruption: Canal irrigation in South India." *Journal of Development Studies* 18, no. 3: 287–328.

—— (1985) "The market for public office: Why the Indian state is not better at development." *World Development* 13, no. 4: 467–97.

—— (1994) *Village Republics: Economic Conditions for Collective Action in South India.* San Francisco: ICS Press.

Watson, Gabrielle (1995) *Good Sewers Cheap? Agency-Customer Interactions in Low-Cost Urban Sanitation in Brazil.* Washington, DC: World Bank, Water and Sanitation Division.

Watson, Gabrielle, and N. Vijay Jagannathan (1995) "Participation in water and sanitation." Environment Department papers participation series No. 002. Washington, DC: World Bank.

WECS/IIMI (Water and Energy Commission Secretariat, Nepal, and International Irrigation Management Institute) (1990) *Assistance to Farmer-Managed Irrigation Systems: Results, Lessons, and Recommendations from an Action-Research Project.* Colombo, Sri Lanka: IIMI.

Weissing, Franz, and Elinor Ostrom (1991) "Irrigation institutions and the games irrigators play: Rule enforcement without guards." In Reinhard Selten (ed.), *Game Equilibrium Models II: Methods, Morals, and Markets,* 188–262. Berlin: Springer-Verlag.

———— (1993) "Irrigation institutions and the games irrigators play: Rule enforcement on government- and farmer-managed systems." In Fritz W. Scharpf (ed.), *Games in Hierarchies and Networks: Analytical and Empirical Approaches to the Study of Governance Institutions,* 387–428. Frankfurt: Campus Verlag; Boulder, CO: Westview Press. Reprinted in M. D. McGinnis, ed. *Polycentric Games and Institutions* (Ann Arbor: University of Michigan Press, 1999).

Whitaker, Gordon P. (1980) "Coproduction: Citizen participation in service delivery." *Public Administration Review* 40:240–46.

Wilson, James Q. (1989) *Bureaucracy.* New York: Basic Books.

World Bank (1988) *Adjustment Lending: An Evaluation of Ten Years of Experience.* Washington, DC: World Bank.

———— (1994) *World Development Report 1994: Infrastructure for Development.* Washington, DC: World Bank.

Wunsch, James, and Dele Olowu, eds. (1995) *The Failure of the Centralized State: Institutions and Self-Governance in Africa.* 2d ed. San Francisco: ICS Press.

Part IV
Polycentric Governance

CHAPTER 16

Artisanship and Artifact

Vincent Ostrom

The *Public Administration Review*, and the American Society for Public Administration more generally, have been dedicated "to advance the science, processes, and art of administration." For many years I construed this motto as providing a rationale for the joint participation of both practitioners and scholars within a professional association that was concerned with the theory and practice of public administration. It has slowly dawned on me that this motto has deeper implications than simply relating the interests of scholars and practitioners to the theory and practice of public administration.

My earlier perspective had been shaped by the presumption that the methods of the natural sciences applied to the study of public administration. Based on this presumption, scholarship is concerned with the development of theory as basic knowledge and practitioners are primarily concerned with applications: theory comes first and applications derive from theory. But reflection leads one to become much more puzzled about the complexity of the relationships in theory and practice.

I have gradually come to conclude that the study of public administration should not be treated as strictly natural phenomena. The methods of the natural sciences are not fully appropriate to the study of public administration. Instead, we need first to look upon administrative tasks and administrative arrangements as works of art or as artifacts. Understanding works of art or artifacts may require somewhat different perspectives than understanding natural phenomena.

I shall define an artifact as anything created by human beings with reference to the use of learning and knowledge to serve human purposes. I shall refer to the task and processes involved in the creation of an artifact as

Originally published in *Public Administration Review* 40, no. 4 (July–August 1980): 309–17. Reprinted by permission of the American Society for Public Administration and the author.

Author's note: This essay draws upon work I am currently doing in preparing a book-length manuscript on *Leviathan and Democracy*. Extensive discussions with Vernon Greene, assistant professor of public administration, School of Business, University of Arizona, Tucson, Arizona, have contributed substantially to these reflections. I also wish to acknowledge the generous support of the staff of the Workshop in Political Theory and Policy Analysis and of Indiana University.

artisanship: artisans create artifacts. Several interesting implications follow when we explore the relation of artisanship to the creation and use of artifacts. In developing these implications I shall first explore the relationships involved in the development of a relatively simple artifact. I shall then extend the discussion to more complex relationships involved in organizations as artifacts. Finally, I shall pursue some implications for the study and practice of public administration.

Simple Artisanship

In exploring the relationships of artisanship to artifact let us use the example of a potter who is making a pot. The potter makes use of certain materials derived from nature. By knowing how to work with these materials and to transform them through an appropriate technology, a potter uses knowledge to yield a desired result. This knowledge draws upon the laws of nature in producing certain physical and chemical transformations. Knowledge of these physical and chemical transformations contributes to the artisanship of a potter.

An artisan does much more than mix ingredients and transform them from one state to another. In shaping a pot, a potter has a conception in mind about the purpose to be served by a pot, a feel for his materials, and a sense of proportion about what constitutes a good pot. These considerations are built into the pot just as much as the material ingredients that are used.

However, we should be careful not to assume that all of these different elements are somehow mixed together in the same way. The material elements used to make the pot are fashioned and transformed by an artisan. The knowledge, purpose, skill, and sense of proportion that are drawn upon by an artisan affect the way that he or she shapes and transforms the materials. The product represents the result of these various elements and processes. A pot can be both a practical utensil and a thing of beauty. Its utility need not detract from its beauty nor its beauty from its utility.

In reflecting upon these considerations, we might want to characterize the material and technology used in pot-making as having reference to factual elements. The factors that entered into the artisan's expression of preference, standards of choice, and sense of proportion might comparably be referred to as "value" elements. Both become an integral part of the pot. It simply does not make sense to speak of a value-free pot.

We can generalize these relationships as being involved in all artisanship and as embodied in all artifacts. Artisanship involves consideration of both facts and values. Both become integral parts of any artifact: an artifact is a union of both. Artisanship is never a value-free endeavor and artifacts are never value-free.

The values that are embodied in an artifact are derived from what I shall refer to as the "intelligibility" of an artisan. An artisan imparts elements derived from intelligibility to an artifact as he conceptualizes, shapes, and fashions it. If we assume that this intelligibility reflects a "similitude of thoughts and passions" characteristic of all mankind, as Thomas Hobbes (1960: 6) expressed it, each person can draw upon his own intelligibility to comprehend the purpose and meaning of the artisan who created an artifact.

In a painting, the material elements may assume essential but relatively insignificant proportions in comparison to the meaning that an artist is trying to impart. That meaning has significance to other human beings to the degree to which others can have reference to their own intelligibility. The intelligibility shared by different human beings derives from the similitude of thoughts and passions shared by all mankind. A painting can impart to *me* a level of insight and meaning that gives me a fundamental appreciation for the insight experienced by its creator. This meaning is independent of the words that might be used to express the same insight and meaning.

In referring to the similitude of thoughts and passions that are characteristic of all mankind, Hobbes quite explicitly rejects the notion that this similitude extends to the objects of human thoughts and passions. These are profoundly affected by education and cultural circumstances. Rather, Hobbes is pointing to a more fundamental structure that affects the way we think and feel. As a result, he suggests that we can come to understand others only as we come to understand ourselves. As human beings come to understand those characteristics that they share in common with other human beings, they are coming to understand characteristics that are universal in human nature. Such possibilities imply that human beings share an underlying sense of meaning that contributes to a universal appreciation of both the utilitarian and aesthetic qualities of human artifacts.

Organizations as Artifacts

If we turn to a consideration of human organizations as works of art or artifacts, we confront problems of rather substantial proportions. The first problem arises from the circumstance that, again in Hobbes's words, human beings are both the "matter" and the "artificers" of organizations (Hobbes 1960: 5). Human beings both design and create organizations as artifacts and themselves form the primary ingredients of organizations. Organizations are, thus, artifacts that contain their own artisans.

The second problem arises from the circumstance that artifacts that contain their own artisans depend upon words for ordering relationships among those artisans. Words themselves are human artifacts and involve substantial limitations that in turn place constraints upon what human beings can accomplish with and through organization.

A third problem arises from the circumstance that word-ordered relationships depend upon potential recourse to coercive sanctions to bind human actions to the constraints implied by words. If we use the metaphor of the "sword" to refer to sanctions, then we need to think of the sword as a necessary ingredient of all organizations.

Organizations, in turn, always function as tools or instruments in the creation of other artifacts. The design of a tool is always a function of what it is designed to do. Since tools vary with the nature of the task, a consideration of this relationship would concern a complex set of variables. Constraints on space do not permit me to undertake that analysis here.

Instead I shall limit consideration to problems that relate to: (1) organizations as artifacts that contain their own artisans; (2) organizations as word-ordered relationships; and (3) rules, rulers, and ruled. In considering the last topic two different models of authority relationships will be described that have radically different implications for organizational design. Finally, I shall develop some implications for the study and practice of public administration in the concluding section.

Organizations as Artifacts that Contain Their Own Artisans

Organizations, whether commonwealths, administrative agencies, or any other form of human institution are works of art in which human beings function both as their designers and creators, and as their principal ingredient. The first order of importance to those who are concerned with the design and creation of organizations is to come to some basic understanding about human nature. Perhaps the most distinctive characteristic of human beings is their capability for learning. Learning involves the development of an image about the order of events and relationships that occur. Where constraint exists, a learning organism can take advantage of that constraint by inducing variety in its own behavior so as to improve its adaptive potential. By the use of language, human beings have radically amplified their capabilities for learning and sharing their learning with one another. The aggregate pool of knowledge, the potential repertoire of adaptive behavior, and the resulting harvest of effects assume extraordinary proportions.

Each individual can calculate the probable consequences that can be expected to flow from alternative courses of action. These are the calculations that derive from the instrumental forms of knowledge that we associate with science. In addition, each individual has an independent capability to weigh alternative possibilities in relation to the internal indicators that might be referred to as preferences. Choice then is a process of selection that derives from the weighing of alternatives in terms of preference. Presumably, in all forms of voluntary action each individual will take account of their own preferences as reflecting essential interests. As a result, human beings are never perfectly obedient automata. Wherever discretion is exercised individuals can be expected to consider their own interests in the actions they take.

How do we then take account of the strategies that individuals can be expected to pursue? Two methods would appear to be available. One is to rely upon the presumption that human beings share a basic similitude of thoughts and passions, and by taking the perspective of others, attempt to understand the basic structure and logic of their situation and infer the strategy that they are likely to pursue. This is essentially the strategy that is inherent in methodological individualism.

Another method, which complements the above method, is to provide individuals with opportunities to communicate their preferences so that they can explicitly be taken into account when individuals relate to one another in the context of human institutions. The use of prices in market transactions provides essential information to both buyers and sellers. Experience in buying and selling enables those participating in market transactions to become aware of patterns of supply and demand. One consideration in the design of organizational arrangements involves the elucidation and transmission of information so that human beings can constructively take account of one another's interests as they interact with each other. They can then make their respective choices about what to do in light of the opportunities perceived to be available to them.

The problems of elucidating the appropriate information are especially difficult in conflict situations where individuals may have incentives to conceal information and resist efforts to explore their mutual and reciprocal interests. Surmounting these difficulties by appropriate methods for elucidating information and clarifying mutualities of interests is essential if the methods for processing conflict are to be conducive to conflict resolution.

Reliance upon organizations as ways of elucidating and processing information is especially important when we understand the implications that derive from human capabilities for learning. The capacity to anticipate the future course of events is critically dependent upon knowledge. The future as perceived by human beings is always a creation of the mind: an artifact of human intelligibility. The future course of human development is always influenced by the generation of new knowledge. New knowledge opens possibilities that could not have been comprehended without access to that new knowledge. So long as new knowledge continues to accrue, long-term planning is an impossibility. New knowledge contributes to the erosion of technologies based upon prior knowledge. The further plans are projected into the future, the less confidence we can have in their reliability. Any creature that has unique capabilities for learning and generating new knowledge inevitably faces an uncertain future. Learning and the generation of new knowledge are themselves marks of fallibility. Infallible creatures would have no need to learn and generate new knowledge. Fallible creatures need to accommodate their plans to changing levels of information and knowledge.

These problems of elucidating and processing information are greatly magnified when we recognize that organizations are instruments or tools that enable human beings to engage in forms of joint artisanship. The joint effort is to create some product or artifact. This implies that basic calculations made by artisans in creating artifacts must be jointly made by a number of individuals where the division of labor in the joint effort may imply that no two persons jointly involved make precisely the same calculations. Underlying that joint endeavor is the need for a shared understanding of the joint task that enables human beings to coordinate their actions with one another. Yet each is an artisan accountable to his own sense of artisanship as he functions in the joint endeavor. This problem of coordination gives rise to a somewhat different use of language that has substantial implications for human organizations.

Organizations as Word-Ordered Relationships

The creation of organizations as artifacts depends upon the use of language to formulate rules for ordering relationships among the individuals who interact with one another. Rules are intended to constrain some forms of behavior and facilitate other forms of behavior. By acting with reference to rules an individual can anticipate how others may be expected to act so that human beings may maintain orderly relationships with one another. Rules are also important in facilitating opportunities so that human beings might be of mutual help to one another. While substantial advantage accrues to human beings from the use of language to create orderly and mutually productive relationships with one another, there are, nevertheless, a number of problems associated with the use of language to create rule-ordered relationships.

Words are artificially created symbols that name, and thus, stand for classes of things and relationships. Language always involves some measure of ambiguity because words apply to general categories. All use of language involves simplification. Furthermore, the use of words to name classes of things and relationships depends critically upon a shared understanding of the meaning of words. Language is easily subject to abuse when the same word is used to mean different things. Such abuse can lead to confused thought and senseless discourse. As John Dewey has observed, "the moment we utter the words 'the state' a score of intellectual ghosts rise to obscure our vision" (Dewey n.d.: 8). We need not even utter the word if our thinking is informed by a theory of "the state" and its correlative theory of sovereignty. The same intellectual "ghosts" or mental images may still be there either to clarify or obscure our vision.

The normal ambiguities inherent in language are exaggerated by the circumstance that the language of rule-ordered relationships always has reference to implicit criteria pertaining to what is right and wrong, legal and illegal, just and unjust. The language of law is loaded with such value-laden terms as rights, duties, wrongs, remedies, benefit, and injury. None of these terms refer to an objective measure that can be used as a standard for reaching an unambiguous definition. Rather, definitions of these basic value terms must necessarily rely upon human intelligibility to derive a sense of meaning. My sense of right and wrong has no special significance or meaning unless concurred in by others. To make legal what is viewed as wrong and unjust is to offend one's basic sense of integrity about the right ordering of human relationships. Only as we gain concurrence in criteria for distinguishing right from wrong, just from unjust, and legal from illegal can we aspire to a right ordering of human relationships. Human societies are grounded in a shared understanding both of instrumental knowledge and of basic human values.

Unfortunately, the patterns of human cultural development with the growth of new knowledge, and the development of new possibilities, mean that the exigencies to which rules apply are themselves subject to change. Applying language to changing configurations of development increases the ambiguities and threatens the shared criteria of choice with an erosion of their appropriate meaning. Under such circumstances error and disagreement can be expected to abound. Methods for processing conflicts and searching out constructive resolutions to conflicts become important for resolving ambiguities and reestablishing consensus about fundamental criteria of choice.

Reliance upon language as the basic instrument for ordering human relationships also poses problems because rules are not self-formulating, self-determining, or self-enforcing. We always have to rely upon the agency of human beings to formulate rules of law, determine their application, and enforce performance in accordance with rules. Furthermore, rules are soft-constraints, and human beings are perfectly capable of acting at variance with them. The problem then is how to bind human beings to act in accordance with words. To make words binding in human relationships requires a special assignment of authority where some formulate rules, determine their application, and enforce performance. This is the special province that applies to human governance. But the exercise of governmental prerogatives also requires the mobilization of sanctions and the imposition of penalties when individuals fail to conform to rules.

Rules, Rulers, and Ruled

Rules, thus, imply rulers and those who are ruled. The maintenance of rule-ordered relationships in all institutions implies a fundamental inequality with reference to rules. Those who are assigned prerogatives to govern are assigned prerogatives that are radically unequal to those who are subject to rules. The most fundamental inequalities in human societies derive front the prerogatives of rule. Attributes of justice ascribed to equality under law say nothing of the inequalities between those who exercise governmental prerogatives and those who are subject to governmental prerogatives. As Alexis de Tocqueville has emphasized, increased demand for equality under law is simultaneously a demand for increased inequality between rulers and ruled (Tocqueville 1966).[1]

The radical inequality between rulers and ruled is reinforced by the use of sanctions as instruments for enforcing rules. Laws "without the sword," to use Hobbes's metaphor, "are but words and have no strength to secure a man at all" (Hobbes 1960: 109). The threat of penalties or punishment becomes a way to bind human beings to the requirements of word-ordered relationships. But the imposition of penalties implies the deprivation of others. Deprivation implies that evil is done to another. This is justified on the grounds that the evil is necessary for the common good if human beings are to realize the benefits of a rule-ordered society. But such a justification does not alter the circumstance that evil is being used as an instrument to do good.

All organizations, then, are Faustian bargains where instruments of evil are used to do good. Those who have legitimate access to use such instruments of evil have unique opportunities to exploit others and dominate the allocation of values in a society. It is entirely problematical when the use of an instrument of evil may come to dominate social relationships so that rules become oppressive rather than liberating. The greatest evils inflicted upon humanity have been the work of those who are so confident of their effort to do good that they do not hesitate to use the instruments of evil available to them on behalf of their righteous cause. But the problem is a general one and not limited either to self-serving or cause-serving individuals: all organizations rely upon instruments of evil to do good.

A question remains as to whether people can develop appropriate precautions in the use of such instruments of evil and constrain them from dominating organized activities. Whether this possibility remains open for consideration depends upon how we conceive the essential nature of authority relationships. One set of conceptions proceeds on a presumption that any system of law depends upon a single source of law that exercises ultimate authority and has the last say pertaining to all matters of government. Another set of conceptions proceeds from a presumption that people can fashion rules to rule rulers, and that rulers can themselves be bound by rules of law. The one set of conceptions is articulated in Hobbes's theory of sovereignty. The other set of conceptions is articulated in the American theory of constitutional rule. Each attempts in its own way to develop precautions that would constrain the use of instruments of coercion in human relationships.

Hobbes's Theory of Sovereignty

Since laws are human artifacts, Hobbes reasons that human societies must rely upon human agents to exercise the prerogatives of government. Since such agents are the source of law, they are above the law and cannot themselves be held accountable to law. For there to be one system of law there must be one ultimate source of law that has the last say in both enforcing law and modifying rules of law. Human societies, thus, depend upon an absolute inequality between those who rule and those who are subject to the rule of law. Authority to rule is inalienable to those who rule and that authority is indivisible. Rulers are accountable only to God; and the peace and prosperity of a people derive from their obedience and concord.

For Hobbes the accountability of sovereigns to God implies a substantial constraint. An understanding of God is derived from a love of knowledge. A love of knowledge, Hobbes says:

> draws a man from the consideration of the effect, to seek the cause; and again, the cause of the cause; till of necessity he must come to this thought at last, that there is some cause, whereof there is no former cause, but is eternal; which is it men call God. (1960: 68)

Hence, men are led to consider how God might rule by covenant. This knowledge might be derived by revelation as in the case of the Hebrew prophets, or it might be derived from reason as in Hobbes's formulation of the laws of nature. Both give expression to God's law.

Hobbes argues, "that subjects owe to sovereigns, simple obedience, in all things wherein their obedience is not repugnant to the laws of God" (1960: 232). But this poses a problem for determining:

> when he is commanded anything by the civil power, whether it be contrary to the law of God or not; and so, either by too much civil

obedience, offends the Divine Majesty; or through fear of offending God, transgresses the commandments of the commonwealth.

To avoid the horns of this dilemma Hobbes draws upon the common Latin sources of the terms *worship* and *culture*. To culture the minds of children or to culture the earth requires a loving care of that which is being cultivated. Artisanship is best expressed as loving care exercised by an artisan with respect to the materials used and the work performed in the creation of an artifact. To worship God is to express a loving care to eternal providence. Hobbes then goes on to suggest that obedience to God's law is "the greatest worship of all" (239). The neglect of God's law is, in turn, the greatest of all contempt. The proper discharge of sovereign prerogatives requires loving care for the well-being of subjects. Their neglect leads to what Hobbes calls the "natural punishments":

> There is no action of man in this life, that is not the beginning of so long a chain of consequences, as no human providence is high enough, to give a man a prospect to the end. And in this chain, there are linked together both pleasing and unpleasing events; in such manner, as he that will do anything for his pleasure, must engage himself to suffer all the pains annexed to it; and these pains, are the natural punishments of those actions, which are the beginning of more harm than good. And hereby it comes to pass, that intemperance is naturally punished by diseases; rashness, with mischances; injustice, with the violence of enemies; pride, with ruin; cowardice, with oppression; negligent government of princes, with rebellion; and rebellion, with slaughter. (240–41)

The exercise of sovereign prerogatives to the neglect of eternal providence yields diseases, mischances, violent enemies, rebellion, and slaughter. These burdens are borne by subjects as well as by sovereigns. This potential for the failure of commonwealths raises a basic question: Is there an alternative way of conceptualizing the nature of authority relationships so that the natural punishments suffered from the negligent government of princes might be avoided?

Constitutional Rule

The American system of authority relationships was based upon a contrary presumption, stated in the *Declaration of Independence,* that:

> Governments are instituted among men, deriving their just powers from the consent of the governed,—that whenever any Form of Government becomes destructive of these ends, it is the right of the People to abolish

it, and to institute new Government, laying its foundations on such principles and organizing its powers in such form, as to them shall seem most likely to effect their Safety and Happiness.

To attain such a solution requires that Hobbes's theory of sovereignty be foreclosed. If people are to rule in a meaningful way, there must exist a system of rules that pertain to the conduct of government itself. Such a system of rules might be characterized as a constitution, and the processes for formulating the rules applicable to the conduct of government might be characterized as constitutional decision making. We might then contemplate how people could rule in a democratic society if they exercised essential control over constitutional decision making, devised appropriate structures of government so that all authority is subject to limits, and enforced the limits of constitutional law against those who exercise governmental prerogatives.

Such a system of rule depends upon a careful allocation and distribution of authority so that each assignment of authority is limited. If limits are articulated with reference to veto points then actions are possible only within the conceptual space that is confined within the constraints of potential veto points. No single center of authority is required to dominate the rest. Rather, an equilibrium can exist within potential veto positions and a lawful order can be maintained within a system of distributed authority without the dominance of a single center of authority. A polycentric order can be maintained so long as all centers of authority can be constrained to operate within a system of enforceable constitutional law.

Rules of law, however, are not self-enforcing and collusion among officials to use the powers of government to exploit others offers sufficient opportunities that the viability of a system of constitutional rule is subject to continual threats. In the face of such threats the survival of a democracy depends upon the willingness of people to resist the usurpation of authority by officials and maintain the effective limits of constitutional law. "Too much civil obedience," to paraphrase Hobbes, is offensive to a democracy where those who command the civil power transgress the limits of constitutional authority. In challenging the usurpation of authority by governmental officials, it is essential that citizens do so on reasoned grounds. Otherwise the moral foundations of constitutional law and civil life are abandoned to terror and violence. Citizens in a democracy must also endure the natural punishments that follow from the neglect of eternal providence.

If the essential limits of constitutional law can be enforced against officials, it then becomes possible to have governments that exercise concurrent authority with one another in which all units of government are constrained by principles of constitutional rule. Under these conditions people can participate in diverse communities of interest and have access to multiple structures of authority relationships. This is what we refer to as a federal system. Principles of federalism can be indefinitely extended so that the relationships among governing authorities need not yield to patterns of warfare among unlimited sovereigns.

The crucial question is whether citizens can maintain effective limits through an enforceable system of constitutional law. If they cannot, then those who usurp authority become effective sovereigns and citizens become no more than subjects. Democracy no longer exists when people no longer rule.

The viability of a democratic system of government is, at best, problematical. Citizens need to know the moral and metaphysical foundations upon which human societies can be organized as mutually productive relationships, and an appropriate theory of constitutional choice to inform their decisions. If they use such knowledge to solve their problems of collective organization and maintain appropriate limits to the exercise of governmental authority, democracies become viable possibilities. When decision-making processes in a democracy are organized to facilitate a continuing inquiry pertaining to basic problems of constitutional choice, we might have some small measure of confidence that these conditions could be met.

* * *

When organizations are viewed as artifacts a complex structure of relationships is implied. Organizations involve a variety of technical considerations built around word-ordered relationships. These involve human beings both as the basic material used to construct organizations and as artisans who use organizational arrangements as tools to accomplish joint tasks of artisanship. The use of language in ordering human relationships is prescriptive in nature and has quite different implications than that used to calculate causal relationships in creating artifacts. But the choice of rules for creating rule-ordered relationships depends upon the existence of a knowledge of the probable consequences of different types of rule-orderings. It is this last form of knowledge that lays the foundations for a theory of constitutional choice and serves as the basis for organizational analysis and design.

When organizations are viewed as natural phenomena, we are likely to neglect the role of artisanship in their development and use. The problem is what conceptions inform the design? Without knowing those conceptions, we are in the position of observing an experiment without knowing what conceptions informed its design. Theory and practice are intimately associated, both in the creation and use of artifacts and in the study of artifacts. The theory used by artisans in creating an artifact is an element in its creation. Scholars need first to learn the theory that informs artisanship before they can contribute to new potentialities of artisanship.

Some Implications for the Study and Practice of Public Administration

Administration is a form of artisanship that has many dimensions to it. Organization, as one aspect, involves a complex structure of artisanship. Values get built into organizational arrangements at every turn. The very language of rule-ordered relationships is built upon a host of value terms. These terms are so fundamental that persons who cannot distinguish right from wrong are presumed to be incompetent to function in an organized society.

The alternative to developing a value-free science of administration is to become explicitly aware of the fundamental role that values play in all forms of artisanship in general, and in the forms of artisanship involved in the organization of human societies in particular. We must come to a better, albeit tentative, understanding of the moral and metaphysical foundations of human endeavor and human organization. One possible route in such a quest is that suggested by Hobbes when he proposes that we can learn to read others by first learning to read ourselves. This suggestion is based upon a presumption that there is a basic intelligibility that is characteristic of all mankind. If we can identify that which is common to all human beings we can come to know what is universal to human nature.

The understandings that we generate through the use of this method must, if true, meet with the concurrence of others. If we established commonly accepted criteria for distinguishing right from wrong, I would have criteria for considering in my own actions with reference to others the same standards I would have others use in considering their actions in relation to me. But this method is always subject to error and one can learn from one's errors only as others are allowed to articulate their own interests. Conflict can permit one to learn from one's errors and better approximate common standards of value as criteria for choice.

Any society that makes any pretense of being a democratic society depends upon the development of a basic consensus about underlying values that can be used as criteria of choice in social situations that involve the interests of others. When people share common standards of value pertaining to right and wrong, and to justice and injustice, and a common theory of constitutional choice, we might then anticipate that citizens could know the proper bounds for their relationships with one another and with officials. "Too much obedience," as Hobbes would say, can be offensive to both the requirements of a democracy and to God. The maintenance of a democratic society seems improbable to me unless citizens can have reference to shared standards of value and a commonly understood theory of constitutional choice.

Much the same problem applies to the social scientist. Rather than assuming oneself to be a value-free observer of other human beings, one might instead use one's resources as a human being to attempt to understand the basic criteria of choice that are utilized by people as they relate to one another. Social structures can then be specified as rule-structures that might enable human beings to relate to one another in mutually beneficial ways. We can view social institutions as representing a structure of incentives and deterrents and come to understand the logic of the situation by anticipating how representative individuals will behave in such situations. Such a strategy should enable social scientists, in turn, to contribute to a theory of constitutional choice.

We must be cautious not to assume that human motives or purposes are directly realizable through organization. It is entirely possible for patterns of human organization to generate results that are contrary to the motives of the individuals who are involved. In some circumstances, this discrepancy between individual motives and organizational results may assume pathological proportions associated with institutional weakness or institutional failure. Garrett Hardin's (1968) tragedy of the commons is a case in point. The public goods paradox developed by Mancur Olson (1965) is another example. Gordon Tullock's (1965) theory of bureaucracy is still another.

But there may be other circumstances where the discrepancies between individual motives and organizational results yield beneficial consequences. A competitive market is an example of this dynamic. Each producer seeks to maximize his profit. Market competition forces prices downward, reduces profits, and increases consumer surplus. Producers would prefer to reduce competitive pressures, increase profits, organize cartels to dominate markets, and exclude new competitors from entering a market.

This discrepancy between individual motives and the organizational results achieved, implies that artisans concerned with the design and creation of organizational arrangements cannot assume that a simple means-ends calculus, expressive of human motives, can be used to attain joint objectives. Rather, a means-ends calculus needs to be informed by a science that recognizes the possibility that rule-structures may transform individual behavior either in a perverse or benign way. A knowledge of how these rule-structures transform human conduct is a fundamental element in any theory of constitutional choice.

Relationships between rule-structures and the effects that they produce are among some of the fundamental issues confronting students of public administration. Where elements of institutional weakness or institutional failure can be reduced, we might contribute to improvement in human welfare if our theoretical presumptions are correct. However, if those presumptions are incorrect, we might err and contribute to the erosion of human welfare.

A case in point is the presumption that fragmentation of authority confuses responsibility: the more authority is divided the more irresponsible it becomes. This diagnosis of institutional weakness associated with divided authority presumes that the unification of authority would result in increased responsibility. Yet we face the paradox that the elimination of fragmentation of authority would also eliminate the conditions that are necessary for the maintenance of an enforceable system of constitutional rule. Such a paradox raises rather fundamental questions about the theoretical warrantability of assertions that fragmentation of authority reduces responsibility.

Another presumption identifies overlapping jurisdictions as a major source of institutional failure in the American system of government. The argument runs to the effect that overlapping authority involves duplication of effort, and duplication of effort involves waste and inefficiency. Presumably waste would be reduced and efficiency increased by eliminating overlapping jurisdictions. Yet the defining characteristic of a federal system of government is one of overlapping jurisdictions.

We have come to reiterate these propositions as self-evident truths, but if we give them serious thought we see that they are far from self-evident. We then confront the serious task of determining how we might test such propositions for their warrantability. Improvements both in a science of administration and the artisanship of organizational design depend upon the warrantability of the propositions we use in the theory and practice of public administration.

Every idea or concept has its limits, and students and practitioners of public administration need to be vigilant in their efforts to discover those limits. During the Great Depression, governmental control over the supply of money and credit became a major tool to regulate the economy in an effort to reduce unemployment. This power over money and credit has been used to create an illusion of command over infinite wealth through an accelerating growth of money and credit that is not matched by increased productivity. The illusion of infinite wealth has been used to justify massive fiscal transfers and a fundamental redistribution of power. One of the costs of this artificial creation of wealth is reflected in an erosion of the value of money and an accelerating rate of inflation. Inflation, however, works to grind the less well-off into increasing poverty. This illusion of infinite wealth can, in the end, result in the collapse of financial institutions, and constitute a fundamental threat to the survival of democratic institutions. The problem we face, then, is how to devise constraints so that those who exercise control over money and credit do not enhance their own power to the detriment of others. This is a basic issue in constitutional choice that we all face during the closing decades of the twentieth century.

Another potential problem arises from identifying constitutional choice narrowly with processes of constitutional decision making in constitutional conventions, constitutional referenda, and constitutional amendments. A constitution is simply a set of rules that apply to the conduct of government. Some of these rules may be articulated in a document called a constitution. But such rules may also be articulated in legislation, court decisions, administrative reorganization plans, collective bargaining contracts, or conventional understandings. The Administrative Reorganization Act of 1939 involved a radical alteration in the constitutional authority of Congress. Congress transferred major legislative power to the President subject to a 60-day veto. In the reorganization plan establishing the Domestic Council and the Office of Management and Budget, the president vested himself with authority to reorganize as he saw fit. Reorganizations of the Domestic Council and the Office of Management and Budget are, thus, no longer subject to the Administrative Reorganization Act. The Administrative Reorganization Act can easily become a tool for fashioning a new system of presidential government that is no longer constrained by effective limits. If that is allowed to happen, democracy will cease to exist and the imperial presidency, will reign as sovereign.

A proper use of tools depends upon a knowledge both of their capabilities and limitations. In the case of public administration in a democratic society, the knowledge appropriate to the analysis and design of organizations is not privy to scholars or administrators alone. A knowledge appropriate to organizational analysis and design is part of the public knowledge shared with citizens in a democratic society. Artisanship in organizational analysis and design in a democratic society should draw upon the same theory of constitutional choice that informs citizenship. Unless administrators are aware of their own limitations and the need to participate in an enlightening dialogue with their fellow citizens, they are apt to become self-serving oppressors who threaten the viability of democracy itself. The worst oppressors are those who have the greatest confidence in their capacity to use instruments of evil to do good. The Faustian bargain need not, however, inextricably lead to tragedy if human beings become critically aware of the burden of being fallible.

NOTE

1. See especially the fourth book of volume 2. There Tocqueville states the general conclusions to his two-volume study.

REFERENCES

Dewey, John. N.d. *The Public and Its Problems*. Denver, CO: Swallow.

Hardin, Garrett. 1968. "The Tragedy of the Commons." *Science* 162 (Dec.): 1243–48.

Hobbes, Thomas. 1960. *Leviathan.* Ed. Michael Oakeshott. Oxford: Basil Blackwell.

Olson, Mancur. 1965. *The Logic of Collective Action.* Cambridge, MA: Harvard University Press.

Tocqueville, Alexis de. 1966. *Democracy in America.* Ed. Phillip Bradley. New York: Alfred A. Knopf.

Tullock, Gordon. 1965. *The Politics of Bureaucracy.* Washington, DC: Public Affairs Press.

CHAPTER 17

Problems of Cognition as a Challenge to Policy Analysts and Democratic Societies

Vincent Ostrom

So that in the right definition of names lies the first use of speech; which is the acquisition of science: and in the wrong or no definition, lies the first abuse; from which proceed all false and senseless tenets; which make those men that take their instruction from the authority of books, and not from their own meditation, to be much below the condition of ignorant men, as men imbued with true science are above it. For between science and ordinary doctrine, ignorance is in the middle. Natural sense and imagination are not subject to absurdity. Nature itself cannot err; and as men abound in the copiousness of language, so they become more wise or more mad than ordinary. Nor is it possible without letters for a man to become either excellently wise, or, unless his memory be hurt by disease or ill constitution of organs, excellently foolish. For words are wise men's counters, they do but reckon by them; but they are the money of fools that value them by the authority of an Aristotle, a Cicero, or a Thomas, or any other doctor whatsoever, if but a man. (Hobbes 1960)

Policy analysis is an effort to address problems impinging upon members of societies and requiring collective choices with commensurate effects upon collective actions. The presumption exists that appropriate forms of collective choice and collective action will contribute to a more effective resolution of common problems and an advancement in the aggregate well-being experienced by members of collectivities.

Thomas Hobbes, in the conjectures appearing in the headnote, is warning that such a presumption may be incorrect. A critical factor turns upon the way that language is used or abused in human cognition. Speech,

---

Originally published in *Journal of Theoretical Politics* 2, no. 3 (1990): 243–62. Copyright 1990 by Sage Publications Ltd. Reprinted by permission of Sage Publications Ltd. and the author.

or language generally, consists of assigning names to that which is being named. A proper use of language in scientific inquiry is not an exercise in free association but a reasoned discourse grounded in computational logics.

There is a danger, however, that names (symbols, words) may be incorrectly associated with referents, and it is entirely possible that human imagination driven by an improper use of language is vulnerable to extreme errors. "Erroneous doctrines" can yield errors greater in magnitude than simple ignorance. Those who are "learned" in an inappropriate language of discourse may become, as Hobbes asserts, "excellently foolish," or proportionately "more mad" than ordinary human beings.

"Men who take their instruction from the authority of books" are especially vulnerable to the madness of becoming "excellently foolish." Hobbes suggests that the authority of one's own meditations may be a way of alleviating this abuse of language. These meditations, implicit in his discussions, require reference not only to the way that words are used in relation to one another but the way that words are related to referents (that which is being named) and the way that referents are associated and related to one another. Hobbes's meditation presumes a critical reflection which ties theoretical discourse to empirical inquiry and to the connectedness not only of a language of discourse but to the world of events characteristic of natural phenomena.

The problem is radically compounded by human artisanship where the instruction derived from the "authority of books" is applied to an artifactual realm in which the world of nature is transformed into human habitations, human relationships as constituted into diversely ordered societies, and how human beings shape their own aspirations and their own character structures. Languages of discourse permeate thought, and action is always grounded in thought because the way that motor facilities shape actions is hard-wired to the cognitive processes of the central nervous system. All human beings have the potential for being "excellently foolish" and "excellently wise" and those who "take their instruction from the authority of books" are especially vulnerable to the madness of being "excellently foolish."

I pursue this inquiry about human cognition because 1989 is likely to be marked as a point in time when major changes occurred in the unfolding of human civilization. It is possible that the twentieth century may be viewed as an era that was "excellently foolish." Diverse doctrines were spun off and called "ideologies" implying a knowledge of ideas but disassociated from experience and critical reflections.

True believers of the doctrine associated with the teachings of Engels, Marx and Lenin, for example, engaged in experiments to construct societies upon a new basis and achieve the liberation of mankind. One of those true believers, Milovan Djilas, cast profound doubt about the warrantability of the doctrine when he asserted that:

> Everything happened differently in the USSR and other communist countries from what the leaders—even such prominent ones as Lenin, Stalin, Trotsky, and Bukharin—anticipated. They expected that the state would wither away, that democracy would be strengthened. The reverse happened. (1957, 37)

When an experiment is conducted and the reverse happens, something excellently foolish pervades such a doctrine. The events of 1989 might be identified with a widespread recognition and response to this particular form of foolishness.

We must presume that other societies are vulnerable to comparable forms of foolishness. The events of 1989 imply that many societies are open to inquiry about the constitution of order in human societies. However, societies remain vulnerable to the forms of madness that derive from the abuse of language. These forms of madness are as likely to afflict democratic societies as any other societies.

It is for this reason that I undertake this inquiry about problems of cognition which place democracies at risk. In pursuing this inquiry I first draw upon Alexis de Tocqueville's critical assessment of democracy in America where he presumes that patterns of cognition, characteristic of democratic societies, place them at risk. I then turn to dangers of cognitive biases in policy analysis. These dangers have strong methodological implications about the cognitive character of policies as hypotheses and reforms as experiments. In conclusion I advance some conjectures about the language of discourse in policy analysis which might be used to reduce the risks of being excellently foolish and enhance the prospect of developing a language that can better serve as tools for reckoning about collective action. What is named "theory" is the use of words for reckoning.

Tocqueville's Analysis and Critique of the American "Experiment"

The Nature of the American Experiment

In the last paragraph of the first chapter of *Democracy in America,* Tocqueville (1945, 1: 25) suggests that the critical focus of his inquiry is concerned with a "great experiment" being attempted to "construct society upon a new basis." He further asserts that "it was there, for the first time, that theories hitherto unknown, or deemed impractical, were to exhibit a spectacle for which the world had not been prepared by the history of the past." The implication is that this experiment was of major theoretical importance and achieved a significant level of success.

The magnitude of the experiment is indicated in the last paragraph of chapter 4 where Tocqueville suggests that societies are predominantly governed by reference to two types of structural arrangements: (1) where a power exists which "though it is in a degree foreign to the social body, directs it, and forces it to pursue a certain track"; or (2) where "the ruling force is divided, being partly within and partly without the ranks of the people" (1945, 1: 57). I presume that the first implies an autocratic state which rules over society and the second implies the participation of popular representatives who share in the governance of society as, for example, a king in parliament. "But," Tocqueville asserts, "nothing of the kind is to be seen in the United States; there society governs itself for itself." This implies that a self-governing society exists without having recourse to a state— single dominant center of authority—which governs over society.

Tocqueville sees the key idea for conceptualizing the design of the American experiment as arising from the covenantal theology of Puritans. The concept of covenantal relationships with God and with one another was accepted as the principle for constituting civil bodies politic for the governance of human relationships. Ideas were translated into institutional arrangements where covenantal methods were applied to processes of constitutional choice in setting the terms and conditions of governance with reference to multiple units of government and multiple decision structures in each unit of government. Sovereignty conceived as the right to make laws resided with the people in diverse communities of relationships since people set the terms and conditions of government in constitutions and reserved unto themselves inalienable rights to govern their own affairs by voluntary associations with one another.

The first volume of *Democracy in America* is primarily an elaboration of the institutions of local, state and national governments and the ways that popular participation is activated through the intermediate institutions of political parties, press and voluntary associations. The volume is concluded by an analysis, critique, conclusions and prognosis.

In drawing his conclusions, Tocqueville attempts an assessment of three factors that contributed to the viability of the American experiment. These are (1) natural endowments and locational circumstances—"the peculiar and accidental situation in which Providence has placed the Americans"; (2) "the laws" or institutions; and (3) "the manners and customs of the people" (1945, 1: 288). The first is identified as being important but of the least relative importance. The second is of an intermediate order of importance and among these he ranks first the "federal form of government," second, "township institutions" and third "the constitution of the judicial power." The manner and customs of the people are ranked of the first order of importance.[1] These he conceives as applying to *"the habits of the heart"* and "to the various notions and opinions current among men and to the mass of those ideas which constitute their character of mind" (299). I refer to both of these as habits of the heart and mind. In this context religion is viewed as "the first of their political institutions" but taking "no direct part in the government of society" (305). Religion had a profound place in shaping the habits of the heart and mind so that individuals might function first as their own governors and have recourse to voluntary association and civil bodies politic organized through covenantal processes establishing the terms and conditions of government.

The priority given to the habits of the heart and mind implies that problems of cognition are of central importance in the constitution of democratic societies. An analysis of problems of cognition is central to Tocqueville's assessment of the long-term viability of American democracy. This is the primary thrust of his misgivings in the second volume. For democratic systems of governance to be viable over time it is necessary that appropriate habits of the heart and mind be reproduced through successive generations so that democracies avoid becoming "excellently foolish," to use Hobbes's terms, and become possessed of forms of madness that place democracies at risk. Tocqueville's analysis is important as we face a world in transition if human civilization is to advance beyond the tragedies endured in the twentieth century.

A basic challenge existing in any democratic society is to achieve a sufficient level of knowledge and civilization to solve problems at the levels of collective choice and collective action. Tocqueville recognizes that there exist societies that are "unable to discern the causes of their own wretchedness and . . . fall a sacrifice to ills of which they are ignorant" (1945, 1: 231). Such societies are incapable of a diagnostic assessment of problematical situations and the conceptualization of alternative ways of remedying those problematical situations. Democratic societies turn critically upon the mobilization of modes of policy analysis that allow for the choice of alternative ways to address problematical situations occurring in those societies. A danger is to draw upon erroneous conceptions which are "excellently foolish." A due process of law requires reference to a due process of inquiry which enables human beings to learn from their past mistakes and to achieve error-correcting capabilities. Serious problems arise in Tocqueville's analysis because he anticipates that the cognitive limits applicable to human beings under conditions that are constitutive of democratic societies will be subject to an intergenerational transformation in the habits of the heart and mind which reduce problem-solving capabilities and place democracies at risk.

The Problem of Cognition

Tocqueville presents the problem of cognition by first positing a state of perfect vision and contrasting this to the human condition. Perfect vision is associated with the Deity who "does not regard the human race collectively":

> He surveys at one glance and severally all the beings of whom mankind is composed: and he discerns in each man the resemblances that assimilate him to all his fellows and the differences that distinguish him from them. God, therefore, stands in no need of general ideas; that is to say, he never feels the necessity of collecting a considerable number of analogous objects under the same form for greater convenience in thinking.

The human mind cannot deal with the immensity of detail to address both similarities and differences in all their heterogeneities and complementarities. Instead human beings rely upon "an imperfect but necessary expedient" of associating classes of events with names in a many-to-one relationship characteristic of human languages. Reliance upon language then is "no proof of the strength, but rather of the insufficiency of the human intellect; for there are in nature no beings exactly alike, no things precisely identical, no rules indiscriminately and alike applicable to several objects at once" (1945, 2: 13). A problem necessarily arises from the disparity between knowledge grounded in the formal use of language—the authority of the books—and the tacit understanding that accrues from the skills of citizenship associated with the practical experiences of dealing with particular exigencies applicable to the world of events in discrete settings.

This problem is compounded by the circumstances that human cognition can have access to only a limited domain of knowledge. It is necessary for human beings to draw upon the knowledge and skills of others as a complement to the limits that prevail in the competence of each individual. Human beings depend upon the knowledge and skill of others, however imperfect these may be.

The existence of societies, then, depends upon a shared community of understanding:

> without some common belief no society can prosper; say, rather, no society can exist; for without ideas held in common there is no common action, and without common action there may still be men, but there is no social body. (1945, 2: 8)

Ideas held in common depend in part upon presuppositions that are the grounds upon which coherence is achieved among the diverse fields of knowledge presuming that a unity of knowledge exists. The more fundamental these presuppositions the more tenuous their relationships to practical experience. Human knowledge turns upon presuppositions which cannot themselves be subject to empirical inquiry but serve as the basis for the pursuit of inquiry and what is presumed to be an epistemology. There are levels of analysis where the appearance of contradictions in a language of discourse may give way to complementarities in differently formulated languages of discourse.

The quest for general ideas specifying universal propositions, characteristic of the scientific enterprise is recognized by Tocqueville as a possibility. He indicates that such generalizations are the result of a slow, minute and conscientious labor of the human mind, and the development of these general ideas extends the sphere of human knowledge. However, he indicates that people in democratic societies acquire a taste, if not a passion, for general ideas which, in Hobbes's terms, would represent an abuse of language. It is important then to recognize cognitive biases that accrue in democratic societies and place those societies at risk by the way language may inappropriately serve the purposes of policy analysis.

Cognitive Biases Characteristic of Democratic Societies

The passion for general ideas, which Tocqueville sees as characteristic of democratic societies, arises from a basic presumption of equality among persons or citizens that are constitutive of such societies. In the words of the American Declaration of Independence, "all men are created equal." Such concepts draw upon the covenantal theology of Jewish and Christian traditions. While human beings in their individual characteristics and capabilities have their discrete individualities, democratic societies presume essential equalities in the standing of individuals as members of a society.

The requirements of rule-ordered relationships in systems of governance imply that some will be assigned prerogatives of rulership pertaining to the formulation of rules of law, and the proper application and enforcement of law. A system of rules for the proper ordering of human relationships necessarily requires an unequal assignment of rulership prerogatives. These inequalities can be subject to limits, provided that constitutional provisions about the exercise of governmental authority can be maintained as enforceable rules of law.

When the presumption of equality prevails in the constitution of society, Tocqueville asserts that certain tendencies come to prevail in the ways that citizens think in democratic societies. Each fixes "the standard of their judgment in themselves alone" (1945, 2: 4). "They commonly seek for the sources of truth in themselves or in those who are like themselves" (9):

They readily conclude that everything in the world may be explained, and that nothing in it transcends the limits of the understanding. Thus they fall to denying what they cannot comprehend; which leaves them but little faith for whatever is extraordinary and an almost insurmountable distaste for whatever is supernatural. (4)

They are no longer bound together by ideas, but by interests. (3)

The idea of human equality is grounded, however, in theological presuppositions. How to relate to others in what is presumed to be a covenant with God, the eternal, and to act with reference to God's law means that basic moral precepts which serve as the foundation for methods of normative inquiry are abandoned for expedient interests that are more concerned with results than the appropriateness of means.

Since each is presumed to be like all of the rest, the intellectual horizons shift from discrete communities of relationships to a society as a whole. The larger the society and the more diverse the country, the greater the propensity for error. Further, "the intellect of democratic nations is peculiarly open to simple and general notions":

Complicated systems are repugnant to it, and its favorite conception is that of a great nation composed of citizens all formed upon one pattern and all governed by a single power.

The very next notion to that of a single and central power which presents itself to the minds of men in the ages of equality is the notion of uniformity of legislation. As every man sees that he differs but little from those about him, he cannot understand why a rule that is applicable to one man should not be equally applicable to all others. Hence the slightest privileges are repugnant to his reason: the faintest dissimilarities in the political institutions of the same people offend him, and uniformity of legislation appears to him to be the first condition of good government. (1945, 2: 289)

The method of covenanting with one another in establishing, maintaining and revising the constitutions of civil bodies politic and other associated relationships is abandoned. Constitutions become mere formalities: words on paper. The habits of the mind become preoccupied with societies as a whole and they come to look upon "government" as a "sole, simple, providential, and creative power" (291). Individuals assuming themselves to be like all of the rest, no longer look upon themselves as fallible creatures subject to limited comprehension, but as omniscient observers addressing themselves to problems in the society as a whole. Government then becomes an omnicompetent, universal problem-solver capable of responding to all of the problems of the society as a whole.

The preoccupation is with results to the neglect of means. "This disposition of mind," Tocqueville asserts, "soon leads them to condemn forms, which they regard as useless and inconvenient veils between them and the truth" (1945, 2: 4). This preoccupation with results—payoffs—leads to neglect of forms—the institutional arrangements for the structuring of human communication in due deliberation, the elucidation of information and the shaping of a common understanding appropriate to the resolution of conflict and taking collective actions. Institutional arrangements concerned with the terms and conditions of governance and with a due process of inquiry in coping with conflicts symptomatic of problematical situations are essential conditions to a self-governing society. Those who presume to know the greatest good of the greatest number claim a mandate for action, for achieving results without delay. Tocqueville considers this puzzle at length:

> Men living in democratic ages do not readily comprehend the utility of forms: they feel an instinctive contempt for them. . . . Forms excite their contempt and often their hatred; as they commonly aspire to none but easy and present gratifications, they rush onwards to the object of their desires, and the slightest delay exasperates them. This same temper, carried with them into political life, renders them hostile to political forms, which perpetually retard or arrest them in some of their projects.
>
> Yet this objection which the men of democracies make to forms is the very thing which renders forms so useful to freedom; for their chief merit is to serve as a barrier between the strong and the weak, the ruler and the people, to retard the one and give the other time to look about him [and to think]. Forms become more necessary in proportion as the government becomes more active and more powerful, while private persons are becoming more indolent and more feeble. Thus democratic nations naturally stand more in need of forms than other nations, and they naturally respect them less. This deserves most serious attention. (325–26)

The cognitive biasing toward results is accompanied by a shift from the equal standing of individuals as persons or citizens to a preoccupation with equality in the outcome of human endeavors. Differences in monetary incomes, occupational status, educational achievement are standard measures used. Standards like equal protection of the laws shift from access to institutional facilities to differences in individual achievements. Legal standards shift to a new terminology stressing "affirmative action" meaning a form of discrimination which implies that preference is to be given specifiable characteristics if a choice is to be made among otherwise equally qualified persons. The basic language of discourse changes with commensurate changes in the character of collective action and the meaning of public policy. Justice is conceived as social justice implying equal shares in social outcomes rather than equal standing in access to the games of life. Given individual differences among human beings, equal access would imply inequalities of outcomes. To achieve equality of outcomes in light of individual differences would require the introduction of a discriminatory system of assigning handicaps.

The preoccupation with equality of results is strongly reinforced by the ease of making interpersonal comparisons with reference to objective standards that apply to the distribution of payoffs. These comparative assessments are significantly reinforced by feelings of anxiety, envy and guilt. Cognitive biases lead to a gradual transformation from a concern for an equality of standing with reference to law to a fundamental change in the habits of the heart and mind that in turn leads to a basic transformation in the way that problems are conceptualized as applying to a society as a whole, and the concept of government shifts to a "sole, simple, prudential, and creative power" that has general jurisdiction for the society as a whole.

Tocqueville anticipates that the cognitive biases characteristic of democratic societies will yield a new form of democratic despotism which he portrays in the following way:

> an innumerable multitude of men [will exist], all equal and alike, incessantly endeavoring to procure the petty and paltry pleasures with which they glut their lives. Each of them, living apart, is a stranger to the fate of all the rest; his children and his private friends constitute to him the whole of mankind. As for the rest of his fellow citizens, he is close to them, but he does not see them; he touches them, but he does not feel them; he exists only in himself and for himself alone—and if his kindred still remain to him, he may be said at any rate to have lost his country.
>
> Above this race of men stands an immense and tutelary power which takes upon itself alone to secure their gratifications and to watch over their fate. That power is absolute, minute, regular, provident, and mild. It would be like the authority of a parent if, like that authority, its object was to prepare men for manhood; but it seeks, on the contrary, to keep them in perpetual childhood: it is well content that the people should rejoice, provided they think of nothing but rejoicing. For their happiness such a government willingly labors, but it chooses to be the sole agent and the only arbiter of their happiness, it provides for their security, foresees and supplies their necessities, facilitates their pleasures, man-

ages their principal concerns, directs their industry, regulates the descent of property, and subdivides their inheritances; what remains, but to spare them all the care of thinking, and all of the trouble of living? (1945, 2: 318)

People spared the cares of thinking and the troubles of living abandon their rational facilities.

Should such conditions come to prevail, Tocqueville anticipates that a democratic people will place democracies at risk. "By dint of close adherence to mere applications, principles would be lost sight of; and when the principles were wholly forgotten, the methods derived from them would be ill pursued." The cognitive biases of a democratic people, and their preoccupation with equality, transform their habits of thought in ways that diminish collective problem-solving capabilities and allow civilization to be "trample[d] underfoot" (1945, 2: 47).

The Transformation of American Society

The transformation in the habits of the hearts and minds of Americans over the course of successive generations has been accompanied by major transformations in American society. Instead of functioning as a self-governing society where people have recourse to covenantal methods for constituting civil bodies politic appropriate to diverse communities of relationships, the society is becoming highly nationalized. The national government is identified as "the government" and the form of that government is identified as "presidential government." Instead of presuming that human beings are fallible creatures of limited comprehension, human beings presume to be omniscient observers capable of comprehending society as a whole where equal protection of the laws is presumed to apply uniformly to individuals in the society as a whole. The greatest good of the greatest number measured by calculations of preferences on a scale of utility in relation to results achieved is assumed to be the basis for collective action. National legislation is presumed to be the supreme law of the land applicable to all forms of collective action. The central government, referred to as "the government," is presumed to be a universal problem-solver. Citizenship is equated with voting and democracy is equated with majority rule. Winning elections is presumed to convey a mandate to rule; law is viewed as command and good citizens are viewed as obedient subjects. All societies are presumed to be nation-states in which "states" rule over societies. Democratic societies are transformed into sovereign states where a sole, simple, provident and creative power is presumed to rule over society. Such a power is viewed as the source of law, above the law and cannot itself be held accountable to law. Democracy gives way to autocracy.

Dangers of Cognitive Biases in Policy Analysis

The conjectures that Tocqueville offers in *Democracy in America* with reference to the three basic analytical categories—(1) the "peculiar and accidental" circumstances with which "Providence" endows people; (2) the laws (institutional arrangements) which people use in ordering relationships with one another; and (3) the manners and customs of a people (their habits of the heart and mind) and the reverse order of relative priority that apply among these categories in establishing the long-term viability of democratic societies—imply that cognitive biases will place democracies at risk. As habits of the heart and mind change, the meaning associated with the use of language changes. There is a shift from a concern with means—from methods and processes of inquiry and problem solving to the ends of results to be achieved—to a preoccupation with material conditions over metaphysical and moral considerations that informs the meaning of value terms and gives coherence to systems of knowledge and the language of law. Some of the critical works in the social sciences address themselves to dangers that arise from the way that choices are ordered in human societies. I shall explore the dangers of cognitive biases associated with establishing foundations for moral judgment and the meaning of value terms, the uses and abuses of knowledge in human societies and the problem of using multiple levels and units of analysis.

Foundations for Moral Judgment and the Meaning of Value Terms

Adam Smith (n.d.) in *The Theory of Moral Sentiments* indicates how a concern for the happiness of others and a "love of humanity" can generate "a spirit of system" which exaggerates the fellow-feeling associated with discrete communities of interest and inflames these feelings "even to the madness of fanaticism." Those infected with such a spirit of system "are commonly intoxicated with the imaginary beauty of [an] ideal system of which they have no experience, but which has been represented to them in all of the most dazzling colors in which the elegance of leaders could paint it" (379).

A transformation occurs where artisans no longer cope with the practical exigencies of common problems but take on the perspective of omniscient observers who presume to address the problems of societies as a whole. Such a "man of system" is apt to be very wise in his own conceit and is often so enamoured with the supposed beauty of his own ideal plan of government that he cannot suffer the smallest deviation from any part of it. He goes on to establish it completely and in all its parts, without any regard either to the general interests or to the strong prejudices which may oppose it; he seems to imagine that he can arrange the different members of a great society with as much ease as the hand arranges the different pieces on a chessboard; he does not consider that the pieces of the chess-board have no other principle of motions besides that which the hand impresses upon them; but that, in the great chess-board of human society every single piece has a principle of motion of its own altogether different from that which the legislature might choose to impress upon it. If those two principles coincide and act in the same direction, the game of human society will go on easily and harmoniously, and is likely to be happy and successful. If they are opposite or different, the game will go on miserably, and the society must be at all times in the highest degree of disorder. (380–81)

Smith's metaphor of society as being a great game in which each of the pieces has a potential for acting independently of each other piece might better be thought of as a supergame composed of many games which can be simultaneously and sequentially played in relation to one another. A sequential ordering would depend upon taking time out to allow one game to have priority in reaching a resolution before the play of another game can be resumed.

If a society is to achieve self-governing capabilities so that standards of liberty and justice are to prevail under conditions of equality, then methods of normative inquiry must exist for establishing distinctions between right and wrong. Smith's *Theory of Moral Sentiments* and David Hume's (1948) treatment of justice as an "artificial" virtue both argue that sympathy or fellow feeling can be used as a basis for developing such a method of inquiry. The first step is to know thyself and to come to appreciate that human beings acting to their own advantage characteristically find themselves in conflict. How to act to one's advantage requires a knowledge of the situation in which one is acting and the way that diverse interests can achieve resolution by searching out the most effective complementarity to one another. This requires a knowledge both of the situation and the complementarity of the diverse interests in that situation.

Sympathy or fellow feeling opens the potential that human beings with the use of speech can, in light of one's own experience with characteristic situations, inquire about the perceptions of others and how they relate to the structure of opportunities in prototypical situations. A method of inquiry to clarify the interests of individuals in interdependent situations would require each person involved in conflict to clarify one's own perceptions. The method advanced by Hobbes, Smith and Hume is for each individual who is party to a conflict to take the perspective of the other and strive to reach a common understanding that would enable each to address the situation and the interests of the respective parties as impartial observers. Hume explicitly recognizes that cognitive biases enter into fellow feelings. The bonds of fellow feelings are, for example, proportionately stronger with proximity. The method of taking the perspective of the other and striving for impartiality is critical to an appreciation of the interests of others and the development of a common understanding about the nature of the situation. There, thus, exists a method of normative inquiry on the part of people who acknowledge each other's standing as equals and are willing to communicate with one another about the resolution of conflict situations. Hobbes conceives this method of inquiry to be an application of the general rule: *"Do not that to another which thou wouldst not have done to thyself"* (1960: 103). This explains Tocqueville's concern with religion as a key political institution even though it has no formal part in the government of society. It may be possible to establish a common understanding about the nature of that situation, a basis for distinguishing right from wrong in rendering moral judgment, and for distinguishing that which is to be prohibited from that which is permitted and that which is required in the language of law. Smith suggests that a man of system presumes to function as an omniscient observer who knows what is good for others and is prepared to impose his conception of what is good upon others. Such a possibility may destroy the basis for common understanding in taking collective action when men of system exercise a power of command over a society as a whole.

Jeremy Bentham's *An Introduction to the Principles of Morals and Legislation* (1948) conceptualizes patterns of order in human societies which place reliance upon Smith's men of system to exercise governmental prerogative. Bentham presumes that human preferences can be registered and summed in relation to a common cardinal scale called *utility*. He conceptualizes the maximization of utility to occur when the greatest good of the greatest number prevails. Bentham further conceptualizes "good will" as "the most extensive and enlightened (that is well advised) benevolence" (231).

There is a presumption that men of good-will can know the conditions that are most conducive to the greatest good of the greatest number. Bentham, thus, views the motive of good-will as "giving birth to an imaginary kind of law or dictate" enjoining one to act or not act accordingly (1948: 231). The core of law then is viewed as command conceptualized with reference to punishment. There is no need for a theory of moral sentiments nor for a method of normative inquiry so long as men of good-will can be presumed to exist and exercise the powers of command consistent with the greatest good of the greatest numbers. The greatest good of the greatest number will be achieved when ordinary mortals act in obedience to the commands of those who exercise the prerogatives of government. What is presumed to be the most general and enlightened benevolence may, however, be based upon the fanaticism of Smith's man of system.

Lenin presumed that he could know what is good for others and exercise a dictatorship of the proletariat to reconstitute societies and achieve the liberation of mankind. The human casualties killed, tortured and imprisoned in this effort to constitute Soviet society have probably far exceeded the casualties suffered in the "wars" of the twentieth century. When sovereigns war on subjects, the cognitive biases of the twentieth century do not consider that to be warfare.

Fallible human beings using sympathy or fellow feeling as a mode of inquiry have the potential for fashioning a shared understanding about the characteristics of a problematical situation and the complementarity of diverse interests among those in problematical situations (Ostrom 1986). A resolution may then be possible for formulating a set of rules for ordering relationships among the community of persons implicated in conflict situations. However, the formulation of a just set of rules is taken by persons aspiring to impartiality while actions in rule-ordered situations are taken by individuals who act in light of strategic opportunities available to them in specific time and place circumstances. Temptations always exist to act at variance with rules to which one would agree as an impartial observer.

The method of normative inquiry expounded by Hobbes, Hume and Smith might apply to the problem of constitutional choice. To cope with the problem of temptations, those who exercise the prerogatives for enforcing, adjudicating and revising law might use the same method of normative inquiry and establish shared communities of understanding about the meaning of value terms, but standards of unanimity can no longer apply at the operational level if temptation strategies are to be curtailed. However, much of the burden of enforcement falls upon citizens monitoring one another in accordance with their common understanding.

The danger arises that the method of normative inquiry in covenanting with one another to create and maintain civil bodies politic will be displaced by less stringent rules of collective action presuming that standards of liberty and justice accrue from those who exercise the prerogatives of government. James Madison (n.d.) presumed that the principle of opposite and rival interests might prevail throughout the system of human societies—that contestation, conflict and conflict resolution are the keys to the political process organized by reference to constitutional choice rather than by principles of dominance. Reliance upon majority voting as a mandate to rule shifts from consensus as the foundation for a just system of law to patterns of dominance by the formal instrumentalities of government in the governance of society. A self-governing society yields to a state-governed society.

The Uses and Abuses of Knowledge
in Human Societies

Walter Eucken in *The Foundations of Economics* (1951), originally published in Germany in 1939, addresses the way that language is used by economists. Much the same problems exist in policy analysis. In referring to the "economic reality" of a stove heating his study, Eucken asserts that the stove and its operation depended upon coordinated chains of actions linking the activities of multitudes of actors involved in the production, distribution and use of the stove, and its supply of fuel. The way that such a "reality" is addressed by economists is subject to two different modes in the use of language. The theoretical economist typically builds increasingly abstract models of the way that an economy is organized. By contrast he sees economic historians as using language to heap facts upon facts in word pictures of economic "reality." The result yields a "great antinomy": theorists who increasingly distance themselves from economic reality and economic historians who paint idiosyncratic word pictures lacking a language of theoretical discourse.[2] Much the same allegations might be made about policy analysis where increasingly abstract models of a state are used to conceptualize how a state rules over society. Descriptive studies, by contrast, heap facts on facts leaving an immense gap between theoretical and empirical inquiries. There is no way for critical reflection to establish conceptual-computational logics among the elements and relationships that might be used to establish a scientific language of discourse.

Eucken is arguing that a scientific language requires reference to basic elements and relationships which are applicable to all forms of economic relationships. Different types of economies might be constituted in different ways. A common language referring to basic elements and relationships for dealing with different economic systems and levels of analysis would permit comparisons across differently structured economic orders. The use of a common framework would provide the context for an appropriate account of historical experience so that language might be formulated in a scientifically more meaningful way.

This problem is greatly simplified in the so-called experimental sciences. Different fields of inquiry treat "nature" as isolable systems which can deal explicitly with an identifiable level of analysis. Experimentation in a laboratory can hold parameters constant while allowing for variability in relation to a single element treated as a variable. Different conditions apply to practical experiments conducted under field conditions. There, the amount of information will be variable rather than the constant it is presumed to be in many models.

F. A. Hayek (1945), in an essay on "The Use of Knowledge in Society," stresses that there are two different uses of knowledge in economics. One pertains to general ideas which are presumed to have universal application. These might then be referred to as general laws. The effort to articulate such general laws is the preoccupation of theoretical economists and is the rationale for the development of an abstract model that is presumed to have universal applicability. Hayek, however, recognizes that anyone engaged in economic activity is also required to come to terms with local knowledge that has time and place specificity. This is the equivalent to Tocqueville's "peculiar and accidental" circumstances set by "Providence." The natural experiment conducted in a field setting requires attention to particular values to be assigned to parameters and how those parameters may function as variables in what may uniquely apply in particular field settings. A laboratory is not available to set parameters at fixed values. In a field setting parameters cannot be treated as constants. They may function as variables in interactive configurations of relationships. To treat policies as hypotheses and reforms as experiments requires reference to general categories of relationships and local time and place specificities.

The use of language implies that human beings cannot be omniscient observers even though citizens and policy analysts may presume that they can relate themselves to a society as a whole and have access to a central government which can serve as a universal problem-solver. This is an impossibility, and any society which operates upon such presumptions places itself at risk.

Ludwig Lachmann, in *Capital and Its Structure* (1978), begins to indicate the magnitude of the problem confronting those who draw upon science and technology to produce goods and services. Any productive effort will require the use of a great diversity of tools, resources, and methods to achieve desired results. This he refers to as a *principle of heterogeneity*. How these diverse elements are put together requires a *complementarity* among those heterogeneous elements. A knowledge of both general relationships in a production technology and the time and place exigencies applicable to the heterogeneous elements is essential in achieving the most effective complementarity among those heterogeneous factors. Lachmann confines his analysis to "material conditions." The concept of capital can also be applied to the skills and capabilities of human beings: *human capital*. Further, the way that human beings relate to and draw upon one another's capabilities is identified by James Coleman (1988) as *social capital*. The ways the institutions of family, church, and community organization complement the educational function of schools are important variables in assessing the performance of schools (Coleman and Hoffer 1987). Different institutional arrangements that facilitate a complementarity of teamwork, exchange relations and ways of resolving conflict imply that various forms of associated relationships can have important effects upon productive potentials.

In such a context, "policy analysis" can no longer be confined to a choice about what "the government" should do. Education cannot be confined to schooling. The productive potential of schools may turn upon the complementarity that is achieved on the part of people working in diverse associated relationships, all of which are involved in the production of human capital—enhancing the skills and capabilities of human individuals. Developing skills that are appropriate for individuals to function as their own governors may turn more upon the social capital of family organization, religious associations and/or local units of government and community organizations than upon what "the (central) government" does.

Any diagnostic assessment of problematical situations requiring collective action must necessarily be conjectural. Various conjectures need to be considered on their merit rather than presuming that policy analysts can accurately identify the alternatives that are available. To presume that differences are "ideological" (ideal plans by Smith's man of system) is to fail to address the relationship of a language of discourse to empirical exigencies.

The generation of languages which rely upon models that are increasingly abstract such as "markets" and "states" means that a language is relied upon which cannot be subject to the critical reflection in light of empirical inquiry. To assume that the basic unit that is constitutive of human societies is a state is increasingly absurd. Systems of governance in human societies get put together in different ways and national boundaries are increasingly permeable to communities of relationships that transcend those boundaries.

There can be no universal problem-solver capable of addressing diverse problems as applying to societies as wholes. Rather, human societies require diverse patterns of association to cope with problems of varying scales under variable time and place exigencies. Principles of heterogeneity and complementarity imply that all human associations occur in the context of what W. R. Ashby (1956) has identified as a law of requisite variety. Given time and place specificities, achieving complementarity among heterogeneous and diverse elements implies that uniform rules of law are not appropriate for the governance of all associated relationships in human societies.

Different forms of teamwork in the production and distribution of goods and services need to be a complement of exchange relationships. Different forms of teamwork may be required for organizing the joint use of public goods. Complementarity among heterogeneous elements may be easier to achieve in market economies than centrally managed economies. But these diverse arrangements are required to take account of monetary institutions, the formulation, application and enforcement of law, the processing and resolution of conflict, the provision of public facilities and the management of common-pool resources. The achievement of complementarities requires recourse to multiple levels of analysis among diverse patterns of organization. Whether such systems are constituted by the dominance of a single center of ultimate authority or by achieving concurrence among diverse decision structures in autonomously organized units of government implies diversely organized systems of governance. Different modes of inquiry in establishing a due process of law would be expected to apply to policy analyses applicable to unitary or pluralistic systems of rule-ruler-ruled relationships.

The Language of Discourse in Policy Analysis

In the author's introduction to *Democracy in America,* Tocqueville asserted that "A new science of politics is needed for a new world" (1945, 1: 7). Eucken's critique of work in the social sciences, which relies upon generalized models presumed to have universal applicability, creates a circumstance where theorists increasingly distance themselves from social reality. Such a language of discourse generates an increasing gap between theoretical inquiries and empirical inquiries. Without a theoretical language that can be used to "penetrate" social reality, Eucken anticipates that advancements cannot occur in theoretical inquiries because the quality of theoretical discourse cannot be improved unless the use of language is perfected in light of a critical reflection in relating theory to practice.

Human beings can rely neither upon intuitive impressions nor upon inappropriately generalized models for developing a language that enables them to come to terms with an increasingly complex and interdependent reality. All human beings experience the general impression that the sun rises and sets. An inference can plausibly be drawn that the sun rotates around the earth. Inferences drawn from universal impressions may be false. The important contribution of scientific inquiry is to establish that counterintuitive patterns of relationships may exist. The impressions of those who look upon themselves as omniscient observers capable of seeing societies as a whole are likely to yield the grossest of errors. A theory of sovereignty based upon a presupposition that the constitution of all societies requires recourse to a state where some single ultimate center of authority exists may not hold for all societies. Such a theory is incompatible with a society that has a multitude of different units of government and multitudes of decision structures in each unit of government. Societies organized in relation to a plurality of power relationships need to draw upon different conceptions. Pluralistic systems of authority relationships may be based upon presumptions that the terms and conditions of government can be set in constitutions and the structure of those arrangements can be set so that constitutional law can be enforced in the discharge of governing prerogatives.

Instead of relying upon intuitive impressions and overly abstract universal models, it is possible to build languages of discourse specifying elements and relationships that are constitutive of diverse levels of social reality (Ostrom 1990). Conceptual-computational logics can be established for dealing with different levels and units of analysis. In this way elements can be dealt with as variables. Human societies might be put together in different ways. To characterize all societies as sovereign nation-states is not a satisfactory way of characterizing systems of governance and of informing choices about policy alternatives that apply to collective choice and collective action. Going back to fundamental elements and relationships means that commensurate elements can be used to constitute incommensurable systems of order in human societies.

A language appropriate to a science of astronomy has gradually emerged in light of empirical inquiry. Scientific languages emerge as human beings presume that human cognition is itself problematical and requires recourse to theoretical conceptions specified with reference to elements and relationships that apply to the diverse levels and units of analysis that are constitutive of "reality." The limits of language in coping with similarities and differences require redundancies in building diverse levels and units of analysis.

So long as human beings think of and experience themselves as living in societies constituted as nation-states, we can expect much of the madness characteristic of the nineteenth and twentieth centuries to persist. Tocqueville's analysis of democracy in America placed priority upon the use of covenantal methods to constitute civil bodies politic, upon religion as a key political institution even though religion had no formal part in the government of society. The institutions associated with a federal system of government, townships and the constitution of the judiciary played the most important formal role in the governance of American society; but the manners and customs of the people—the habits of the heart and mind—were considered more important.

Where do these elements fit in the analytical scheme of policy analysts? Until we have a language that is appropriate to an understanding of what it is that is constitutive of democratic societies, people cannot learn how to maintain such societies in a world of increasing complexity and interdependence. A new science of politics for a new age calls for a language that can be used to penetrate social reality and perfect our understanding of how ideas relate to practice in the exigencies of human experience. Words like *socialism* and *capitalism* may be without meaning. People may talk to one another without communicating with one another. When that happens languages cannot enhance problem-solving capabilities. The events of 1989 call for the development of languages that enhance problem-solving capabilities.

NOTES

1. I presume that Tocqueville's order of importance may be variable with circumstances. The "peculiar and accidental situation" of Poland in the eighteenth century certainly had a more adverse effect upon the viability of a constitutional republic than those existing in North America.

2. Wilson (1982) makes a related argument about economic theory.

REFERENCES

Ashby, W. R. (1956) *An Introduction to Cybernetics.* New York: Wiley.

Bentham, J. (1948) *An Introduction to the Principles of Morals and Legislation.* New York: Hafner.

Coleman, J. S. (1988) "Social Capital in the Formation of Human Capital." *American Sociological Review* 9(4): S95–S120.

Coleman, J. S., and T. Hoffer (1987) *Public and Private High Schools: The Impact of Communities.* New York: Basic Books.

Djilas, Milovan (1957) *The New Class: An Analysis of the Communist System.* New York: Frederick A. Praeger.

Eucken, W. (1951) *The Foundations of Economics: History and Theory in the Analysis of Economic Reality.* Trans. T. W. Hutchins. Chicago: University of Chicago Press.

Hayek, F. A. (1945) "The Use of Knowledge in Society." *American Economic Review* 35:519–30.

Hobbes, T. (1960) *Leviathan or the Matter, Forme and Power of a Commonwealth Ecclesiasticall and Civil,* ed. M. Oakeshott. Oxford: Basil Blackwell.

Hume, D. (1948) *Hume's Moral and Political Philosophy,* ed. H. D. Aiken. New York: Hafner.

Lachmann, L. M. (1978) *Capital and Its Structure.* Kansas City: Sheed Andrews and McMeel.

Madison, J. (N.d.) Federalist 51. In Alexander Hamilton, John Jay, and James Madison, *The Federalist.* New York: Modern Library.

Ostrom, E. (1990) *Governing the Commons: The Evolution of Institutions for Collective Action.* New York: Cambridge University Press.

Ostrom, V. (1986) "A Fallabilist's Approach to Norms and Criteria of Choice." In *Guidance, Control, and Evaluation in the Public Sector,* ed. F. X. Kaufmann, G. Majone, and V. Ostrom, 229–44. Berlin and New York: Walter de Gruyter.

Smith, A. (N.d.) *The Theory of Moral Sentiments.* Indianapolis: Liberty Press.

Tocqueville, A., de (1945) *Democracy in America.* Vols. 1 and 2. Trans. H. Reeves. New York: Alfred A. Knopf.

Wilson, J. A. (1982) "The Economical Management of Multispecies Fisheries." *Land Economics* 58(4): 417–34.

Suggested Further Readings

The best place to start reading is Elinor Ostrom, *Governing the Commons: The Evolution of Institutions for Collective Action* (New York: Cambridge University Press, 1990). This award-winning book summarizes a large amount of field research and lays out the "design principles" shared by all the cases in which communities successfully managed their common-pool resources over long periods. *Rules, Games, and Common-Pool Resources* (Ann Arbor: University of Michigan Press, 1994), written by Elinor Ostrom, Roy Gardner, and James Walker with the assistance of four Workshop colleagues, is a truly unique book that fully integrates field research, formal models, and laboratory experiments, all focused on the management of common-pool resources.

Institutional Incentives and Sustainable Development: Infrastructure Policies in Perspective (Boulder, CO: Westview Press, 1993), by Elinor Ostrom, Larry Schroeder, and Susan Wynne, is a textbook that emphasizes the importance of common-pool resources for development policy, with particular emphasis on the development and sustainability of rural infrastructures. Steven Hackett's *Environmental and Natural Resources Economics: Theory, Policy, and the Sustainable Society* (Armonk, NY: M. E. Sharpe, 1998) is a basic text on environmental economics by a Workshop-affiliated scholar.

The study of irrigation systems has played an important role in developing and extending the Workshop approach to institutional analysis. Two books that emerged from doctoral dissertations on this subject are Shui-Yan Tang, *Institutions and Collective Action: Self-Governance in Irrigation* (San Francisco: Institute for Contemporary Studies [ICS] Press, 1992); and Wai Fung Lam, *Governing Irrigation Systems in Nepal: Institutions, Infrastructure, and Collective Action* (Oakland, CA: ICS Press, 1998). The general implications of Workshop research for the practical establishment and maintenance of irrigation systems are summarized in Elinor Ostrom, *Crafting Institutions for Self-Governing Irrigation Systems* (San Francisco: ICS Press, 1992). William Blomquist, *Dividing the Waters: Governing Groundwater in Southern California* (San Francisco: ICS Press, 1992) provides a good overview of problems relating to water management,

including the systems that Elinor Ostrom studied in her doctoral dissertation, long before the Workshop was established.

Readings in this volume have concentrated on irrigation systems,
watershed management, and fisheries, but Workshop-affiliated scholars
have investigated many other types of common-pool resources. *Making the
Commons Work: Theory, Practice, and Policy* (San Francisco: ICS Press,
1992), edited by Daniel W. Bromley et al., collects papers that apply the
Institutional Analysis and Development framework to several different
substantive examples of common-pool resource management. Clark Gibson,
*Politicians and Poachers: The Political Economy of Wildlife Policy in
Africa* (Cambridge: Cambridge University Press, 1999) examines the controversies associated with wildlife management in Zambia. Arun Agrawal,
*Greener Pastures: Politics, Markets, and Community among a Migrant
Pastoral People* (Durham, NC: Duke University Press, 1999), evaluates the
efforts of pastoral groups in Nepal and northern India to manage a diverse
range of common-pool resources, not all of which are under their exclusive
control. Robert McC. Netting, *Smallholders, Householders: Farm Families
and the Ecology of Intensive, Sustainable Agriculture* (Stanford: Stanford
University Press, 1993), demonstrates the effectiveness of the many techniques that peasants in all parts of the world adopt in order to cope with their
uncertain environment.

Forestry resources are the focus for much of the research currently
underway at the Workshop, as part of the International Forestry Resources
and Institutions (IFRI) Research Program. A brief volume that lays out the
overall structure of the IFRI research program is James T. Thomson, *A
Framework for Analyzing Institutional Incentives in Community Forestry*
(Rome: United Nations Food and Agriculture Organization [FAO], 1992).
The first major edited volume to emerge from this extensive research
program is Clark Gibson, Margaret McKean, and Elinor Ostrom, eds.,
*People and Forests: Communities, Institutions, and the Governance of
Forests* (Cambridge: MIT Press, forthcoming).

By this point it should be apparent that the single most important
influence on the Workshop approach to institutional analysis has been
Alexis de Tocqueville's *Democracy in America*, the classic work on self-
governing associations in democratic societies. A modern classic on the
crucial roles played by informal institutions in development is Hernando De
Soto, *The Other Path: The Invisible Revolution in the Third World* (New
York: Harper and Row, 1989). Janet T. Landa, *Trust, Ethnicity, and
Identity: Beyond the New Institutional Economics of Ethnic Trading Networks, Contract Law, and Gift-Exchange* (Ann Arbor: University of Michigan Press, 1994), applies institutional analysis to the informal networks
formed by diverse ethnic groups.

In *The Meaning of Democracy and the Vulnerability of Democracies: A Response to Tocqueville's Challenge* (Ann Arbor: University of Michigan Press, 1997) Vincent Ostrom examines the prospects for developing self-governing societies in all the major world civilizations. The informational problems inherent in autocratic rule are scrutinized by Antoni Kaminski in *An Institutional Theory of Communist Regimes: Design, Function, and Breakdown* (San Francisco: ICS Press, 1992). T. S. Yang's *Property Rights and Constitutional Order in Imperial China* (1987) is an award-winning (but as yet unpublished) doctoral dissertation that explicates the basic structure of Chinese society over several centuries.

Kathryn Firmin-Sellers, *The Transformation of Property Rights in the Gold Coast: An Empirical Analysis Applying Rational Choice Theory* (Cambridge: Cambridge University Press, 1996), covers a specific example of the historical development of the centralized constitutional order typical of postcolonial Africa. The general problems of governance in contemporary Africa are surveyed in *The Failure of the Centralized State: Institutions and Self-Governance in Africa,* 2d ed. (San Francisco: ICS Press, 1995), ed. James S. Wunsch and Dele Olowu. Contemporary crises in Liberia are placed in historical perspective in *The Emergence of Autocracy in Liberia: Tragedy and Challenge* (San Francisco: ICS Press, 1992) by Amos Sawyer, a former president of that country.

The benefits of polycentric governance are most apparent when analysts draw explicit connections between local and national governments. The best and most succinct summary of the Workshop perspective on metropolitan governance is Ronald Oakerson's *Governing Local Public Economies* (Oakland, CA: ICS Press, 1999). *Local Government in the United States* (San Francisco: ICS Press, 1988), by Vincent Ostrom, Robert Bish, and Elinor Ostrom, is an overview of the U.S. political system originally written for an Italian audience. Mark Sproule-Jones, *Governments at Work: Canadian Parliamentary Federalism and Its Public Policy Effects* (Toronto: University of Toronto Press, 1993), shows that institutional analysis works north of the border as well, in this integrative evaluation of the constitution of order in Canada at the local and national levels.

The broader implications of Workshop research for development issues are explored in *Rethinking Institutional Analysis and Development,* 2d ed. (San Francisco: ICS Press, 1993), ed. Vincent Ostrom, David Feeny, and Hartmut Picht. This book also includes a mixture of micro-level and macro-level applications. The Workshop approach to institutional analysis is one of several analytical approaches to the study of governance included in *Guidance, Control, and Evaluation in the Public Sector* (Berlin: Walter de Gruyter, 1986), ed. Franz-Xaver Kaufmann, Giandomenico Majone, and Vincent Ostrom.

The current volume was prepared in conjunction with two other volumes of previously published articles and book chapters by Workshop scholars. *Polycentricity and Local Public Economies* (Ann Arbor: University of Michigan Press, 1999) includes classic works on the nature of polycentric order and a series of research reports comparing the performance of large and small police agencies in selected metropolitan areas of the United States. *Polycentric Games and Institutions* (Ann Arbor: University of Michigan Press, 1999) includes technical essays that develop formal models and experimental tests of the conditions under which self-governance is likely to be successful. This latter book nicely complements the current volume because most of the models and experiments developed there are based on a generic representation of the problems associated with managing common-pool resources.

Scholars interested in the study of common-pool resources are encouraged to consult a comprehensive set of reference materials developed by Workshop librarians. Four volumes of *Common-Pool Resources and Collective Action: A Bibliography* have been published by the Workshop. Volumes 1 (1989) and 2 (1992) were compiled by Fenton Martin; volumes 3 (1996) and 4 (1998) by Charlotte Hess. By the time this book appears in print we plan to have all four volumes available in a single file on CD-ROM. Meanwhile, scholars can search these bibliographies on the web page, <http://www.indiana.edu/~iascp/library.html>. For the IFRI project, Charlotte Hess has also edited volumes 1 (1996) and 2 (1998) of *Forestry Resources and Institutions: A Bibliography*. Also, abstracts of recent papers presented at meetings of the International Association for the Study of Common Property (IASCP) are available at the web page, <http://www.indiana.edu/~iascp/abstract.html>. Finally, readers are encouraged to check the Workshop's web page, <http://www.indiana.edu/~workshop> for recent updates and for links to other reference and teaching materials.

Contributors

William Blomquist is Associate Professor of Political Science at Indiana University's Indianapolis campus and currently chair of the department. He was a graduate student in the Workshop from 1983 through 1987. He is the author of *Dividing the Waters* and the 1991 U.S. Advisory Commission on Intergovernmental Relations report *Coordinating Water Resources in the Federal System*. His areas of research interest have been water resources policy, theories of the policy process, and the organization of local government in the United States.

Kathryn Firmin-Sellers is Assistant Professor of Political Science at Indiana University. She received her Ph.D. degree from Duke University and began teaching at Indiana University in 1994. Her first book is entitled *The Transformation of Property Rights in the Gold Coast*. Her current research explores the evolution of property rights institutions in colonial Africa, linking Africa's contemporary property rights system to the historical struggle between indigenous actors and colonial officials to claim African land and the profits emanating from that land. She has been a Workshop Affiliated Faculty member since she joined the Political Science faculty at Indiana.

Wai Fung Lam is Assistant Professor of Public Administration at the University of Hong Kong. He received his Ph.D. degree in Public Policy from the Joint Program of the Department of Political Science and the School of Public and Environmental Affairs at Indiana University in 1994. His research focuses on institutional analysis, resource management, public organizations, and public sector reform. He is the author of *Governing Irrigation Systems in Nepal*.

Michael D. McGinnis is Associate Professor of Political Science and Co-Associate Director of the Workshop in Political Theory and Policy Analysis. After receiving a B.S. degree in Mathematics from Ohio State University and a Ph.D. degree in Political Science from the University of Minnesota, he joined the faculty at Indiana University in 1985. His initial research on arms rivalries and international conflict was published in several articles and in a book manuscript *Compound Dilemmas,* coauthored with John Williams. He became a Workshop Research Associate in 1990 and Co-Associate Director in 1997. His current research interests concern institutional arrangements for the provision of humanitarian aid to communities displaced by conflict and famine.

Claudius Bamidele Olowu teaches at the Institute of Social Studies in The Hague, Netherlands. He was Professor of Public Administration and Local Government Studies at Obafemi Awolowo University, Ile-Ife, Nigeria. He received his education at the Universities of Ibadan, Ife (now Obafemi Awolowo), and Birmingham, England. He has served many African governments, international organizations, and the United Nations Economic Commission for Africa in Addis Ababa. Dele (as he is known by friends and colleagues) was a postdoctoral fellow at the Workshop in Political Theory and Policy Analysis in 1985-86 and returned in 1987 to finish *The Failure of the Centralized State,* coedited with James Wunsch. Dele's other publications include *Local Government in West Africa, African Local Governments as Instruments of Economic and Social Development, Lagos State: Governance, Society and Economy, Nigerian Public Administration,* and *African Perspectives on Governance.*

Elinor Ostrom is Arthur F. Bentley Professor of Political Science, Co-Director of the Workshop in Political Theory and Policy Analysis, and Co-Director of the Center for the Study of Institutions, Population, and Environmental Change, all at Indiana University in Bloomington. She received her Ph.D. degree from the University of Southern California in 1965 and began teaching at Indiana University the same year. She has served as chair of the political science department and as president of four professional associations: the American Political Science Association, International Association for the Study of Common Property, Midwest Political Science Association, and Public Choice Society. She has served as consultant and member of advisory boards for several local and national organizations. She is a Fellow of the American Academy of Arts and Sciences and received the Frank E. Seidman Distinguished Award in Political Economy in 1997. She was a cofounder and coeditor of *Journal of Theoretical Politics.* Her best-known book is *Governing the Commons,* and she has authored, coauthored, and edited numerous other books as well as many journal articles and book chapters.

Vincent Ostrom is Arthur F. Bentley Professor Emeritus of Political Science and Co-Director of the Workshop in Political Theory and Policy Analysis. He received his Ph.D. degree from the University of California at

Los Angeles in 1950. After teaching at the Universities of Wyoming and Oregon and at UCLA, he joined the political science faculty at Indiana University in 1964. Throughout his career he has kept active in resource policy, serving, for example, as consultant for the Wyoming Legislative Interim Committee, the Alaska Constitutional Convention, the Territory of Hawaii, and the National Water Commission. He was Editor-in-Chief for *Public Administration Review* (1963-66) and President of the Public Choice Society (1967-69). He is the author of several books and numerous articles and book chapters. Among his principal works are *The Intellectual Crisis in American Public Administration, The Political Theory of a Compound Republic, The Meaning of American Federalism,* and *The Meaning of Democracy and the Vulnerability of Democracies.*

Edella Schlager is an Associate Professor in the School of Public Administration and Policy at the University of Arizona, Tucson. She received her Ph.D. degree in Political Science from Indiana University in 1990. She was a research associate at the Workshop in Political Theory and Policy Analysis. Her dissertation focused on institutional arrangements designed by fishers to govern their use of coastal fisheries. Currently, she is studying how local organizations in the western U.S. acquire and coordinate their ground and surface water supplies to meet a variety of goals, from environmental protection to drought protection.

Shui-Yan Tang is Associate Professor at the School of Policy, Planning, and Development at the University of Southern California. He obtained his Ph.D. degree in Public Policy from the Joint Ph.D. Program from the Department of Political Science and the School of Public and Environmental Affairs at Indiana University in 1989. During his doctoral study he was a research assistant for the Workshop's Common-Pool Resource Project. His book *Institutions and Collective Action* is a result of his work in the project. His current research focuses on the institutional contexts of pollution control enforcement in Asia and on micro-credit programs in the United States.

James S. Wunsch is Professor of Political Science and International Studies at Creighton University. He received his Ph.D. degree from Indiana University in 1974. He returned to the Workshop in 1985-86 for his sabbatical year, where he spent his Saturdays with Bill Blomquist and Lin Ostrom helping develop the conceptual framework and coding scheme for the common-pool resources project . . . and had a lot of fun doing it. At Creighton he has served as Department Chair and Director of the African Studies Program. He has held a Fulbright Grant in Ghana, a Council on Foreign Relations Grant, and served for two years at the U.S. Agency for International

Development as a Social Science Analyst. He has worked for Associates in Rural Development, Inc., and as the Director of the Nigeria Local Development Project. He is coeditor of *The Failure of the Centralized State* and author of articles in *Public Administration and Development*. His research interests concern using institutionalist frameworks to explain decentralization, local governance and administration in the developing world, and democratic reform in Africa.

Index

Tanzania, 219–20, 223, 224, 229, 230
Technological externalities, 97–98,
104–5, 108nn.20,22, 116, 119,
141n.18
Tennessee Valley Authority, 34
Thailand, 264, 272
Thulo Kulo, 83–84, 131
Time and place information, 138, 411
See also Local knowledge
Tocqueville, Alexis de, 24, 40, 183,
213, 234n.2, 384, 392n.1, 396–
405, 407, 410, 412, 413
Toll goods, 252
See also Nature of goods
Trade credit, 330, 333
Tragedy of the commons, 2, 188, 390
Transaction costs, 119, 330, 340
Trust, 284, 369n.22
Tullock, Gordon, 57, 58n.1, 189, 195,
234, 318, 390
Turkey, 12, 92

Uganda, 13
United Gold Coast Convention
(UGCC) party, Ghana, 191, 192–
205
United Kingdom, 232
See also British colonial officials
United States
Advisory Commission on Intergov-
ernmental Relations, 120, 232–33
Agency for International Develop-
ment (AID), 244, 367n.10
Bureau of Reclamation, 32, 38, 51
Corps of Engineers, 32, 38
Unity of law. See Sovereignty

Valenca (Brazil), 94–95, 97, 127
Valencia (Spain), 83–84
Veil of ignorance, 189, 204
Voluntary organizations, 51, 52, 66,
70, 209, 221–26, 352–53
See also Tocqueville, Alexis de
Voting. See Elections

Wade, Robert, 79
Watermaster (California), 53, 70, 72

Water resources. See Groundwater
basins, management of
Water rights, 34, 48–51
See also Prior appropriation doc-
trine; Riparian rights
Weber, Max, 44
West Basin (California), water re-
sources and management, 9, 51–
57, 60–61, 69–72, 134–36
Wilson, Woodrow, 16, 159–62
World Bank, 209, 243, 244, 269, 297,
329, 348, 352, 367n.4, 369n.19

Young, Crawford, 186
Yugoslavia, 19

Zaire, 264
Zambia, 218, 367n.2
Zanjeras, 83–84
Zimbabwe, 224–26, 245, 264
Zolberg, Aristide, 186